Joseph Alfred Scoville

Vigor

A Novel

Joseph Alfred Scoville

Vigor
A Novel

ISBN/EAN: 9783337026752

Printed in Europe, USA, Canada, Australia, Japan

Cover: Foto ©Thomas Meinert / pixelio.de

More available books at **www.hansebooks.com**

VIGOR.

A Novel.

BY
WALTER BARRETT, Clerk.
AUTHOR OF
"THE OLD MERCHANTS OF NEW YORK CITY."

NEW-YORK:
Carleton, Publisher, 413 Broadway.
MDCCCLXIV.

I Dedicate this Book

TO

JAMES GORDON BENNETT, Esq.,

Proprietor and Editor of the New York Herald.

Who has carved for himself a record in Journalism that will last as long as newspapers are published—because he first told me that I had those peculiar imaginative qualities that would enable me to write a successful novel. This will test his sagacity. Long years ago, he asserted in the most positive manner that I had qualifications that would give me marked success as a novelist. I laughed at him because I did not believe him. He asked me if I had read many of the great novels, and when I replied in the negative, he gave me money to purchase novels written by Scott, Bulwer and others. I read their works, but I did not write a novel then, though I thought much of what Mr. Bennett had said. Since then I have done more than write for the daily bread and butter for my family, and have found leisure to write this novel, which may or may not verify the predictions of Mr. Bennett.

WALTER BARRETT, Clerk.

Washington's Birth-day,
February 22, 1864.

VIGOR.

CHAPTER I.

The Introduction.

HOLLAND has sent to our shores many of her best citizens. She has the merit also of having commenced two hundred and forty years ago, and some of the best families in New York are of the *Neder Duitch* stock. The country is overstocked with *hock deutschers* of more recent importation.

Not many years ago I made a visit to Holland. I resided for some months in Delft, the capital of Delftland in the Province of Holland. Having business at the Royal Academy, where I was having various models made, I endeavored to procure a residence in a private family. Through the exertions of Professor Lipkins I succeeded; and the second day after my arrival, found myself installed into a quiet country villa about half a mile from the city. It was located upon the bank of the canal that connects Delft with the Hague. My host, whose name was Van Hagen, was a man of great age, and his *vrouw* was still younger. They had no children, but occupied this beautiful villa alone. It had a large and well cultivated garden attached to it, and its neatness and luxuries still leave a pleasing impression upon my mind.

Over the gate was a motto—but whether it was indicative of the mind of the owner, or his coat of arms, or indicated the character of the place, I never inquired. It was in gold letters, or made of brass, gilded—LUST EN RUST—or Hope and Repose.

It was a pleasant morning's walk from my host's country villa into the city of Delft, and the sudden transition from the tranquility of the country to the busy hum of men was very striking. The canals, with their numerous drawbridges in the heart of the city, lined with Treckschuiyts of all sorts and sizes, gave a relief from country quietness.

The first meal of which I partook at my new home was a solitary one. Every thing was neat, and the victuals well cooked. I had a silver fork by my side, and the table cloth was of snowy whiteness, and in the room in which I dined was a glass China cupboard, and every article within it bore shining testimony of its having received a due proportion of diurnal care. After my meal was finished I was joined by my aged host and his worthy lady. They had dined previous to my arrival. He addressed me in English, somewhat to my surprise, and remarked—" You are an American."

I replied that I was, and he added, " Had you not been, I should not have consented to entertain you even at the request of my old friend the Professor of the Royal Academy." "You seem to be partial to Americans, and I certainly feel thankful that it is so, for Delft is a gloomy place, while here I am already at home. But why are you so friendly to America?" I asked. He replied, "I once thought of going to America. My brother went out there many years ago, with a young wife. It was during the time that the French occupied Holland, and our king was then Louis, the brother of Napoleon. He was ambitious to restore the fallen fortunes of our house, for we are one of the oldest families in Holland; and some day when we visit the city, I will show you a monument in the " ould kirk " at Delft of one of our name, who was buried in 1562, and was a famous scholar in his day. Now, my young friend all of our old race are in America except myself. Had my brother not died, I should have sold my property here, and followed him over the sea. I am not rich, but in comfortable circumstances, and as a Director appointed by the Government to keep the dams and roads in repair I receive a handsome fixed salary, and am content to live and die where my ancestors for five hundred years before me have lived and died."

I listened to the old gentleman's remarks with the very deepest interest, and after he had concluded I asked, " What part of America did your brother and his wife go to?"

" To Charleston, in the Southern part of America," replied the old gentleman with great simplicity.

" To Charleston in South Carolina, you probably mean."

" Yes, that was the place."

"You have heard from your brother frequently, I presume, before he died?" I asked.

"Yes, frequently, until somewhere about the time that Waterloo was fought. That was when?"

"In 1815," I added.

"Yes. Soon after then I got a letter from him. He had been very successful in business, and had acquired considerable property as a merchant. He owned a plantation and negroes, but he wrote me that his health was failing. He had two children, both girls. Not long after I received the letter in which he stated he was sick, I got another from my brother's widow. She wrote that he was dead."

"Was that the last you heard from your relatives in Charleston?" I asked.

"No. I received a letter occasionally for several years, describing the growth of my two nieces, one of whose name was Margaret, and the other Mary, who was some years younger than her sister, and was not born until the year in which my brother died. For twenty years I have not heard a word or received a line from any of them. I wrote frequently, but no reply came, and I suppose they are all dead."

When I parted with the venerable Van Hagen, I told him that very probably I should at some future day, after my return to America, visit Charleston—and in such an event I would diligently seek out any of his race or name, and if I ascertained that any were living, I agreed to write and inform him fully in reference to what so nearly concerned his family love.

Years passed away before I found myself in a position to redeem my promise. I had occasion to go to Charleston, and while there had rooms at the Charleston Hotel, kept then, and I believe now, by a most excellent landlord of the name of Mixer.

With his assistance I obtained a clue to the locality where I would probably find the relatives of my ancient Dutch friend, I was obliged to undertake a short journey into the country, and to reside for some time in a spot that at certain periods of the year is a modern Garden of Eden. Fruits and flowers flourish in the most luxuriant manner. Game is abundant, and the rivers and creeks are stocked with fish ready to bite at the most insignificant bait.

I returned to Charleston, and immediately devoted my time for several days in writing a letter to the aged Van Hagen in Delft, Holland. I enclosed the letter to William S. Campbell,

Esq., the United States Consul at Rotterdam, a city only one hour distant from Delft.

After dispatching my formidable document, I left for the North. I had not been in New York a great while when I received a private letter from Consul Campbell, informing me that old Adam Van Hagen was dead, and had not received my letter.

Luckily I kept a copy of the letter I had sent to Holland. I determined to re-write it in a book form. A faithful narrative required me to embrace the adventures of one of the descendants whose spirit of enterprise led him to New York. As a consequence I had to bring in other names, and use many other matters of interest indirectly connected with one of the family.

I will now relate in a regular manner what I have to say. But in order to do so with spirit, I will commence a new Chapter.

CHAPTER II.

[This Chapter was written before the outbreak in 1861.]

South Carolina and her People—Marriage of Henry Monck to Miss Van Hagen—Monck's Corners—Country Fever—Birth of Marion Monck.

SOUTH CAROLINA was the State in which the descendant of the old Holland Van Hagen was born, and who is also the principal hero of this narrative. *The* State, as her leading sons affectionately designate her, in Congress and elsewhere, has ever been regarded as the most aristocratic State in the Federal Confederacy, and her sons and daughters as the very *elite* of the great American population. Even the F.F.V. or "first families of Virginia" by general consent, back down gracefully and give place to an old South Carolina family. In the North, Southern travellers who can assert with truth that they are South Carolinian, hold their heads at a more lofty elevation— and their right to do so is never disputed. Northern people cave without a murmur to South Carolina pre-eminence.

The actual opinion of a genuine South Carolinian of his State, and of him or herself, is not put on for show, while travelling or while conversing upon the subject. They honestly believe what has the appearance of being egotistically asserted

—and the humiliating idea that South Carolina is not *the* genteel and *the* most powerful State in the Union, if not *the* only State of any account, and her population the most enlightened, most wealthy, most happy, most prosperous, and the best educated, is never entertained for an instant in the breast or brain of a genuine South Carolinian.

South Carolinans are a singular and an exclusive sort of aristocracy. They believe in their own institutions of all kinds, and have a holy horror of Northerners in general. It is true that this Japanese sort of exclusiveness is not so intense as it was a few years ago. Yankee pedlers, Northern merchants and storekeepers have emigrated into South Carolina, made fortunes, and in many instances made alliances by marriage with some of the best blood in the State. Both parties have gained by these marriages. Families of two or three hundred years' standing, but broken down, so far as finances were concerned, have been married into by men of business habits, literary merit, or property qualifications, and the happy result has been a much healthier progeny, intellectually and physically, than when the descendants of the old families married with each other exclusively. Such marriages have done a great deal also to soften the prejudices of South Carolina against the people of the more Northern States.

South Carolina may be said to be divided into three parts—the upper, the middle, and the lower division. In the latter are to be found the largest planters, and those who own the greatest quantity of slaves. These planters reside near the banks of the Cooper and Ashley rivers, both of which pass Charleston on each side, and then unite and pass onward to the sea.

It was on the banks of the Cooper river that my principal character was born.

I have already mentioned that in the early part of the century, a Dutch gentleman and his wife emigrated from Delft, in Holland, to Charleston, South Carolina. Delft, already alluded to in the introductory chapter, was famous many years ago for its crockery. The city is located about midway between the Hague and the city of Rotterdam. Martin Van Hagen, as well as his brother Adam, was born in an old house stretched upon the mainland, and directly opposite to the old church in which William, Prince of Orange, was assassinated.

When Martin and his wife decided to try the United States, they took passage in an American ship at Rotterdam, bound directly for Charleston. They reached their destination in safety. Ere they had been ashore a month, Mr. Van Hagen, who had cash capital, had engaged in mercantile business, and he had also secured a small wooden dwelling-house on the corner of King and Warren streets. The building is still standing. In this house the family resided several years, and their affairs prospered. They were blessed with two daughters. One named Margaret and the other Mary. A considerable interval elapsed between the birth of the eldest and the youngest. Shortly after the birth of Mary the father died, and left a widow and two children.

They continued to reside in the old house long after the father's death, but before the eldest reached the age of sixteen, she married a young American of the name of Henry Monck, and shortly after his marriage he conveyed his bride to his own home on Cooper river, in the parish of St. John Berkley, not far distant from the celebrated Monck's Corners, a name derived from his ancestors, one of whom emigrated from England at a very early period of the history of South Carolina. The Henry Monck who emigrated to South Carolina was the second son of that English Admiral Monck, who, in 1640, fought the great battle that lasted three days with the Dutch Admiral de Ruyter in the time of Charles the Second. It was under permission of the Admiral Monck that Vandervelde, the great maine painter, plied between the fleets, so that he was enabled to represent every movement of the ships, and every material circumstance of the action with astonishing minuteness and truth. But to return to young Monck. When he married Miss Van Hagen he was not twenty-two years of age. His father died when he was very young, and by some rascality of his guardian, before he became of age he was robbed of nearly every negro that he had inherited at his father's death. When he married he was only the owner of two negroes, a dwelling-house, and about three hundred and sixty acres of land. This quantity of paternal acres would have been a great property if located in some parts of the Union, but at Monck's Corners, where land in those days was as reasonably cheap as "seven pence" an acre, the value of the land only amounted to about forty-seven dollars.

The dwelling house was large and commodious, with a wide hall through it, and a spacious piazza in front. All the outbuildings were good. The store contained about five hundred dollars" worth of merchandise, of a suitable and assorted character for that region, so that the young couple started on their marriage career under very favorable auspices. The' lands owned by Henry Monck bordered on Cooper river, and he had only to seat himself in a boat, and it would float down with the ebb tide to Charleston City, about thirty miles distant by water, The State road passed his door, and a drive of twenty-eight miles would take him to Charleston by land. It was very easy, under such circumstances, to replenish the stock of goods in his store whenever it was called for. The young couple were also blessed with health, and though poor white people, yet they had no reason to envy their more prosperous neighbors, the rich rice planters of Cooper river. It frequently happens in the state of South Carolina that those who appear to be most rich are in reality the most poor, while, on the contrary, those who are comparatively poor, but out of debt, are the most independent. Our agricultural readers will be somewhat astonished with the information that rich lands, teeming with luxuriant vegetation, located both by land and water within thirty miles of the queen city of the south, should ever have been at low a figure as twelve and a half cents the acre. Yet such has been the fact, and even now, fifty-four years later, rich lands, capable, by proper attention, of producing as valuable crop as are made on the best land on Long Island, and valued at five hundred dollars the acre, can be bought for one dollar and fifty cents to two dollars an acre, with a dwelling-house upon them. But Northern farmers, although well aware that rich lands are to be had in South Carolina at a very low figure, refuse to emigrate to South Carolina as they do to Virginia, because—not slavery—but the country fever. It is worse than yellow fever, African fever, or any other fever but itself. It is a scourge—a terrible scourge, and wo to a Northerner or Southerner who places himself in the way of country fever. If he takes it, and escapes with his life, it breaks his constitution forever. Our readers have got so far this tale as where Henry Monck carried his bride up to Monck's Corners. They were married in December, and at that season the country in the neighborhood of Charleston is a paradise. The bride was delighted with her new home, and all went on pleasantly and prosperously with the new couple until the month of August of the year succeeding their marriage. When May came, Henry told his wife of the danger that she would incur by residing on their place in the summer months, and proposed that they should go into the Pine lands some ten miles distant, and there erect a log cabin for their residence in the summer nights. He told her that he did not fear the country fever, and that she might escape it if she would go to the Pine region before sundown and spend the night there, returning to the plantation and store in the morning, after the dew had been driven off the grass by the rays of the sun. So they arranged matters, and for weeks and months until far into the summer they left their dwelling before sunset to go to the log hut in the Pine region, and there escaped the danger of the miasma worse than that of the pontine marshes. Mrs. Monck enjoyed excellent health, and could scarcely credit the horrible but truthful stories she heard related of the immediate effects of the country fever. When told of Mr. Smith, who had accidentally been caught out at night, and slept in the woods, only succeeded by the long sleep that knows no waking—it seemed to her a dream. When told that to sleep, unless a large fire was kept burning all night, was certain death, she could not credit it; and finally, as the summer passed into autumn, and it became necessary to use extra exertions to get in the crops of their small farm, which was cultivated by her husband and the two old negroes Phillis and Toney that remained out of the wreck of his property, she found it so inconvenient to go to and fro night and morning between the two places, she told her husband that she did not believe there was any danger, and refused to leave her dwelling to go any more to their log cabin in the pine woods. He begged her to wait until the "black frost" came, the only sure remedy or preventative of South Carolina country fever. No. Before September closed she had it, and though it ran nine days before it was broken, yet she recovered, after months of suffering.

On the second of December, 1814, a year after their marriage, Mrs. Monck gave birth to a son.

She had visited with her husband the grave of General Marion, in St. Stephen's Parish, had been over the grounds where he had fought his battles, and she insisted that her child should be baptized in Biggin Church, famous in revolutionary history, and that he should be named after the hero of whom she had heard so much;* and so the boy was baptized by the Rev. Mr. Howe as

"MARION MONCK."

He was an only child, and father, mother and son vegetated at Monck's Corners, with more or less prosperity every year, until Marion had reached his eighth year.

CHAPTER III.

Young Monck's Boyhood—Jack Bird and Mr. Negro Black—Wild Turkey Hunting and Fishing.

When Marion Monck was eight years old, like other southern boys, he was capable of playing almost the game in life of a man. He could hunt, fish, ride a horse, or drive a team, and was a great favorite not only of his own relations, but of many of their neighbors. Some of these became Marion's instructors in all manly arts. One of the names of these men was Jack Bird. He was a fine specimen of a man. His age was over 60, and he stood six feet and a half without boots, and his frame was well proportioned. He could neither read nor write, but he would secure more wild turkeys and deer in twenty-four hours than any other man in South Carolina. Jack was a fair specimen of many poor white people. His den or cabin was in the Pine woods, some three miles from the Santee canal, and there he kept his wife and eleven children, all growing up in the ways of old Jack. Jack Bird owned no cows, or hogs, or poultry. Why should he? His neighbors on Cooper river owned large herds, and—well, Jack could steal as many as he needed for home consumption, or as he could safely sell.

Marion had always been an immense favorite of Jack's, and although the position in life of Mr. Monck was several degrees above that of Jack Bird, yet the latter did not envy or injure him, and would have gone some distance out of his way to have done Mr. Monck or his wife a service. The mother repaid Jack for all his kindness to her son, by giving him choice bits of tobacco occasionally out of the store, and he frequently returned the compliment by leaving her a fat wild turkey, a brace of wild ducks, or when these were scarce, a dozen pigeons, partridges, or robins. Whoever else Jack Bird plundered was of no consequence—he left the denizens of Monck's Corners unmolested, and they were grateful whenever occasion offered.

Charleston people frequently visited Monck's Corners to have a hunt, and Jack was always to pioneer on such occasions; but wo to any unlucky favorite pen-knife, pencil-case, or fish-hook that fell in his way! It was sure to be missing if it took the fancy of six-foot Jack.

Jack had trained Marion until he had become one of the best wild turkey hunters in the parish. He could discover, with little trouble, where the wild turkeys came to feed. He would then prepare a hiding-place in the neighborhood, and fix a gun loaded, so as to command a reach of ten or twenty feet in a trench by the side of a log. This trench he would bait with corn, and then trail the corn off in several directions to places where the wild turkeys would be likely to see it. A day or two only would pass when Marion would discover that the turkeys had found the trench and had ate the corn. This he would refill, and so do every morning for a week, until the turkeys had made a regular business of crowding the trench. Then Marion would select a particular morning, go early to his hide, and conceal himself, with the barrels of his duck gun loaded with buck-shot, bearing directly upon the track. Bye-and-bye he hears a noise—one, two, twelve, twenty, fifty wild but unsuspecting turkeys arrive—they jump over, and on, and around each other, to get at the corn. Marion quietly pulls one, and then the other trigger—bang, bang! Some turkeys get off, but nearly all remain. Twenty-eight are dead, and Marion goes home for a negro—Toney and the one horse cart to convey his spoils home.

Another especial friend of Marion Monck's was Negro Black. His original name was John Black; but besides being a poor white man, a hunter and day laborer, he added to his slender income by catching negroes. Hence his nick-name of Negro Black, by which he was known not only throughout St. John Berkeley, but by many planters in other sections who had runaway negroes to catch. Like Dick Bird, he had a wife and eight or ten white-headed children. Mr. Black had one source of revenue, and it was always a sure and profitable one. It arose from successfully hunting wild cats. When a prowling wild cat made the fact apparent that he was in the neighborhood, by catching up chickens or small pigs, the planter upon whose premises the animal had made a demonstration was seen to dispatch a summons to Mr. Negro Black.

It is a very curious fact in respect to the habits of a wild cat, that when he approaches a plantation, or rather the dwellings on a plantation, where his designs lay, whether it be to catch poultry, chickens or pigs, he goes to work in a regular, scientific business manner. The cat exhibits no greediness. If he lights upon an old sow that has a litter of eleven or more nice little delicate pigs, wild kitty commences with using up one a day, and no inducement of appetite can force him to increase the quantity. If no discovery is made by the owner of the poor old sow, at the end of the eleventh day she is pigless. The instant the overseer discovered by the regularity of the thefts that a wild cat was about, he sent for Negro Black. Perhaps it took one, two or three days, but Negro Black was a sure coffin for the cat. He and his dog Victor never failed. The cat was a doomed cat, and Mr. Negro Black received the skin and $10 as his fee for the operation. Negro Black had a jealousy of Jack Bird, and he maintained that the mode Jack had of catching wild turkeys, by a hide, was deliberate murder. It gave the turkeys no show; and he taught Marion another method. At a certain season, when the wild turkeys got scattered, he would go into the woods with Marion, and pile up a lot of brush wood.

"Get behind that with your gun, pull the brush wood over you, and use the whistle."

It was many days before Marion succeeded in shooting a solitary wild turkey; and even before that event took place, Negro Black's patience became quite exhausted;—for while Marion's gun was idle, and not a wild turkey would come nigh him in answer to his whistle, Negro Black would be off in a different part of the woods, and kill several. At last he broke out—

"Why you no whistle as I do, when you go for catch wild turkey? Take your whistle and blow leetle bit—turkey hear him—wait—no blow again until you hear turkey answer—then blow a leetle harder—wait—turkey answer again—then blow one soft, slow blow, and don't blow any more. Wait—turkey come bye-and-bye sure—den pop him. Turkey like young girl. If young man want take young girl for his wife, he give one call—little girl don't answer—it no use. Young man hab patience and wait. Bye-and-bye little girl make reply. Young man call again—wait until the young girl come, like turkey, and say, 'I'm yours.'"

Another and a third mode of killing wild turkeys, taught Marion by his hunter teachers, was to watch in the woods to hear where they roosted. He would hear a turkey fly at sundown, and very soon would trace a flock. If it was moonlight Marion would go for his gun, and four or five turkeys would be his reward. Or if it was very dark, he would wait patiently for the first glimmering of daylight, and then pop off a few turkeys before they had left the "turkey roost."

Marion's two friends were both fishermen as well as hunters; and where in the world is there such sport with the finny tribes as at Monck's Corners? Hours, day and night, Marion used to spend on the banks of the Biggin creek, or on the side of the old Santee canal. Sometimes with a small dip net he would catch one, two or four shad, as they dashed up to the waste way of the canal, and in the months of February, March, April and May, with the hook and line, in Biggin creek, he would catch trout of the size of eleven pounds, rock fish, perch, brise, catfish, and mullet by the million. O, such sport as he had in these well-filled waters. Every fish that belongs to salt or fresh water is caught in the Biggin creek, or Santee canal, when the tide is running in or out. Thousands of nights could Marion have been found with his dip net on the bank of the Biggin creek, the whole scene made as light as day by the "light wood" bonfires, and sometimes he and his companions would be thus engaged, with more or less luck, until daybreak.

CHAPTER IV.

Marion's Education—Death of Grandmother—Aunt's arrival at Monck's Corners—the Store—Negro Customers.

WHILE Marion Monck, by violent exercise, was developing his physical powers, his mental were neglected, so far as education was concerned, during these years of child and boyhood, or until he was over ten years of age. At that time he had not acquired the first letter of the alphabet. His grandmother came up from Charleston occasionally to spend a few days, but our youth never returned to town with her. About this period, the grandmother, who had came over from Holland with her husband, died in the city of Charleston. Her remains were taken to Monck's Corners for interment. So soon as her affairs were settled, the eldest daughter left Charleston and went to Monck's Corners to reside permanently with her sister, Miss Monck. This event had a very important bearing upon the education of Marion. She was a very intelligent lady, had reading many books, and possessed a very general knowledge of what it was now highly important that young Monck should know.

The Aunt found in her nephew, a well developed handsome boy, capable of leading in any manly enterprise, and accomplished in all manly sports. In place of A B C, he knew the number of every fish hook; if he had no knowledge of grammar he could ride a horse, and join in a deer hunt. If he had no knowledge of geography, he knew every spot where game could be scared up, and for arithmetic he could catch fish and game to an extent that even David could not have counted. In a word, he could ride, drive, hunt, fish, or swim equal to any man in St. John's Parish, if thrice his age. He was intelligent, could talk well on many and most subjects, his information having been derived from the conversation with others. His aunt, who regarded a good education as everything in life, became very much alarmed at finding a nephew ten years of age who could neither read or write. She determined to remedy what she regarded as a degrading evil. Marion felt that it would at least be convenient to read at last, and willingly became a prompt pupil to his aunt. His progress was very rapid, for he had an iron memory. The A, B, C, was soon acquired, and night and day did he devote to learning, until he could read anything, wrote a plain hand, could " do " any sum in Daboll's arithmetic, and had Murray's grammar by heart. Moore's geography was soon mastered, and Marion had acquired at least as good a foundation in useful and necessary learning, as is given in the District schools of the North. It is needless to add that he had acquired from his mother and aunt the Dutch language, and as his teachings from the aunt were partly in that language, he could read and speak it as well as he could English. His father devoted most of his time to the plantation, and to raising horses, cattle and hogs. His mother superintended the household matters, and also attended to the store. When Marion was able write and reckon, he became of vast service to his mother, and spent a great portion of his time in the store, and when customers were rare, he had a book in his hand. He literally learned it by heart, and what " he knew, he knew."

He continued until he was nearly fourteen years old. The store was quite an affair. The stock of goods was limited, and articles were bought in Charleston once a month, or ordered by letter. The maze consisted of coarse dry goods, bacon, coffee, sugar, rice, whiskey, tobacco, pipes, cigars, crockery, soap, lead, butter, spices, tin buckets, and coarse wooden ware.

The customers were in part the poor white folks, and second the negroes from the adjoining plantations. Fifteen thousand negroes at least, looked to that store for their little luxuries, and the happiness that this store conferred, can hardly be realized. Here, sometimes, the slave would come at midnight, having travelled ten miles, with ten more to go before he got back again to his home, and perhaps he would have walked all the distance to get a "fourpence" worth of tobacco for his little bag of corn. When he got it, he was a happy fellow. Sometimes forty or fifty would come together, and then some care and caution had to be exercised, for in such a force in the store at one time, the temptation to steal was too great to be resisted. Each took his turn, while the rest remained outside. Marion became quite a favorite with these negroes, and it was really a pleasure to him to get up and wait upon a tired customer even for the most trivial article. The pay was in corn. Sometimes the negro had received money for his corn, and then he had cash. If it was a bill of five or ten dollars, the slave asked it to be changed into silver, and when that was done, he knew what he was about, and trade commenced. "How much for dat tin biggin?"

"Seven pence."

"I tax um," and the quarter would be handed in by the purchaser, and then change given. Trade would then commence again.

"How much you ax for dat spider?"

"Quarter dollar."

"Quatah dollah. I gib ten pence for him."

"Take it." Pay and take change again.

"Gib me one and ninepence worth of tobacco."

And so trade goes on, paying for every article as he buys it, from a dollar's worth of homespun to a cent cigar, and perhaps he goes to the plantation where he belongs loaded with small things—and no father of a family, or patronesses of Stewart in New York, ever enjoyed spending money so much as these slaves. If it was corn he brought to trade with, then he had it measured. Suppose it was two bushels. The price has been seventy-five cents, and never varies in the negro trade if corn is worth in Charleston only fifty cents or a dollar. Then he pays for his goods with corn—a peck, four quarts, two quarts, as the case or price may be of the article bought, and never makes a blunder.

Now and then two negroes are in partnership, or some negro who could not come, has sent his corn by a friend. The bearer of the corn for another gets what is wanted, and never mixes it up with his own transactions. How it is done, no bookkeeper in a bank could tell. Sometimes in financial transactions the red corncob is used as a matter of security. One negro owes another. They deposit a red corncob in the hands of a third party as an evidence of money loaned or a debt due. The person who receives this corncob never gives it up until the debt is paid or cancelled, and then it is done in the presence of the two parties interested. It is a sort of red corncob bond and mortgage, and the parties can't get over it. It is rarely set aside, even by poor white people.

The attachment of the negroes to this store was wonderful. It was what they looked forward to, when they had cash or corn, as a great blessing in their existence. As an evidence of this, when Marion was about twelve years old, the family were woke up about two o'clock one morning, by a bright blaze. The store was on fire—and in less than two hours, being built of pitch pine, it was in ashes. Five thousand negroes were on the ground before it finished burning, and then came sympathy and anxiety for it to be rebuilt. The negroes for two weeks poured in from all quarters at odd hours which were their own. Carpenters from all the plantations volunteered. Others went into the woods with axes, and cut down trees, and hewed them into their proper size.

Before two weeks had passed the store was rebuilt again, twice its former size; and when it would have cost, under ordinary circumstances, four hundred dollars to rebuild it, it did not cost Mr. Monck fifty dollars—and then it was for nails, and things the negroes could not furnish. When it was ready to receive goods, Mr. Monck went to Charleston and bought them, and when the store was re-opened again, there was as general a rejoicing among fifteen thousand negroes and negresses, young and old, as if each one had had an individual interest in the affair. It was a "want." They missed it. It was their place of resort for luxury and comfort, and they could not get along without it. The dark lover, when he was about to wed a darkey bride, could get the rings at the store, and a bottle of cologne, a comb, papers of pins, or any little article, that, when purchased, gave more real happiness than a thousand dollar shawl in other circles of society.

CHAPTER V.

Parting from Home and from Parents—His stay in Charleston—Arrival in New York.

To leave a loved home, loved parents, loved friends, and long-loved associations, at the age of fourteen, to wander forth into the great world with the design of acquiring an education, a livelihood, a profession, a fortune, or any other of the thousand and one objects of human ambition, is a serious matter. Long and earnestly had Marion Monck communed with himself, and dreamed by day as well as by night of his future. His mind was made up to leave home. Young as he was, he knew and felt that his father, his family and himself could only hold a second rate position in white society. He could not rank or associate on an equality with the rich planter, and he was somewhat in advance of the poor white class. He was occupying a sort of mongrel white rank, betwixt and between the two white extremes. Marion felt within himself that he had talent and genius, and it urged him on to seek a larger field.

At last he gained the consent of his parents that he should leave home, and seek an occupation elsewhere, where he could see and learn more of the world. Worthy Mr. Monck wished his son to seek employment with some merchant in Charleston, as he honestly thought that Marion's experience in the store at Monck's Corners would have been a good preparatory school for a merchant's counting-room. Marion promised that in six months he would come back and see them—perhaps sooner. The mother packed his trunk, placing a Bible in a flannel shirt carefully, gave her son a few crying kisses, and Mr. Monck drove off with him *en route* for Charleston. On their arrival at their destination Mr. Monck found quarters for Marion with a friend, and the same day started on his return home.

Charleston was then, is now, and will be fifty years hence the same Charleston. The quicksand bar is still there, shifting and changing about—the old houses grow a little older—the mass of the old wooden tenements gets thicker and more impervious every year—the bell to call in the negroes rings at a quarter to nine, and the drum beats at the guard-house at a quarter to ten, to say that all negroes out after that hour without a pass from their masters, if they are slaves, or from their guardians, if they are free, will be locked up in the guard-house for the night, and taken before the Mayor in the morning. The yellow fever makes its appearance every two or three years, just when the Charleston people, because it has missed a year, have begun to indulge the hope that it will keep away five years, and give their favorite city a chance to loom up in the commercial world. But no—it seems almost hopeless; and the dread of yellow fever is like an incubus upon the city, and it is doubtful whether it will ever be taken off.

For more than a week Marion Monck roamed about Charleston, seeking employment in some commercial business. Perhaps it was lucky for him that he found no vacancy. No one wanted a clerk of his size, shape or make. One beautiful morning he wandered down about the wharves, and was admiring a stately ship. She was loading for New York. The idea flashed across his mind whether his chances would not be better in New York than in Charleston. He answered it by going on board and ascertaining the price of passage. It was within his means, and would still leave him something in his pocket to keep afloat a few days in New York. The ship was to sail the next day. Her name was the Saluda, and her commander was the man who had traded so long between Charleston and New York, that in the latter place he is known by no other name than the Charleston "Berry." Long ago he left the ship line, and has built and commanded every steamer that has voyaged from Charleston to New York. May he command steamers between the two cities for a thousand years more!

Marion returned from Adger's wharf to the house where he boarded, and announced to the worthy Mrs. Ferguson, the landlady, that he had half made up his mind to put out for New York the next day.

"Who do you know there, young Monck?" was her immediate question.

"Nobody."

"Indeed! And pray how will you get along without being acquainted with anybody or somebody?"

Marion reflected, and replied, "Well, I have had no success to my wishes in this town, where I do know a great many people, who knows but that I may find a situation among those who don't know me or that I don't know?"

And quick as lightning, the idea made him decide to go to New York; and he told the worthy lady, in the most flat-footed and decided manner that he should embark for New York in the good ship Saluda, Captain Berry, the next day.

"Well, my brave boy, if you will go, I will give you one letter that may be of service to you. I have a niece in New York who is married to a merchant there. She is a Charlestonian, named Bessy Nordheim, and will give a helping hand, if need be, to a South Carolina boy."

Marion expressed his thanks, and immediately returned to the ship and paid his passage. That night his landlady wrote the letter, and he placed it carefully in his trunk. The next morning, bright and early, he and his trunk were on board the Saluda, and before meridian the ship had passed over the bar, bound to New York.

It is useless to give a description of a sea voyage of eight days' duration. Marion was intensely sea-sick for two days, and it did him more good than fifty boxes of Brandreth's pills would have done. On the afternoon of the eighth day, the ship Saluda was moored alongside the dock in Burling Slip, and Marion hired a cartman, and with his trunk proceeded to a boarding house in Liberty street near Greenwich, to which he had been recommended by a fellow passenger. It was nearly dark when he got fairly established in his room, and after he had taken a boarding-house tea, he did the most sensible thing a young stranger who made his first visit could do at night, viz., he went to bed.

CHAPTER VI.

Marion Monck in New York—Presents his Letter of Introduction—Procures a situation with Granville and Nordheim—Home of Mr. Nordheim, in Bond Street—The Character of the Wife.

WHEN Marion arose from his bed on the morning after his arrival, his head was so confused by the multiplicity of noises which he had listened to from long before daybreak, that he could with difficulty comprehend where he really was. But at last his lonesome position, in a strange city, broke with full force upon his mind. He thought of his distant home and loving parents, and cried. He could not help it. He was in a great city, without one solitary friend. Bye-and-bye he dressed himself, descended to the breakfast room, and after drinking a cup of strong coffee, felt decidedly better, and much more energetic than he had felt since he left Monck's Corners.

The landlady cautioned him against getting lost, as soon as Marion told her that he had never been in the city before, and he started out to try his fortune in New York. He wandered about until dinner-time, staring at the million of novelties that his eye encountered, and then he returned home, and went at once to his trunk to get the letter of introduction that his Charleston landlady had given him. He had hardly looked at the address before, but now he regarded it as of some importance. It was directed to a house in Bond street, and he found his way up there, and before five o'clock in the afternoon he had presented the letter of introduction to the lady to whom it was addressed. She received him in a very cordial manner, insisted that he should stay to tea, and become acquainted with her husband, Mr. Nordheim, who, she said, had resided in Charleston some time, and who was engaged in a large business in Broad street. Marion felt that there was a hope, and so he did as Mrs. Nordheim wished.

It was nearly half-past seven before the husband came home, and then the wife introduced Marion, and showed the letter from her Charleston relative. Mr. Nordheim was very cordial, and joined his wife when she insisted that Marion should take tea with them and spend the evening. It was not long before Marion discovered that Ferdinand Nordheim was an Israelite.

Conversation turned upon Marion's prospects; and when he stated that he was anxious to get a situation in a counting-room or store, Mr. Nordheim observed that the firm of Granville and Nordheim, of which he was a partner, wanted a clerk. "I leave these matters to my partner," said he; "but in this case, if you will meet me at my store at ten o'clock to-morrow morning, I will make you acquainted with my partner, Mr. Granville, and I dare say some arrangement satisfactory to you may be made. I will tell him how I became acquainted with you, and your own rather prepossessing appearance must do the rest. If he is willing to engage you in our service, I shall make no objection; on the contrary, I will willingly employ you."

The heart of Marion beat quick—and after the evening meal was concluded, Mr. Nordheim, that there might be no mistake, wrote down the address, "Granville and Nordheim, corner of Broad and Garden street," and Marion took his leave.

At precisely ten o'clock he was in the counting-room of Mr. Nordheim. That gentleman introduced him to Mr. Granville, with such explanations as were necessary, and Mr. Granville led the way into his private office. After cross-questioning Marion for some time, he appeared to be quite satisfied as to his capability, and observed "It will take some time before you can be of much service, but you look as though you would try and learn fast; and although it is not customary with heavy houses to pay any salary for two or three years—(Marion was all aghast)—don't be alarmed; in your case, under the circumstances, we will vary from the custom, and give you a salary the first year. What will it cost you to live here?"

Marion had no idea. Supposed he could board for one or two dollars a week.

Mr. Granville smiled.

"Probably four or five dollars will be nearer the mark.

However, we will make an engagement with you for four years, and give you $250 the first year, $300 the second, $400 the third, and $500 the fourth year. After that your services will be worth whatever you choose to make them, if you get a thorough knowledge of the business meanwhile. Are you satisfied?"

" Perfectly, and am very thankful," said poor Marion.

" Very well—then come with me." And he left his private office for the general counting-room, where seven or eight clerks seemed to be very busy. He addressed an elderly clerk:

" Mr. Wilson, this young gentleman will come into our office to-morrow. His name is Marion Monck. You must try and make something of him."

Mr. Wilson bowed, and after having given some instruction to Marion as to the hour next day when he would be expected, went on writing his books. Marion quietly took his departure, and went at once to his room, and wrote a letter to his father and mother. The next day he was regularly installed as a clerk with Granville and Nordheim.

Mr. Wilson, the bookkeeper, explained to him his duties, and stated that as he was the junior clerk, it would be necessary for him to commence at the bottom of the ladder, and work his way up. He was obliged to open the store, put the books in the safe at night, lock it up, and give the key to the bookkeeper, and stay and see the porter shut up the store at night. He was also post-office clerk, had to go with letters to the office, and bring all letters in Box 910 to the office of Granville and Nordheim. Marion went through the first day with real satisfaction to himself and his employers. His modest willingness to do anything that he was called upon to do, had already secured to him the good feeling of the bookkeeper and the other clerks.

The store was closed before dark the first day. In fact, such was the usual habit, except on " packet nights," and then it was kept open until ten or eleven o'clock. Marion received the keys from the porter, and proceeded to his home, No. 119 Liberty street. He told his success to the landlady, Mrs. Birch, and she congratulated him warmly, adding, " You owe much to the lady who received you so kindly, and who was the means of procuring you the place. I have known young lads wait months to get a situation, and then not so good a one as you have secured in two days. Have you been up town to thank the kind lady in Bond street?"

Marion replied that he had not.

"Then you ought to go at once. Gratitude costs but little in your case."

These few words set Marion to thinking. He was merely a clerk. Was it right to go and pay a visit at the private residence of his employer? "Well," thought Marion, "she asked me kindly to call when I got fixed in a place. I am fixed, and through her kindness, I will go up and see and thank her to-night." An hour afterwards he was on the steps of a large three story brick house in Bond street, and had pulled the bell-knob. A negro woman came to the door and opened it.

"Is Mr. Nordheim at home?"

"No—Massa hain't come in yet. Missis is in."

"Go and tell her Marion Monck would like to see her."

In a moment Mrs. Nordheim herself came out of the parlor, and taking Marion by the hand, led him back into it, and placed him by her side on a luxurious sofa.

"Well, what luck, Marion?"

"Thanks to you, dear lady, I am engaged for four years by your husband's firm—but has he not told you?"

"He—my husband—no. I have not seen him since morning. Sometimes I do not see him for two or three days and nights together"—and noticing Marion's look of astonishment, she added, "He has so much to do at times, and frequently has to visit neighboring cities on business—but never mind him. I am so glad you have come up to-night. I want to talk to you about Charleston—about your home and parents, and South Carolina matters generally. But you must have some tea"—and she jumped up, and pulled the bell. It was answered by another negro girl, who took the order.

Marion again thanked her for being the means of getting him a place, and told her that she did not know how happy it had made him—that but for her he should have had a wretched, anxious time of it. "And you must tell me how to show my gratitude," he added.

Again she took both of his hands in her own delicate white ones, and pressed them closely. "Say no more about it. I need just such a friend as you will be, and if you are grateful, as you say, you will be able to do a thousand kindnesses for me. You must come here as often as you can. I am sadly in want of a beau; and as you are so young, and from my own State too, I am sure Mr. Nordheim will not be jealous of you, and will let me go out with you for an escort whenever I please. It is very rare now that he goes out with me himself."

The ice was broken, and before the tea was served they were chatting as familiarly as a couple of children—and, in truth, they were both children.

"How old are you, Marion?" she asked.

"I was fourteen last second of December, and it is April now, Mrs. Nordheim."

"There, stop—don't call me Mrs. Nordheim—say Bessy, and I shall like it and you a great deal better."

Marion laughed, and added, "Well, Bessy, how old are you?"

"Guess."

"I cannot. You are married, and "——

"Very well. I am just two years older than your most venerable self, Master Marion. I am but sixteen now—just old enough to be your loving elder sister." And with one hand pressed around Marion, with the other she parted the dark brown hair on his white forehead, and pressed it with a pure, loving kiss. "Now, that christens you my brother," she playfully added. "And this," said Marion, throwing one arm fondly about her neck, and putting his lips to hers, "makes you my loved sister."

The blood rushed to the face of the young wife, and slowly disengaging herself, she sprang up and said, "Now for tea;" and they sat down to the well-served table.

"Take Mr. Nordheim's seat, opposite me," said the lady.

Marion complied.

"Have you no sister, Marion?"

"None—and no brother either. I am an only child."

"And that is my case precisely, and now we will be brother and sister to each other. I will love you and you shall love me, and Mr. Nordheim "—— She stopped. "Well, Mr. Nordheim don't trouble me with any of his doings, and I don't see why I should bother him with telling that I have adopted a brother;—so, dear Marion, when Mr. Nordheim is at home, you must call me 'Madam,' and be as respectful to my ladyship as if I were Queen of England. But you won't be much troubled with this formality on his account. Now drink another cup of tea. I suppose your clerkship is very anxious to know how I came to marry Mr. Nordheim, and all about it?"

Marion smiled, and looked anxiously at the beautiful creature opposite to him. She took her hands, and flung back from each side of her face the masses of dark, beautiful curls that partly concealed her features, and completely covered her snow-white neck and shoulders.

"I look more like a wild girl than a dignified wife, I suppose. No matter. Mr. Nordheim was pleased with my chit of a face, and my long dark hair. I was very poor—dependent upon my aunt, and I was tired of it. True, Mr. Nordheim was an Israelite, but my aunt, like a good prudent woman as she is, before she consented—no, before she sold me, that is the right word—made Mr. Nordheim settle $2000 a year upon me for life; and I feel independent, at least, if I don't love him. As he don't beat me, I am as comfortably off or more so, than I was when dependent upon my aunt. I believe he behaved handsomely to my aunt—that is, he gave her $1000 the day we were married.—Why, what are you looking at me so earnestly for, Marion?—I married Mr. Nordheim, became his wife, and he brought me on to this big house. The furniture is elegant, is it not? But you have not seen it all yet. Now, have you finished your tea? Then let us go back to the sofa."

Marion went with her and took a seat by her side.

"What do you think of all I have told you?" she pleasantly inquired.

"Why, what should I think, except that you have done what pleased you, and I hope you will be very happy."

Bessy Nordheim drew a long sigh, and then made Marion tell her all his history, his plans and prospects.

"I don't like your being in that boarding-house. Why, it would be much more—— We have plenty of room in this house. Why should you not come here? I will speak to Mr. Nordheim about it, but not just yet."

A key was heard turning in the door, and she jumped up and flew towards the hall. It was her husband.

"Here is your new clerk, come to thank you and me for his situation, Ferdinand."

Mr. Nordheim entered the parlor, and without further notice of his wife, commenced talking to Marion. "I hope to find you very attentive to business. I have a great many things of my own to attend to, independent of the firm, and I hope I shall find you ready to lend me a hand when I need it."

"Certainly," replied Marion. "Anything that I can do for you it will give me great pleasure to do. I owe you my situation."

Mrs. Nordheim had taken a seat, and listened, but said nothing.

"Where are you boarding?" he asked.

"At 119 Liberty street."

Mr. N. made a note of it, and carefully placed it in his pocket-book. "I may want to find you at night. Are you busy evenings?"

"No sir. I have nothing to do."

Very good. I will call at your boarding-house, and some time it may be necessary for you to do some writing for me up here at my house. In such cases Mrs. Nordheim will have a room fixed up for you, and you can stay all night. I will explain the necessity to your landlady when I call at the house."

Marion rose to take his leave—and as he approached Mrs. Nordheim and took her hand, he felt a gentle detention and pressure, and a glance of those beautiful soft eyes, which said as plainly as if they could have talked, "Don't forget your sister Bessie." Mr. Nordheim did not extend his hand, but accompanied Marion to the door, and kindly bade him good night. He had made up his mind that the handsome intelligent boy should be made useful to him in more ways than one.

When he returned to the parlor, he said somewhat surlily, "That boy owes his place to me. I only hope he will be grateful. He is a stranger here, and I must go to his boarding-house and see if he is comfortable. It is my duty to do so, Mrs. Nordheim."

"It is very kind of you; but I suppose boarding-houses are not very comfortable."

"You ought to know;"—and Mr. Nordheim sneered very severely. "I believe your excellent, but somewhat sharp aunt, Mrs. Ferguson, was engaged in keeping a house of that kind, when I was so fortunate as to be struck with your silly face."

Bessy's eyes were flashing fire under their long dark lashes.

"Now, madam, I do not expect that my young friend will be very comfortable at his present location. You heard me say to him that I shall probably require his services up here occasionally to do some private writing for me, and that I should require you to fix a room for him. Now madam, let me tell you, that it is my intention, if he is not comfortable where he is, to ask him to come up here and make it his home altogether; and let me add decidedly, madam, that I expect you will submit to my wishes in this respect, and make no opposition to them. You have objected to my bringing any of my relatives to this house. He is not a relative, but a young boy that will be useful to me, and I prefer to have him in the same house with me. Don't say a word, madam—I *will* have it so." And Mr. Nordheim, who had worked himself into quite a passion, in order to silence any objections that he took it for granted his wife would make, bade her good night, went into the hall, seized his hat, and then passed out into the street.

What a world! Could Mr. Nordheim have looked back into the parlor, and have seen that elegant form, with one foot pressed forward, her figure erect, her eyes sparkling with excitement, as she flung back the long curling tresses which she had allowed to cover and conceal her delighted face while he was talking with her, he might have thought that his determined purpose was not so obnoxious to his girlish wife as he imagined. She burst out into a merry, happy laugh as she heard the street door close, and exclaimed, "Dear, dear Marion! I shall have a brother with me, after all. Who would have thought that Mr. Nordheim himself would insist upon his being here, when I hardly dared to ask it!" She was as innocent and pure as an unborn babe, and it was a sister's love she thought she felt for the handsome boy.

CHAPTER VII.

Mr. Monck moves to Bond Street, and resides with Mr. Nordheim—The Mercantile Library Association—How to learn Languages.

THE new clerk improved in his capacity for general usefulness every week, but he had been nearly a month at his new place, before Mr. Nordheim carried out the idea expressed to his wife. He then called on Mrs. Birch, in Liberty street, and apparently was not satisfied with the place selected for Marion. He informed the landlady that it would be more convenient to have Marion at his own residence. He paid her bill, and when he returned to the office of Granville & Nordheim, he informed Marion of what he had done, and told him to hire a cart, and remove his baggage to Bond street that night. It was Saturday.

"Here is a note, Marion, that I wish you to deliver to Mrs. Nordheim. It informs her that I am obliged to go to Philadelphia this evening, and may not return until the middle of next week. I wish you to take good care of matters at my house. If any thing is needed, get the money from Mrs. Nordheim and procure it. If she wishes to go any where—to church—to any place of amusement, you will go with her. In this note to her, I have written my wishes as I have verbally stated them to you; I hope you will be pleased with your new home."

He bowed and left the office before Marion had any time to

make any comment. As soon as the store was closed that evening, he engaged a hack and went to Liberty street, bade his landlady good bye, and with his trunk proceeded to Bond street.

The hackman had carried his trunk into the hall before Mrs. Nordheim made her appearance. She seemed a little surprised at the trunk, but when Marion had shaken hands with hed, and she had read her husband's note, her features assumed a different apperrance, and were covered with rosy blushes.

"How beautiful you do look, Bessy," was the involuntary exclamation of Marion as he was led by her into the parlor.

"Now, Mr. Truant, give an account of yourself, why have you kept away from here a long month?"

Marion said he did not see how he could come with any propriety, as Mr. Nordheim had told him weeks ago, that he was to come—until the latter directed him to do so, as definitely as he had that day.

"And now that you have come, I am going to make the most of you, brother dear. Mr. Nordheim writes that you are to escort me wherever I want to go, and be my protector while he is gone. Good. I am very much obliged to my husband. Next. I am to fix up your room in the most comfortable manner, and not to fail to treat you with the utmost kindness—you see, sir, I quote from the note. In the first place, I fancy that I have already made your room very cosy, as I had a hint this morning from my lord and master, that you would probably come, and as for treating you with kindness, why, you ungrateful brother, after such a long absence, and such sisterly kindness, have you no reward to offer me?" and, as she put her pretty pouting red lips in close proximity to Marion's, he could do no less than put his arms around her, draw her close to his breast, and press the lips to his own.

"There, dear Marion, that will do, and now I will go and superintend the making-tea department, and you shall have a supper such as I dare say you need."

Had Marion Monck and Bessy Nordheim really been brother and sister, it is not probable that they would have exhibited a stronger attachment for each other. The next day was Sunday. Marion accompanied her to church, and almost every night he went with her to some place of amusement, or called with her upon some of her extremely limited circle of acquaintances. Mr. Nordheim did not come to his home for a week, and during his absence Marion had made himself completely at home, and his attention to the duties of the store were from very early in the morning until sometimes a late hour at night. Mr. Wilson the book-keeper had promoted him to copying letters, and to making duplicates of letters and invoices. As Marion wrote a neat mercantile hand, it was no great hardship. Marion also found work at the dwelling house of Mr. Nordheim. That gentleman was, as I have stated, an Israelite, and had inherited a large property from his father, who had died about two years previously at Amsterdam in Holland. When he discovered that Marion could read and write Dutch, he was overjoyed, and Marion for months worked several hours at night in copying important papers in that language of a private nature for Mr. Nordheim. The latter bought a nice desk, and had it placed in Marion's room. Frequently Mrs. Nordheim would sit and chat with him, while hard at his work. She was as fascinating in her conversation as she was beautiful and attractive in her appearance, although she did not seem to be aware of it. Marion regarded her as a sister, and treated her as he would a sister. He would catch her and draw her upon his knees, and make perfectly free with her balmy mouth and lips. Sometimes if her magnificent hair had been carefully arranged, he would pull out the combs and fastenings, throw it loose over her, and comb it with the finger of one hand, while he continued writing with the other. Bessy would call him her teasing brother, and then select one of her combs, would carefully comb his hair, without preventing his writing. Did a thought of wrong cross their minds? No. She had been isolated first in her aunt's boarding-house, and secondly in the cold home of her husband. She placed Marion on the footing of a brother. He had brought the first sunshine to her cheerless home. She had something to pet, fondle and caress. She never thought it wrong, never analyzed her feelings, and hardly took the trouble to control or conceal them before Mr. Nordheim. Marion was in a new home—he who had been petted all his life, and Bessy was the only one who brought love and home—or home love, back again to his mind. He appeared to regard her affectionate kindness and caresses as he would those of his aunt or his mother. He was too young to dream or think of love. Both were happy, for both were innocent in thought or word as well as deed.

Mr. Nordheim was a man whose age must have been nearly forty years. He was of small stature, with dark, piercing, oriental sort of eyes, and a nose that clearly told his Hebrew origin. He spoke English with great purity, and one could hardly have imagined that Dutch had been the language of his boyhood. He was short-sighted, and wore a pair of gold spectacles. His habits were very irregular, although it was many months before Marion discovered that he was one of the worst of libertines, and that his frequent journeyings to other places for business purposes, and also his frequent absence for the same reasons, were not so. On the contrary he was off in the country, or anywhere else where he could carry on his numerous intrigues without discovery. As he was the principal capitalist, his partner, Granville, if he knew Nordheim's weakness, did not notice it in any manner.

Marion Monck had not been in the counting-room of Granville and Nordheim over two months, before Mr. Wilson, the bookkeeper, asked him how he was off for books?

"Books?" replied Marion. "I have no book, save one, and that is a Dutch Bible which my mother placed in my trunk when I left home." Mr. Wilson smiled. He probably remembered his own mother having made for him, when a boy, (perhaps fifty years before this) a similar provision. "That is a valuable book, no question of that," said Mr. Wilson, "but, Master Marion, what I meant is this, is there any one you know who is the possessor of books who will lend them to you to read, otherwise you will have many an idle hour hang heavy upon your hands." Marion said he knew no one who would lend him books such as he desired. "Mr. Nordheim has books at home." "Then I propose that you should at once join the *Mercantile Library Association*. It was established for merchants' clerks, and when once a member you will have access to any book or paper that you need." Marion asked the expense of joining, and when told that it was only the small sum of two dollars per annum, agreed to go with Mr. Wilson and be made a member that very night. The counting-room was closed before six o'clock, and Marion did not go home, but went to get his tea with Mr. Wilson, at Clark & Brown's eating-house, in Maiden Lane, where Mr. Wilson, with many other Englishmen, boarded, and took his meals when and where he pleased. They each had a cup of tea and hot muffins, and after these were despatched, they proceeded to Cliff street, where the Mercantile Library Association occupied the first floor of number eighty-two. It was then poor and in its infancy. Not long after, it was removed to a building in Beekman street, Clinton Hall. Since then, it has been removed to the old Opera House in Astor Place.

But to return to the visit to the Mercantile Library Association. Mr. Wilson introduced Marion to the Treasurer, Librarian, and one or two of the Directors, and after he had paid the fees, received a certificate of membership. "Is there any particular book you desire?" asked the Librarian. "Yes," replied Marion, and he named a French work by Voltaire. It was given him with a catalogue and the last report of the Association. As Mr. Wilson and Marion went out into the street, Wilson remarked, "Why, Marion, the book you selected is printed in the French language. Do you understand it?" "Not a word," was the reply. "You may think it queer, Mr. Wilson, but I will read that book before I return it. The fact is, Mr. Wilson, I will read French, Spanish and German before I am two years older. I understand Netherland Dutch now as well as English. I will learn a language after my own method, or rather one taught me by Aunt, who taught me low Dutch."

"What is the method?" enquired Wilson.

"In the first place, I can repeat the New Testament almost word for word from beginning to end. I have read it so often, and got so many lessons from it in former years to oblige a very excellent mother. You comprehend that part."

"Very well."

"Within three days I have been to the Bible Society, and they *gave* me for a trifling sum a New Testament in French. I shall read that in French until I have it almost by heart. By the time I am through, or before I have been at it a few hours, I shall understand perhaps a thousand French words, and the mode of placing them without having to refer to a French Grammar or Dictionary."

"That is very clear," remarked Wilson.

"Now I shall get a dictionary and grammar, read the work by Voltaire, and what words I cannot acquire rapidly in the New Testament, I shall get out of the dictionary. It will not be long before I have mastered the French, and the Spanish and German will follow."

"But how will you learn the pronunciation of the language?"

"By placing myself where I can hear one or the other spoken incessantly. But we are up to Broadway, and I must bid you good-night, and hurry up to Bond street."

CHAPTER VIII.

*The Business Excursion of Mr. Nordheim—Birth-place of Clara Norris—
Her Advent into New York.*

It has already been mentioned that Mr. Nordheim made frequent excursions to neighboring cities. He gave out that these frequent trips were for commercial purposes. His partner, Mr. Granville, did not contradict such announcements, and his family were unable to do so.

October had arrived, and Marion Monck had been living at the residence of Mr. Nordheim more than four months, when the latter informed him that the next morning he should leave for a distant State, and would not probably return for some weeks. Mrs. Nordheim was in the parlor engaged upon some embroidery when her husband made this business sort of announcement, and, as usual, she made no comment upon it. Turning to his wife, he said, "Of course, my love, if you want money, you can send word to the office by Marion in the usual manner, and he will bring it up to you." This was said in a very sarcastic manner, and a slight bend of the magnificent head of the young wife was the only reply. Soon after he left the house to go to Pat Hearns', or some other equally well known "Hell," or a worse place.

The carrying out of our story requires that the reader should be carried out of New York, and taken to one of the most northern counties of the state of New Jersey. It is again evening, and only two days later than when Mr. Nordheim told Marion that he was to make a business excursion the next morning. It was night, the tallow candles were lit, and in the bar-room of a country inn in Sussex county was the well-dressed Nordheim. Several rough-looking countrymen were loitering about the bar-room, and two were engaged in playing dominoes at a pine table in the corner of the room. A young and rather pretty girl was behind the bar, waiting upon such customers as required a glass of cider, or the more potent cider brandy. Mr. Nordheim was smoking a cigar, and seated near the fire place, in which a wood fire was burning, for the weather in October in a village two thousand feet above the level of the sea was intensely cold. The girl was evidently about fifteen years of age, but fully developed. Every now and then she cast an anxious glance towards Mr. Nordheim, and as his eyes caught her own, she would suddenly drop them and blush, scarcely conscious why. Mr. Nordheim was evidently an object of curiosity to her, and the contrast between his elegance and the rough customers in the room made her wonder what his business could be there. Presently another person entered the room, and as he stepped into the bar he said, sternly, "Susan, go into the kitchen and help your mother get supper."

"Have you ordered a fire in my room?" demanded Mr. Nordheim of the new comer, who was evidently the landlord.

"I have just finished making it myself, and your supper will be ready presently," was the reply.

"Thank you," was the reply of Nordheim, and he continued to puff away at his cigar. Soon after Mr. Nordheim obtained supper and then retired to his room. He found a good fire blazing upon the hearth, and almost at once the girl called Susan made her appearance with a candle, which she placed upon the table.

"Any thing else, sir?" she asked.

"No, my dear—stay, yes—there is—I want to ask you a few questions. Are you acquainted with a young lady in this neighborhood whose name is Clara Norris? Sit down, Susan."

Susan took a seat before she replied, in a very low tone of voice, "Oh, yes, sir; I know her very well."

"Indeed. Here, Susan, is a little something to spend when I am gone." He placed in her hands half a dollar, patted her cheeks pleasantly—"and now tell me all about Clara. Is she very beautiful? is she as pretty as you are?"

Susan simpered and replied, "Oh, yes; a thousand times prettier. Every body calls her the Sussex Lily, and indeed, sir, she is the sweetest girl in this region."

"How old is Clara, should you think?" asked Mr Nordheim.

"I know precisely. She is just one month younger than me, and I shall be fifteen next month. Do you know her, sir?" and Susan paused to hear the answer.

"No, not exactly, that is to say, I have not yet seen her. I became acquainted with her father last summer, and I have heard him speak of Clara so frequently that I was almost tempted to say I know her, but I do not."

"Oh, she is a charming girl. You will like her very much. She is not at all like me. Her hair is light auburn, and very long, and when she wears it in ringlets it is pretty. She has a beautiful figure, and her cheeks are as red as roses, and her skin is as white as snow."

"Why, Susan, you are quite eloquent in your description," said Mr. Nordheim, and he continued, "Is Miss Clara comfortable in her home?"

"Oh, no indeed, sir. Her father is a drunkard, and her mother is not much better—in fact—worse, some say, but I don't know any thing about it. I see poor Clara every Sunday at church, and she looks very unhappy, I don't know how she stands it. I wouldn't. If my father licked me as her'n does her, I'd run off and go to York, but I must go and help get supper for the other boarders."

"Stay one moment, Susan," and as the girl stopped he slid his arm around her and gave her a long kiss upon her mouth. "Oh, don't, sir—what—will"—but a half dozen kisses in succession stifled her voice, and when Mr. Nordheim placed in her hand another silver half dollar, Susan wiped her mouth, smoothed her ruffled hair, and promised Mr. Nordheim that she would come back as soon as supper was over to see if he wanted any thing. Any of her country beaux might have fiddled around Susan six months before her lips would have given one kiss. Girls like the man, be he old or young, that impudently takes what he wants without trifling or beating around the bush. She had left the room but an instant when her father made his appearance. "Well, Van Ness, what is it?" asked Nordheim.

"Did you send a message by the stage-driver to old Bill Norris, up the road, that you wished to see him?"

"I did. Has he come?"

"Yes, sir. He is down in the bar-room."

"Van Ness, have you any really good liquor, any wine fit to drink? That cider brandy is vile stuff."

"Yes, sir, as good as any gentleman need have, I don't care who or what he is. I have got the best French brandy, but it comes at two dollars the bottle."

"Bring it along if it was five dollars, and here, by the way, is a five dollar gold piece, and if you have a bottle of champagne, bring that up also, and never mind the change. Old Norris may prefer some other drink besides brandy or wine."

"Not he, sir. He will never leave this room as long as there is another drop of that French brandy in the bottle."

" Show him up at once, and then put some more wood on the fire."

A few moments more and the heavy boots of Bill Norris approached the door. "Come in," exclaimed Nordheim, and the old drunkard entered. "Take a seat, Norris. I am glad to see you. I told you at Dover last summer I would come and see you before Christmas day."

"So you have. I like to see a man who sticks to his word. It looks like business."

"True, Mr. Norris: but here is some liquor I have ordered. It is no use talking with dry tongues. Here is champagne, and here is French brandy. Which will you try?"

"Oh, give me the brandy. I don't want any new fangled stuff down my throat," and he helped himself to a stiff glass of raw brandy, and drank it off at a gulp. It did not even make the old toper wink. "Prime!" he exclaimed. "Now I will take another with a little water into it," and he helped himself while Mr. Nordheim knocked off the neck of the bottle of champagne, and as he poured it foaming into the glass tumbler he said, "Now, Norris, I want you to drink with me to the health of that young girl we talked so much about at Dover. Here is Clara's health." Old Bill Norris again emptied his glass and took a seat, and turning his face full upon Mr. Nordheim, said, "So, so, mister, yer hain't got off that notion, eh?"

"No, indeed; the more I hear of her the more anxious am I to come to some understanding with you in regard to her future welfare. Where is she now?"

"At hum, or was there half an hour ago."

"Bill, can any one overhear our conversation?"

"No, I reckon not." Bill opened the door and looked into the entry to see that the coast was clear.

"When you see my darter, if as how you likes her, and she takes a kind of liking to you, what do you intend to do with her? Do ye mean to marry her? That's the pint."

"Mr. Norris, we will talk of that presently, meanwhile, I want to enquire kindly of you whether five hundred dollars, if given to you by some kind friend, would really be of any service to you?" remarked Mr. Nordheim in a whisper.

"What? Just say that over again," and Bill was on his feet.

"Keep perfectly calm, Mr. Norris. I have five hundred dollars that I can get by driving up to the Sussex Bank after nine o'clock to-morrow morning, and I could give it to you without feeling the loss."

"Five hundred dollars. Sussex Bank bills! and"—

"Stop one moment more. I am anxious to do that for you to-morrow. I am anxious to do *more* than that for Clara, if you aid me in the matter. I want to take her away from here, however, and you will lose her services. Of course I expect to pay you for that loss."

"That's fair. Five hundred dollars. Of course I'll let her go for that. She will never bring me any thing like that. Five hundred dollars! Whew! What a sum. Why, it will buy a good sized house and farm, won't it? But you hain't told me one thing. What do you want to do with the girl? Marry her?"

"Mr. Norris, you know it would be imprudent to do so now. What I may do when I have sent her to school, I cannot tell. I shall take her to New York, place her with a rich aunt, and she will be taken good care of. What can I do more?"

"That is all on the square. I don't see what you can do fairer, Mister. What am I to do?"

"Go home very soon. Talk the matter over quietly to your wife. Get her consent. In the morning I will be up at your house, and have a talk with Clara, if she consents to go with me, and the matter is fairly understood among you. She goes to Dover in the stage with me to-morrow evening, and I will hand you and your wife five hundred dollars before we leave."

"It's a bargain. Shake hands upon it. You are a gentleman, and do up your business brown. I will go now."

"Take some more brandy."

"Not a drop," and Mr. Norris left—he was really sober; the five hundred dollar proposition had fairly neutralized the effects of the strong potions of alcohol which he had drank.

He had hardly got down stairs before a light step came up them, and Susan came in, shutting the door behind her. "I came up to see if you needed any thing," she observed.

"Yes, Susy, come here," and he pulled her towards him.

"Don't—don't—I"—

"All I want, Susy, is to hear more about your friend Clara. Kiss me, now, and then tell me, has she any beaux?"

"You kiss me so hard I don't like it. No; Clara hasn't got any fellows. She is too proud for that. None up here are good enough for her."

"Indeed. I am glad to hear that,"—here Susan began to squirm in a very uneasy manner, for Mr. Nordheim was resorting to all sorts of means to stir up the young girl's passions, and probably he would have succeeded had not Susan said, "If you are so anxious about Clara, what do you want to fool with me for?" It was enough. "I was wrong. Now kiss me, to show that you are not angry." Susan complied, and he led her to the door. She had escaped that time, but the poor chirping bird was marked for a shot, and only got away because a beautiful quail was to be looked after.

When Mr. Nordheim was alone, he lit another cigar and then went down to the bar-room. Bill Norris had gone. The room was crowded. Mr. Nordheim had an object—it was to make popularity. Time after time did he treat every man in the room until all but himself were drunk—roaring country drunk, and then he went to bed. How little his elegant wife dreamed of the nature of her husband's commercial negotiations!

The next day opened bright and beautiful. It was much warmer, and Mr. Nordheim rose early. He had ordered a horse and buggy to be ready for his use immediately after breakfast. It came as he had drank his last cup of coffee. He settled his bill, paid for a day's use of the horse and buggy, observing that he might not return. The carpet bag was placed in the buggy, and after a few enquiries as to his route to the house of Mr. Norris, he bade his host "good morning," and started on the main road. He had to drive a distance of two miles. He occasionally stopped to gaze on the woods and the water. The forests were covered with colors as variegated as the rainbow, and he passed two long sheets of water that he could not but stop to admire. Between the two first lakes stood a cottage embowered in a grove of large drooping willows, and not far off was a long row of poplars. He enquired what place that was. "Poplar Farm," was the reply, and he drove on. He had nearly reached the head of the second lake, and was coming in sight of the third, when he noticed a log-cabin that seemed hardly capable of holding up itself. It was large, but every thing about the spot looked poverty-struck and desolate. He was passing on by it when out started a man that he recognized as Bill Norris.

"Hallo. What, you was a-going by, eh? That won't do."

"Have you a place to put my horse, Norris?"

"Yes; I got a little snuggery down under the hill. Drive around the road a little way, and I will come and help you unhitch."

Mr. Nordheim complied, and when the horse was put in

the miserable apology for a stall, Nordheim asked if the mother had been spoken with.

"Yes; and she is willin'. She thinks it the best thing that can be done."

"And Clara—does she know any thing of what is proposed?" said Nordheim, anxiously.

"I rather think the old woman had something to say to her about it, but I don't know. Women folks can't keep a secret, you understand."

Nordheim felt relieved. Half his work was done. The two now reached the log-cabin. Norris entered first, but no sooner had Nordheim followed over the door-sill than he actually started back with astonishment. Never had his eyes been placed upon such a vision of female loveliness. He could not speak. She was dressed in rags, but there was a form, a complexion, a skin that rags could not hide. She had been trying to do up her splendid hair, but lacking combs and material, it had fallen like a golden cloud over her shoulders and reached nearly to her knees. Nordheim jumped towards her, took her hand, and observed, "This is Clara. I need no more of an introduction—don't be scared on my account," and then, with the grace of a man of the world, he placed all at their ease by talking of their future. There was a little boy and a little girl, brother and sister of Clara. To one he gave a pearl-handled knife, and to the other a gold pencil-case. "Now then, Mrs. Norris, I am going to dine with you, and here is some money to buy any article you need. I suppose Mr. Norris will go and get it for you." She took the money. "Miss Clara, as I was riding up, I could not help admiring the mountain in front of us. There must be a beautiful view of the lake from the top of it. Suppose you accompany me, and point out all that is to be seen," requested Mr. Nordheim, kindly.

"Get your bonnet and go with the gentleman," came from the mother's mouth.

"I am in no hurry," observed Nordheim. "Take your own time, Clara." This he said so kindly that the poor girl burst into tears. A few moments after he was following her up the side of the mountain. "Clara," called Mr. Nordheim. She stopped, and he took her hand in his own. "Don't let us go too far and get tired. Here seems to be a nice quiet place, where we can take a seat and talk over certain matters." Clara seated herself by his side. He still kept her hand. "Clara, will you answer me a few questions honestly and truly?"

"I will."

"Are you happy here? Do your parents treat you kindly?"

"No—I am miserable, and they treat me horribly."

"Would you like to leave here?" he asked, kindly.

"With all my heart! But my poor parents!"

"Clara, suppose I say that I will give your parents the sum of $500 to-night, to make them comfortable. Will you then place yourself under my charge?"

"Will I? Try me. But what am I to do?"

"This is all, Clara, if you will make me your husband to-night—that is, you will treat me in every way as if I were your husband."

"But will you marry me to-night?" said the girl, who was covered with blushes. "Speak plain," she continued. "I know what you mean. You will *not* marry me, but you wish me to become your mistress; you have money, and you would buy me! Now repeat the offer," said Clara, determinedly.

"Yes, Clara, that is it. I will take you from here to New York as speedily as possible. To-morrow morning we will start. Then I will get you handsome clothes—I will procure you a home—I will get you teachers, and I will make a lady of you."

Clara smiled, and said, "Listen to me, Mr. Nordheim. There is no need of words. I am a decided girl. I am as pure as ice—but I can't lead such a life. I want to see my father comfortable. Do what you said, and the next night I will return to my wretched room, remain in your arms until morning, provided you then hurry me off to New York. If you do what you promise then, you will have a mistress that will be true to you till death. If you deceive me, or do not make good your promises, woe be on your head! Now let us return to our humble home."

"Stay a moment, Clara. If you are anxious to go, why not start to-day?"

"No—I will not move until I see my mother and father in possession of the price you have agreed to pay for me."

"And then"——

"I am yours, body and soul, and I do not care what you do with me."

"I have the money ready. See, here it is, in Sussex Bank bills. Count it."

He handed her the money. Clara did count it, and then slowly drawing her hand across her face, she asked,

"And when you give that to my parents"——

" Then, Clara, I expect you to regard yourself as mine. We will stay here to-night, or we will go to Dover, just as you decide. Now shall we return home?"

" Be it as you wish—I have no choice," said Clara, mournfully.

Nordheim attempted to kiss her lips.

" No, no," she exclaimed, while pushing him aside. " Not now. Pay the sum to my parents, and then I am yours altogether."

Not a word was spoken until they reached the log house. Clara took a seat.

" Well?" said the father.

" Everything is pleasantly arranged, and Clara and myself have decided to leave for New York city either to-night or to-morrow morning. But I have something for you."

He took out of his pocket-book a roll of bills, and laid it upon the table. Clara jumped up and seized the money. She selected from the roll five fifty dollar bills, and placed them in one pile. " Father, take the money;" and then an equal amount she handed to her other parent, adding, " Mother, take this. God bless you both!"

They each took the money. Then she kissed her mother, and afterwards her father, crying as if her heart were broken. When she had found voice, she said, " Now you have money, spend it wisely. Father, don't drink any more; and when you think of doing it, think of poor me, and perhaps at what an awful cost I earned the money." Then turning to Mr. Nordheim, she added, almost hysterically, " Come sir, you have not yet decided whether you will stay here to-night or go to Dover. Follow me, and I will show you my delightful bed-room. Up this ladder."

She was followed up by the exquisite New Yorker in astonishment. As he reached the floor of the open garret, he exclaimed, " Why, Clara, *where* do *you* sleep?"

" There, she exclaimed, pointing to a pile of rags in a corner of the garret; and she ran towards it, and loosing her hair so as almost to cover her entire figure, she flung herself upon the rags, and said, " Well, what do you think now? This must be our bridal bed if you stay here to-night. My parents have no other."

He went to her, calmed her excitement, and kindly coaxed her to descend the stairs. " We will start for Dover in a few minutes. Fix up Clara the best you can," said he kindly to her mother.

Clara did not cry any more. She spoke kindly to her mother, and helped her to spread the table with a few eatables. An hour later she took her seat in the buggy beside Mr. Nordheim. That same evening they reached Dover, after a few hours' drive. They were just in time to catch the mail stage for New York via Newark. The next night at about ten o'clock the two reached a private house in the upper part of the city, where Mr. Nordheim seemed to be perfectly at home.

Such was one of the business transactions of Mr. Nordheim. It was the opening history of a beautiful girl, who in after years made a sensation as the haughtiest as well as most magnificent courtezan that ever walked the streets of New York.

CHAPTER IX.

The first year over—Dinner at Mr. Granville's—The Family of Mr. Granville—Col. Mac Neil.

LIFE in a counting-room during the period of junior clerkship is without much of interest. The routine is about the same from day to day. A year had now elapsed since Marion arrived in New York, and he had become quite expert in his clerical duties. He was a favorite with Mr. Granville, he continued to reside at the residence of Mr. Nordheim, in Bond street, and oftentimes was of great service to that partner. Young Monck was a hard student, and rarely retired to bed before twelve o'clock at night. He could read French well, and availed himself of every opportunity of speaking it. This was the more easy, as the business of Granville and Nordheim was principally a foreign commission business. They received consignments of vessels and cargoes from many ports in the Mediterranean, and wine and assorted cargoes from Cette and Marseilles were regular. By such means Marion became acquainted with French captains and French passengers that brought letters of introduction to the firm, and he used to show them the hospitalities of the city. His progress in pronouncing French was extremely rapid from these facilities, so that at the expiration of his first year in New York he was a fair French scholar. The foundation was laid, and by practice he improved until he could write, read or speak French equal to a Frenchman. Mrs. Nordheim was his fellow student in French, and her progress was equally rapid with Marion; for Mr. Nor heim spoke French well, and when she expressed a wish to that effect, he would converse with her in that language. Frequently Marion would take part in their conversation.

It was a very curious fact, that for some months Mr. Nordheim had not found occasion to be absent from the city, and he was much more kind and sociable at his home than before Marion came there. He was absent almost every night, but no curiosity was ever expressed by his wife or Marion as to the cause of such absence.

Marion had had very few opportunities of knowing much of Mr. Granville or his family. The intercourse between them was only at the counting-house; and although Mr. Granville appeared to be pleased with the attention which Marion showed to his business, yet he rarely noticed him save to give orders or instructions. Marion had observed to Mr. Nordheim that Mr. Granville did not seem to be aware that he was in existence, save in the office.

"Never mind, Marion," was the reply. "An old merchant like Mr. Granville does not waste much time on the youngest clerk in his employ. Wait."

He took his advice. Precisely one year from the day he entered the office, Mr. Granville in the morning called him into his private office, and somewhat abruptly remarked,

"It is a year that you have been with me."

Marion was astonished. He could not conceive that the haughty merchant by any means should stop to remember such a fact. He did not know the man—and he replied "Yes sir."

"Then to-morrow your salary will begin at three hundred dollars."

Marion bowed and added, "I have not drawn my salary of two hundred and fifty dollars. There is nearly one hundred and fifty dollars due me now."

"How is that?"

"I have been living with Mr. Nordheim, and he has not said anything to me about what he should charge, and I did not think it would be right to draw under such circumstances."

"Go and call in Mr. Wilson."

It was done.

"Wilson, fill up a check and bring it to me to sign for the balance due on this young man's salary up to date. In the coming year it will be three hundred dollars. Now, Mr. Monck, I have nothing to do with my partner taking you to his house. I understand that you speak and write low Dutch, and he has made you useful to him to a greater amount than any board he would charge: Make your mind easy on that score. He will make no charge against you—or if he does, give the account to me, and I will pay it out of my own pocket."

By this time Mr. Wilson had brought the check. It was for one hundred and sixty-five dollars, and Mr. Granville signed it. As he handed it to Marion, he laughingly said, "You will be quite rich. What will you do with so much money, eh?"

"Send it to my parents, sir," replied Marion.

"Very right and proper; and now, sir, will you do me the favor to come and dine with me to-day at five o'clock? I wish to make you acquainted with my family; and you will meet at my table one or more of my friends worth knowing. You know where my residence is, I suppose; and be before the hour rather than later, whenever you are invited out to dine."

"I shall be pleased to dine with you sir, and will not be later than the hour."

Before we present Marion at this dinner with his senior employer, it will be interesting to the reader to learn something of Mr. Granville. William Pitt Granville was the grandson of a man who was once speaker of the English House of Commons. He had been educated commercially in one of those extensive commercial firms in England, whose business connection extended over the world. The firm had sent Mr. Granville to New York to attend to some special business, and his keen eye saw an opening in New York, and he wrote home to that effect. The London firm of Prescott, Grote & Co. had a correspondent named Nordheim, who had a son that he was anxious to place in business in some American port. The London firm saw that they could benefit these parties, besides their own firm, and the result was that old Nordheim agreed to put $50,000 in cash in the firm for his son, and young Nordheim in less than six months became the partner of Mr. Granville. Mr. Granville was the business man. His energy was unceasing. Connexions and agencies were made in every part of Europe; and what with Mr. Nordheim's cash capital, and the facilities extended by the London firm and the elder Nordheim, business rolled in upon the New York firm from every quarter, and their profits in a short time were more than double their original capital.

Mr. Nordheim, as we have before observed, was not much of a business man, and Mr. Granville persuaded him to go to Charleston, S. C., to procure shipments of rice and cotton to New York and to his father's house in Amsterdam. As he had money to advance on all such shipments, he was very successful in procuring them, and his sojourn in Charleston was of great benefit to all parties. It was while residing at Charleston that he became fascinated with Elizabeth Ferguson, and married her, as has been detailed in a former chapter.

To return to Mr. Granville. He was English in his appearance, habits, mode of thinking, and in every other way. He believed that this was a great country to make money in, but that England was the only country worth belonging to; and he never would take out papers to become an American citizen "British I was born, and a Briton I will die," was a favorite expression. He was six feet in height, and well-proportioned. His forehead was very high, and his head almost bald. He was fifty years of age when Marion joined him. His nose was curved like the beak of an eagle, and he felt much flattered when told that this feature very much resembled that of the great Duke of Wellington. It was true, too. He had married in England, and brought over with him, when he decided to remove to America, a wife and two children, the one a girl named Isabella, and the other a boy named Walter. His residence was in a house which is still standing in State street, fronting the Battery. At that time it was the residence of some of the most prominent merchants that New York has produced. It was a venerable double house, painted yellow, with a door in the centre, and an old-fashioned stoop supported by two wooden pillars, with red stone steps on each side, leading up to the doorway. It had a large, spacious hall, four times the size of a hall in a modern house. On the right was a large reception room, or parlor, and on the left was another of equal dimensions. In the rear of the hall was a dining-room, with large bay windows, extending nearly the width of the house, and overlooking a large yard, which was filled with plants and shrubbery of every description. The view from the front parlors, or from any room in the front part of the house, was magnificent beyond comparison. The windows overlooked the Battery and the bay, and the view in the summer season was unsurpassed in the world. There was nothing to equal it in New York. Mr. Granville had good taste.

Besides his wife and children, Mr. Granville had a younger brother residing in the old English mansion. This brother Thomas was as eccentric a being as ever drew breath; and we shall have much more to say of him as our story progresses.

Mrs. Granville and Thomas were the only persons in the dining-room when Marion arrived. It was to them that Mr. Granville introduced Mr. Monck.

Mrs. Granville appeared to be about forty years of age. She was very small in size, and extremely pale. She looked as though a good strong gust of wind from the Battery would blow her away. She put out her hand to Marion, and kindly greeted him, saying,

"I have heard of you often from my husband, and expected you would have visited us before this; I am glad to see you now, and I trust you will come and see us as often as you have leisure."

Poor Mrs. Granville, her days were numbered! Marion soon learned that her seclusion arose from the fact that she was dying of consumption.

"I shall be most happy to continue the acquaintance, believe me, Mrs. Granville; for I know very few families in the city."

"Here comes Isa—my daughter, this is Marion Monck."

And a beautiful girl sprang forward and gave her hand to Marion.

"O, I have seen Marion a hundred times when I have skipped in and out of the office, but I am so glad Pa has brought him here. I am sure we shall be excellent friends."

A moment after Walter, the son came in. He was a handsome lad, of about Marion's age, but extremely reserved. He had already become acquainted with Marion, having seen him many times at the office. A gentleman came in just before the family rose to go to the dining-room. Mr. Granville introduced him to Marion as "Col. Mac Neil, a very old and valued friend."

The Colonel in a very gentlemanly manner expressed great gratification at meeting Marion. Soon after the party that had assembled in the parlor adjourned to the large dining-room. Covers were placed for seven, and when all had taken their seats a dinner was served in a very simple manner, and Marion felt completely at his ease. His seat was directly opposite to Isabella Granville, and before he had received a dozen of her laughing glances, poor Marion began to feel that he was getting in love.

"Bell," as her Pa called her, was a sweet little creature, very girlish in form and figure. Her eyes were black, and she had a profusion of soft black hair, which was partly taken up on the back of her head, and the front portion was arranged in curls. Her mouth was small and pretty. She was ready to fall in love with anybody that there was a spark of romance about. Although only fourteen, she had had two lovers since she was twelve. One was a West Point cadet, and the other an unfledged midshipman; but her father, kind and gentle as he appeared, was a stern, despotic man in his own house, and most fully imbued with the English ideas of marriage. He considered children as merely a means of extending "connections," and deemed it his duty to select a suitable husband for his daughter, and a proper match for his son, where settlements could be made on both sides. He detested cadets and midshipmen, lawyers, doctors and clergymen. He had his own views for "Bell." Mr. Granville was a merchant, in the true meaning of the word, and he looked upon every man outside of the commercial profession as not belonging to *his* world, and as a nobody. He believed in the English nobility, noble blood, and all that sort of thing. He also thought that there might be a nobility in the United States; but if there was any, that no class could justly lay claim to it except the commercial class. A great merchant was an object of profound respect: the President of the United States he regarded as the principal Custom House officer in the nation, and he had a contempt for all Government officers, high or low. He deemed them a pack of useless suckers. There was one class of the world that he respected next to merchants—they were actresses and actors. A celebrated English actress was a Mrs. Granville, a century ago. He was descended from her. This was the clue to the secret, that there was no actor or actress, from Kean the elder to Vandenhoff, and Ellen Tree to Mrs. Wilson and Miss Sheriff, that he did not invite to his house. James and Henry Wallack were his intimate friends. Hackett found a banker in him when he needed one. In a word, no actor or actress came to this country from England without a letter of introduction to Mr. Granville. That was his weakness, if he had any.

When the ladies retired from the dinner table Walter Granville went with them, and the conversation continued until a late hour. Marion was delighted. Mr. Granville treated him as if he had been the richest merchant in the city, conversed with him, drew him out, made him at his ease, and yet not one word was said about the store, his own position, or business. The shop was sunk in the house of Mr. Granville. It was nearly ten o'clock when Marion took his leave, and when he reached Bond street Mrs. Nordheim made him tell her all the events of the dinner, and particularly all that Colonel Mac Neil had said. But Colonel Mac Neil is is too important a person to bring in at the close of a chapter.

CHAPTER X.

Colonel William Mac Neil—Duel of Mr. Graham and Colonel Barton.

"BESSY, pray tell me something about Colonel Mac Neil, whom I met at the dinner at Mr. Granville's yesterday," exclaimed Marion, at their early breakfast next morning to Mrs. Nordheim. "I am sure you know something of his previous history."

"Not so much, perhaps, as you may imagine. What I do know, I obtained from Mr. Nordheim. The fact is, the Colonel is a very gallant man, and regards himself as quite a lady-killer. He made love to me before I had been in New York three weeks. I rather astonished him by repeating some of his love speeches before him at dinner, when Mr. Nordheim was present. The gallant Colonel did not make any more sweet speeches to me, I can assure you. Mr. Nordheim was excessively pleased with my *tact*, as he called it, and in gratitude, I suppose, for its display, told me somewhat of my gallant gentleman's antecedents. The Colonel is Scotch, and of a very good family. He must have been born somewhere about the year 1800, and I have heard him say he was only fourteen years old when his father, who commanded a regiment of Highlanders at Waterloo, was slain. The young Mac afterwards emigrated to Canada with his mother, who married a second husband, and ten years ago came to this city. He was about twenty-one years of age, and had about ten thousand pounds Sterling in money. By Mr. Granville's advice he formed a partnership here and went into the wine business with a Mr. Gillespie, who had no capital but great experience. Colonel Mac Neil is a dashing, fashionable man about town. He goes into the best society, boards at the City Hotel, is a manager at the City Assembly balls, and, though he has made some seductions, and one of his victims he keeps as a mistress in very good style, and has had two children by her, yet he is well received wherever he goes, and he is engaged to be married to the wealthy and accomplished Miss Grasper."

"If he spends money in so princely a manner, I should think he would need to marry an heiress unless his business is a source of great profit," remarked Marion.

"Mr. Nordheim says unless the Colonel marries money, that his high flown game will soon be up, that he gambles tremendously at Washington Hall every night. He is a good hand at cards, I dare say, and it may be that his luck and skill as a gambler is the secret of his having so much money to carry on the war with. You know what a noise he made some years ago as the second in a duel."

"No; I do not. Never heard of it."

"It was a sad affair. By the way, Marion, I do not wish to prejudice you against Colonel Mac Neil. He is a great friend of both Mr. Granville and of my husband. He is a perfect man of the world, and when you are a few years older, it will be in his power to be of great service to you. I recommend you to cultivate an intimacy with him, and receive any advances of a friendly nature on his part with cordiality."

"Thank you. I will not forget your advice. But about the duel?" asked Marion.

"I had nearly forgot it. A Mr. Graham, connected with the *Daily Courier*, had some difficulty with Mr. Barton, who is more famous as the husband of Cora Livingston, a daughter of the great Edward Livingston, than any other act of his life. It led to a demand for satisfaction on the part of Barton. Graham accepted the challenge. Barton, who was intimate with Col. Mac Neil, requested him to act as his second. The principals met, and Mac Neil's advice to Barton saved his life and killed Graham."

"What was the advice?"

"Don't aim, Barton, but raise your pistol to a dead level with your stomach, and fire at the word."

"Mac Neil must be a very cool sort of person on such occasions?"

"It is much easier for the seconds to be cool than it is for the principals, I should suppose. This affair, and the noise about it, made Mac Neil quite a hero among the girls—and all the young bloods about town, if they get into a quarrel when drunk, go to consult Mac Neil about their honor when they are sober. Keep on the right side of Colonel Mac Neil, Marion. I feel that he will be of use to you some day. I did think that Mr. Granville had an idea in his head to marry pretty Isa to Mac Neil. I don't think so now. Why, Marion, how you wince."

"I — nonsense! What difference would it make to me? But why would not Mr. Granville marry Bell to Mac?"

"Because Mac is getting on too fast for Mr. Granville. He

wants Bell to marry a man who has got money and a steady business. Don't you begin life by falling in love with that little face. She is the most arrant little coquette in existence, and don't know her own mind ten minutes. Or if you do choose to get up a flirtation with her, don't make it serious, for she will marry, at ten minutes' notice, any man 'Pa' chooses, and he will not choose you. Another prudent reason for not falling in love with Isabella is this—Mr. Granville would make short work with your clerkship if it was to get to his ears. *Prenez garde.*"

Marion laughed, and thanked Mrs. Nordheim for the information she had given him, and then hurried down to the office.

CHAPTER XI.

Cows and Mocking Birds in South Carolina—The French Coffee House in Warren st., and its visitors.

NEARLY a year had gone by since the close of the last chapter, and two years since the arrival of Marion in New York. Not a week had passed without his writing a letter to his parents, or receiving one from them, and every now and then, he would get some present from home, to remind him that he was not forgotten. He had remitted one hundred and sixty dollars to his father. The latter acknowledged its receipt, and while he thanked his son for sending it, declined to use it for his own purpose.

"We have no need of it, my son, but I have placed it where it will *grow*—in other words—cows are worth here at present only eight dollars. I have bought and branded M M, twenty cows, and have registered them in the parish as yours. Four or five years hence my son will be quite a cattle proprietor. I have taken to Charleston four cages, each containing a valuable mocking bird; they will be sent to you by the first ship."

The ship arrived, and Marion gave one of the birds to Wilson, the book-keeper, one to Mrs. Nordheim, one to Isabella Granville, and the fourth—Mr. Nordheim offered to buy it. Marion refused to sell it, but begged Mr. Nordheim to accept it, adding—

"I have already given one to Mrs. Nordheim."

"I aware of that, Marion, but I wish you to procure the

handsomest cage you can find. Put my bird in it. I will give you the address to which I wish it taken, and you shall accompany it with a note from me. I have to ask an additional favor. You need not mention the circumstance of the bird, or any part of this conversation, or to whom I have given the bird."

"Certainly not, if you do not wish it."

As the office was closing that night, Marion asked Mr. Wilson if he would go and take a cup of coffee with him. The offer was accepted, and they strolled off to No. 9 Warren street. At that time there was a French coffee-house there, kept by a sleepy-looking Frenchman named Blinn. When Mr. Wilson and Marion had taken their seats at one of the small tables, Marion ordered coffee and omelettes for two from Blinn himself, who attended to all orders. The order was given in French. Mr. Wilson remarked it.

"Yes, I must confess that such is my anxiety to perfect myself in French, that I come here every chance I get to practice. There are some very remarkable men, Mr. Wilson, that visit this place daily. Fitz Green Halleck, the poet, who has rooms at 45 down the street; Charles Fenno Hoffman, and several others. I have become well acquainted with Mr. Halleck, and have been to his rooms at Mr. Martine's, where he has roomed for fifteen years. I like him very much. With Mr. Hoffman I am not so well acquainted. He must be preparing himself for death or the mad-house."

"Why do you think so?"

"Because I have seen him drink at one sitting, and that not once, but a hundred times, four or five cups of this French coffee, as strong as lye; but that is not all. He places a large lump of sugar in a teaspoon, puts it across the top of his cup over the coffee, then pours over it a wine glass of *Kirchwasser*, and burns it, the sugar melting and running into the coffee. It is a devil's dose, is it not?"

"Yes, I should think so, if old Lucifer ever stimulates. I should think a few such cups of coffee, with the burnt sugar and Kirchwasser, would waken the old chap up."

"While we are waiting for our omelette I propose to read you a letter from my father," and Marion read the letter about cows and mocking birds.

"Cows are cheap in South Carolina, are they not?"

"Extremely so. But it costs nothing to keep them. If my father does as he says, (and I never knew him do otherwise,) I may own a hundred cows before five years are over."

"It will cost some money and fodder to keep such a stock in the winter," observed Mr. Wilson.

"Not a cent. Those cows will go off in the woods, and perhaps not be seen until next spring. Then father will hunt them up, for they will run with his stock. They will be found with calves; all the bull calves will be selected, fattened, and sent to Charleston, where they will bring seven dollars each. The heifer calves will be branded M. M., and turned adrift again with their mothers and the bulls."

"How do you manage to keep them out of your neighbor's land? Do they break down fences?"

"Fences! Fences are somewhat rare in the great swamps and forests in South Carolina. Our neighbors do as we do with their cattle, and they feed themselves from one end of the year to the other. We only keep up a few cows for milking purposes. Why, we raise hogs and colts in the same manner. What do you think of Mr. Nordheim's asking me for a mocking bird extra, eh?"

"I think he intended to give it to his mistress."

"His mistress!" and Marion jumped up; "mistress! what, does he keep a mistress?"

"A mistress. By the Lord Harry I don't think he keeps a mistress, I think it more likely that he keeps three or four. You seem perfectly astonished."

"I am, and can hardly credit it. His wife knows nothing of it."

"I dare say not. At least I should presume it would not be a very frequent or agreeable subject of conversation in the family circle between man and wife. Don't you remember about four months ago asking me about a beautiful girl with light hair that called to get some money?"

"Very well. She was a beauty, I do remember."

"That was one of the mistresses of our worthy Mr. Nordheim, and she occupies a handsome two-story house in Broome street, not far from Hudson. Nordheim has had her about a year. He picked her up somewhere in the country, and pays house rent, furniture bills, &c. for her."

"It is a shame and a sin," said Marion.

"Not at all. Nordheim is rich, and the firm is coining money. He can afford it, and if a man can't do what he pleases with his own money, what is the world coming to in a financial point of view? I dare say you will see the lady with your own eyes, for I judge that the junior partner intends that you shall carry the bird up to Miss Norris, for that is her name.

Don't those birds cost your father some money? I would not take twenty dollars for the bird you gave me. I have him hung up in Clark & Brown's bar-room, and the chap goes it with a perfect looseness."

"No, they are as thick at Monck's Corners as robins are here in the Spring. They build nests all about our house, and as soon as they are hatched, we take the nest and put it into a cage. The old birds follow, and then they feed the young birds in the cage until they are able to fly. Then we have to be careful—for the old birds, when they find their young *old* enough to fly, and unable to get out, go into the woods and select some poisonous berries, which they administer, and kill the little birds, if not prevented."

"That is queer, and bad in a financial point of view. It is getting late, and I must go," said Wilson.

Marion was extremely embarrassed when he reached Bond street. He had made a discovery in reference to Mr. Nordheim that he would prefer not to have made. He felt guilty himself, and when Mrs. Nordheim asked him what the matter was, or if anything unpleasant had happened, he tried to laugh it off, and only made matters worse. Finally, he concluded that come what would, he would keep the secret, and Mrs. Nordheim remarked, "Very well, Marion, you have made a discovery of some kind that affects me, and you will not tell me what it is. That is not brotherly. I am the best friend you have in the world, and you ought to trust me as such."

When each retired for the night, there was a certain degree of coldness. Marion felt that he must regain her confidence at any cost.

CHAPTER XII.

The Home of the Kept Mistress—The Opinion of a Wife of her Husband's Follies.

TRUE to his word, the next morning Mr. Nordheim, who was absent from breakfast at his own house, met Marion at the office, and handed him a note. It was addressed to " Miss C. Norris, No. 591 Broome street."

"Did you get the cage as I wished?" he asked.

"I did, sir," replied Marion.

"Take the porter and go with it and the bird to the number where this note is addressed. Send him off when you reach there, and deliver the note yourself to the lady with the bird and cage," said Mr. Nordheim.

Not many hours elapsed before Marion was at the residence designated. He inquired for the lady, and a negro girl received the bird cage, and asked Marion into the parlor. He handed the note to the girl, and bade her take it up to her mistress with the cage and bird. While she was doing this errand, he had time to look around the parlor. It was luxuriously furnished, a double parlor, with mahogany doors between, which were furnished precisely alike. The walls were covered with paintings, that at a glance Marion knew to be by the old masters. The carpets were so thick that you hardly heard your own footstep. In both the front and back parlors were centre tables of black Egyptian marble, and they were covered with books, bound in the most costly style of binding. Sofas, lounges and ottomans were in every part of the parlor, and covered with the most costly blue velvet. Marion had no time for further examination, for the girl returned and said, " Missus wants you to come up stairs." Marion followed her, and was shown into a sleeping room extending the whole width of the house on the front part of the second story. His eye rested upon the same beautiful face that he had seen once before, and he recognized her at once. There was a splendid bedstead in the room, but the lady was dressed in a rich silk dressing-gown, and reclined upon a lounge near one of the windows. She raised her head as Marion entered. In her hand she held the note, and by her side upon the floor was the cage and bird.

"Oh it is you, Mr. Marion, you do not know how very glad I am to see you. Mr. Nordheim has often spoke of you, and I have to thank you for for this charming present. There, don't say a word. I know all about it. Come and sit down by me. Do you know that I had to threaten Mr. Nordheim before he would consent that you should come up here ?"

Marion bowed and took the seat.

" I have not had my breakfast. Do ring that bell, and you must take a cup of coffee with me."

Marion was about to decline, but the impetuous girl declared he should. The negress came in, and she ordered a double breakfast. She gazed at Marion.

" How old are you ?"

" I shall be seventeen before many months are over."

" You *are* handsome and good, and I shall like you very much. There, don't blush and look foolish. Wait until you hear me through. You know my relations with Mr. Nordheim. There—don't say a word—that is enough. Mr. Nordheim is kind—very kind—yet he is very jealous. There are things that I need—must have—I crave them. I will have them. I crave knowledge. I read—read—read every thing that I can get hold of. You see what a quantity of books I have got"— (the room was littered up with books.) " I have read them all. Mr. Nordheim says that you are learning different languages. Is that so ?"

" Yes, madam, I am learning languages."

" How many have you acquired ?"

" Two—Dutch and French. I am now learning German. I mean to learn more before I have finished," observed Marion in reply.

" That is capital. I am crazy to learn French, German, Spanish, and Italian. Now tell me, how do you manage ?"

Marion related to her his mode of learning a language.

" You have given me a new idea, and I shall not lose it. But now answer me another question. I cannot go about to coffee houses and French places. How can I acquire the pronunciation ? I know—don't talk. I must have a teacher. Now you can find me a proper person who can teach me French, German, or Spanish. I know you can. Nordheim says so, and he is willing that I shall have one of your selection. Why, Marion, you *are* handsome ! What a fool Nordheim is, to be sure. He might with reason be ten times more jealous of you than any man he has ever brought here yet."

Marion looked confused.

" You need not be afraid of me, Marion. I know your position at the home of Mr. Nordheim. I will not mention the name of that lady—it is too pure for my lips. I hope she is happy. There—don't say any thing. You can serve me in many ways. Will you ? That is enough. I frequently need money. Nordheim will always give it to you, or I will write a note to you when I want any special favor. Now about the teacher. Will you find one for me ? Some oldish man who is poor." Marion promised that he would do so. " Find one, if you can, who can teach me several languages—a German, Pole, or Russian. I understand those people speak three or four languages equally well. Did you notice my piano in the rear parlor ? If I was dressed and down stairs I would play and sing to you. Nordheim has had me taught me the piano, and to sing—also to play on the guitar an accompaniment to myself when I sing. Oh what pleasure ! I should not have

been allowed to learn that, but I could have a woman to teach
me those accomplishments. Pshaw! what am I talking about.
You don't understand such restraints," said Miss Norris. Marion did, though. He was wiser than she thought. "What
delight that bird will give me! What shall I call him? Oh,
I know—Marion. That's a good name. I want you to get me
a quantity of books—will you? You say 'Yes.' I will send
you a list in a note, and you must get the money from Mr.
Nordheim. Look, here is my hand-writing. What do you
think of it? 'Neat and lady-like,' you say? Will you believe me when I tell you that when Nordheim—when I became acquainted with him, I could not write my own name?
I have cause to be grateful to him for some things, if not for
others. Now I know you are anxious to get off to that horrible office. Here is the breakfast. Help me to devour that,
and then you may go. Not till then." She poured out a cup
of coffee, made him eat some nice toast, and when he had finished said, "Now you may go, Marion, but have mercy upon
my mania to learn French, and get me a teacher suitable to
my circumstances." Marion promised, and soon after took his
leave. The reader who remembers chapter eighth of this book
will not need to be reminded that the country girl Clara Norris, who eighteen months previous had been brought by Mr.
Nordheim to the city, and who was then innocent and ignorant, was now the luxuriously located, and the well read and
somewhat literary kept mistress. Nordheim had bestowed
upon her every accomplishment that he could, consistently
with his jealousy of male teachers. Miss Norris had led a life
of seclusion, and devoted herself to study and to reading. Her
mind was maturing for the most deadly purposes. She was
armed with beauty, and needed but the sharper weapons
which the mind's accomplishment would give her, to make her
vengeance felt whenever she should repay upon man the injury she had received from his sex. Marion reflected well
upon his position as he walked from Bond street down Hudson, and when he reached St. John's Park one of the gates was
open, and he passed in and took a seat in an arbor. There he
remained over an hour, endeavoring to satisfy his own conscience as to what was right and proper for him to do under
the peculiar circumstance in which he was placed. "I am
living in the house with the pure wife of my employer. She
is like a sister to me, and here I am forced by her husband
to be a sort of platonic friend to his kept mistress! Now
mind, Marion Monck. Do what is right. You are obliged to

do what your employer civilly asks you to do, but as the only person affected is the wife—and situated as I am, in the house with her, I will not lose her confidence, come what will. If she acts upon what I shall tell her, why then, there will be a pretty general smash up and breaking of things, and I must take my chance." He found Mr. Nordheim at the office. The latter quietly enquired if he delivered the bird and note, and when answered in the affirmative, made no further comment.

Mr. Wilson, the book-keeper, nodded to Marion and whispered, "Been up in Broome street, eh? Expensive in a financial point of view, eh?" Marion smiled and went at his work. When evening came he hurried home, and although anxious, yet as he opened the door of the tea-room in a cheerful manner, he caught the attention of Mrs. Nordheim, who congratulated him in being in so good spirits. "I am, dear Bessy, and I will tell you why."

She gazed into his face a moment, and then said, "Tell me why."

"Because I am placed in an awkward situation. I have not shown that confidence in you that I ought to have done. Come what will, after tea I want you to go up in my room. I have some writing to do, and when we get up there you shall know all." She smiled. Tea was soon over, and Marion went to his room. He was soon followed by Mrs. Nordheim. "Now be seated, Bessy, and I will tell you all that I have kept from you. It may make trouble, but you shall never say I concealed any thing from you, in any way or shape, or look coldly upon me as you did last night." Marion took her hand and told her *all*. Every thing that Nordheim—her husband had said and done, and all about the beautiful mistress and her well furnished home. She never spoke a word. "Well, Bessy, what is the matter? Why don't you say something? Are you angry with me?"

"No, no. God bless you, Marion. You have made me very, very happy by what you have told me. I could not bear the thought that my loved brother—my Marion, my friend, that I would trust with life, could be a traitor and keep back any secrets from me. No—angry? No. Why should I be with you? But I should have been outraged if you had not told me. So they would get you into the meshes of that lady, would they?"

Marion was astonished, and asked, "Well, Bessy; it don't seem to annoy you at all, what I have told you?"

She smiled. "Brother mine, I have known it all along.

All I cared about was your learning what I already knew, and keeping it a secret from me that you did know it. As for *that* girl—or Mr. Nordheim, I don't care the weight of a feather what they do. Did I love him, I might feel different. I married him to obtain two thousand dollars a year. It is settled upon me, and as long as I act right it cannot be altered. Let him do as he pleases. Keep as many women as he pleases. Seduce as many girls as he chooses, or corrupt as many married women as he sees fit. It is none of my business so long as he don't sport them in my face, or bring them into my house. Now that perfect confidence is restored between you and me, I rather like the idea that Mr. Nordheim should have selected you to get books and language teachers for Miss Clara. It will be extremely funny for us to know how my moral husband progresses. But Marion, mind you "—what she was going to say—whether to caution Marion against being entrapped in the golden hair of Miss Clara, it is not our province to reckon. "Marion, you may kiss me to-night as long as you please." Marion drew her upon his knees, unfastened her hair, and availed himself of her offer, saying, as he almost smothered her with his loving caresses, "Dear Bessy, I imagined you would be outrageously angry with Mr. Nordheim and the lady, and that at least you would get a divorce or do something very dreadful. I am agreeably disappointed."

"Marion, you need not have had any such fears. He is not worth the trouble. Now stop kissing me. Go to work at your desk. It is nearly twelve o'clock, and I must go to bed, for I am weary and tired. Good night, Marion; you have shown that you are a dear good brother, and I will never be angry again with you a moment. So she told you that you were very handsome? She is a fool, and ought to know that you are merely a child."

She left the room, and he went to work with his pen.

CHAPTER XIII.

The Marriage of Thomas Granville—General Jackson—The party from New York.

There was a gay party assembled in an old fashioned dwelling in the city of Baltimore, on Christmas eve, 18—. The building was in the old portion of the monumental city, and was known as "the Castle." Few of our readers that have visited that city, but what will remember it. The rooms were spacious, and crowded with guests, who comprised some of the oldest and best families in Maryland. There was more beauty in that assembly than had been gathered together for many years. Washington, the capital, had sent down several guests, among whom was the venerable President, whose slight figure and stern military aspect made all who approached him pause with respect and reverence. It was General Jackson. Several senators and members of the House of Representatives had come down with him.

There had been a wedding at five o'clock that afternoon in the Cathedral, and Archbishop Eccleston had performed the ceremony which made Thomas Granville the husband of Catherine Pinckney. The venerable edifice was crowded with spectators, who had been invited to the wedding, for Granville had troops of friends, and the beautiful and accomplished bride had been the belle of Baltimore. She had refused scores of offers, for she had long given her heart to Tom. To be refused by Kate Pinckney was a part of a Baltimore young man's education. His education was not deemed complete unless he had offered his hand and been refused by Kate. The more intimate friends had been invited to a large evening party at the Castle, given by the venerable grandmother of the bride, whose age was nearly ninety, and yet she was as gay and as lively as any one of the youngest in that gay party. She was the widow of one of the signers of the Declaration of Independence, but had outlived her worthy husband half a century. She was rich, and although eccentric, and at times very penurious, yet when a favorite grandchild married, she spared no pains or expense to make a brilliant display. A daughter had married one of the most gallant of our commodores in the last war, and from this marriage came seven lovely girls and two sons. It was one of those beautiful girls whose marriage had taken place that day.

All the other sisters were present, and their names were somewhat remarkable. The mother had named the younger daughters after leading men. There was Miss Madison Pinckney, next to Kate in years; then came Miss Monroe Pinckney, Clay Pinckney, and Calhoun Pinckney. The sisters, from the eldest, Kate, to the youngest, Calhoun Pinckney, were not less celebrated for their beauty than their superior education and accomplishments. Their father, when alive, had been a devoted friend of General Jackson, and the mother was not less so after his death. Hence the presence of the President on this occasion. He was in good spirits, and seemed as happy as though no cares of State, no United States Bank, or no disunion troubles preyed upon his mind. He even danced a reel with the venerable old dame, whose age lacked but five years of reaching a century. The President offered his congratulations to the bride and her husband with a hearty good-will, and observed to the bridegroom,

"Tom, I understand that you are about to engage in mercantile business in New York. I hope you will be successful; but merchandizing is but a species of gambling, and should you not succeed, come and see me."

Tom had visited Washington—he had told stories and anecdotes, sung songs at the President's fireside, and made many a gloomy, anxious hour pass merrily to the old hero, with whom he became a great favorite. "Come and see me" meant worlds when it came from Andrew Jackson's lips; and when, not many years after, Tom did go and see the old man at the White House, he made him dine with him; and when Tom felt almost discouraged at his future prospects being so gloomy, and was about leaving after the dinner, General Jackson told him to wait a moment. Tom complied, and walked to one of the windows that overlooked the Potomac. The President touched his elbow.

"Tom, that recitation you gave after dinner, which you say is from a play of our friend Howard Payne, was very good—very capital. Appropriate to you, Tom, eh? Pronounce it again here. I like it."

Tom repeated :

"I can believe that beauty such as thine
May possess a thousand fascinating snares to lure the
Wavering and confound the weak; but, what is his
Honor, that a sigh can shake, or his virtue, that a
Tear can move? Truth, valor, justice, constancy
Of soul, these are the attributes of manly natures.
Be woman e'er so beauteous, man was born for
Nobler purposes than to be her slave."

"So he was, Tom—so he was. You and Kate have parted. Very bad—d——d bad. But, cheer up. What do you intend to do? Brother won't help you, eh?"

"No, General, he will not. I believe I am abandoned by all—have got no friends. Don't know what I shall do, unless I turn actor."

"You would make a first rate actor, Tom, but wait a while. You are wild, Tom—everybody says so—I think so myself. But you must keep straight with me. Have you any money?"

"No, General, not fifty cents."

"I will give you thirty dollars—lend it to you. To-morrow I will send your name into the Senate for confirmation as consul to the second city in France. Here is the money to get out of this place with. Come and see me before you go abroad. You will have plenty of friends as soon as your appointment is in the Globe. Good-bye."

But we are getting in advance of our narrative. Our readers must return from this little digression to the wedding party and supper. All the Granville family were there, except Mrs. Pitt Granville. Mr. W. Pitt Granville, his son Walter, and his daughter Isabel, had come on from New York to be present at the wedding. Isabel was one of the six bridesmaids of aunt Kate—her sisters and Miss Benson making the other five. Walter was making the best use of his time with Miss Madison Pinckney, with whom it may not be out of place to mention that he was desperately in love—and these young people were actually engaged to be married. This was a secret kept from the elder Granville, who would have murdered his son in cold blood if he had suspected such a thing for an instant. Miss Margaret Benson, a daughter of Colonel Benson, had come on with the party from New York, as a friend of Isabella and her aunt Kate. She acted as one of the bridesmaids, as before stated.

Tom had six chosen friends from New York who acted as his groomsmen. The first was Colonel W. Mac Neil; the others were Doctor Carnochan, a young surgeon who at that period had but little else to do than attend weddings, or any other amusing affair, though now the leading surgeon of the country, if not of the world. A third was an Englishman of good family, a Mr. Sidney Herbert Cedar, who wrote tales for magazines, and gained by " hook or crook a living." The fourth was Mr. Francis Popinjay, who lived off his wits and his wife's allowance from out of a bankrupt estate swindled out of the Government by a notorious tea importer. The fifth was a character well known in New York as Colonel Le Grand Peacock, and the sixth was Walter Granville, Tom's nephew.

All the New York visitors were putting up at Barnum's Hotel, and late at night, when the party at the Castle was broken up, another elegant repast was spread by direction of Mr. Granville, under Barnum's superintendence. Some of the guests kept it up until daylight, in the long dining-room of the hotel.

It was decided that immediately after the wedding, the

bridal party should return to New York, and then the bride and groom should go to housekeeping at once, in a house prepared by Mr. W. P. Granville, and there spend their honeymoon. We ought here to mention, that the engagement between Thomas Granville and Kate Pinckney had been of some duration. It would have been still longer, had not Mr. Granville senior opened a negotiation with the venerable grandmother of the bride. Mr. W. Pitt Granville agreed that immediately after the wedding he would take Tom into the firm of Granville and Nordheim, and give him an interest in the business; and the relict of the signer of the Declaration, who was a shrewd business woman in her way, agreed to place $25,000 in the concern for Tom, if he kept steady and devoted to business one year. This proved a prudent and safe clause.

The elder Granville was delighted with the wedding. He saw hope for his favorite brother, "Master Tom," as he called him, and he never dreamed that Tom would sport with such brilliant prospects, or pursue a course that would dash his hopes to the ground. The elder Granville confessed to Colonel Mac Neil that he had never witnessed a bridal that opened with such brilliant prospects as that of his brother. Tom was gifted, clever and amiable, and although somewhat eccentric and extremely lazy, yet Mr. Granville concluded that when he became the husband of the brilliant, beautiful, and well descended Kate Pinckney—one who brought money to him and a powerful connexion—one who actually worshipped the very ground which Tom trod upon, and whom Tom professed to love deeply and devotedly in return, they would be happy. These were hopeful prospects for the new beginners in married life; and what would have been the fate of any one of the brilliant crowd at that wedding, if he or she had prophesied that ere one year had passed, Tom would have left business and his brother, separated from his wife, so recently a bride, and that in that space of time she would have applied for a divorce, and that ere two years had passed, it would have been granted by the Legislature of Maryland. Such is life, under the most happy auspices.

The morning after the wedding, all of the party that had come on from New York returned thither with the bride and groom; and as soon as they arrived in that city, Mr. and Mrs. Tom Granville left for Niagara Falls.

CHAPTER XIV.

The Supper at the City Hotel—The Count Falsechinski.

MARION did not go to Baltimore to attend the wedding of Thomas Granville, although the latter gave him a cordial invitation to do so. His opinion of Tom was not very flattering to that gentleman in a business point of view. He thought that Tom was gifted, could tell a good story and sing a song very prettily; but in all other respects he regarded him as a very light and silly fellow. He had a good excuse for not accepting the invitation to the wedding. In the first place the elder Granville would not have allowed Marion to leave the counting room when he himself was absent. He was now seventeen years of age—almost fully developed in stature, and his features possessed a dignity that made him appear older than he really was. Two years and a half in the counting-room had made quite a change in the South Carolina boy. He had been promoted step by step for his devotion to business, and now he ranked next to Mr. Wilson, the head clerk or book-keeper. Marion entered vessels and goods at the Custom House when they came consigned to the firm; he made sales of merchandize, purchased produce for foreign orders, and chartered vessels when needed. He also wrote most of the domestic business letters of the firm, and not a few foreign ones. He had assisted Mr. Wilson so often with his books, that he told Marion as a great mark of his esteem and respect, "Marion, if I were to die, the best thing the firm could do in a financial point of view, would be to put you in my place. You can keep the books as well as I can."

Mr. Nordheim did not go to the wedding. He was obliged to remain and sign checks and papers during the absence of Mr. Granville. Marion, since his interview with Miss Norris, had received several notes from her, giving him commissions to purchase books, papers, journals, and many other things. He had frequently taken them up to her himself, and sometimes sent a note, with the article ordered, by the porter. Mr. Nordheim had frequently given him money to pay for such orders, and sometimes two hundred dollars were called for in one sum. He never refused a demand from that quarter, and thanked Marion for relieving him of trouble and bother. — He was really grateful.

Marion had made several attempts to procure a proper person as teacher of languages to Miss Norris, but the summer and autumn had passed since the request was made, and he had been unsuccessful. He almost despaired of finding one, and he wrote an apologetic note to that effect. The reply was, " Don't give it up. I will wait."

"After the return of Mr. Granville from the wedding at Baltimore, Marion was relieved from many duties that became his while Mr. Granville was absent, and he found more leisure to attend to his own studies and amusements. About a month after the marriage, he was invited by Colonel Mac Neil to pay him a visit at his room in the City Hotel, and to meet a few friends. Marion accepted the invitation, and at nine o'clock was at the place designated. The Colonel had invited a dozen people to a supper which was arranged to come off in his own parlor, for he had a handsome suite of rooms in the City Hotel, which was then kept by Chester Jennings, and was the principal hotel in New York. It was here that all the great balls and famous dinners came off, and it was at the City Hotel that strangers of any note stopped when they came to the city.

The supper was truly a *recherche* affair, and did credit to the Colonel's good taste in ordering it. It is a secret that few men possess, but Col. Mac Neil was an old traveller. There were present at it several bloods and fast young men of the town, and they drank, sang, and seemed to enjoy themselves amazingly. Dr. Carnochan was at the table, and so was Mr. Cedar, the story writer; and to these gentlemen Marion was formally presented. There was a Mr. Wolcott, a son of an ex-Governor of Connecticut, a foreign count with an unpronounceable name, and an Irish gentleman, that Mac introduced to Marion as Mr. John O'Doemall. After the supper had been disposed of, the Colonel introduced cards, and parties were made up in different parts of the room. Marion was seated near the foreign Count, and as he noticed that he did not seem disposed to join himself to any of the parties at the card tables, he determined to form a more intimate acquaintance, and asked,

" Count, do you not intend to play ?"

" No sare."

" I believe I was introduced to you in a somewhat informal manner by our host, but your name escaped me. May I ask you to repeat it ?"

" The Count Adolphus Falsechinski, at your service, sare."

"Count, I am really pleased to make your acquaintance;" and Marion opened upon him in French. The Count spoke it like a French native. Dutch—low Dutch came next. That the Count was at home in, and you could not doubt but that he had lived in the Netherlands from boyhood. The Count was equally pleased to find some one who could speak Netherland Dutch, as it was a somewhat rare accomplishment in New York.

"Pray, sir Count, are you a Dutch Count?"

"No sare—I am a Polish nobleman. I left my own country after the late revolution."

"Then you speak other languages—perhaps better, if that were possible, than you do Dutch, French, or English."

"Sare, I speak the English, the French, the German, the Russian, the Danish, the Spanish, the Italian, the Portuguese, the Holland Dutch, and of course the language of my own beautiful loved country, which is Polish. I am also a good Greek as well as Latin scholar, and having resided in Greece some time, I speak the modern Greek."

Marion bowed to the Count with the most profound respect, and the thought came to him that it was extremely unfortunate that the Count was not poor, as he would be just the person to engage as language teacher to Miss Norris. He took a good look at the Count, and examined his dress. He wore *white* pantaloons. It was January, and the night was bitter cold; but Counts and other distinguished foreigners are permitted to do queer things. Still Marion would not have been much less surprised had the Count wore no unmentionables at all. The coat was a military arrangement, and buttoned close up to the throat. Although it was warm in the room, yet the coat clasped its owner closely, and showed no signs of unbuttoning. Conversation commenced again, and Marion devoted himself to the Count until the party broke up. Occasionally he watched the luck of the players, and particularly the Colonel. He could not exactly tell who was the winner, until he heard the Count remark,

"Ah, what a happy dog! The Colonel Mac Neil has won three thousand dollars this evening. It will pay for many suppers."

As the guests of the Colonel were passing through the hall of the hotel, Marion found himself walking by the side of the handsome Count.

"Do you go up or down town?" he asked.

"Up," replied the Count.

"And as I am going the same way, suppose we keep each other company?"

"It will give me the very greatest of pleasure to do so," said the Count; and so they walked up Broadway. It was a bitter cold night. Marion wore a thick overcoat, but before the two pedestrians had got as far as Canal street, he was almost perished. The Count had no cloak or overcoat, but he did not seem to feel the cold. Marion chatted away about the parties with whom they had spent the evening, and the Count gave him a great quantity of very useful information. He was quite indignant that the young blades who lost their money should have been so green as to lose it to Colonel Mac Neil.

"I am sure, Count, from some of your remarks, that you understand 'bluff' better or as well as any gentleman who was in that parlor. How comes it then that you did not play and win some money yourself?"

The Count replied that there were many reasons, and some day perhaps Marion would be convinced that *one* reason alone was enough to prevent his playing.

The wind blew down Broadway so cold and so piercing, and withal so wild and fierce, that Marion remarked it could not have long left the region of the frozen North, where icebergs abounded. On, on they went up Broadway. Prince and Houston streets were passed, and when they came to the corner of Bond street, Marion stopped, remarking,

"Well, Count, we must part here, for I turn up this street to the Bowery."

"So do I," answered the Count.

The weather seemed to become more intensely cold. They reached the residence of Mr. Nordheim. Again Marion stopped—so did the Count. "At last I am home," said the former. "How much farther are you going, Count?" demanded Marion.

"Me?—well, I really don't know. I shall walk down town again, and if I do not find some place open that keeps open all night, I shall have to keep walking, unless I get so very cold as to make it necessary for me to warm my toes in the watch-house."

Marion was thunderstruck. "Count, I wish you to come in. I have a good fire in my room. It is too cold to talk out here."

The Count declined.

"Psha! no nonsense with me—you don't know me. You can rest yourself a few moments, and then if you wish to go, you shall. It is near two o'clock."

The Count followed Marion into the house, and with little noise they ascended to his room. There was a cheerful fire in the grate. Candles were on the table ready to be lighted, and in addition there was a light supper waiting for Marion.

"Seat yourself, Count, and be at home."

The Count drew a chair to the fire, gave a slight shiver, and remarked, as though he had just found it out, "It is quite cool to-night."

"Decidedly," said Marion, who had got off his overcoat, and had taken a seat in a cozy cushioned rocking-chair. "Now, Count, I want you to deal frankly with me. I am of the opinion that you have no room to go to to-night."

"You are perfectly correct. Such is the fact."

"Excuse me, Count, I do not wish to pry into your affairs; but when a gentlemanly person like yourself makes such an admission, it is high time that some friend should find out what it means."

"You are right. You noticed that I ate very heartily to-night at the supper?"

"I did—and wondered at it."

"This night food passed my lips for the first time in three days."

"Count, Count, this is too bad!" and Marion looked at the supper. The Count understood it.

"No, no. I have ate enough for three days more."

"How is it that I find you in such company, and without a home to go to?"

"Simply this, that I have kept up appearances to the last. Col. Mac Neil knew me under other circumstances. He knows that I can handle cards better than he can. He knows that I am too poor to play. He invited me to-night, with the understanding that if he was beat by any of his rich opponents, I was to take his place, he was to furnish me with means, and my share of the plunder would have been whatever he chose to give me. He was lucky all the evening, and my services were not needed. I was too proud to even tell the person whose supper I had eaten, that I had not a cent, or a place to lay my head to-night. Had I done so, I dare say he would have handed me a five, as he would have done to a beggar, but would never have met me as an equal again."

"Count, do you know that you cannot get out of this room to-night?"

The Count insisted that he would go—that he was sure that he should be a trouble, and made a thousand apologies.

"I would cheerfully let you have money to-night, Count, but no hotel is open, and I really have business for you to do in the morning."

"Business for me!" the Count repeated, as though anything for him to do was an utter, and very absurd idea. He had lost all hope.

"Yes. Business—occupation. Something that will employ your time, and that will give you an income that will support you like a gentleman, as I believe you are. Yonder is a large double bed—you have got to occupy one side, I the other."

The Count would not—he would sit by the fire. But no—Marion would not consent to anything but that the Count should immediately undress and go to bed. The Count was in despair. He would not undress—he would lie down upon the carpet, but he would not trespass so much upon the kindness of Mr. Monck. Marion became really angry, and the Count saw that it was so. He rose from his seat, and with quiet dignity, said,

"Be it so. But you might have spared me from showing my disgrace." As he said this he slowly unbuttoned his coat and removed it from his body, and burst into tears.

So did Marion. "My poor Count, is it possible!"

The Count was vestless and shirtless. Not a rag covered him but that old military coat and the close-fitting military stock. He quietly took off the pair of white pantaloons and his boots. He had not even a pair of stockings.

"Do not be angry with me, Mr. Monck. This is not my seeking—you made me do it;" and as Marion continued silent, he added, "I ought not to have come here, and then I should not have been exposed."

"Exposed!" repeated Marion. "Why, Count, you don't know me. Thank God, you are not far from my size. Now Count, I want you to oblige me;" and he opened a bureau, and took from it two pair of thick woolen under shirts. "Put them on, Count." Two pair of woolen drawers. "Put them on." A pair of thick socks, and last a fine linen shirt were laid across the chair. "All must go on."

The Count consented.

"Now these pantaloons—this vest, Count. Last, not least, this coat. Here is a new stock. Now Count, don't stop yet—I am master here. Put on this cloak—I never wear it. Now Count, you can take all these things off, and go to bed as soon as you please, but all have to go on in the morning; and to relieve your mind of all obligation, let me say this—that before to-morrow night I mean that you shall have employment. Then, if you choose, you can pay me."

The Count was leaning his head on a chair, crying. He could bear up with the thermometer at twenty degrees below zero, but the kindness of a heart that beat at ninety in the shade melted him. He was like a child. "Don't laugh at me, Count," continued Marion, who delicately wished to spare the Count's feelings, " but I have done you the most gross injustice; and I beg your pardon a million of times."

"You, Mr. Monck? Why, in what manner?"

"Tell me, Count, you really wore those white pants this cold January night because you had no other?"

"Certainly: but they were respectable, and no one would notice them at a party."

"Why, Count, I think a hundred thousand times more of you than I did before I knew all this. I did you gross injustice about those pants. I never for a moment dreamed of the real state of the case. I supposed you were a stuck-up foreigner, that wanted to come some new dodge over us unsophisticated Yankees, and out-do us; and that you had put on those white pants to astonish the crowd. You did astonish me. Some day, Count, you will tell me how all this has come about. Not to-night. Now let's to bed, and get a good though short night's sleep, for it is after three o'clock."

Both slept better than usual—the one with the sweet consciousness that he had performed a good action; the other, that he had found a true friend and some comfort in his dreary walk. What passed in the morning in that room must be left to another chapter.

CHAPTER XV.

The Count gets a Place.

THE sun was pouring his most brilliant beams into the room of Marion Monck when he awoke the morning after the supper at the City Hotel. He heard breathing near him, and as he turned his eyes to the spot from whence the curious noise proceeded, he saw the pale face of the Count. He was buried in deep sleep. Marion then recalled all the circumstances of the past night. He immediately arose, dressed himself without making any noise, and descended to the breakfast room. There he found Mrs. Nordheim, who received him very cordially, and then enquired, "Who in the world, Marion, did you bring home with you last night? You were out very late." Marion took her hand and commenced an apology. She interrupted him. "Stop all that. I do not need any explanation. I have the most unbounded confidence in you, Marion, and am perfectly satisfied that when you do any thing out of the usual course of things, it is capable of being properly explained."

"But I must tell you the whole story."

Mrs. Nordheim listened with the most profound attention until Marion came to the part where he had to tell of the Count's real destitution, and then she cried in sympathy.

"Poor fellow! and to bear up so bravely, too! We must do some thing for him. What can be done?"

"Leave it to me, dear Bessy. I have a plan in my head, but have no time to detail it to you now."

"Don't attempt it. Go up and call the Count down to breakfast. I have a nice one all ready, and it needs but an extra plate, or he can take Mr. Nordheim's place. He did not come home last night, and I suppose he will breakfast down town to-day, or in—Broome street. Never mind."

Half an hour later the Count was seated at the breakfast-table. He was a fine-looking fellow, about Marion's size, and the clothes he had received made him look much better than he did the night previous in the white pants. His moustache and imperial were properly arranged, his hair carefully combed, and he was altogether a different person. His conversation was amusing, and Bessy Nordheim was much pleased with him. Breakfast was over.

"Now, Count, I expect you to go down with me, and as I am late, I must hurry you." Marion sent the girl up for his cloak and his overcoat, and after the Count had flung the cloak over his person, they left for Broad street.

Mr. Nordheim was already at the store, and alone in his office. Marion entered, passed the usual compliments of the day, and, after closing the door, asked Mr. Nordheim if he could have a few moments' private conversation with him.

"Unquestionably, Marion. Is there any thing the matter at the house?" said he, somewhat startled.

"Nothing, except that I took a guest there last night, entirely unauthorized."

"Is that all?" and Mr. Nordheim looked listlessly out of the window. Marion continued, and did not stop until he had given in detail all that could operate favorably for the Count, adding, "You know, sir, Miss Clara has been very anxious for a person to teach her languages. I think this is the very man, if it meets your approval."

Mr. Nordheim was wide awake. "You have said nothing to the person about Miss Norris?"

"Not a word."

"Nor to her about the Count?"

"How could I? I have not seen her."

"True, true. Where is the person?"

"Seated in the front office."

"Stay where you are. I will go and have a look at him."

Marion remained. Mr. Nordheim was absent but an instant, and then he returned and resumed his seat, and reflected a moment.

"What do you propose to do in the matter, Marion? He seems a very nice person. Is he capable, think you?"

"I have no doubt about that, and I think that he is in such need that he will be very faithful to you, sir, if you pay him pretty liberally for his services."

"Indeed. You may be right. Suppose you engage him, then. Hire him for the office."

"For the office?" repeated Marion, in surprise.

"Yes, sir. Engage his services at fifty dollars a month, to copy, translate, or do any work required about the counting-room, and make one of the conditions that he shall teach Miss Norris any language that she wishes to learn. I suppose he can support himself very well on six hundred dollars a year, and I will have it charged to my private account. I will speak to Mr. Granville about the matter, and you can tell Mr. Wilson to give him a desk and find something for him to do. Draw a check for fifty dollars, and give him in advance, and take his receipt. When this is done, you had better take him up to Miss Norris. No. Go up yourself, and see what she thinks of it, and if she agrees, the Count can go to give her the first lesson to-morrow."

Mr. Nordheim was a prudent man; if he paid for teaching, he meant to make the most of the teacher.

"When you get things fixed, Marion, you can let me know."

What the junior partner said to the senior, rests with them. Marion informed Mr. Wilson that the Count Falscchinski was to be a clerk from that date, and then introduced them to each other, first telling Mr. Wilson all about the Count, and after he had asked the Count if six hundred dollars a year would keep him afloat, the Count could not contain his joy. He was almost annoying in his expressions of gratitude. "Keep calm, Count, and wait here until I return."

Marion went at once to the residence of Miss Norris, informed her of his success, and told her that now she could learn ten languages, if it pleased her to do so. He informed her of all that had passed. "Poor fellow. I know I shall like him, and you may tell Mr. Nordheim that I thank him very much. When will he come up?"

"To-morrow."

"Oh, no. Send him up this afternoon."

Marion returned to the office, where he found the Count already at work translating some invoices.

"Count, I have some other work for you to do. The junior partner, Mr. Nordheim, has a relative that he wishes to be taught French and other languages, if she wishes it. You will go there this afternoon. I will give you a note, and you can commence your instructions immediately."

"I like that very much, indeed."

"You will devote all the time necessary to the young lady, and purchase such books as she may need. You will get the money from me. Here is a receipt for you to sign for your first month's wages, and here is fifty dollars; and I also recommend you to get a boarding-house without any delay."

The Count promised to do any and every thing. Marion gave him a letter to the lady at No. 591 Broome street, and he delivered it that day, and then returned to the office. Mr. Wilson did not like the new arrangement. He was intensely English, and hated *foreigners*, particularly if they had moustaches.

"I will make that fellow do more work than he ever did before, but I am sorry he is coming into the office. I don't mind his teaching the young woman, although *that* is very bad, in a financial point of view."

The Count selected a boarding-place in John street before night, and gave Marion a very pressing invitation to come and see him. The latter promised to do so the very first opportunity.

"Mr. Monck, I have no words that can express my gratitude to you. Last night I was almost in despair. I meditated suicide. I met you—I found rest—clothes—food—an income, and a home, and a bright prospect of independence. What can I do for you? What can I say?"

"Say nothing at all, Count. Go to work with a good will

Teach that young lady all that you know in languages. Be faithful in that quarter, for your income of six hundred dollars is more for what is expected of you there, than for office work."

"I know that already, Mr. Monck, and rest assured I will teach as no teacher ever taught pupil before, and I will do all that can be found for me to do at the office. God bless you, I say again and again."

CHAPTER XVI.

Tom Granville's Extravagance—Washington Hall, and an evening at a Faro Bank.

AGREEABLY to the engagement made between old Mrs. Chase and Mr. Pitt Granville, Thomas became a partner of the firm a month after his marriage. Mr. Nordheim agreed to it, on one condition, that his share of the profits was to continue the same, viz: one half. It was a generous act on Mr. Granville's part, to relinquish his own half share or any portion of it to his brother, but he did so—to what extent was only known to the brothers. The style of the firm remained unchanged. We have already stated that Mr. Granville had rented a house and furnished it previous to the marriage of his brother. To this house, which was located in Chambers street, the new married couple removed on their return from Baltimore. The house was crowded with visitors, for Tom invited every body that he had ever known, to come and see him, and he gave a dinner party every day of the week, and before March had given two large parties at night, and the doings got into the newspapers. Mrs. Thomas Granville became the talk of the town. Tom himself attended to business for about a month, and then he neglected to come to the office until one or two o'clock in the afternoon. His brother remonstrated, and plainly told him that such neglect would be ruinous; and Tom, to show how he appreciated such brotherly advice, did not come down at all, except it was to draw money. Luckily for the house of Granville & Nordheim, the partnership, so far as Tom was concerned, was a matter between him and his brother. No notice was publicly made, nor was it intended to be until the grandmother of Mr. Tom Granville paid the twenty-five thousand dollars. The way that Tom was going on—spending money at the rate of ten thousand dollars a

year—made it pretty certain that the old lady would back out
of her promise, for it was not probable that Tom's extravagance could long be kept from her. Still the Senior Granville determined to keep his brother within bounds, and
agreed to allow him at the rate of two hundred dollars a
month, and no more. January and February passed, and Tom
rather increased than diminished his expenses, for he told
Mr. Granville on the first of March, only two months after his
marriage, that he required a thousand dollars to pay off what
he already owed, and that if W. Pitt Granville would let
him have that amount, he would solemnly promise after that
to live within two hundred dollars a month. Poor Tom. The
Elder Granville gave him the one thousand dollars, but Tom
was incurable. He flung away the money by the handful, and
did not use the one thousand dollars to pay old claims, but
spent it in new extravagancies.

About a month after the one thousand dollars had been advanced by one brother, and squandered by the other, Tom
called at the counting room to make a fresh demand. It was
evening. The next was packet day, and this was called packet
night. In these days of steamers, the word may not be understood by the reader. In the days of sailing packets, nearly all
the foreign merchants kept their offices open the night before
a packet sailed for Liverpool, London or Havre, those being the ports to which regular foreign packet lines were
established. When Thomas Granville reached the office, he found his brother had left, and was not expected
to return. Mr. Nordheim was in the private office,
and as soon as he became aware that young Granville was
there, he came out, and invited him to go in the private room.
Tom accepted. When they were alone, Mr. Nordheim kindly
inquired after his handsome lady, adding—

"I think you are a very lucky man, Mr. Granville, in securing as a life partner so charming a person."

Tom said he was satisfied with his choice.

"I understand, Mr. Granville, that my partner has given
you an interest in his partnership, and I was given to understand that you would take an active part in the management
of our business."

Tom replied:

"I believe something of the kind was talked about, but I
don't like business. I think it a most infernal bore. My
brother thinks I ought to be down here at ten o'clock, but I
find it utterly out of the question. I never get up until

twelve, and it takes an hour before I get my breakfast down, consequently it is after two o'clock before I could possibly get to the office. My brother found fault, and I gave up coming at all."

"You do not appear to be as fond of commercial business as my partner. He is always at his post before nine o'clock."

"He is, excuse me, a great fool for his pains. No, I don't think business agrees with me, and I shall cut it."

"You married a lady of some wealth, I believe."

"Not a red cent, as yet. She has an old witch of a grandmother who is as rich as black mud. She is ninety-five, and ought to have died long ago, but really she is so dried up and withered, that I think she may outlive me. When she dies, if the old fool will ever oblige her grandchildren so much as to die, she will cut up well, and my wife will get her slice."

"Meanwhile, Mr. Granville, how are you to live? I suppose my worthy partner allows you a pretty liberal sum, eh?"

"So, so, but I am spending more, much more than my allowance of two thousand four hundred dollars, and I came here to-night on a *beg*—disagreeable, is it not?"

"Very, Mr. Granville. People say you are one of the most fascinating dogs alive. Is that so?"

"I am overrated, I fear. I never tried to be very fascinating."

"Now, Mr. Granville, if you were so disposed, you could do me a great favor. I want to get rid of a woman, and if you would exert your fascinations in my favor, with a very beautiful creature, and take her off my hands—get me clear of her, I will not only be very grateful, but I will, as my worthy man Wilson says, make it an object to you in a financial point of view."

"Nothing will give me greater pleasure. Your wife, I suppose?"

"D— it, *no*, man, not so bad as that comes to. No. It is a very beautiful, but terrifically expensive mistress that I have. In a word, I am tired of her. I want to get her off my hands, and yet I will not cut the connexion myself, but if you can gain her affection—get her to leave me, and run off with you in such a way that she can have no possible claim upon me, I will give you, as soon as the work is finished, two thousand dollars. More than that. If you consent to do what I require, I will give you to-night five hundred dollars to commence the war with."

"I will do it, as sure as my name is Thomas Granville."

"You will have hard work. She has an easy time of it and every comfort and luxury, and—and—I think she really loves me;" and Mr. Nordheim stroked his whiskers with great satisfaction.

"How am I to get acquainted with her ladyship?"

"She has a Count Falsechinski, who is a clerk in this office, and who is also employed in teaching her French. You must get him to take you there, or Marion Monck. Do it any way you can, except through me. She is very honorable. Were I to introduce you, and you were to make love demonstrations, she would feel called upon to inform me. That will not do. Is it a bargain? Will you undertake it?"

"With the greatest pleasure; but I must have some money immediately. I shall succeed. Have no fear of that. Three months from this I will claim the other fifteen hundred dollars—perhaps sooner."

"I have not five hundred dollars with me; but I will draw a check for the amount, and go with you to the City Hotel, and Jennings will cash it to-night. He has frequently accommodated me in that manner after bank hours.

The check was drawn and signed, and then these two conspirators left the office in company for the City Hotel. Jennings cashed the check. "I am walking up Broadway, and will keep you company, Granville, if you have no objection." Tom agreed, and on they passed until they came to Chambers street, when Tom invited his companion to go home with him. This was what Mr. Nordheim anxiously desired, and they walked down Chambers street to Tom's residence. When they entered the parlor Mrs. Granville was alone. She bowed to Mr. Nordheim, and then, in a very anxious manner, asked, "Well, did you see your brother? and with what success?"

Tom placed a roll in her hand, and replied, "No, Pitt was out, but Mr. Nordheim advanced me what I needed, and you can thank him for relieving our pressing necessities."

Kate Granville was somewhat surprised, and she thanked Mr. Nordheim, although somewhat coldly, for she had met him on several occasions, and there was something in his manner that did not please a virtuous wife. She was afraid of him, and almost wished that Tom could have procured the money somewhere else. But the money must be had, and she took it and used it.

Tom made no stay at home. Other guests came in, and he left, apologizing to Mr. Nordheim, and saying he would return soon. He called Kate out into the hall. As soon as they were alone, she said,

"No, no, Tom. I know what you want, but I need every cent to pay what we must pay, or be turned out of house and home, and be disgraced."

"Only a hundred, Kate. I must have it. Why, woman, it is mine. I earned it—yes, earned it.

"Tom, you will lose it at gambling. I know you will; you have no luck, and—but here, take it and go; I must get back into the parlor."

Tom got into the street, and with a hundred dollars in his pocket. He turned around into Warren street, and into No. 9.

"Blinn, give me a glass of brandy and water. Has the Count Falsechinski been here yet?"

"No, Monsieur Granville. The Count has not been here yet."

While Tom was sipping his brandy the Count entered: "Ah, Count, I am glad to meet you. What in the name of Lucifer has come over you? Have you discovered a gold mine, a new tailor, or what is out?" asked Tom Granville.

The Count smiled, and took a seat. In a moment, an idea seemed to flash across Tom's mind, for he asked, "Have you got employment to teach French to a young lady—a Miss Clara Norris—eh?"

"And suppose I have, Mr. Tom Granville, have you any objection to my making an honest living!"

"None in the world, Count, for I like you very much. I knew that this coffee-house is one of your haunts, and that you came here every evening. I had heard of a Count being employed in my brother's office and that he taught French to a very dear friend of my brother's partner, Mr Nordheim, but I did not know that you were that Count. You remember your promise some weeks ago?"

"Name it, Mr. Granville."

"You promised that for a small sum you would teach me how to play with the chances in my favor against a Faro Bank."

"Excuse me, Mr. Granville—with the chances *not* in your favor. Ten weeks ago, when I made that promise, I was very poor. I needed money, and I was aware that you were losing money every night at a Faro Bank. I could have saved you from losing, but you did not avail yourself of my offer. I am in different circumstances to-night, and I might decline your offer, but I will not. But I must do one thing. I assist you to-night. I will dictate my terms. First answer me this question: how much money have you in your pocket to lose to-night? Precisely, tell me."

"That is a queer question, Count. But I will answer it. One hundred dollars: no more, or no less."

"Now I will tell you what I will do. Give me that money in my own hand. You can come with me to Washington Hall—to the Faro Bank room. I will play for you, with your money. If I lose it, you are not to say a word. If I win, you will follow me out, and I will pay you one-half of the winnings."

"But, Count, that is rather severe. I put up the money, lose it, if it is lost, and if it wins only get one-half. Oh, no."

"Very well. Then I will not play for you. I put up my experiences against you with your money. It is worth *more* than your money if I win, as you know. Say no more. Those are my terms."

"There, Count, try it. Here, take the hundred dollars; but I will go with you, and if I say stop, or"—

"If you say one word to me, I will knock you down."

"Why, Count, what is the matter with you?"

"Nothing at all. Remember, not a word to me, for I will not only strike you, but I will deny that I have received a cent from you and call you a liar; and, Mr. Tom Granville, the word of the Count Adolph Falsechinski with money in his pocket, will outweigh the oaths of Mr. Tom Granville, penniless as you are now. Trust me as a gentleman, and half the winnings are yours. If we miss each other when we leave the gambling table, I will come directly here. Do you follow."

The Count had the hundred dollars, and the conditions were arranged. Then the Count ordered a strong cup of coffee, and the pair left the French coffee-house for Washington Hall, then the headquarters of fashionable young New York John Mariner kept it then. It has long ago been torn down and its site occupied by Stewart's great dry-goods store. The Count and Tom went into the bar-room. Several of their acquaintances were there, and they all took a drink at the Count's expense. As Tom Granville kept near the Count, the latter whispered, "Don't come near me, or speak to me again, until we meet at the French coffee-house. Don't go to the Faro table with me. Keep by youself."

The Count shortly afterward separated from the party who had drank at his expense, and quietly slipped into the great hall, and then passed to the third floor, and on the right hand side, knocked at a green baize door. A question was asked by some one inside. The Count replied, and his answer appeared to be satisfactory, for the door was opened just sufficiently wide to admit him. When he had entered, the door was closed and fastened. There were two large rooms, separated only by large folding doors. In one of the rooms were several tables, and surrounding them were parties of two or more engaged in card-playing. In the other room was a long table. To this the Count approached. Twenty more persons were seated about it. One man, to whom the Count bowed, was dealing from a small silver box. On the table before the dealer, covering nearly the whole table, was a suit of cards, commencing with the ace and ending with the king. By the side of the dealer was a man who acted as banker or treasurer. He had a box filled with piles of white, red and purple chips. Each white chip was worth one dollar. The reds were fives, and the purples twenty dollars each. Another person sat close by the cashier, with a little box filled with white and black checks on wires. As a card was dealt, he moved a corresponding check in the little box. This was the man who kept the game. The play was running high, piles of red chips were upon the cards, and the luck seemed to favor the bank, for the dealer raked pile after pile of the red chips towards him, and then deliberately restacked them in the mahogany box. Presently Mr. Granville entered. The Count was still standing up. He did not notice him. The play went on. One—and then another, left the room—had lost all. Their faces were haggard and despairing. The Count smiled. He was not ready to play yet. He was noticing one man, behind whose seat he stood. He seemed scarcely conscious of any thing. He placed a pile of red chips upon the ace; the cards were dealt. He had lost. He rose from his seat, and with horrid curses and imprecations upon himself, cards, and every thing else, left the room. The Count took the seat left vacant by this person, who had lost fifteen hundred dollars in half an hour.

"Hand me a hundred dollars' worth of red chips, if you please," said the Count—and as they were delivered to him he deliberately counted twenty, and piled them up before him. A new deal commenced. The Count placed a red chip on the ace —another on the seven-spot. It was some time before either turned up. He was a winner. Meanwhile the Count had watched other cards; the king had been dealt out three times and the deuce-spot twice. He placed ten red chips on the king and five on the deuce. The king won. He had doubled ten red chips. The deuce won. The Count then placed twenty red chips upon the last deuce; it was a bet, and won. He looked at the game board—there was but one five spot in. All the rest had won for the bank. The Count placed fifty red chips upon it, and won. That deal was over, and the Count piled up his winnings, but was perfectly cool. There was no limit to the betting allowed at that faro bank. If it bet fifty thousand dollars, it would be good.

Another deal began. The Count scattered one or two chips on different cards—and they won and lost, until he noticed that but two aces—one seven and one ten—were left in the dealer's box. He put down five piles each of twenty red chips on the ace, and won. He was paid in purple chips. He left all the purple chips on the ace again, and it won. There was but one turn more, and the Count placed five hundred dollars on it. It won. Another deal followed, and the Count played heavier yet. When there was but one ace left in the box, he placed fifteen hundred dollars upon it.

"That is my last play to-night," said the Count sternly.

The cards were dealt.

"He has won," said Samuel—and so he had.

"Pay me," said the Count, and he received from the smiling banker four thousand two hundred dollars, and it was paid as pleasantly as though he would not have cared if it had been four hundred and twenty thousand dollars.

The Count placed the money about his person, waited a few moments, looked at those who continued to play, and then left the room and descended to the bar-room. Several gentlemen who were broke followed him, and begged a small loan.

"No, it is not my money," said the Count.

In the bar-room he asked several up to drink. Then Granville came up, expecting of course to be invited.

"If you drink, let it be at your own expense, Mr. Granville," quietly observed the Count.

Tom took the hint and sheered off. After the drinks had been settled for, the Count walked slowly to the French coffee house in Warren street. As he entered, he saw Tom Granville with a glass of brandy before him. The Count took a seat opposite to him.

"You are lucky to-night, Count," remarked Tom Granville.

"I played my own game, sir," replied the Count.

"You must have won a couple of thousand dollars."

Tom had got so excited before the last deal that he had descended to the bar-room to get cool, and was not present when the Count placed fifteen hundred dollars on one card.

The Count placed roll after roll of money on the table.

"Hands off!" he exclaimed, as Tom put out a hand to clutch some.

The Count then counted it, for there were three bills of one thousand dollars each.

"Four thousand two hundred," said the Count.

Tom Granville ordered another glass of brandy.

"Four thousand two hundred," repeated the Count—"and your share is twenty-one hundred dollars," and he handed him the precise amount.

"Waiter, bring me a cup of coffee and a cigar." He lit the latter, and turning his face to Tom, quietly asked, "What was your meaning to-night, when you asked if I was *the* Count who was teaching French to Miss Norris?"

"Oh, nothing in particular. Count, how can I express my gratitude for this sum of money?"

"By saying no more about it. It is but a trifle, Tom Granville."

"I suppose you will now play on your own hook and win a good deal more."

"You never was more mistaken in your life. I never play at faro when I have plenty of money. I only play with my last dollar, or when I have other people's money to lose or win with. What do you want to know about Miss Norris?"

"I hear she is very pretty. I should like amazingly to get acquainted with her."

The Count laid down his cigar, and gazed into the face of Tom for a minute ere he replied,

"I will take you there."

"When?" asked Tom.

"Now—to-night. It is not late, and as you are a good musician, we will have music, and a gay time of it."

At twelve that night, if Mr. Nordheim had called upon Miss Norris, he would have had the pleasure of listening to a delicious concert. Clara played the piano, the Count accompanied her with the guitar, and Tom Granville, who would have made money as a tenor singer in opera, sang some of the sweetest songs in the English language; and in some few both the Count and Clara joined.

The Count, from some hidden motive, told a little anecdote, how Tom had lent him one hundred dollars, and how he had employed it; and added, "My share was twenty-one hundred dollars, and Mr. Granville has an equal amount in his pocket. I think, Miss Clara, you ought to teach him how to spend it." What was the object of the Count?

Miss Norris regarded Tom as a flat, and she determined to take the Count's advice. She led Tom on so far as to promise that he would take a private box and accompany her to the Park Theatre the next evening.

The two gentlemen left the house together; and as they came down town, the Count told Tom that he had evidently made an impression upon Miss Norris, and advised him to follow it up. What was the Count driving at?

The Count saw Tom safe at his own house, and saw him enter; then he walked down to his own rooms in John street, and enjoyed a good night's repose.

CHAPTER XVII.

Prime, Ward & King—Teaching French—The Thousand Dollar Bill—The Park Theatre.

THE morning following the successful gambling operation of the Count at Washington Hall was a delicious April morning. Eight o'clock found the Count Falsechinski at the counting-house of his employers. Mr. Wilson had already arrived and opened the safe. The Count volunteered to assist him in transferring the massive ledger and journal and other books of a great commercial firm to the long mahogany desk occupied by the book-keeper. When the work was done, Mr. Wilson thanked the Count, who asked, "What shall I commence doing?" The Count wrote a hand that was almost like copy right. Wilson had become aware of the fact.

"If you have no particular objection, Count, I will get you to assist me in the books. You can copy my day entries into the journal."

Mr. Wilson showed him how it was to be done, and the Count cheerfully went to work. The stock of the Count advanced fifty per cent. that morning in Wilson's mind. After some little time had elapsed while working, the Count asked Mr. Wilson to name to him the most responsible private bankers in the city.

"I have not much to deposit with them, but I have this small amount that I should like to have placed in safe hands, where it would be drawing interest," and the Count laid down on the desk two thousand dollars. He took out one hundred dollars. "This I will keep. The two thousand dollars I wish to keep at the bankers."

"Prime, Ward & King, No. 42 Wall street, are the firmest bankers. I would recommend them, but I am not certain that they will take your account. Who could you get to go and introduce you to them?"

"I know of no one," replied the Count.

"Then, Count, I will tell you what I will do. Their book-keeper, Charles Christmas, is a particular friend of mine, and I flatter myself that *my* introduction to him will be as good an opening as you could have. I will vouch for you, Count. About ten o'clock, if you will go with me to that banking house, I will do the needful, and get an account opened with you by that firm."

When Marion arrived, he was somewhat surprised to see the Count and Mr. Wilson on such familiar terms, and he was rather pleased than otherwise.

The bankers alluded to, Prime, Ward & King, were at that time regarded by the commercial community here, and, in fact, in every city of the Union, as the most solid house on this continent. Their bills of exchange on London or Paris would bring one per cent. higher than any commercial firm. The partners of this celebrated house were men of originality. The senior was old "Nat Prime," as he was familiarly designated. He started life in a humble capacity, and rose to be the head of a great banking house. His residence for many years was at No. 1 Broadway, now occupied as a hotel. "Sam Ward," the second partner, built a house on the corner of Fourth street and Broadway, and added to it a gallery of paintings, that was the wonder of the people in that day. James Gore King, the junior partner, was born in England, where his father, Rufus King, was Ambassador from the United States to Great Britain. He was named after James Gore, a celebrated merchant. All these partners died long ago. The Count and Mr. Wilson went to the banking office of this firm. Wilson introduced the Count to the book-keeper with a request that he willingly complied with. In a word, the Count was introduced to Mr. Ward, one of the partners, his account was received, and he deposited two thousand dollars, and wrote his signature upon the signature book. He also received a bank book, on the leather cover of which was printed Prime, Ward & King in account with, and written underneath, the Count

Adolph Falsechinski, and inside he was credited April fourth with two thousand dollars, bearing interest at four per cent. per annum. When this was all done, the Count took his leave, but not until he had made a very favorable impression upon Mr. Ward, who begged to serve him in any manner. The Count was a deep planner, and knew the world. In opening an account with Prime, Ward & King, and getting one of their bank books with the name of Count Adolph Falsechinski upon it, and a sum to his credit, he had procured a credit, a consequence, an endorsement, backers, position—that would be valuable in any part of the Union. There was no disputing it. It was worth more than a reference, for either of the partners would have said they knew nothing of the Count. An authorized banking book, with a credit of cash in with so respectable a firm, told its own story. It was the best kind of a reference. The Count had his opinion of it. It was near twelve o'clock when all this was completed, and the Count, instead of returning to the counting house, parted from Mr. Wilson, and went to Broome street to give a French lesson to Miss Norris.

He found Tom Granville already there. Miss Norris received the lesson, which occupied nearly two hours. Tom remained quiet until it was finished, and then insisted that Clara should read French with him an hour. Tom was a good French scholar, for he had in early life resided two years in France.

"By-and-by. I will not now. I want to scold the Count for not coming earlier. I waited for you two hours this morning."

"I am sorry for that, Miss Clara. I will be more punctual in future, but the fact is, I was obliged to visit my bankers, Prime, Ward & King, this morning,"—here he displayed carelessly his bank book,—" and I was detained talking with Mr. Ward longer than I expected."

Tom opened his eyes, and even Miss Clara felt a greater respect for her teacher. Here was more mystery. A count, and a book account with Prime, Ward & King.

"Count, Mr. Granville has secured a private box at the Park Theatre to-night. Shall we have the pleasure of your company? You will be welcome."

"What is the novelty? What is to be played?"

"The Opera of La Somnambula. Mr. and Mrs. Wood and Mr. Brough, with his magnificent bass, all appear in it."

"I shall accept your invitation with pleasure. I knew the Woods in London."

"The deuce you did. Tell us all about them, Count. Is Mrs. Wood his wife?"

"To be sure she is, but she was divorced from her first husband, who was Lord Lennox. Lady Lennox procured a divorce, and then married the tenor Wood. Lord Lennox used to beat her, it was said. I must go now, but will be here precisely at seven o'clock to accompany you to the theatre."

"Mr. Granville," said the fascinating Clara, after the Count had gone, "how much have you left of the two thousand dollars you won last night? They say you are a terrible fellow to spend money. I dare say you have spent it all."

"No, I have not. I have had no chance. See, here it is. Count it."

Clara did as she was desired to do. She took a thousand dollar bill. "Tom, I will be your banker, and keep this for safety. You will squander it. It will do you no real good. With me it will be quite safe."

Tom looked anxiously—

"What, afraid of me! Here, take your old trash. What I proposed was for your own good, and you know it well," and the fair girl pouted as though she was angry in earnest.

"My dear Miss Norris, you entirely mistook me. Keep it, by all means. I have the most perfect confidence in you. Indeed, I insist you shall be my banker."

In the struggle to force her to keep it, her face came near Tom's, and he kissed her.

"You naughty man. That is the first time I have been kissed, except by Mr. Nordheim, since I was a country girl. I do not see how you dared to do it. I will take good care of this money, if you wish it, but really, I had rather you would take it back."

But no, Tom Granville would not consent to do any thing of the kind.

"Very well, then, I will keep it safe, and you can have it whenever you wish. I should serve you perfectly right if I never gave it back to you. It was very wrong for you to kiss me. What would Mr. Nordheim say, if he knew it? But to show you that I forgive you, I will read French with you an hour, and then I must go, for I expect Mr. Nordheim, and he must not see you here."

Clara procured a book of French plays, and lay down on the lounge. Tom drew an ottoman near her head, and they read together. Tom was completely lost. That reading finished him. He was madly in love with Clara Norris. She saw it— her pride was gratified, and she allowed him more kisses, and when he left he was perfectly insane about her. Wife, brother, business, all were forgotten. No sooner had he passed into the street than Clara took from her bosom the thousand dollar bill. Then she walked to a black walnut bureau, unlocked a small drawer, and took from it a bank book. Outside on the cover was marked "The American Savings Bank in account with Miss Clara Norris." She opened it, and read off various sums. Five dollars, ten, fifty, eight, twelve, thirty-two, fifty, seventy-five, one hundred, two hundred.

"Very good. This is a changing world. We do not know what may happen. Mr. Nordheim thinks I am very extravagant. So I am—this book says I have already squandered in that Savings Bank eleven hundred dollars;" and she rang the bell. The colored girl answered it.

"Cheeky, I am going out to be gone an hour. If Mr. Nordheim calls, say that if he will walk down Broadway to Stewart's dry goods store, he will meet me coming up."

The lady went out. In less than an hour she returned, and took the same book from her bosom. Another one thousand dollars had been placed to her credit; and she carefully locked the book in the drawer, and placed the key around her neck.

"Now I must dress for the opera to-night. What will Nordheim say? But Tom Granville is brother to his partner. Surely he can't object to my going with him—and if he does? What a fool Tom Granville is! And yet I rather like him. So I do my mocking bird Marion. But that Count—heigho! I wish I knew his history—it must be a strange one."

There was a curious grouping of people in the old Park Theatre that night. Stephen Price was the manager, assisted by quiet Simpson. The Woods were cramming the house every night, and the treasury was overflowing. On this particular day the Woods had dined with Mr. Granville at his residence in State street, for he had been very kind to them, and was their banker. Colonel Mac Neil was at the dinner, and one or two more. Mr. Wood insisted upon placing a private box at the disposal of Mr. Granville and his family, and the offer was accepted.

Mr. Nordheim had also secured a front bench in the dress circle. He had invited Mrs. Tom Granville and her sister Miss Madison Pinckney to go with him. He knew that Walter Granville loved the latter, and so to have Mrs. Tom all to himself, he invited Walter to go with him.

Mrs. Nordheim, the day previous, had expressed a wish to hear the Woods, and Marion had been able to secure three prominent seats—and he invited his old friend Wilson to take tea in Bond street, and then go with Mrs. Nordheim and himself to the theatre. This was agreed to.

When the curtain rose that night, the pit, the dress circle and the galleries presented from the foot-lights one sea of human heads, and they were all in raptures with the performance. Brough sang "My Boyhood's Home" as it never has been sung since, and Mrs. Wood enchanted the audience with "False one, I love Thee Still."

When the curtain descended, people began to look about them. Marion was the first to utter an exclamation of surprise. The front seats occupied by his party were directly opposite the centre of the stage. A little to the left was Mr. Nordheim, Mrs. Kate Granville, Walter Granville, and Miss Madison Pinckney. On the right hand stage private box was Mr. Granville and his family, including Col. Mac Neil, and in the opposite box was Mr. Thomas Granville, the Count Falsechinski, and Miss Clara Norris. Mr. Nordheim smiled, and came around and spoke to his wife. Marion, when Mr. Nordheim had left, pointed out Miss Norris to Mrs. Nordheim. The only person who felt particularly foolish was Tom Granville. Mr. Nordheim informed Mrs. Tom who the lady was that Master Tom had chartered a private box to accommodate. The eyes of the brilliant Kate flashed fire. She felt humiliated and disgraced, the more so, as Mr. Nordheim expressed the deepest sympathy, and mentioned the fact that the senior Granville and his party had been informed that Tom was in company with a kept mistress, and that it must be very annoying to his brother! Poor Kate! Her love was fast changing to contempt; and Tom was more confirmed in his mad love for the beautiful woman by his side, as he noticed the withering glances that were bestowed upon her by those nearest and dearest to him. Isabella Granville leaned on the front of the box, and attracted universal admiration. Marion seemed particularly struck with her loveliness, and made some very enthusiastic remarks in her favor to Mrs. Nordheim. She sighed, and in a tone of voice that was overheard by honest, tenderhearted Wilson, remarked,

"Have a care, dear Marion; don't fall in love with that trifler, or you will feel more sorrow than you ever yet have known."

Wilson seemed struck by the sigh and the remark with a new idea, and he turned his eyes from the one to the other, but he did not say what he thought of it, even in "a financial point of view."

Walter Granville did the worst thing he could have done. He tried to escape the observation of his father, and yet not actually neglect the fair Miss Pinckney by his side. It was of no use, for the senior Granville had a pair of eagle eyes, and his course was decided upon in his own mind.

At last the opera was finished. Tom and the Count went to a supper party at a Broadway Saloon. The rest of those that we have grouped together returned to their homes.

CHAPTER XVIII.

A Marriage Arranged—Departure of Walter Granville—Death of Mrs. Pitt Granville.

It is not our purpose to write a philosophical work; if that were the case, we might philosophise upon the foolish but notorious fact, that a majority of parents, especially those who are possessed of wealth and aristocratically descended, or in position, deem it a parental right to interfere in the marriages of their children, and if these children happen to form any attachment, and the object of such attachment does not happen to come up to the parents' standard of the husband or wife, they have arranged for their child, they or one of the parents goes to work to break it off.

Walter Granville was an only son. His father was most anxious that he should tread his own footprints, and be able to succeed him in business, and to keep the name of Granville in the commercial world for another century at least. The father had given him a good education, and "Master Walter" had recently graduated at Columbia College, with considerable credit to himself. It was now the purpose of the father to place his son in the counting-room, and to have him settle down in life, as he termed it. He had determined that Walter should marry at once. True, he was not out of his teens, but that fact was of no importance to the senior Granville. He had a horror of Walter falling in love with any young woman that he, the father, did not deem a suitable connection. He had been driven almost to madness for several months, by having hints given him, that Walter was in love, and engaged to Miss Madison Pinckney. True, she was a very beautiful and a very accomplished girl. That is all very well so far as it goes, but to a mind like old Granville's, there was nothing tangible either in beauty or accomplishments. He wished for his son's wife, something more reliable. He could give a business and settle money on his son, and in choosing a wife for him, he wanted the other side of the house to be able to do the same thing. He had other objections to a marriage between Walter and Miss Madison Pinckney. His brother had married one of the sisters, and one of the family was quite sufficient, as there was no money and never might be any. It all depended upon the caprice of a "mean, mad, woman" as Tom designated the grandmother of his wife.

"If Walter will marry, I have a girl in view, that he shall marry, and I will make him do it at once, or know the reason why." Thus spoke Pitt Granville to himself. The party that he had fixed upon was Miss Margaret Benson, the daughter of Colonel Benson, and one of the bridesmaids at the wedding of Kate Pinckney.

Colonel Benson had served in the English army, but he had married an American widow lady of wealth, who owned a plantation and several hundred negroes on Ashley River, near Charleston, South Carolina. He had resigned his commission in the British service and settled in New York, where he became a special partner in a commercial firm, largely engaged in the English trade. The Colonel held some sort of special agancy for the British Government, which gave him no small income. His wife had one son by her first husband, whose name was Glen Hammond. The latter was a wild harum scarum fellow, who was travelling in Europe. By Colonel Benson she had two children, a son and a daughter.

The name of the son was Middleton Benson. He was nearly of age, and was devoted to business, being engaged as a clerk where his father was a special partner. The daughter Margaret was a tall, dignified girl of eighteen years of age, very haughty, and proud of her descent and her position. She worshiped her father and was not likely to fall in love with any man, except such a one as her father would approve.

Colonel Benson and Mr. Granville were on the most intimate terms. If the latter had needed for any sudden emergency half a hundred thousand dollars, the Colonel would let him have it any day before three o'clock. They dined, supped and made excursions together, and almost every evening if one did not come to the the house of the other, that other was sure to know the reason. The marriage of Walter and Margaret, had often been a topic of conversation between these two fathers. But while Walter was at college, there was no need of being in a hurry. But the public attentions of Walter to Miss Pinckney at the Park Theatre had brought matters to a climax, so far as Mr. Granville was concerned, and the next morning he sent a note to Colonel Benson, asking him to dine in State street that day. The result of that dinner was, that Mr. Granville agreed to place Walter in business as soon as he was of age—to settle immediately upon him, real estate that should produce two thousand dollars clear income, and the Colonel agreed to give his daughter a house, and furnish it, and settle upon her and her children the income of thirty thousand dollars, two thousand dollars a year addition, and these conditions were to be complied with at once, and the marriage to take place without any delay. Both parents shook hands cordially when these preliminaries had been arranged, and then they agreed to drink an extra bottle of choice old Madeira to the health and prosperity of the 'to be' married couple.

The same evening Mr. Granville called Walter to his room, and informed him of what he had done to settle him for life. Walter listened, but did not say a word until his father had amplified and explained all the advantages of the match; he concluded, " Now, Walter, I want to hear your opinion."

" My opinion or wishes seem to have been little consulted."

" You do not mean to say that you are not pleased with the arrangement I have made for you ?"

" Has Margaret Benson been consulted ? Is she aware of the honor about to be conferred on her ?"

" What in the world has she got to do with the matter, so far as we are concerned ? Her father will arrange with her. It is my duty to attend to your welfare and happiness. Now, Walter, speak out like a man. Don't have any foolish modesty. Of course you authorize me to say to Colonel Benson that you are delighted with the prospect, and all that sort of thing, eh, Walter ?"

" Father, I believe you love me. I do not think you have any thing nearer to your heart than my happiness. Is it not so ?"

" Of course it is, my boy. I love you better than I do myself—and I flatter myself that if any proof were wanting that I love and care for you, this arrangement between Colonel Benson and myself made this afternoon, is enough to convince you of the fact."

" Father I cannot marry Margaret Benson—I do not love her."

"Pooh, pooh, is that all? You will soon learn to do so. You must marry her—I have given my word."

"There is still another reason. I love another, and I have promised to marry that other."

"You have! I think, Master Walter, that I have one or two words to say about *that*. You mean Madison Pinckney. She has not got a cent, and is very extravagant, or will be so, if she ever gets a chance. No, no, Walter—drop all such nonsense. I will give you until to-morrow before I go to dine with Colonel Benson to think it over, and then I think you will do as I wish."

"Father, let it be settled now. I cannot give up Miss Pinckney, and I *will* not. My word is given to her, and my affections also. If you do not sanction my marriage with her, I must do without it, or wait until you do. I will not marry Miss Benson under any circumstances. I do not love her, nor could I have done so, had my love to Miss Pinckney never existed."

"Now hear *me*, Walter Granville. From this moment I disown you as entirely as if you had never been born. Go out of this house forever. Go and marry Miss Pinckney to-morrow if you choose, or go to the devil. You have disobeyed your father, and I will disinherit you. You have mortified me beyond measure. How can I look Colonel Benson in the face? You need not go penniless. Take this money."

Walter took it, and then flung it upon the floor.

"Perish your money—I want none of it, and I will get out of the house before an hour. I merely wish to bid my mother and my sister good-bye—and farewell, Sir. The day may come when you will regret this harsh treatment."

"Never, sir. If you should change your mind, and come back obedient to my wishes, you will be my son once more. Until that day comes, I care not to see you again. Begone!"

Walter Granville bowed and left the room. He was not long in packing a trunk with clothing. That done, he went to his mother, who was an invalid. What passed between mother and son is only known to them. Isabella was not at home. An hour after a hack conveyed Walter and his trunks to the City Hotel. He selected a room, and then hurried up to Chambers street to his Aunt Kate's. Madison Pinckney he felt could sympathize with him. He found her alone.

Walter had yet to learn another lesson. Madison Pinckney was perfectly cool and very calm, while Walter, whose mind was frenzied, narrated all that had passed. At last Miss Madison spoke.

"You are a silly boy, Walter. Quarrelled with your father, and he has turned you out of doors."

"It was for your sake, dearest Madison. I could not marry Margaret Benson and continue to love you."

"And pray, who wished that you should? But, Walter, you certainly have no idea that I am such an immense simpleton as to dream of marrying you, after you have been cast adrift by your father. I would do nothing of the kind. We would starve in six weeks. Love is very fine if you have money or business enough to keep house and be comfortable. Now I advise you to forget me as quick as possible, for if your father has fairly made up his mind against me, and in favor of another young lady as your wife, further words are useless. He is not a man to change, and although as his son, you are of some account in the world, yet cast off by him I don't know what you will do."

"But, Madison," exclaimed poor Walter, who was completely heart-broken, " your letters—your caresses — your promise—your "—

"Do, for mercy's sake, stop repeating that lover's catalogue. I dare say I have been very foolish, but I did not dream that your father would oppose your marriage with me. Now be a good boy. My advice is to go to your papa. Tell him you have been to see me, and that you have told me that you cannot marry me, and promise your father that you will marry Miss Benson any day that you are called upon to do so."

"My dream is over," exclaimed Walter. "Past—gone."

"That is right, Walter. Wake up and get over dreams as soon as possible. They are extremely unhealthy, and make people nervous. Come and see me as a friend any time that you have leisure. I must say good-night, now," and she left the room. Walter seized his hat and hurried back to the City Hotel. He was enraged and mortified at himself. He did not go home to State street again. That evening he met with a wild young fellow that he had known for some years—a regular New York boy.

"I'm off to morrow," said Charley King.

"Where to?" enquired Walter.

"On board a whaler bound round the Horn."

"Could I get any berth aboard?"

"Certainly; and the skipper would be glad to get you. Have you got any money?"

"Plenty."

"Then let's have a regular night of it."

Walter agreed. They visited every drinking place as long as any was open, and then returned to Walter's room. The next day Walter had shipped for a whaling voyage. The ship Dorothea went to sea the next day, and it was many months before Mr. Grunville ascertained what had become of his son.

Meanwhile Mrs. Granville became worse. The loss of Walter preyed upon her mind, and her strength failed daily. May arrived, and one morning Mr. Granville did not come to the office. It was whispered that Mrs. Granville was worse—dying. Then a note came for Marion Monck to come at once to State street. When he arrived, the servant said he had orders to show him up to Mrs. Granville's sick room, where Mr. Granville was. He entered the room. The proud merchant was weeping and kneeling by the bed, with a hand of his wife in his. Isabella, too, was sobbing as though her heart would break. Marion was about to retire from so sacred a scene when the eyes of the dying woman fell upon him. "Come here, Marion," she whispered, "give me your hand, and promise me that you will be a faithful friend to my two children, and find the lost one, and tell him his mother blessed him before she died." Marion promised. "They will need a true friend some day. Be a brother to my poor Isabella. God bless you." Marion left the room, but not the house. He remained in the parlor. Some time elapsed, and then Mr. Granville came into the room, still sobbing.

"It is all over. She is dead. Close the office, and then come back for further directions. Bring Mr. Wilson down with you."

CHAPTER XIX.

The Cholera—Summer—Changes.

The funeral of Mrs. Pitt Granville was plain and simple, and according to the English mode. She was buried in a vault belonging to Mr. Granville, in St. Thomas' Church Yard. The office was closed the day she died and the day the funeral was celebrated. All the connexions went into deep mourning, and for a few days Mr. Granville forgot his usual gaiety. The spring months passed away, and then came the summer, that terrible summer when the Asiatic cholera made its first appearance in New York. What a scattering of people when the facts became apparent that the long dreaded scourge was here! Mr. Granville took his daughter to the residence of Colonel Benson after Mrs. Granville's death, and when the cholera broke out she was with Colonel Benson and his daughter at Niagara Falls.

Mr. Nordheim closed up his house in Bond street, and found a refuge for his wife at the village of Woodbury, some twenty miles north of New Haven, Connecticut. He did not remain but a week with his wife, and then started off on a tour of pleasure. Mrs. Tom Granville and her sister went to Saratoga, while Tom accompanied Clara Norris to her early home in Sussex County, New Jersey.

Mr. Granville concluded not to leave the city, and his example was followed by Mr. Wilson, the Count Falscchinski, and Marion Monck. Although the Count continued his lessons daily to Miss Norris up to the day of her departure, yet he had regarded them as a secondary affair. Save when absent to give these lessons, he had devoted every hour to business. He was at the office early and late. At last he became so useful to the book-keeper, that he made him his assistant, and Mr. Granville ordered his salary raised to eight hundred dollars per annum, and to be paid by the house, and not out of Mr. Nordheim's private funds. Mr. Granville invited Marion to take up his residence at his house in State street to keep him company.

It would be a melancholy chapter if I were to relate all that occurred in the city while the cholera raged here. It did not make Marion falter or flinch. At that time there was scarcely a store in Broad street except the one occupied by Granville & Nordheim. The street was filled with private residences and boarding-houses. Opposite to Mr. Granville's store, at No. 24, was a boarding-house. Marion counted in one day nine coffins taken out of the one house, and that very evening he felt convinced that he had the cholera. Mr. Granville was alarmed, and made him go to bed, and sent for funny old Doctor Francis. He was shown into Marion's room. There Marion lay groaning with the cholera. The Doctor felt his pulse, asked some questions, and Marion related how many coffins he had seen come out of No. 24 Broad street. The Doctor smiled, and ordered up a slice of bread. When it came up, he made up two or three small pills with it. Marion looked at his proceedings with astonishment.

"Take these pills; they will cure you," said the Doctor.

"Why, they are nothing but bread," said Marion, and he jumped up in a rage at the idea of the doctor making fun of him.

"Why, the very sight of my pills has cured you," and the Doctor laughed heartily. Marion commenced dressing, and he could not help laughing also. It was catching. Mr. Granville laughed, and so did the servant. "Nothing serious is the matter with you. You have no cholera. You have seen so many coffins to-day that your nerves have become excited, and you fancied you had the cholera. It's lucky for you, my boy, that I discovered the fact, or you might have had it in earnest, and perhaps died with it," said Doctor Francis, solemnly.

The Doctor descended to the parlor, accompanied by Marion Monck and Mr. Granville. A glass of old Madeira made Marion quite well, and when the Doctor departed, he went part way home with him. Many persons in the hands of less sensible doctors died that summer with the cholera who had no more cholera at the commencement than did Marion. The doctors treated such cases as cholera, and they died of cholera.

While the epidemic lasted, only once did Marion leave the city, and then he obtained leave of absence for a week, and he spent it at the village where Mrs. Nordheim had gone.

There are some lovely villages in the State of Connecticut, and none more so than the beautiful town of Woodbury, in the County of Litchfield. It is on the mail route between New Haven and Litchfield, and about fifteen miles south of the latter town. The town extends three miles, with houses prettily laid out along the whole line. There are three places of public worship, and one, the Episcopal, is located in the corner of a burying ground that has been used as such for over two centuries. At the south end of the burying-ground is a neat, well-kept inn, with a large garden that adjoins the burying-ground. It was at this inn, or hotel, that Mrs. Nordheim had obtained quarters during the prevalence of the epidemic in New York. When Marion obtained leave of absence for a week, he hurried up to this town, and he was delighted with it. It was such a contrast with a town in his own State of South Carolina. In the village where he was born there was not a school-house, and, in fact, not one within thirty miles. In this Connecticut town there were no less than five district schools, and one academy kept by one of the clergymen of the aforesaid churches. Marion soon became acquainted with the principal people. He attended singing schools, went on fishing excurcursions, clambered over rocks, bathed in the river, and almost every day accompanied Mrs. Nordheim to spend the afternoon or evening with some one of the families with whom she had become acquainted.

The week of absence soon passed away, and he returned to the city. Mrs. Nordheim continued to reside at the village inn until the cheering news reached there that the cholera had abated in the great city. Arrangements were made for her return, and one lovely October morning she left the quiet country life to take her part again in the city of New York.

One by one, family after family, returned to New York, and about the close of November the principal part of the absentees had returned, and were as gay and devoted to worldly pleasures and pursuits as though the Almighty had not sent a destroying angel into the city to remove by sudden and horrid deaths a large portion of the unthinking population.

CHAPTER XX.

The Commercial Success of Marion Monck—The Count Falsechinski speculates and makes money in Stocks—The bargain of Mr Granville with Mr. Nordheim—Marion is nineteen years old—Mrs. Nordheim propo es a party—The Irish Adventurer, John O'Doemall—Anecdote of h s Arrival in New York.

A YEAR passed away from the time when the scattered and scared persons alluded to in our story returned to the city after the cholera summer. During that year few changes or occurrences took place worth noticing. The duties of the counting house of Granville and Nordheim were carried on as usual, and their business increased rapidly. Mr. Nordheim was absent from the city, or engrossed with schemes of his own personal pleasure. After the death of his wife, and the departure of his son Walter, Mr. Granville seemed to lose a portion of that business energy that so strongly characterized him. These two facts flung a greater responsibility upon Marion Monck, and Mr. Granville had already entrusted him with a power of attorney to sign the name of the firm. It was a great trust for so young a man, as Marion was not quite nineteen years old. But he was of the right metal, and this confidence served as a more powerful incentive to renewed activity and devotion to the business of his employers.

The Count Falsechinski, during the eighteen months that followed the cholera summer was not idle. He devoted his time to the duties of the office, and by a careful economy had increased his deposits with his bankers, Prime, Ward and King. He had become acquainted with the different members of that distinguished firm, and one of the partners made a suggestion to the Count, in reference to taking an interest in a purchase of stock, which was to be " cornered," which proved valuable ; for the Count availed himself of it to quite a large amount, at least to four times his capital; his bankers making the purchase, and retaining as a " margin " the funds of the Count in their hands. One December morning, the Count received a note from his bankers, requesting him to call at the banking house, No. 42 Wall street, early in the morning, and Mr. Ward surprized him by saying,

"Count, you are aware that our firm purchased for your account ten thousand dollars' worth of Morris Canal stock. It has advanced fifty per cent. on the price we paid. Shall we sell it at the Board to-day? I think it has reached a high limit. It may go higher, but you will make a good thing of it at yesterday's quotations. What do you say?"

The Count had very little to say, except to authorize the sale at the Board that day. His orders were complied with. The stock had advanced still more, and when the Count's bank book was wrote up and handed him next day, he found that he had to his credit over eight thousand dollars. This did not move him. He was the same quiet, smiling, unobtrusive Count. He attended in Broome street, and gave his lessons to Miss Norris regularly; and that young lady was already an excellent Spanish and German scholar, as well as French, which was the first language he taught her. Frequently he met Tom Granville at the residence of Miss Norris, but the Count took very little notice of him on such occasions, nor did the notorious fact that Tom was perfectly fascinated with the beautiful and accomplished girl seem to disturb the usual placidity of the Count. Occasionally, when he called to give a lesson, he met Mr. Nordheim in the house of Miss Norris, and he seemed pleased with the progress that his protegé had made.

Our readers will remember that Tom Granville had made an arrangement with Mr. Nordheim to take Miss Norris off his hands in a specified time. He had signally failed; for although it was quite apparent that Clara liked Tom, yet her ambition to learn, and the advantages she had in her present relations with Mr. Nordheim, made her decline in the most positive manner all overtures to change, or make any arrangement with Master Tom. Now and then, when Tom became clamorous for funds, Clara would give him a few tens from the amounts she received from Mr. Nordheim, but she never went to draw money from the Savings Bank. She received Mr. Tom Granville's attentions without the slightest objection. She allowed him to escort her to public places on all occasions, and it would almost seem that she was aware of the secret purpose of Mr. Nordheim, but she kept her own counsel in this respect. Tom occasionally spoke of his progress to Mr. Nordheim. The latter merely smiled, with a few words, such as, "Well, Tom, more money, I suppose." Tom would leave with a hundred dollars in his pocket. He still kept house in Chambers street, but left his wife to get on as well as she could; but when she needed advice, she found an adviser in Mr. Nordheim, who was a regular visitor in Chambers street, and escorted Mrs. Tom Granville to nearly every private party which she attended. Many who had met them frequently in public, thought that they were Mr. and Mrs. Nordheim.

Meanwhile Marion Monck was residing in Bond street, where he had removed when Mrs. Nordheim returned from the country after the cholera. Marion and Bessy were like brother and sister.

Another visitor now made his appearance in Bond street, and not a Sunday passed that he did not dine at Mrs. Nordheim's. This was no less a personage than our serious, methodical old bookkeeper, Mr. Wilson. His attachment to Marion, his sterling integrity and good sense, had rendered Mr. Wilson a great favorite with Mrs. Nordheim, and a welcome visitor. He was a safe man, and the lady felt that he was one of those that could be relied upon in a case of emergency, should such a case ever approach her home. The Count Falsechinski was also a regular visitor at Bond street. He was accomplished, and helped to while away many an hour pleasantly that without his music and animated conversation would have been dull and cheerless.

December had arrived, and it was near the anniversary of Marion's birth-day. Mrs. Nordheim had determined to make some preparations for the day when her "brother Marion" would be nineteen years old. She had consulted with the Count and with Mr. Wilson, as to what she should do to make the occasion an agreeable one, and to be remembered. They advised a party in the evening, and this was decided upon.

"Marion," said the lady, a few days before the event was to happen, "I am going to give a small party on the evening of your birth-day. I hope the idea will please you."

"Most unquestionably; whatever you do, dear Bessy, pleases me. I have a happy home, and I ought to be very thankful to you. I wish you would tell me how I can be sufficiently grateful for all your goodness and kindness to me."

"By telling me who to invite that you know, and that I do not. See, here is the list of those I have already invited."

Marion took the list, and carefully read over the names.

"Why, you seem to be better acquainted with the names of my friends, Bessy, than I am myself; and yet there is *one* name that is not on the list, and I wish you would invite the person. I have met him frequently, and he has behaved with great civility to me. I know of no way to return it except by inviting him here. I will take the invitation when you have filled it up, and deliver it myself. Here is the name." And Marion wrote in pencil upon a slip of paper, "John O'Doemall."

The name was transferred to an envelope, and in the course of the day Marion delivered it to the party for whom it was intended. He found Mr. O'Doemall in his room at the City Hotel, for this Irish gentleman never stopped at any place except it was *the* first-class hotel.

As Mr. O'Doemall will be frequently introduced into this local history, it will perhaps be as well that I should give a brief narrative of his career from the time he reached our hospitable American shore, until he makes his appearance as one of the leading characters in our story.

Ireland never sent to the United States a more perfect gentleman than John O'Doemall. He claimed to be an Irish peer, but in disguise. He spoke the Spanish language as well as English, was really handsome, very aristocratic in his bearing, dressed well, had the manners and used fluently the language of an educated gentleman. He was a fascinating lady-killer. He could discourse of beautiful scenery, Moorish palaces, the Alhambra, Mount Zion, and the river Jordan, life in Spain, in Germany, France, Holland, Greece and the East, including Jerusalem, Grand Cairo, and Mecca. There could be no doubt but that Mr. O'Doemall had been a very great traveller. Exclaim suddenly "Jack—you Jack!" and Mr. O'Doemall would jump up hastily and reply, "Ay, ay, my Lord!" This was tried on frequently by doubtful people, who had heard of this peculiar trait in this original Irish character. There seemed no possible way of accounting for it, except by surmising that gentlemanly Jack had been, at no very remote period, a valet to some Irish or English peer, and had travelled with the said peer in those countries which Mr. O'Doemall could talk so learnedly about. This was probably the true secret of the former occupation of the Irish adventurer. Doubtless he had committed some rascality that had parted him from his noble patron, and rendered it necessary that he should try the American continent. He landed from a Liverpool packet ship of the Black Ball line, but as his name never appeared in the list of cabin passengers, it was reasonably supposed that he came in the steerage. Before he had been in New York a week, he could have been found at the City Hotel, located in a comfortable apartment, and perfectly at home.

One day at dinner his agreeable, gentlemanly language

made an impression upon a neighbor at the table who formed one of a group of gentlemen that were sipping their wine together after most of the other diners had left the table. This gentleman invited John to take a glass of wine with him, and finally to draw his chair nearer and join the drinking party. John cheerfully accepted the invite, and before another hour had passed he had made a still more decided impression upon the individual alluded to. The conversation became general, and John was brilliant. One of the party having made a statement that anybody could earn a living in this country, was asked by John O'Doemall the following question :

"How can a reduced Irish gentleman earn an honorable living ?"

"Easily enough ; provided he is not too proud to take any situation that offers."

"What position could I get ?" asked John.

"I have but one that I could offer you," was the reply. "I keep a hotel at West Point, and I need a bar-keeper."

"And if you think I would suit you I accept the situation," said O'Doemall.

The bargain was concluded, and Mr. O'Doemall received a sufficient sum to pay his hotel bill. The next day he left the city in company with his new employer, and before the week had passed he was concocting drinks for the pupils of Uncle Samuel's great military establishment near the Highlands.

This worthy hotel proprietor had a young and very beautiful sister. Of course it was not long before Mr. O'Doemall became acquainted with this sister, and also with the fact that she had the snug little sum of ten thousand dollars in her own right, which sum would become hers the very day she married. What arts so accomplished a traveller as Mr. O'Doemall used with a simple country girl to fascinate her, it is needless to mention. They can be easily guessed. How quietly and how adroitly everything was managed was wonderful. Had a thunderbolt pitched into the brain of the worthy landlord, he could not have been more astonished, than when one afternoon, just as he was preparing to take a siesta after dinner, his barkeeper requested a private interview. Somewhat astonished at the request, the landlord complied. When they were alone, Mr. O'Doemall remarked,

"I believe sir I have been with you three months ? Perfectly satisfied with my manner of performing my duties ?"

"I have no particular fault to find, Jack," said Mr. Cozzens.

"Well, sir, I shall leave you in the down boat this evening, and shall take my wife with me."

"Your wife! I didn't know you had a wife! Where the devil have you kept her?"

"I have only been married about a week, sir. Perhaps you will have the kindness to read this certificate. It slightly concerns you, and when you are satisfied, I shall expect some sort of arrangement in reference to the trifling sum of about ten thousand dollars that you are trustee for, and I will henceforth relieve you of the duties of trusteeship."

"Intriguing, d—— scoundrel!" was the only comment uttered by the landlord, as he read the certificate. "Bring your wife here immediately."

"With pleasure."

The girl came. But why prolong such a scene? The brother's horror—a woman's faith. O'Doemall secured her property—had it placed in his wife's hands, and a few days after the husband and wife came to New York. Before six months, O'Doemall had the whole sum in a bank in his own name. He had wheedled his poor wife into giving him the money. He took a store down town, and commenced business as a wine merchant. Before a year had expired, the poor wife died in giving birth to a child. O'Doemall was all right. He had secured the money safe by proper deeds and gifts, and was now a regular boarder at the City Hotel—as more than a year had elapsed since the death of his wife.

Had Marion Monck been aware of these interesting antecedents, I question whether Mr. O'Doemall would have been invited to his quiet home. Marion knew nothing of them. He had first met O'Doemall at the rooms of Colonel Mac Neil. He had been introduced to him as a merchant of capital, and he had perceived that he was an agreeable man of the world. Mr. Nordheim also associated with and recognized him, and besides Mr. O'Doemall had bought of the firm a large bill of wines, and he had paid the cash for them. With such and other collateral evidences of respectability, what occasion had Marion to hesitate about introducing him to his home circle? He had none.

CHAPTER XXI.

Mrs. Nordheim gives a Party—Marion Monck is nineteen years old—John O Doemall—James G. Bennett at a party—Henry W. Cedar—Mrs. Woodruff—Marion and Isabella Granville—An offer and an acceptance—Secrecy enjoined—An anecdote of the Author's "first love"

THE eventful day arrived. Marion Monck was nineteen years old. He did not make his appearance that day at the office of Granville & Nordheim, except for an hour or two in the morning, and he returned to Bond street to assist Bessy Nordheim in the event of her needing such assistance.

"Bessy, I have invited more people without your permission."

"Pshaw. What do I care for that? I have invited a few more than I had on my list. But we have room—plenty of room, and I shall have a gay, happy time of it. Our party will be a regular old fashioned party, Marion. I will not have one uncomfortable if I can help it. But pray, Marion, whom have you invited?"

"First. Mr. John O'Doemall; but you know all about that. Next, a person connected with the press—with one of the daily papers. He is a young Scotchman, and used to live in Charleston."

"That alone, to a Charleston girl, is almost a sufficient letter of introduction, without any other. What is his name?"

"Bennett—James Gordon Bennett. I was introduced to him at Mrs. Coffin's, the large boarding house on the corner of Broadway and Wall street, opposite Trinity Church. I like him very much. He is quiet—very intelligent, and you will be pleased with him, Bessy."

"Very likely. Who else have you invited?"

"Then I frequent Ned Windust's Shakespeare, near the Park Theatre. I have invited two friends from that region, although I had previously met them both at Colonel Mac Neil's room at the City Hotel. They help fill up, and are perhaps as much my friends as many others that will be here. One is a literary man named Cedar. He writes for the Weekly Mirror, and for some of the monthly journals, and he also writes novels. He promised me one, which I will give to you when I get it. The other is a young doctor and surgeon named Carnochan. He is also Southron like you, only born in Florida instead of South Carolina. He has been quite a traveller in getting surgical knowledge. He studied in Scotland three years—in Paris he walked the hospitals four years, and was several years the favorite pupil of one of the first surgeons in this city—Doctor Mott."

"Then I suppose he has a large practice."

"In playing billiards, I dare say yes, but as for private practice, I do not, Bessy, believe he has a solitary patient in New York. He is a gay man—good looking—rather careless—has a prospect of property, and—well, I think he lives off those prospects, and a few dollars he gets now and then from a rich uncle."

"I like him already. He must be an original, and when night comes, if your three friends come also, I will try and make them at home, and that is all I can do. Have you no curiosity to know who I have invited?"

"To be sure I have. Do I know them?"

"Yes and no. You have observed the wealthy widow lady that lives next door to us."

"Certainly—Mrs. Woodruff is the name on the silver door-plate. I am glad she is to be here. Do you know I have a great admiration for her? She lives so quiet, no noise, sees few friends, has her pet rabbits, parroquets and parrots, mocking birds, canaries and dogs. Why, I have tried to steal her beautiful fawn colored Italian greyhound half a dozen times, but I did not like to be so unneighborly."

"I am glad that you are pleased with my inviting her, for you will share the responsibility of the act with me to Mr. Nordheim. I do not know how it is, but on one or two occasions when I have mentioned the name of our lady-like neighbors in his hearing, he has turned up his nose one degree more, and then followed such a curious expression upon his face that I asked him once if he knew any harm of Mrs. Woodruff."

"Pray, what reply did he make?"

"Nordheim said he did not know any harm of her, on the contrary, that he believed she was highly connected, and that her husband was a man of great genius, and died wealthy, leaving her a princely fortune and no children."

"She has some of the handsomest equipages in town call at her door," observed Marion.

"That is true. We have occasionally spoken when we have met at the door, and this morning I boldly asked her to be present this evening, and she accepted. In addition, I have invited Mr. and Mrs. Parker and their beautiful niece Julia. They live up the street, and called upon me and Mr. Nordheim yesterday. They are immensely rich, have retired from business, and are very desirable people to know. Mrs. Parker prides herself upon being one of the principal leaders of fashion. She is only twenty-five years old, while he is fifty if he is a day. The niece is but seventeen. But who is ringing away at that door-bell? Is there nobody to answer it? Go, Marion, to the door yourself."

Marion went and opened the door, and returned, leading by the hand, Isabella Granville. The look of intense admiration with which Marion gazed at the beautiful girl whose hair fell over her face, her cheeks red with excitement, and her eyes dancing with joy, was not lost upon Bessy Nordheim. She was rather cool at first, but it did not last long.

"I have come to help you, dear Mrs. Nordheim. Papa said I might come, and I will do all in my power to relieve you of your care about the party," said Isabella.

"Thank you, Isa; but I must be at work, so I will leave you and Marion to amuse each other."

Mrs. Nordheim left the parlor to go and look after the servants. Poor Marion. Isabella Granville took off her bonnet, then her shawl, and then Marion seated himself by her side. They chatted and laughed, and finally Isabella adjourned to the piano, played several favorite airs, and sang the words. Marion stood by and drank in every note. Isabel looked up at him, when she had finished. "Isa." It was all he said, and then he took her hand in his, and led her back to the sofa. He put his arm around her waist, and again repeated, "Isa, I love you." She did not make any reply, but leaned her head over on his shoulder. The perfume of her hair almost took away his breath. He kissed her forehead, and then, more bold, he pressed her pouting, cherry-ripe lips—not once, but a dozen times, and—she returned it.

Mrs. Bessy Nordheim, where were you all this while? Down in the kitchen—the sweat pouring out of your face, as you gave hurried directions about the baking and cooking arrangements; and he for whom you were making all these extra preparations, was only over your head, giving away his first, his puppy love, to a silly little coquette who did not know her own mind five minutes.

"Isa, I love you. Do you love me in return?"

"Oh, yes; very much indeed. I love you a great deal more than I ever did Frank Clacksome, or that stupid William Senless, although I did love them once, but I don't now. I have loved you ever since—let me see—ever since my mother died. But you must not tell any body that I love you," simpered Isabella.

"Of course, dear Isa, you will let me speak to your father and"——said Marion, earnestly.

"Oh, no. Certainly not. The idea of such a thing is perfectly frightful. Why, he would lock me up, beat me—I don't know what he wouldn't do. He would very likely make me marry Middleton Benson at an hour's notice, as he tried to make Walter marry his sister, and you know I could not run away and go to sea, as Walter did. Now don't look so cross, Marion. Kiss me again," was Isabella's reply.

Marion complied, and told Isabel that he thought she was alarmed without cause. "Why should your father object to me? I am only nineteen, it is true, but you are very young. We can wait, dear Isa. However, I will do as you wish; but will you promise to marry me when your father gives his consent?"

"To be sure I will. But then you are not to ask him and not to say a word to a soul alive until I tell you that you may. I will be very angry if you do," observed Isabella.

Marion promised. All further conversation was interrupted by the entrance of Mrs. Nordheim, who was too much excited by her culinary troubles to give any heed or even to notice the sheepish looks of the two young friends. She called upon Isabel to go up stairs with her, and Marion was alone. It was his first love. There was a pretty face, his employer's daughter—and imagination must do the rest. He thought Isabella perfection itself; but he was only nineteen years old, and as ignorant of the sort of partner he had been making love to as though he had never seen her. Youth must love something. If it is not a reality, it will be an ideality. I well remember that my first love was a young girl that I first saw in St. George's church. I attended that church in Beekman street two years for no other earthly or heavenly purpose except to see her every Sunday. I did not know her name even. Then I went to the East Indies—to Canton—was gone a year. Eight months of that period I was at sea, and I walked the deck at night and indulged thoughts of her. I dreamed of her. All my aspirations of future success in life were associated with her. When I returned, I hurried to that church, for it was Sunday morning when I landed from my Canton voyage. I found her there. That Sunday I cultivated the sexton, and ascertained her name and where her parents lived. It was opposite St. John's Park. There for weeks after dark, I used to go and sit on the stone foundation of the iron railing, and look at the house that contained the object of my admiration, and so four years passed. Then I commenced sending her anonymous but costly presents; I wrote her poetry, and used up another year, but no hope dawned. I began to see daylight. I had lent two hundred dollars to a wretched cousin of my fair flame, and he agreed to introduce me to the family. "When?" I asked. "One of the daughters is to be married next week, and I will get you an invitation." "Capital," I replied. "But what is the name of the daughter that is to be married?" I asked, with a shiver. "Susan," was the reply. The universe seemed to me to have capsized for about five minutes. "Susan" was the name of the daughter that I had so long loved, and that I had regarded as my wife. She was to marry, and did marry a man named Wilson. I have hated that name ever since. I contemplated having Susan arrested for spiritual bigamy; but was too much occupied to commence proceedings. Then, again, as I had never spoken spoken a word to her in my life, it made it so odd. That was my first love—my puppy love—and it was deep in the heart. Susan has children—ay, grandchildren—now, but I never see her in the street, meet her in church, but soft, pleasant memories will steal over me of my long-tried love. The only thing painful about it is that I did not say something to Susan at the time. It was all one side. I ought to have let her know something about it, and the chances are decidedly in favor of the supposition that the abominable, plodding Wilson that made *my* Susan Mrs. W. would have been nowhere.

But to return to Marion Monck. He was obliged to fall in love with somebody or something. He was honest as the day was long. He would not commit a wrong. He liked Bessy Nordheim. He never dreamed of loving her, because she was his employer's wife; and for want of a better real to his ideal in soul, he fell in love with Isabella Granville. She remained until afternoon in Bond street, and then Marion accompanied her home in State street, where she went to dress to return to the party that evening. That party must commence another chapter.

CHAPTER XXII.

The Evening Party comes off at Mrs. Nordh-im's—The guests—Mr. Bennett's Conversation—Mr. and Mrs Parker and niece Julia—Old John Grasper, the millionaire—Col. Mac Neil and Miss Irene Grasper—Mr. Bennett's family and birth place in Scotland—Col Mac Neil offers his hand to Miss Grasper, is accepted by her, and rejected by her father—"No man is rich enough to support two families"—Mrs. Woodruff's Residence—Her horses and carriages—Her pew in Grace Church, and her piety—The Count Falsechinki at the party—He offers to go to church—The party breaks up.

THERE was a vast difference between an evening party thirty years ago, and now. In those days, the hour in the evening when the guests assembled at the hospitable mansion was much earlier, and the hour when the party dissolved was not later than midnight. The refreshments were of a different order. Then there were the solid, old-fashioned mahogany sideboards, filled with good things, and covered with substantial eatables and drinkables. There was choice old Southside Madeira that had been in cask forty years. There was old cider for old-fashioned people, and quantities of cut glass dishes overloaded with cracked hickory nuts. Rhode Island Greenings and Spitzbergen apples were piled up on famous large crockery open-work dishes, and the young people could eat nuts and do courting at the aforesaid sideboards. Then the supper was a substantial supper, with oysters done in every style, and cold turkey and chicken, and knives and forks and plates, and above all, room for all the guests to partake of the good cheer in comfort. There was a room for the supper. There was room for those who danced, and room for those who played whist, or who wished to converse.

Those were good old days, but they have changed for the worse. Few of our readers but what know from personal experience the difference between such a party as we have described, and one in the modern times, when all is heartlessness, claptrap and show.

Before eight o'clock on the evening of Marion Monck's birthday, the two large parlors of Mr. Nordheim's spacious residence in B nd street were partly but not uncomfortably filled with the persons to whom invitations had been sent. There was not one missing.

Mr. Nordheim could act the gentleman when he chose to do so, and on this occasion he spared no pains to make every one feel at home. His partner, William Pitt Granville and Isabella were among the first to arrive; and soon after, Mr. and Mrs. Tom Granville, accompanied by Miss Madison Pinckney, were announced. Tom had no sooner entered than he was hurried to the piano by Miss Benson, who knew how delightfully Tom played upon that instrument. Colonel Benson joined Pitt Granville, and with Colonel Mac Neil and Mr. Cedar the author, a whist party was made up.

Marion did the honors to a certain extent, for as fast as those arrived to whom he had specially given invitations, and who were personally unknown to Mrs. Nordheim, he presented them by name to the latter lady. Mr. Bennett and Mr. Wilson came in together, and after the former had been presented to the hostess, he retired quietly to an ottoman in a corner of the room, and there remained until Mr. Wilson went and took a seat by his side.

"I suppose you will join the dancers presently," said honest Wilson.

"No indeed. I don't dance. I prefer looking on. It is very rare that I go out to a party, and when I do I have my own way of enjoying myself. As you seem to know most of the people here, you will confer a great favor upon me if you will tell me all about them. I am very fond of studying characters, and I am much deceived if you have not some originals here to-night. Mrs. Nordheim is a beautiful woman—which is her husband?" asked Mr. Bennett.

"That Jewish-looking man talking with Mr. Thomas Granville," replied Mr. Wilson.

"I've seen him before. I conversed with his lady a few moments about Charleston; I must have seen him at the South," was Mr. Bennett's observation.

"Very likely: and Mr. Nordheim is a man, that if you see him once, you are not likely to forget him. He is not remarkable for his beauty, but he is clever in a financial point of view," said Wilson.

Here Mr. and Mrs. Parker and Miss Julia Parker were announced, and soon after were cordially received by the host and hostess. The latter introduced Marion, and he offered his arm to conduct Miss Julia to a seat. Mrs. Parker and her husband followed. Soon after, Mr. Nordheim, accompanied by

Mr. O'Doemall, introduced him to Mrs. Parker, and the husband went off to find Mr. Granville, who was an old acquaintance. These parties are disposed of, and we now return to Mr. Bennett and Mr. Wilson. Mr. Bennett remarked,

"Those last arrivals seem to create quite a sensation; who are they, Mr. Wilson?"

"Oh. Mr. Parker is as rich as Crœsus—retired from all sorts of business, married a handsome wife only one third as old as he is, and they live up the street in princely style," was the reply of Mr. Wilson.

"Their daughter is an elegant girl," said Mr. Bennett.

"She is only a niece, and the aunt is very jealous of her. Do you see that nice young man who is paying such devoted attention to Mrs. Parker?" asked Mr. Wilson.

"Yes; who is he?" asked Mr. Bennett.

Mr. Wilson rolled up his eyes as he replied, "From all accounts, he is a hard case, in a financial point of view. I don't know much about him. He is able to make the female sex believe black is white, and—well, in a financial point of view, he is said to be a regular Jeremy Didler. He goes on change, and he gets into society somewhere or other, and no Englishman of any account comes to this town but what Mr. O'Doemall gets into his good graces. Why, man, I don't believe but what he owes every hotel in town except the one where he resides. He comes to our office occasionally, but I don't like him."

Mr. Bennett smiled and observed, "He seems to be making himself very agreeable to Mrs. Parker."

"He make himself agreeable! Why, sir, he has already explained to her all about our Savior's tomb at Jerusalem, and promised her a fragment of the rock which covered our Savior's sepulchre, which he has at his hotel, and which he got from a monk when he was last in Holy Land. I'll bet two to one that she has already invited him to call to morrow with it at her residence," said Wilson.

"Do you suppose he has a piece of the rock?"

"Rock be hanged. No; doubtful if he was ever nearer Jerusalem than I have been. As for the rock, he will smash a piece off the curb-stone as he goes up to her house, and take it along with him. He is a bad customer, in a financial point of view, and if he once gets a foothold in the house of Mrs. Parker, she will never get him out," said honest Wilson.

Mr. Bennett queried out of the book-keeper the name and occupation of nearly every person in that room, and then they left it together to join the dancers, who were busily occupied on the floor above. They had hardly procured seats before Mr. Bennett was much struck by the appearance of an elderly person who was watching the dancers. He asked Wilson who that was.

"Old Grasper, the millionaire," was the reply.

In those days, thirty years ago, millionaires were very few and far between in the city of New York. Now they are as plenty as pickpockets in a great assemblage. Old John Grasper was considered about as rich as any other man, with one, or perhaps two exceptions. Astor could set several numerals to the word millions. Old Nat Prime, of the firm of Prime, Ward & King, was getting up rapidly towards a million, and would have overreached it by the rise of city property had he not died suddenly. Then there was Stephen Whitney, who was running up on the hundreds of thousands, but did not touch "million." Thirty years ago Bobby Lennox, who made his first property while a clerk to the Commissioners of the British prison ships, could count up to three or four hundred thousand, and John Grasper was not far behind the richest of them (save Astor) in those days. He had recently built him a house out of town of granite, and people wondered at such extravagance and folly as to put up so costly a building way up Broadway, above Prince street. But old John finished it, and in spite of opposition moved into it from his brick house on the north-east corner, where the Astor House now stands, and took a position as one of the aristocratic families in New York. He had two children—one a boy and the other a girl, or rather, these children were a young man named Francis, who sported his money around town as one of the exclusives, and a fair girl named Irene, who, with her pecuniary prospects so flattering, was acknowledged as one of the elite and most fashionable young ladies about town. Old Grasper had other children, but they have no connection with this story, and need not to be alluded to. Mr. Grasper was a man of strict business habits. He had acquired property in the fur trade, and he judiciously invested it in real estate and bank stock. After he retired from active commercial life he was elected president of a city bank. The position was a respectable one, and the income from this office was well worth having by even one of the richest citizens.

On the present occasion old Mr. Grasper was watching every movement of his daughter Irene, who was dancing with Colonel Mac Neil. His eyes scarce wandered for a moment from them. Mr. Bennett and Wilson took seats near him.

"So that is old Grasper, who is so rich—the millionaire, as you say, Mr Wilson," said Mr. Bennett.

"Yes, Mr. Bennett, and judging by the way he is watching the attentions of Colonel Mac Neil to his child, I should think something was broke. He evidently don't like Colonel Mac Neil's sweet demonstrations upon his daughter—it is bad in a financial point of view; for my own opinion of Colonel Mac is that he is not worth a cent."

"He may be a good man, for all that. Scotch—is he not?" replied Mr. Bennett.

"Yes sir. He might be a good man, but he is not, in a financial or any other point of view. He is a very immoral man. But you are Scotch too, are you not?" asked Mr. Wilson.

"I certainly was born in Scotland, and lived there until I was sixteen, when I came to this country, and have been here ever since. I am from a different part of Scotland than where this Mac Neil's race lived. My family were Catholic Scotch, and believed in the Divine rights of the Stuarts down to this day. My mother was as strongly in favor of the Stuart dynasty as were her ancestors before her, although years had passed since there was the remotest hope of any of that royal race ever reigning again in Great Britain. But tell me more about this Colonel Mac Neil. You say that he is immoral. How so? Gambles, I suppose?" asked Mr. Bennett.

"Worse than that. He seduced in Canada a virtuous young lady named Jane McPherson. She was a soldier's daughter. I have seen the poor old father, McPherson. He came down to New York to try and persuade his child to return home. But no—she would not do it. She loves Mac Neil too well. She lives very retired as his mistress, and has two children by the Colonel. Poor thing! She hopes some day that Mac Neil will make an honest woman of her by marriage. There is no hope of that—the Colonel must marry for money, and he will do it too, if he can."

While this conversation was being carried on, the object of it was deeply engrossed with Miss Irene Grasper. They had finished dancing, and Col. Mac Neil conducted his fair partner to one of the side rooms. They were alone. Irene Grasper was a magnificent girl, stately in appearance, with a profusion of light auburn locks arranged with great taste. Her cheeks were pale—her eyes a mild blue. When she was seated where few were likely to interrupt them, Mac Neil took one hand in his own, and in deep impassioned tones observed,

"You know, dear Irene, how devotedly—how madly I have

loved you. To-night I must know from your own lips my fate. You must have perceived how closely your father watched every motion while we were dancing. Do you love me, Irene?"

"O Colonel, how can you ask me such a question! You know that I do. How could I help it, although I have tried to do so," replied the lady.

"Tried to help loving me, Irene? What do you mean by that sentence? Why do you wish not to love me?" asked Colonel Mac Neil.

"I do—God knows I do. O Colonel, there are so many stories told about you—so many lies, perhaps scandal—and yet I am afraid almost to dream of trusting my happiness in your keeping."

"Do you confess that you love me, Irene?" asked Col. Mac Neil.

"I do," replied the fair girl, her eyes swimming in tears.

"And will you authorize me to make that statement to your father, when I ask him for your hand, which I will do to-night?" said the Colonel.

"O, do not! He will not give his consent, and I shall be more miserable than ever," said Irene.

"That, dear Irene, we shall see. There can be no great harm in my asking. I owe it to myself—to my own self-respect. Why should he not give his consent? I am his equal, except perhaps in point of wealth, and of that he may have more than I."

What reply the young lady might have made is not so certain, for just at that moment Mr. Grasper the millionaire made his appearance upon the scene. Colonel Mac Neil arose.

"Be seated, sir; and you, Miss Irene, go and join your mother. I would like to say a few words to you, sir," observed Mr. Grasper.

Colonel Mac Neil rose and bowed to Miss Irene as she left the room, and then re-seated himself.

"I am waiting patiently to hear the words you mentioned that you wished to address to me," said Colonel Mac Neil.

"Colonel Mac Neil, you have been very pointed in your attentions to my daughter of late, and especially to-night. I am a plain man, sir, and should like to ask you what are your intentions towards her?" demanded old Mr. Grasper.

"Honorable, of course, sir. I would like to see that person who dared say or hint otherwise!" said Col. Mac Neil.

"O—ah—yes. That is all very well, sir. *Honorable*—that means marriage. That is just what I *don't* want. I had just as lief your intentions were what you would call *dis-*honorable. It would suit me as well," sternly observed Mr. Grasper.

"Mr. Grasper, I thank you for opening the way to a proposal I have to make. I love your daughter. You need not sneer, sir. I love her for herself alone. You may think I seek her hand in honorable marriage because she is the daughter of a wealthy man. It is false, sir! I care not for her money. She loves me, sir, and will confess it with her own lips, if you will ask her," said the Colonel.

"Shan't do anything of the kind. I will not consent to your marrying her under any circumstances. If you take her, God curse me if I ever give her, directly or indirectly, dead or alive, a solitary cent to keep her or you from starving. Do I speak plain?" sternly observed Mr. Grasper.

"Perfectly; but really, Mr. Grasper, some explanation is necessary. I have a good business. I can support my wife. My position in society is equal to yours. By birth, I am at least your equal. Pray, Mr. Grasper, give me *some* reason for so extraordinary a refusal to my proposition. I am no beggar!"

"Do you wish me to give you the reason—my real reason?" asked Mr. Grasper.

"I do, most respectfully," replied Colonel Mac Neil.

"And, Mr. Mac Neil, if I do, and if it is satisfactory, will you promise me, as a man of honor, that you will go to my daughter, and say to her that you relinquish her affections, and all claim to her hand?" asked Mr. Grasper.

"I will, upon my honor. And now let me hear, if you please, the reason," said the Colonel.

"Colonel Mac Neil, you may be doing a good business—you may be making money—I care not. I do not believe you or any other man is doing a business sufficient to justify him in *attempting to support two families.*"

Colonel Mac Neil was for a moment paralyzed. He was not prepared for this. "Stop one moment, sir—I am satisfied."

Mr. Grasper passed out of the room.

"What a fool I have been! Who in the fiend's name could have told him that I kept a mistress, and had two children by her? That is what he meant. Well, I am as proud as he is."

A moment after he joined Miss Grasper, and addressed her as easily as though nothing had happened. Ere he left her side, he said,

"Irene, we meet hereafter as strangers. Your father has refused me your hand. I am satisfied, and shall never claim it again. God bless you!" And soon after he took his leave of Mrs. Nordheim, and left the house.

Mr. Bennett had noticed some of these proceedings, and when Colonel Mac Neil took his hasty departure, he gently nudged Mr. Wilson, remarking, "My Scotch friend, the Colonel, seems to have had a rebuff from some quarter."

"Indeed he has. I overheard a few high words between him and old Grasper a short time ago, and I think the Colonel will haul off in that quarter."

He communicated to Mr. Bennett the "two families to support" remark. The latter laughed, and said he had not thought Mr. Grasper had so much keen wit in his composition.

"It was not bad, was it?" said Mr. Wilson.

Marion Monck was not idle for a moment. He introduced such people to each other as he thought would make agreeable acquaintances. Such of his friends as were bashful, he led up to the prettiest girls, and made them select partners for the dance. At last he approached Mr. Bennett.

"Come, come, sir, this will not do. Why, you are destroying Mr. Wilson's usefulness, and it don't pay in a pecuniary point of view—eh, Mr. Wilson? What can you two have to say to each other of so much interest? Mr. Wilson, you must take down Mrs. Nordheim to supper to-night, and as to Mr. Bennett, I must trust him to take charge of my sweet Isabella Granville. Consider yourselves engaged, both Monsieurs, when the proper time comes," and he passed on and joined Mrs. Woodruff, who was seated alone.

"That Marion Monck is a noble fellow, Mr. Bennett. What do you think of him? You have known him some time, he informs me."

"For some months. He came up to the editorial rooms of the Courier to see Colonel Webb one day, and I then had a short conversation with him. I have since met him at my boarding-house," was Mr. Bennett's reply.

"He will make a great merchant one of these days, I am thinking," added Mr. Wilson.

"I have my doubts about that. I do not think he will make a great merchant, nor a small one, either. He has talent of a high order, and fitted for a higher sphere, or I am much mistaken," observed Mr. Bennett.

"Higher sphere!" repeated the indignant Wilson; "what higher sphere is there in New York, I should like to know?"

"I don't wish to be rude, but I think to be an editor requires a higher order of talent than it does to make a successful shop-keeper—or, I beg your pardon—a leading merchant. Young Monck, I dare say, has never written a line in his life, yet I think some day he will make a clever journalist. He will if he can write as well as he talks—but time makes strange changes."

Time proved it, for what that editor prophesied became true in after years to a far greater extent than even he dreamed of at that early period.

Marion was deeply engaged in conversation with Mrs. Woodruff. She seemed grateful for his attention. "I feel almost isolated here to-night, knowing so few, in fact none except the inmates of this house, by seeing you pass in and out of the doors," was her remark.

"You have resided next door to us over a year, have you not? I have always admired that house—it is at least one-third deeper than our house, and the yard is larger, and very beautifully arranged with trees, plants and flowers. You must be fond of flowers, madam?"

"Very, indeed. I love them. My husband has been dead some years, and but for my pets, and my flowers, I should not know what to do," replied Mrs. Woodruff.

"Have you no relatives living with you?" asked Marion

"Not one. I have done with them, and they with me. Not a soul lives with me except my servants and my live stock. I have many acquaintances who call upon me, but they are of the highest character. Mr. Monck, I shall be most happy to have you call and see me whenever it is convenient. I am rarely out. If I have company, it need not discompose you. I shall have a parlor for you, no matter how many may be in the house. I never show one of my visitors into the same parlor where there is another," remarked Mrs. Woodruff, proudly.

Marion thought this was a queer sort of woman; but as she was rich, she had a right to be as eccentric as she pleased. He answered, that he should avail himself of her kind invitation.

"One word more. When you wish to ride, I have a carriage and servants at your disposal. My stable and carriage-house are in the rear of my house in Bond street. I hope you go to church," was the word more of Mrs. W.

"Occasionally," replied Marion.

"You ought to go every Sunday. Religion is an excellent thing for a young man or woman. It keeps the minds of both occupied and out of mischief. Will you go to church with me next Sunday?"

"What church?" asked Marion.

"I own a pew in Grace Church, down Broadway, corner of Rector. We will ride down in my own carriage. Dr. Wainwright is my pastor," said Mrs. W.

"Nothing will give me more pleasure. Perhaps Mrs. Nordheim"——observed Marion Monck.

"Stop, stop. I never ask women to go with me anywhere. I shall be happy to have you go. You will be obliged to return without me, as it is sacrament Sunday, and I always stop to partake of the Lord's Supper. Who is that gentleman conversing with Mrs. Thomas Granville?" said Mrs. Woodruff.

"That? Why, that is the Count Falsechinski."

"Tell me all about him. I am anxious to know his history."

Marion complied with her request, and told her all he knew of the Count, except one or two matters that he had no right to tell.

"Thank you; thank you. Now will you do me one favor more? Bring the Count here and introduce him to me."

Marion stepped across the room, and, after talking a few moments to the eager Count, telling him about the rich lady next door, and so forth, he took his arm and brought him over. "Madam Woodruff, allow me to present to you my noble friend the Count Falsechinski. I will leave him with you."

The Count became almost excruciatingly polite. He bowed almost to his knees, and placed one hand on his heart while he declared that he was perfectly overwhelmed with bliss at becoming acquainted with so perfect a lady—that she reminded him of his sister (he was too polite to say mother,) the Princess Sophinski, the most beautiful woman in Warsaw before the recent revolution. All the extra touches were put on by the Count.

"No more. No more, Count. I cannot bear it. There—stop and sit right down, or you will hurt yourself." The Count took a seat by her side. "There, that is right. You are a dear good Count, and we shall like each other much, when we are better acquainted."

What passed after that between the two last-named persons it is not necessary to recount. Suffice it to say here, that Mrs. Woodruff showed the same anxiety about the piety of the Count, and repeated the same invitation she had given to Marion. She also spoke of remaining to the sacrament, and the Count said he could not possibly permit that, unless he also remained with her,

"But do you wish to partake of the sacrament, Count?" she asked earnestly.

"Nothing, I assure my dear madam, would give me more pleasure. Rather than part with your dear company, I would partake of any thing."

Here supper was announced, and the Count offered his arm and escort. The other quests were suitably arranged, and before ten o'clock all were at the supper-table, and ere midnight the regular occupants of the house were left in it alone.

CHAPTER XXIII.

Miss Norris and her Teacher of Languages— She Threatens Mr. Nordheim —Gives the Count a Fearful History of the Antecedents of Mrs. Woodruff —The Value of Mr. Cedar's Note or Draft upon his Publishers—Doctor Carnochan—The Difference between a German and a Dutchman.

Not many days after the party in Bond street, the Count Falsechinski called in Broome street to give a lesson in German to Miss Norris. He found Tom Granville there.

"Tom," said Clara, "I wish to see the Count alone this morning—so be so obliging and take yourself somewhere else. Money you cannot get from me to-day, nor to-morrow, either— it would do you no good. Go to your brother."

"But you have money of mine in "—commenced poor Tom.

"Stop—no more of that, or I will forbid you the house. I do not owe you a dollar. You put some in my hands, but you have drawn it all," said Clara.

"Surely I have not had "—again commenced Tom.

"Never mind whether you have had it or not. I don't keep accounts. I have not got any of it, and if you have not spent it, I have, so there is no more to be said about it. Now go, that is a good boy," and she rose and gently pushed him out of the room and locked the door. "Now, Count, I have got rid of that poor foolish youth, I wish to talk with you. You are a man. I understand you perfectly, and I tell you candidly, I admire you very much. Hawks must not pick out hawks' eyes. So you were at the party at Mrs. Nordheim's? Never say a word until I finish. Mr. Nordheim was all attention to Mrs. Tom Granville. Don't shake your head. I know better. But what do I care? As long as he allows me what I need, and pays me regularly, he may do what else he pleases, but let the funds stop but a day, an hour, ay, a quarter of a moment, and Mr. Nordheim and me part company forever. Tell me all that you know about Mrs. Woodruff."

This was a subject upon which the Count willingly enlarged, and he gave a glowing description of the rich widow, her splendid mansion, coach, servants in livery, and pew in Grace Church.

"Did Mr. Nordheim speak to her when she was at the party of his wife?" asked Miss Norris.

"I don't think he did. No. I am sure he did not."

"The arch hypocrite! Did Mrs. Woodruff become personally acquainted with other persons at the party beside you and my friend Marion?" asked Miss Norris.

"Oh, yes, to be sure; with many," replied the Count.

"Name them, every one, male and female," said Clara.

"She talked with Miss Irene Grasper, with Mrs. Parker, and her niece, Miss Julia, and she was also introduced to Mr. Doemall, an Irish gentleman. Some say he is a peer," replied the Count.

"Are those all?" demanded Miss Norris.

"Upon my honor, Mademoiselle Norris, I think those I have named are all," was the Count's reply.

"Count, I like you. I wish you to steer clear of the breakers. May I confide to you a secret for your own good, not mine?" asked Miss Norris.

"You may," replied the Count.

"You say Nordheim did not appear to know *that* woman. He lied by his actions, and is worse than I dreamed him to be, to introduce *her* to his home," said Clara.

"He did not invite her there. It was done without the knowledge of Mr. Nordheim. I know that to be a fact. I had it from Marion, and he will not lie."

"That is true, and Nordheim is not quite so black as I thought him to be. Count, listen to me, but never repeat it. Use the knowledge for your own purposes, but do not use it to save others. Count, you know that I was bought by Nordheim and brought to the city. You do *not* know, but now I will tell you, the first week that I spent in New York, before this house was ready for me, I spent in *that* luxurious mansion now, as then, occupied by Mrs. Woodruff."

The Count did not trust himself to speak for several moments. His eyes were busily engaged upon the rich flowers of the tapestry carpet that covered the floor.

"That carpet cost four dollars a yard, Count. You need not examine its texture more closely."

The Count smiled.

"Mademoiselle, I am too astounded to say any thing. What a game my lady Woodruff must be playing?"

"She is a fearful—a terrible female, Count. It is real friendship for you that has made me open your eyes. She is the more to be dreaded because she moves in the very highest circles, and spreads devastation wholesale. Count, for some purpose you are saving money with all a miser's eagerness. Don't look so astonished. I know it. A little bird tells me all that you do. I, too, am saving money. For what purpose I know not, but this I do know, the power of money. I will never be poor again while there are gulls and pigeons to be plucked. Use the information I have given you. Show this pious lady that *you* at least know her, and make her *pay—pay* —that's the word—if she uses *you*. As you regard me, breathe not a word if you were to see your best friend's wife going into those double hall doors in Bond street," said Clara.

"I thank you, Mademoiselle Clara, a million of times. I will make that lady pay before she has done with me. You shall see what you shall see before the play is over. Now for the German lesson. You will need but three or four more, and then you will speak English, French, Spanish and German. The next shall be the Italian, eh?"

"Yes, Count. Italian next. Answer me one question. Tell me what you think of the intrigue between Mr. Nordheim and Mrs. Tom Granville. Tell me honestly and truly. You are a man of the world. Will that lady succumb to the infamous man?"

"No. Upon my soul. She is too clever—too spirituelle. He pays her money—largely, too. I know that. Five hundred —one thousand. But—she takes it—is civil—goes with him all about, but, lady—that Mrs. Granville *loves* her husband. It is true, and she is honest."

"A precious pup for a sensible man to love, and yet, poor Tom, he is a delightful, harmless fellow. I do not think Tom would hurt a chicken. No; not a fly. But he does not know the value of money. I gave him fifty dollars one morning last week, and what do you think he did that evening? Came to me for more. It is true, and when I asked what on earth he had done with it, he pulled from it a note of that precious scamp Cedar's for sixty dollars, and told me had made ten dollars by cashing it," said Clara.

"Mr. Cedar's note is not, then, worth much?" asked the alarmed Count.

"Not worth so much as the paper was before he wrote his name upon it. Beware of that English genius, Count," observed Miss Norris.

"I will take care of him, and thank you, too, for had you not told me this, I should have given him two hundred dollars for his draft upon his publishers for two hundred and fifty," said the Count.

"And you would have lost every cent. I don't think his publishers owe him a penny. Yet that man would challenge you if you dared insinuate that he was any thing but an honorable man. Count, is not this a very queer world?" sarcastically observed Miss Norris.

"The people in it are very queer—a very curious people. Mademoiselle, tell me about Doctor Carnochan."

"He is a young man of decided talent, and he will one day rise to the very head of his profession, if he lives. He has it in him. At present he is, from the force of circumstances, a wild, dissipated, useless man, and his companions are of the most worthless class. Does he want money of you, too, Count?" asked Miss Norris.

"No. But it may be in my power to throw some practice in his way," kindly added the Count.

"Do so if you can, Count. He will earn more than the usual fee as compared with other doctors. Tell me how Marion Monck gets on with his languages," asked the lady.

"He has already mastered several of the most difficult. His parents were Dutch, so that it came natural to him to acquire the German, which is a sort of first cousin to low Dutch."

"What is the difference between German and low Dutch?" asked Clara.

"The German, or *Hoch Deutsch*, is spoken all through Germany. The Neder Deutch, or Low Dutch, is the language of the Hollanders, or the *Nederlanders*, which, in English, is lowlanders, in contradistinction to the *Hoch* Deutsch or high Germans—or rather high-land Dutchmen. Now shall we proceed with your German lesson?"

"With pleasure, Count," was her reply.

An hour afterward the Count sent a note from the office to Mrs. Woodruff.

CHAPTER XXIV.

Harrison Street—Colonel Mac Neil's private Home—Miss McPherson and her two Children—A Breakfast Scene with Willy and Patsy—The Colonel settles a House on his Children, and places two thousand dollars in the Savings Bank for them—Redeeming traits in a Fashionable Bad Man's character.

SUCH of our readers as are familiar with New York, will remember a street in the lower part of the town, running from Hudson street to the North river, named Harrison street. As it was known a hundred years ago by the same name, it could not have been named after our General Harrison, or more recently President Harrison, but must have honored some English family. Be this as it may, in this same street, at No. 27, the first door from Greenwich street, stands or did stand a small two story brick house. It rented for three hundred dollars a year, and was occupied by two families. The lower part, save a back kitchen, was rented by a worthy butcher and his small family, while the upper or second story was occupied by a lady and her two children, one a boy about five years of age, that his mother called William, and a little girl three years old, with the pretty cognomen of Patsy. The front room of the second story was plainly but comfortably furnished as a parlor. The rear room contained a bed, and between the two rooms was a third small room in which was placed a trundle bed for the children. It was a cold December morning, only a week after the party at Mrs. Nordheim's house in Bond street, when the bell rang at No. 27. The mother of the two children had just placed their and her simple breakfast upon the table in the small back kitchen in the basement, where she had a cooking stove and a pantry. This also was a portion of her part of the house, for which she paid an annual rent of one hundred and twenty dollars. The bell rang a second time.

"Go to the door, Willie; who knows but it is your papa? It sounds like his ring."

The little boy was off like a rocket, and in a moment afterward a heavy footstep was heard descending the kitchen stairs. He entered the room with the boy in his arms, and placed him on his feet; and then the lady flung herself in the gentleman's arms, uttering but one word, "William!" He gently displaced the lady, and then took up the little girl, and kissed her fondly.

"I am just in time for breakfast, Jane, eh?" and he took a seat.

"O William, if we had but known you were coming—we have not a breakfast fit for you to eat," observed Jane.

"Don't you and the children eat that breakfast? and if so, is it not good enough for me?" asked Col. Mac Neil.

"Don't be angry with me, William—I did not mean any thing. But you, who are so used to living at hotels, could hardly expect to enjoy such a breakfast as this. But why have you kept away so long?" she asked.

"Business, Jane. Business, pleasure, every thing. But now let us have a nice breakfast. Here is money—send out and get any thing nice that you can find," observed the Colonel.

"I will go myself, if you will mind the children while I am gone, Colonel," she replied.

"That I will do with pleasure;" and he took a child upon each knee, and kissed, caressed and played alternately with them until the mother returned. It was not long before the good mother had a very choice breakfast smoking on the table, and all partook of it, while the father, for so he was, of those two children exerted himself to the utmost to make a pleasant time of it. An hour elapsed before the happy family had finished the meal. Then the gentleman, who was no other than Colonel William Mac Neil, asked if there was a fire up stairs. Receiving a reply in the affirmative, he continued: "Jane, send Willy and Patsy up stairs—we will follow presently; but I have a few words to say to you alone."

The children went up stairs, little Willy leading by the hand the tottersome Patsy. When they were gone, the Colonel drew out a segar from a rich shagreen segar case, and deliberately lit it.

"Come and sit down by me, Jane."

She complied in silence, her looks expressing wonder as to what was to come next.

"Jane, I idolize those children. I wish to God you were my legal wife, for you are a true-hearted, loving woman. Don't cry, darling, but listen to me. You think I could easily legalize them, and marry you. No, no—that is a dream; it is too late—my cursed pride will not let me do it. That is not all; I must marry a woman who has money, or be a disgraced bankrupt. Yet, you nor those two dear children shall ever want, or be dependent even upon me. I am a rascal, Jane, so far as you are concerned: I know it—I feel it. But, thank God, I have placed you and those dear ones so that you can never want. Are you listening?" said the Colonel, with emotion.

"Surely, Mac, I have not lost a word. Go on—I hope you have nothing worse to tell me," she observed.

"Jane, I have saved up and withdrawn from my business seven thousand dollars, and with it I have purchased a house in Franklin street near Broadway. The lot is twenty-five feet by one hundred, and sixteen years hence, when Willy is of age, that property will be double or treble in value. I have deeded it to you, Jane McPherson, in trust for Willy and Patsy. The house is a good one, and now rents for six hundred and fifty dollars per annum, and has a good tenant. That rent you must draw and live on, in case I am unable to do any thing more for you. That is not all. Here is two thousand dollars that I won in gambling some time ago. It is but a partial return of ten times that amount that I have lost at gambling. It is yours—take it to a Savings Bank, and place it there at interest in your own or in Willy's name—your own is better, and then you will have two sources of income."

The poor young mother was weeping. "O Mac—dear Mac, why do you do this? Are you going away? I don't want it; you allow us all we want!" she exclaimed.

"Listen, Jane. When I signed that deed, I had determined to offer myself that night to a very wealthy young lady. I expected to be accepted, and I then determined to act honorably by her; and to do so I intended that deed as a provision for you and my dear children, and then to bid you farewell, and see you no more," said the Colonel.

"O Mac, could you have the heart to do it? Could you part with those two little precious ones, and never see them more? O, it was a cruel thought!" said Jane.

"Be calm—I am. I have not yet done. I offered myself to the girl, and she accepted me. Don't start off in that manner. Then I saw her father—one of the wealthiest men in the city. He refused to countenance the marriage, and what was still more, situated as I am, he swore before God that if his daughter married me, she should never receive a cent. He had heard of *our* affairs—of *our* children, Jane, and he said he did not think I could support *two* families. That was quite enough for me, Jane. The affair is at an end, and I shall probably never marry."

The mother flung herself into his arms, and kissed the Colonel in the most fond manner.

"Hear me out, Jane, and know the worst. I have secured you from want, and the deed is irrevocable; but Heaven only knows how soon I may be a beggar. The affairs of my firm are in a terrible state. My partner thinks that he can carry the concern through. He is buying produce on credit, and shipping it to Europe, or any where else where he can get cash advances upon the shipments. If those shipments turn out well, we are safe, and shall keep afloat. If not—but I don't dare to think of it. This thought though consoles me—come what will, you and Willy and Patsy are provided for," continued the Colonel feelingly.

"But, dear Mac, if this would serve you, I will deed it back to you, and you could sell it again, and also take the two thousand dollars," observed Jane.

"You are an unselfish being, Jane—but no, no. It would not be a drop in the bucket. Do exactly as I have to d you, and I will continue to give you what funds you need, just as though the nine thousand dollar provision had not been made. If I am fortunate and get through my own difficulties, you will have the interest every year to add to the principal, and in a few years you will have quite a little sum. Now kiss me, and then let us go up stairs and join Willy and Patsy. After all there are some happy moments for the most miserable, and I will come and breakfast with you soon again," said the Colonel.

"Dear Mac, it makes the children so happy."

The haughty Colonel Mac Neil played and romped with his children until dinner was ready, and then he dined with them. Before evening he was again at his hotel.

There are some redeeming traits in even the most worldly of men. And this is a redeeming chapter, and shall stand by itself.

CHAPTER XXV.

The Italian Opera House in Church street—The Character of the Subscribers—Mr. Nordheim a Director—A Tragedy Night—Mr. Nordheim insults a lady in the Dress Circle—His Spectacles driven into his eyes by a Brother—His removal to the City Hospital—Francis Guillard of South Carolina—Mr. Granville dissolves the firm of Granville & Nordheim—The Notice—List of the Daily Newspapers—Feelings of Miss Norris—Her Proposition to Tom Granville—The Days that the Wife of Mr. Nordheim spent at the Hospital with her dying husband—Nordheim's Will—His Death and Funeral.

IN the year 183—, a company of persons who would be extremely exclusive, determined to put up a building and open an Italian Opera House in this city. To carry out their design, they purchased sufficient ground on the corner of Church and Leonard streets, and proceeded to put up a large and handsome building. When this Opera House was finished, an arrangement was made for a manager, and a regular stock Italian Opera Company was established in New York city. It was a mixed-up sort of concern. At first it was a regular stock company. Then private boxes were disposed of to particular families for life, in order to raise money; and then commenced a system of begging, borrowing, and voluntary contributions, until all hands became disgusted, and the building passed from the opera people to the mortgagee, and he leased it for a regular theatre to James Wallack, who opened it under the title of the National Theatre.

But to return to the Italian crowd. The parties who got up the Italian opera were not the old Knickerbocker stock inhabitants. They were a parvenu population—people who had been successful as brokers, merchants, stock gamblers, real estate speculators, and other modes by which fortunes are suddenly accumulated in this great metropolis. Many of the parties had travelled in Europe to acquire business, and form commercial connexions. They had visited Paris and London, and perceiving how aristocratic the Italian opera was in those cities, they considered that to become interested in an Italian opera in New York would give them an aristocratic position These were the motives that actuated most of the patrons of the early Italian opera in New York. It is needless to say that they paid dear for the Italian whistle, and it got broken in a very short period of time.

Among those who took a very active part in the Italian opera was Mr. Nordheim. He spoke Italian fluently, and he was not only allowed to spend his money in the enterprise without stint, but he was also permitted to take a very active part in the details. The Finance Committee knew no more about Italian than they did about Greek, and Mr. Nordheim translated between the false Italian Prince and Princess actors, and their Wall street financiers.

The Italian opera opened during the month of the party at Mrs. Nordheim's, and Mr. Nordheim placed at his wife's disposal a private box, and she filled it almost every night with some of her friends. She was generally attended thither by Mr. Wilson or Marion—sometimes by both. The Count Falsechinski received tickets frequently for Miss Norris and himself, and occasionally Tom Granville made up a party for one of the front seats in the dress circle. It was April. The bill for that night was very attractive. Mrs. Nordheim was in her private box with a party. Marion Monck was there also—and so was Isabella Granvile. On the right side of the dress circle, Miss Norris, with the Count and Tom Granville, occupied three seats.

Shortly after the curtain rose, Mr. Nordheim was seen to enter the dress circle by a door directly opposite the centre of the building. He took a seat on the third bench. Directly in front of him was a gentleman accompanied by a lady of rare and surpassing beauty. It was noticed by those in the neighborhood that Mr. Nordheim endeavored to attract the notice of the beautiful woman who occupied the seat directly in front of him. Once she turned her head almost around, and gazed at him with an expression that denoted the most violent anger, and then seemed absorbed with what was passing on the stage.

I may have omitted to mention that Mr. Nordheim was near-sighted, and wore gold spectacles. He never was without them. Hundreds who were present that eventful evening, well remember the fearful scream of agony which rung through that Opera House, although the extent of the tragedy in the dress circle was not dreamed of that night. Again that lady turned and looked indignantly at Mr. Nordheim, who smiled and partly bowed. It was noticed that the lady whispered to the gentleman with her. She quietly informed him that the person on the rear seat had put his hand upon her person in an improper manner.

" Can you point him out to me distinctly ?" whispered the brother—for so he proved to be.

" Yes, Frank, he is seated directly behind me, with his knees upon the seat where I am sitting. Frank, he has pinched me behind again !"

" Keep perfectly quiet, Emily—don't move," and as he said this he rose to his feet, turned his back to the stage so as to face Nordheim, and rapidly drew back his arm, and with all his force struck his fist directly in Nordheim's right eye. There was one terrific scream. The glass had broken, and the force of the blow had driven several of the particles into the right eye of the unfortunate Nordheim. There was an instant rush, and much confusion. The gentlemen remained perfectly calm and did not move an inch. Nordheim had fainted with the intense agony from the pierced eyeball. Shouts arose from the parterre—" Turn him out !" The gallery re-echoed " Turn him out !" Meanwhile Marion Monck, the Count, and some others of the acquaintance of Mr. Nordheim, hurried to the spot, just as he had been carried out of the boxes. They all saw at once the nature of the wound. Then the gentleman who had inflicted it came out and explained what had occurred —regretting that he had inflicted so terrible a punishment. A carriage was procured. By this time Pitt Granville had learned what had occurred. " Take him at once to the New York Hospital," was his peremptory order. Mr. Nordheim was with difficulty placed in the carriage. His agony was fearful.

" Go and tell Mrs. Nordheim what has happened, and take her home, Marion. I will be up there as soon as Nordheim is better or worse. The hospital is the only place, for he needs immediate surgical aid. Mr. Wilson, go with me."

These sensible orders of Pitt Granville were rapidly carried into execution, and the carriage drove around to the hospital gate. Mr. Roberts, the Superintendent, was an old friend of Mr. Granville, and luckily happened to be in the office. A proper room was instantly arranged, and Mr. Nordheim was taken into it. Then the leading surgeons were sent for. They tried to extract the broken pieces of glass, but only partially succeeded. Mr. Nordheim was a raving maniac.

But I must carry back my readers to the Opera House. When Mrs. Nordheim had learned the particulars of the accident, she refused to go home, but left her party, and with

Marion went directly to the hospital inner gate, where the little house of the gate-keeper is, and asked permission to go in and see her husband. She was refused—politely but positively—and she at once got into a carriage and went home to Bond street. Soon after, a gentleman appeared at the gate and asked permission to see one of the officers of the hospital. He was shown inside to Mr. Roberts.

"Here is my card, 'sir. I am the person who struck the blow at the opera."

Mr. Roberts took the card and read, "Francis Gaillard, at Mrs. Mann's, No. 85 Broadway."

"The accident, sir, I fear will terminate seriously, and I will use this card, as you may be called upon to give some explanation. How did it happen?" inquired Mr. Roberts.

The stranger, whose name was Gaillard, replied, "I am a South Carolinian, on a visit here with my mother and sister. I took my sister to the Italian opera this evening. After the performance had commenced, she told me that a person on the seat behind her had insulted her, and I at once struck him."

"Served the d—— libertine right," was the only comment made by the indignant but honest Mr. Roberts.

"I took my sister to Mrs. Mann's boarding-house, and came at once to give myself up in case of need. Will it be necessary for me to do any thing more?"

"No. Go home as though nothing had happened. If he dies to-night, or within a few days, a coroner's inquest will be held, and you will have to be on hand; but it is a disgraceful affair, and unless Nordheim dies immediately it will be hushed up. Good night."

"Thank you—good night," and the stranger Gaillard passed out of the hospital.

The Count conveyed the horrified Clara Norris to Broome street, and then left her, promising to return as soon as he had paid a visit to the hospital. He, too, was refused admission, but as he was passing out of the gate he was overtaken by Mr. Pitt Granville and Mr. Wilson.

"Count, go at once to Mr. Nordheim's, in Bond street, see Marion Monck, get the keys of the store, and come directly to the City Hotel."

The Count went on his errand, and when Pitt Granville and his book-keeper were walking alone, the former said, abruptly, "Wilson, this sort of thing has got to be stopped. I am tired of it. Such proceedings by one of the members of a mercantile firm are ruinous."

"I think so, sir. It will be known on change to-morrow, and even if Mr. Nordheim gets well, I don't see how he can explain it."

"Explain. There is no explanation needed. I can put up with a great many things, but this is a beastly concern altogether. Come what will, I am not going to associate with him any more as a partner."

"But how are you to end the partnership? You have no right to"—asked Mr. Wilson.

"I know what you mean; but right or wrong, you will see what course I shall pursue under the present painful circumstances. Wait until I get into the office."

They reached the City Hotel, and Mr. Granville ordered whiskey punch for himself and for Mr. Wilson. They finished the first glass, and then Mr. Granville ordered one more for himself, as Mr. Wilson refused, and he requested him to go and find Colonel Benson, and meet him at the office as speedily as possible. Soon after the Count and Marion joined him, and all proceeded to the counting-house in Broad street. It was opened. Then Colonel Benson and Wilson arrived. Books were got out of the safe. Accounts were examined. The consultation was held, and finally Mr. Granville came out of his private office with a paper in his hand.

"Marion, I want you to make several copies of this. Take one to each of the following daily papers:—

"The Daily Mercantile Advertiser,
" Gazette,
" Courier and Enquirer,
" Journal of Commerce,
" Standard,
" Post,
" Commercial,
" N. Y. American."

Marion complied. The next morning the following could have been read in either of the five morning dailies:

NOTICE.—The co-partnership heretofore existing under the firm of Granville & Nordheim is this day dissolved. The liquidation of the affairs of the late firm will be attended to by the undersigned, who will continue to carry on a General Commission Business under his own name.
W. PITT GRANVILLE,
At No. 31 Broad street.

NEW YORK, *April* 10, 183–.

When Marion returned from the publishing offices of the morning journals, he found Mr. Granville and Mr. Wilson in the main office. The Count had left. So had Colonel Benson.

"Have you put those advertisements in the morning papers?"

"Yes, sir. I was in time with all of them."

"When you go home tell Mrs. Nordheim what I have found it necessary to do, with promptness, to save the credit of this concern. She can appoint you or Mr. Wilson to act for her interest, should he die. He may recover his senses enough to make a will. If he does not, Mrs. Nordheim has her settlement of two thousand dollars a year to fall back upon, and one-third interest in his property. He has been spending a fearful amount of money lately, and Mr. Wilson thinks his share of the profits is not only drawn out, but also a large portion of his stock capital in the concern. We shall know in a few days."

The Count Falsechinski, when he left the office, although it was nearly midnight, went up to Broome street. He found Miss Norris waiting for him. Tom Granville was there.

"Nordheim will die, or be insane for life," said the Count.

"Is that your opinion, Count?" asked Tom, who seemed pleased at the idea.

"It is. The firm is dissolved by Mr. Granville, and notices to that effect will appear in all the daily papers to-morrow."

"Then good-bye, Ferdinand Nordheim. You have been a source of good and a curse to me. Now I will fight my own battles and play my own game in life, for you are dead so far as I am concerned in any event. Shall we make up a card party to-night?"

"Thank you. No. I must get home, for I have much to do to-morrow. Are you walking down town, Tom?"

"No; he is not going down town these two hours yet," spoke Clara.

She showed the Count to the door, and then returned.

"This is a funny business, all round, ain't it, Clara?" said Tom.

"Tom Granville, answer me one question. You have stated to me that you believe your wife and Nordheim were engaged in a criminal intimacy. Answer me now, as God will be your Judge. Do you, in your inmost soul, believe that?" demanded Clara.

"I do solemnly," replied the husband Tom.

"Why do you not take steps to get a divorce from your wife, then, if you believe her guilty and faithless to your honor?" asked Miss Norris.

"Never. I have loved that woman. Perhaps love her yet,

but I will never take any steps to get divorced from her," replied good-natured Tom Granville.

"Suppose she, however, should try to get divorced from you. She could do it," said Miss Norris.

"Let her do so. I will make no objection."

"Tom, do you believe I have been true to my master—to Nordheim?" asked Clara.

"I do. I know I can speak for myself, Clara," said Tom.

"Tom, it is true. I have been as faithful to that man as if I had been his wedded wife, but it is all over now. He is no more to me than if he was dead. His money is gone, even if he lives. He has been fearfully extravagant. You say that you will never live with your wife again?" said Clara.

"Never," replied Tom Granville.

"Will you live here, Tom? and devote yourself to my comfort? Go with me when I go out? I need a protector. I will pay for one, but no nonsense with me. No jealousy, or any thing of that sort. I will be as free as a bird, go and come when I please, see whom I please, dance, flirt, coquette, or play the fool with whom I please, and you are not to open your lips. I like you, but I don't love you. You are amusing—a gentleman—and you shall have the means to carry on the war as such. You don't keep me. I keep you. Do you agree to these conditions? and have you force of character enough to stick to them?" she asked.

"I have, Clara," was the reply.

"Very well. Our bargain is made, but mark me, the very first moment you deviate from our understanding, or show any jealousy, or any dislike to my being intimate with whom I please, that moment we part. Now you may kiss me, and seal the bargain," she pleasantly remarked.

Poor easy, good-natured Tom Granville. Little did you dream, when completing this arrangement, that you were signing the death-warrant for your future hopes of earthly domestic happiness, and degrading yourself to the lowest of mankind—the kept man of a fancy woman! Leaving these worldly ones, our reader will go with us to the hospital. Nordheim became worse and worse. The next day his wife spent several hours by his bedside. He did not recognize her. Day after day she visited him, until the inflammation, which had reached his brain, became so certain of ending fatally, that a lawyer, Charles S. Spencer, was employed to remain with him constantly, under the hope that he might become sane for a few moments ere he died. Two weeks after the accident, his wife called, and found him, for the first time, perfectly conscious of every thing around him. His partner was sent for. The lawyer asked the Physician Surgeon how long he might live.

"Until evening."

Then occurred a painful scene—a death-bed repentance. He dictated a will. It was short. He left all to his wife. All— every thing. Except the furniture of the house in which Clara Norris lived, that he gave to her, and also five hundred dollars. He signed articles dissolving the firm, and authorizing his wife to close up the affairs as best suited herself, and he made Mr. Granville give a solemn promise that in case his half interest in the concern should not leave a respectable sum for his wife, that he would give her one-third interest in the future business, or take into partnership any one she should designate. Frank Gaillard was sent for. When he reached the bed of the dying man he was much agitated, and expressed the deepest regret for what had occurred.

"Not a word more. You served me right. Tell your sister that a dying man begs her forgiveness for the outrage he committed."

Mr. Nordheim lingered on through the day, but just after sunset, when twilight was deepening into dark over the trees and around the old hospital windows, Nordheim sank into what appeared a gentle sleep. Mr. Granville first discovered that he was dead. Mrs. Nordheim pressed her lips to the dead man, and was then led out of the room. That night the coffin containing his body was conveyed to Bond street. The succeeding day it was transferred to a cemetery, and the troubles, the pleasures, the rascalities, and the redeeming qualities of the unfortunate Nordheim were over forever.

CHAPTER XXVI.

New Street thirty years ago—The store of Mr John O'Doemall—His Business—The Debt of three hundred and four dollars and seventy-two cents, and how it was liquidated—Mr. Granville's Instructions—The Story of the Irishwoman, and how O'Doemall victimized her out of seventy-two dollars' worth of shirts, and ruined her sister and husband—A Bad Character.

BETWEEN Broadway and Broad street, running from Wall to Beaver, is a little narrow street called the New street, although it is one of the oldest streets in the city. Thirty years ago it seemed to be used for no other purpose than for an alley to the two main streets of Broadway or Broad. A sort of sewer ran through it. Some of the houses on Broadway had stables in the rear, facing on New street. An occasional dwelling house occupied by French dry goods importers on Broad had a solid stone warehouse on New street. No. 20 New street was used as a building of that description. The walls were two feet thick, with small windows, closed by two straight iron bars and an iron shutter. On this store was a large sign, "John O'Doemall, Wine Merchant." There was an office in the rear on the first floor. In it was one desk. The floor contained eight, or perhaps ten gin pipes, whiskey puncheons, and a pile of champagne baskets. All were empty. In the office was a plain table, and upon it was a couple of wine glasses, two glass tumblers, and some sample bottles. Mr. O'Doemall is at his desk. He is seated in a cushioned armchair, with one leg cocked over the desk, and is engaged in reading the Courier and Enquirer.

A customer enters. Mr. O'Doemall drops his leg and removes the paper from his face.

"Oh, ah, my friend Marion Monck. Good morning. Really, I am quite happy to see you. Sit down. Take a seat. Where is my clerk? Here, Thomas."

But the aforesaid Thomas, the clerk, is an invisibility.

"I have called, Mr. O'Doemall, at the request of Mr. Granville, to obtain some sort of a settlement with you. Mr. Nordheim, unbeknown to his partner at the time, sold you goods to the extent of three hundred and four dollars and odd"—said young Monck.

"Exactly. Three hundred and four dollars and seventy-two cents. I know the precise amount. A mere trifle, which ought to have been paid long ago, but I overlooked it. Surely, Mr. Granville would not send you to collect so small an amount as that."

"He did so, and if it is not convenient for you to pay the money, he would like to have you give your note, adding the interest for ninety days, or even four months."

"I forgot to ask you how Mrs. Nordheim is—poor lady—great misfortune. Nordheim was a good fellow. Queer. If Nordheim had lived, he would never have been so mean as to send for that pitiful sum. How do you know but what I have a receipt for it? In fact, I don't think I can pay that note. Nordheim owes me, let me see, three hundred dollars at John Florence's, two hundred and ten dollars one night in Broadway —and—d— it, man, I could not think of paying it at present.

I must look up some of Nordheim's I O Us. I dare say they are in one of my cast off vest pockets," replied the impudent O'Doemall.

"If you have any receipts from Mr. Nordheim, or any claim against him—note—due bill, or positive evidence that Mr. Nordheim owed you a dollar, Mr. Granville will allow it," said Monck.

"Of course he will. I knew he was an honorable man. I have them somewhere. That is a beautiful daughter of Granville's, Isabella. You are to marry her, I suppose? Couldn't do better, and I shall tell my friend Granville so," said O'Doemall.

"Really, Mr. O'Doemall, I trust you will do nothing so foolish. I have no idea—that is, I am not engaged to her, and "— said Monck, embarrassed.

"I will speak to Gran about it. You are a first rate match for his daughter. She is pretty, and will have the rhino, eh?" said O'Doemall.

"Really, Mr. O'Doemall, I cannot converse with you upon such a subject. I called to settle an account. If you will not settle it, I will so say to Mr. Granville when I return to the store."

"Very well, sir. I could pay, I believe, twenty such accounts, if I owed them. I believe W. Pitt Granville is good, and you can say to him that if he wants to borrow eight, or even as high as twelve thousand, I can let him have it at ten minutes' warning," said the audacious Irishman.

"I will mention the circumstance to Mr. Granville, and I wish you good morning," coolly observed Monck.

"Bye-bye. Drop in any time and take a glass of wine," said the indomitable O'Doemall.

"What an infernal scamp," was Mr. Granville's comment upon Marion's report. "Never mind, Marion; I want you to call every day upon that impudent fellow until you shame him into paying it. Nordheim owe him! He never owed any body in his life. He was uncommonly particular in that regard," continued Mr. Granville.

"I think it will be a waste of my time, but as you wish it, I will call until I see there is no hope. *Shame him!* That will be a tiresome job," was Marion's comment upon the business.

The next day Marion went again in No. 20 New street, but at a later hour. The clerk, Thomas, was there, engaged playing marbles on the store floor with another boy.

"Where is Mr. O'Doemall?" demanded Marion.

"Gone to dinner," replied the boy.

"Coming back soon?" asked Marion.

"Immediately. Going to wait? Please tell him, sir, when he comes, that I've gone home," and before Marion could express the least dissent to a proposition that left the responsibility of the store and its goods upon him, the boy was out of sight as well as hearing.

"I am in a fix. Suppose O'Doemall don't come at all? But I will wait awhile, anyhow."

Presently a very respectable-looking, middle-aged woman entered, and enquired for Mr. O'Doemall.

"He is not in, madam, and will not be for some time. I am waiting to see him about some money."

"Oh; do you owe him any money, sir?" asked the woman.

"No, indeed. But he owes me, or rather the firm that I am a clerk with," replied Marion.

"And do you think he will pay you? Do you think he will pay me, or any body else he owes?"

Marion looked at the woman, who was in a state of violent excitement.

"Does he owe you much?" he asked.

"Only seventy-two dollars, but it has ruined me, and my husband goes out now to work at days' work. But perhaps you, sir, can tell me what I ought to do. Mr. O'Doemall served us a dirty trick."

"If you will tell me how he incurred the debt, with all the particulars, if I can give you good advice, I will do so," said Marion, who began to be interested in the matter.

"It is a long story, but I will tell you all about it. Well, sir, you must know that me and my sister Mary used to do fine needle-work in the old country. I married, and came to this country with my husband, and he got a good situation. Then he says to me, 'Now, Bridget dear, I am making a little money, and we have got a little saved up, and as you and Mary can do fine work, I think the best we can do is to take a little store somewhere up town, and you can make and sill shirts and sich like, and gentlemen's underclothing, and I shall be able to send a good many hotel people to buy of you.' Well, we got a little store just big enough to hold us and a few goods up in Broadway, near Broome street. We had not been open a great many weeks, but was doing uncommon well, when one evening, bad luck to him, who should come in but Mr. O'Doemall. 'Ah,' said he, 'fine nice store. Show me some of your best shirts. I must patronise you, and I will buy a dozen. I want the finest linen shirts.' I showed him our best, and asked him two dollars a piece. They would not do, but he said, 'You seem honest young women, and I will trust you to make me a dozen of the finest linen shirts at six dollars each. I must have them in a week; and more than that, if you do them well, and suit me, I will bring young Coster, Astor, Lord Lennox, and some other fashionable young fellows, my friends, and we will get you up a first-rate business.' Oh, sir, that O'Doemall has a tongue in his head, and he wagged it to some purpose. ' He set me and my sister Mary almost crazy. We thought our fortunes were more than made. We took our good cash, and went and purchased the very finest linen to make this dozen shirts, and we both worked night and day until they were finished. One Saturday evening he called for the shirts. They were all packed up ever so nice. He winked and looked at every one, and he talked all the while about his magnificent room, and that he could not bear to stop at a hotel, and I do not know what. I thought he was a marquis at least. At last he says—

"'Seventy-two dollars, eh? That is cheap enough. I have paid, in London, twenty guineas for shirts not half as good. But you must send them round to my house in Prince street, it is only a few doors.'

"I called my husband's little brother, Felix, and he took the bundle. Then Mr. O'Doemall began to feel in his pockets, and he took an old wood cane and laid it upon a chair. He felt—felt.—I asked him if he had lost any thing. He said no, but that he had dressed for dinner, and left two hundred dollars in his vest pocket.

"'It will make no difference,' said he; 'your little boy can be trusted, I suppose, and if so, I will give the seventy-two dollars to him.'

"We told him to trust the boy—we did not like to refuse to let the shirts go, but he went, and the boy too. Presently the boy returned.

"'I want to get the gentleman's cane.'

"'Where are the shirts?'

"'He is holding the shirts while I came back for his cane.'

"The poor boy went away again, but it was a long time before he came back, and then it was to tell us that he could not find Mr. O'Doemall. We could not believe that so gentlemanly a person would commit so cruel a wrong upon two women just starting business in a new country. But next day we found that he had never lived in the house in Prince street. It broke us up at our little place. So great a loss disheartened us; we did not try to do any more. It was long before I found out where he did business. I have been several times, but Mr. O'Doemall laughs at me. Says he will pay me, but that I ought to pay him for teaching me a lesson in not trusting. Oh, I don't know what to do. I am afraid we will never get paid;" and here the poor woman relieved herself by a flood of tears.

"What a rascal he must be, to be sure?"

"But that ain't all, sir. He got acquainted with my poor sister Mary. She was a very beautiful girl, sir, and she met him and took walks in St. John's Park with Mr. O'Doemall, and she has never been herself since, and I fear, sir, she is bewitched after him."

"Is it possible such a man is allowed to walk the streets?"

"But I am not not quite done yet. My husband went to Mr. O'Doemall, and gave him a piece of his mind. The very next day he was turned out of his situation at the hotel, and I do believe that Mr. O'Doemall was the occasion of it. Now he goes out to days' work, when he can get any thing to do. But here he comes, Mr. O'Doemall."

"Aha, my sweetest plant from ould Ireland is it there you are?" laughingly exclaimed O'Doemall—and then noticing Marion, he added, "and the future husband of the delicious Miss Granville."

"Mr. O'Doemall, good-bye," exclaimed the indignant Marion as he left the store. That evening he told Mr. Granville the story of the shirts, and the claim of three hundred dollars was placed in a lawyer's hands. Marion was told that he need not call on the New street wine merchant any more.

CHAPTER XXVII.

Increased Business of Mr. Granville—Mrs. Tom Granville becomes his Housekeeper—The latter discovers the engagement between Marion Monck and her Niece—Communicates it to Mrs. Nordheim—Disappointment and stern Resolve.

THE dissolution of the firm of Granville and Nordheim apparently had no effect upon their extensive business. It was continued to the new house of W. Pitt Granville, who, if there was any change, largely increased their business. Mr. Granville devoted much more of his attention to business than ever. He was at his office early in the morning, and except to go to his meals, never left until ten o'clock at night. Some changes had taken place at his home. Tom Granville had some time previously left his house and home in Chambers street, to devote his whole time to Miss Norris. As soon as it became evident to Mrs. Thomas Granville that her husband had utterly abandoned her, and had openly connected himself with Miss Norris—which he did immediately after the death of Mr. Nordheim—she sent a note to her brother-in-law, Pitt Granville. He came at once to Chambers street.

"Tell me nothing, Kate, about Tom. I know all. What do you intend to do?"

"It is useless my incurring the expense of keeping house alone, I think. I have no one but my sister, and she can take her departure for Baltimore at any moment."

"Then give up the house at once, sell off the furniture to the best advantage, and come and take charge of my house. Isabel is too young to be burdened with a housekeeper's cares and anxieties, and besides she needs looking after. She is very inexperienced, and as her aunt, you are the proper person to take charge of her."

"This is really a proposition that I could not have expected. I do not know how to thank you."

"There is no occasion for thanks—I am the obliged party, and if you say you will come, Kate, there is an end of it. Make your arrangements, and come as quick as you can."

The result of this conversation was, that Mrs. Kate Granville was installed as mistress in State street. Isabel liked her aunt, and was delighted at her taking charge. To Mrs. Kate Granville it was the most acceptable thing that could have occurred. The scandal afloat in reference to her, and the separation between Tom and herself would be silenced, for certainly the world would say there could be no blame attached to Mrs. Tom Granville, if her husband's brother, a large and extensive merchant, should receive her at his house; not only that, but take her to keep house, and take the charge of his daughter.

Mrs. Kate Granville had not resided with her brother-in-law but a few weeks, when her keen eyes discovered that there was some sort of a secret between her niece Isabel and Marion Monck. She was satisfied that notes and letters passed between the two young people. Marion was a regular visitor at the house in State street, and was there a hundred times unsuspected, because he was now the confidential clerk of Mr. Granville, and it was necessary that he should see him frequently. Sometimes Mr. Granville would be confined to the house for a few days, by sickness. Then Marion would be there half a dozen times a day. He never came but Isabel contrived to see and speak with him, if it was only for a moment.

Aunt Kate determined to put an end to this in some manner, for she was not certain her brother would like the idea of an attachment between Marion and Isabel. The former was but a clerk, and although Mr. Granville seemed to be very fond of him, yet she knew that being fond of a youth as a clerk, and approving of him for a son-in-law, was entirely a different matter. She took Isabel to task the first opportunity, and taxed her with being in love or engaged to Marion Monk. The fair girl could only reply to the charge on the instant with a flood of tears.

"Don't deny it, Bella dear. There is no very great crime, and you can tell Aunty all about it—how it happened."

Thus coaxed, Isabel very soon took the advice, and made Aunt Kate her confidant. At first the sister-in-law concluded that it was her duty to inform her brother of circumstances that so nearly concerned his domestic happiness; but when she listened to Bella's pleadings, her anxieties, and her confident assurances that if Aunt did tell Papa, that he would turn her out of doors, as he had done her brother Walter, and not only that, but that he would discharge poor Marion from his employ, and probably ruin him and his prospects for life, and all "for no good," Aunt Kate hesitated. Then Isabel told her that Marion was not to blame, and that it was her persuasion that had made him conceal his attachment from her father. Finally Aunt Kate was persuaded to keep silence so far as Mr. Granville was concerned, provided Isabel would agree to submit the correspondence between her lover and herself to Aunt Kate's inspection, and that no further letters should be sent or received unless she inspected them. Again, it was understood that Marion should be informed that Kate knew all about it, and that she would converse freely with him upon the subject. Isabel affectionately kissed her Aunt after all these preliminaries had been settled upon, and she felt her mind much relieved. She dreaded the anger of her father. With Aunt Kate as her confidential adviser, there was somebody to share with her the furious anger of her father, whenever he was informed of the attachment, should it be displeasing to him, or should he have other matrimonial views for her.

Mrs. Tom Granville, after Isabel left the parlor in which this memorable explanation had occurred, did not feel at ease in her mind. "I have consented to do wrong, but I have promised Isabel not to interfere, and I will not. If it comes to Pitt Granville's ears, as Isabel says, the house would come trembling down, and there would be a general smash up. Pitt has a fearful temper when he gets a going. There is poor Walter too—driven off to sea—never been heard from, and his father never allows his name to be mentioned, and all because he chose to fall in love with my sister Madison, and refused to marry that proud, impudent hussy Mag Benson. No—Isabel may run off with this Marion Monck—I certainly will not interfere. But one thing I will do, without delay—yes, this very morning. This Marion has a warm friend in widow Nordheim. Of course she is aware of his attachment to Isabel, and she has great influence with Granville. I will go and consult her about the matter, and take her advice." She rang the bell. The servant answered it.

"Go tell Thomas the coachman that I wish to go out in about an hour."

Aunt Kate went up to Isabella's room, and informed her that she was obliged to go out for a few hours, but would be home by dinner-time. Isabel was surprised, but said nothing. She little dreamed of the object that Aunt Kate had in view. If she had done so, Aunt Kate would not have been permitted to go on such an errand; for with a keen instinct Isabel had partly discovered a secret that Mrs. Nordheim supposed was safe in her own bosom; and on one occasion the young Miss had almost allowed jealousy to get the better of her, and she came very near charging Marion with loving Mrs. Nordheim better than he did herself.

Mrs. Granville found Mrs. Nordheim at home. She was dressed in deep mourning, and received Mrs. Tom Granville with unusual courtesy. She felt a deep sympathy for her. Both had lost husbands—one by death, the other by the fascinations of a beautiful but bad woman; for Mrs. Nordheim was not aware that there were two sides to the story of Tom's separation from his wife. She had heard that Tom had left his wife to go and live with Miss Norris.

"I am very happy to see you, Mrs. Granville, very indeed; and I cannot tell you how glad I was to hear that you had found a refuge from your domestic difficulties in the house of the elder Mr. Granville. It is an arrangement that must be very gratifying to all parties, for my beautiful friend Isabel is too young and inexperienced to have charge of so extensive an establishment as Mr. Granville's, and you can relieve her of all care, and be a mother to her. Poor girl! She needs a mother, for I think Mr. Granville has an extremely bad temper, although he can be so pleased and smile so amiably in his out-door intercourse."

Mrs. Nordheim spoke with animation, and from the heart.

"I really believe, Mrs. Nordheim, that you do feel what you express; and you have never joined in the lying scandal about me, although my name was connected with your husband's. He was a good friend, and assisted me. What his ultimate motives may have been, he can only settle with his God. I could not do less than be grateful for his kindness, which was bestowed upon many occasions when I assure you I needed kindness. But don't let us talk, Mrs. Nordheim, of what gives me the horrors. I came up this morning for an express purpose."

"Indeed! Can I guess that purpose?"

"I presume you are aware of the relations that exist between Marion Monck and my niece, Isabel Granville?"

Mrs. Nordheim sat rocking herself to and fro in a well-cushioned chair, and when she caught the last words, the chair ceased its motion, and the occupant placed her hand for a moment upon her heart, as if to discover that it beat. Her breath caught for a moment, and her face was as pale as death. It was but for a moment that she hesitated, and then she asked

"The relation between Marion and Isabella?"

"Yes. I suppose Marion has told you that he has long been attached to Isabel, that it is reciprocated on her part, and that they are engaged to be married. They are both fearful that their views may conflict with those of my stern brother, and they are both keeping the arrangement very quiet. I coaxed it out of Isabel this morning, and knowing how warmly you are attached to Marion, I presumed of course that he had at least informed you of it. Is it possible that he has not done so?"

Mrs. Nordheim broke out into a laugh that actually surprised Mrs. Granville.

"Told me—me! No, he did not tell *me*. Why, it is the most comical thing I have heard of for a long time! Marion in love, and engaged to be married to that little girl, Isabel Granville!—ha, ha, ha! It is a good joke, is it not?"

Mrs Tom Granville could not, or did not see the joke; and she replied that her niece was not so very little; on the contrary that she was a full grown young lady.

"O, my dear Mrs. Granville, I meant no harm. To tell you

7

the truth, your information has somewhat surprised me. Marion is not yet twenty years old, and it is rather young to think of getting married."

"It is indeed. But what can be done? I thought I would come up and have an explanation with you."

"You are very kind indeed, but I must decline having any thing to do with the matter. Marion has not told me of it, and therefore I shall say nothing. Your conversation shall go no further. I will keep it in my own breast;" and she placed her hand there for a moment, as if to press the secret in, so that it would be safe.

These two ladies continued in conversation for over an hour upon almost every topic of the day. Mrs. Nordheim took the lead, and Mrs. Tom Granville wondered at such a flow of good spirits. At last the visitor left. No sooner had the door closed, than Mrs. Nordheim fell at full length upon the floor, and rolled in agony.

"O, my God, preserve my reason! I that have so long loved him in secret! I—that now all obstacles to my dreams for years is removed! He—Marion—our Marion—my Marion—to go and fall in love with that chit, simpleton, foolish, nonsensical girl! But I will not give way! No, no, no! Courage, courage! It is better as it is. He nor no living soul shall know what I have suffered! But it is over now, and if Marion were to come home I could receive him as calmly as if he was my brother."

She rose and resumed her seat. The tears silently poured down her cheeks, but after a few moments she descended to the basement and gave orders to the servants as calmly as if her heart had never known aught but the most peaceful pulsations. Such is life!

CHAPTER XXVIII.

The Daily Life of a New York Merchant—Habits and Ideas of one of the Class Mr. Granville—Colonel Benson, the British Merchant—Merchants' Ideas of children—A plan concocted to marry Isabella Granville to Middleton Benson by their parents—Isabella at the piano—Arrival of the ship Dorothea from Bavaria—A profitable voyage—Morion Monck informs Mr. Granville that he has left the house of Mrs. Nordheim—The City Hotel—Captain Watson—The Shades, in Thames street—A pleasant night there.

THE daily life of a merchant in New York is one round of routine. He rises in the morning, gets a hasty breakfast, and before nine o'clock reaches his place of business. If he is a shipping merchant he reads the list of arrivals of that day, and the clearances of vessels the day previous. If he is any other sort of merchant, he reads that portion of the journal that affects his peculiar interest. Half an hour with the newspaper in his hand, and then he puts it one side and goes at his work. The letters come from the post-office—these he reads, and then transfers them to his bookkeeper to be read and noted. An hour later he goes out into the street and attends to his out-door business, and perhaps stops at a refectory, an oyster cellar, or Delmonico's, and gets a stiff glass of brandy and a bite of something to eat, and then is back to his counting-house or store. Business, business, business. Business in his head, business in his actions, business in his thoughts, business at heart. He is nothing more than a body made up of business. He goes home to dine at five o'clock, and reaches his commercial palace filled with thoughts of business. He has left a loved wife—been absent from her nine hours. He has perfect confidence in her, and when he comes home, he tells her how successful he has been in business. He eats a hurried dinner, but delays longer to drink his wine. He returns to his business again after dinner, or if not he takes his hat and goes down to some place of amusement, or to see some friend. At or before eleven o'clock he is found at home, and after he gets his tod goes to bed. The next and ten thousand succeeding days, perhaps as long as he lives, is but a repetition of the one day that we have given as a sample.

He may acquire money, but even that is not all he desires. He is never as happy as when he is admired as the most extensive merchant of his class. He works for that; he battles for it night and day. As a politician he is a nobody. Empires may be overthrown, kingdoms conquered, a republic corrupted—it is nothing to the merchant—it has no connection with his business. He cares not who rules the city, the state, or the nation. He does not vote—it would take too much time, and he would be obliged to indirectly mix with people that he considers beneath him. Sunday is not a working day. He goes to church because it makes a man more respectable, and helps pass away the time. His religion is a part of his regular business. In early life he has married, has a family. They become a part of his business. He leaves his wife, perhaps a young charming woman to get along the best way she can with nothing to do. Most women find something to do, and they have it all their own way, for from morning until night, day in and day out, the wife of a New York merchant can tell at any time where her husband is. But could the veil be removed from the careless husband's eyes, he who is a worse slave than the Jane or Tom of the South—could he imagine for one moment in what manner his wife or the daughters, or the sons occupy their time, his business would lose its charm.

An eminent statesman once remarked that it was a remarkable fact that there should be a virtuous *rich* merchant's wife in New York, and on being asked why he thought this, he answered,

"Because, of all the male inhabitants of God's earth, the merchant is the only known class that abandon their wives and daughters without remorse or fear to be seduced, corrupted and betrayed by the idle and the vile of the other sex."

It was once a good custom in New York for merchants to have their dwellings in the same buildings with their stores. A return to that habit would save from vice thouands of wives. It is a good custom. The merchant can then look after his business and his honor at the same time.

Mr. Granville was just exactly the business man we have described. He ate his meals regularly. He went to church on Sunday. He had a good stock of wines in his cellar, and occasionally gave a dinner. It was a part of his business. Most of those he invited were business men. If he invited others who had genius, it was to make the dinner go off better by having a few intellectual persons mixed in the business eaters.

He had lost all hopes of seeing his son Walter again—that is to say, as he wished to see him. He did not regard him as a son but as a sailor, and as his confidence was lost by what the senior Granville called a gross act of filial disobedience, he determined that his remaining child should be the means of carrying out his design. On one occasion Colonel Benson called in State street. Mr. Granville was alone. Aunt Kate and Isabel had gone out to spend the evening at Mr. Grasper's. Between the Colonel and Mr. Granville, Walter's name had been a forbidden subject by quiet consent. This evening Mr. Granville alluded to him in the following manner: "Colonel, are you aware that I have never been so crossed in any matter, so completely disappointed, as at the overthrow of my plans, or rather of our mutual plans, in reference to our children, Walter and Margaret?"

"Children are inexperienced and great fools, Granville. I confess that I was annoyed for a short time, for Walter was a great favorite of mine. I saw no reason why the match should not have been a happy one. We could have started the young couple fairly in life, and our own minds would have been at rest. I'll tell you, Mr. Granville, that one of the greatest anxieties in a person's mind, if he has sons or daughters, is that they will make an unfortunate match, especially so if you have money. There are so many prowlers about in a city like this—chaps that have got nothing, but dress well and can keep up appearances, and get into society. These fellows keep parents constantly on the look-out. I am never easy in my mind. There is my son Middleton—he is rising rapidly as a business young man. I am delighted with his conduct. He is not fooling about the town at nights, and has formed no bad acquaintances. He will be taken into the firm before he is much older, and I shall give him the capital that I have invested in that house, and withdraw my own name altogether. Now would it not be enough to make a man curse his father, if that favorite son should fall in love with some pretty shop-girl or some angelic book-folder? Yet I should not be surprised at it. It would only be in keeping with the proceedings of sons generally who have wealthy parents."

"I hope Middleton will never take any step, my dear Colonel, that would be so utterly repugnant to you views for his future. I have to keep a careful watch upon my daughter Isabella, but thank God, she is heart whole, and will never disobey or cross my wishes; but as double security, I have got Tom's wife here, and she is a perfect woman of the world, and if there is any young man comes to my house to make love to my daughter, it will not be long before I should be fully informed of it. If your views, Colonel, are not changed, as we have been disappointed in one match between my son and your daughter, suppose we try again, with your son and my daughter."

"With all my heart, Granville; but we must manage somewhat differently. I shall take a warning from your son. I don't like to come directly in contact with mine, or he too might go off a three years' voyage. Consider it a bargain, between us. I will do for my son what you proposed to do for yours, and you shall do the same for your daughter that I proposed to do for mine. Now, if you agree to this, let us go to work and bring about the match as originating with the two young people themselves, and not with us. Come often to my house and bring your daughter with you. I will make it a point to bring Middleton with me when I come here. Miss Isa must display her fascinations to the best advantage and when we find there is a liking, then we can carry out our views; but don't let us try to do in two months what may take two years and we shall see if we don't have more success in this marriage plot, than in the other one, which resulted, I am sorry to say, in losing your son, at least temporarily."

"I agree with you, perfectly, Colonel. I already perceive that your plan is a more feasible one than mine."

The return of Mrs. Tom Granville and Isabella interrupted the conversation of these two worthies, who were a fair sample of nine in ten of the parents of New York, who have marriageable children. Business. Position. Money. These are regarded as the materials for a suitable match. Honesty, talent, health, on the one part—beauty, virtue, amiability, intelligence, on the other, are not counted in the game. If they were, there would be few matches made between rich men's sons and daughters.

Colonel Benson was a man who had moved much in society, and could be very fascinating when he chose to be so. When Isabella had removed her bonnet and shawl, he gazed at her for some time in silence. He was more struck than ever with her extreme loveliness. He drew his chair near her, and engaged her in a very animated conversation for some time. He was delighted with intelligent conversation. Then he asked her to play and sing some of his old favorite English songs, and without a moment's hesitation, or any hypocritical arts, which young ladies frequently use to enhance the value of this performance, she arose and went to the piano, which was an upright English piano, imported expressly from England for his child's use, by Mr. Granville. Isabella played all the English airs that she had learned to play to please her father. When she had finished, the colonel looked at Mr. Granville. There was an expression in his eyes which the father understood. He saw that the colonel was delighted with the prospect of such a wife for his son, and he could not control his feelings, but turned to Isabella and said:

"My dear Isabella, I am very glad I did not bring my son Middleton with me, for had he been in my place this evening, you would have set him crazy. But I will venture him the next time I come."

Isabella shuddered—she hardly knew why, but at that moment the bell rang, and shortly after, although it was late, Marion Monck entered the parlor. He bowed politely to all in the room, and then approached Mr. Granville with some letters.

"The ship Dorothea, Captain Watson, is below, sir. She is just in from Batavia with a cargo of sugar, and is consigned to the late firm. Captain Watson came to the office only a few moments ago. I took him up to the City Hotel. He will go down to the ship early in the morning, and wishes some directions; but I will wait until you have read your letters."

Meanwhile Mr. Granville was occupied in reading his letters, and as he read he commented upon them.

"The Dorothea will make a glorious voyage. Her sugar will bring eleven cents a pound from the ship, and they only cost five Spanish dollars the pecul."

"How much is a pecul, Mr. Granville?" asked Col. Benson.

"One hundred and thirty-three and one-third English pounds. The ship will clear twenty-five thousand dollars in her cargo, and pay a good round freight to her owner;" replied Mr. Granville.

"Is the cargo owned by you?" asked Colonel Benson.

"It is owned one half by my late firm, and the other half belongs to John McGreen of Philadelphia, who also owns the ship. I am his agent here," replied Mr. Granville.

Some general conversation occurred, and then Colonel Benson remarked:

"Well, Granville, I see you have something to do to-night, and I will take my departure."

"You need not be in a hurry, although I shall call on Captain Watson as soon as I have finished my letters," said Mr. Granville.

Colonel Benson took leave of the two ladies, and soon after they bade Mr. Granville and Marion a pleasant good-night, and retired to their rooms. Mr. Granville and his clerk were left alone.

"A capital voyage the Dorothea will make, eh? How does Captain Watson look? I will go up and see the old sea dog presently. You must send a note to Havemeyers and the other sugar refiners early in the morning, and see if we can't sell this cargo of sugar from the dock. It will save us a great deal of expense. You were late at the office to-night. Lucky, too, or you would have missed Captain Watson. How is Mrs. Nordheim?" demanded Mr. Granville.

"Quite well. I am going to leave there."

"Leave there! Why, I thought it was almost a permanent home? What is out? Have you and her quarrelled?" demanded Mr. Granville.

"Not that I am aware of. She told me this afternoon that she should probably give up the house soon, and although she did not wish to incommode me, yet the sooner I procured a home somewhere else, the better."

"Short and sweet. What are you going to do?" asked Mr. Granville.

"I have not made up my mind yet. This sudden notice has taken me all aback. I must try and get a boarding-house somewhere nearer the office," said Marion.

"You will do nothing of the kind. To-morrow do you come here with your trunk. I will have a room fixed up for you, and you will be perfectly at home. It will be very convenient for me. I shall save for you and myself a large amount of boot and shoe leather," said Mr. G.

"Really, you are very kind, but shall I not put you to inconvenience?" enquired Marion.

"What have you got to do with that? You are well acquainted with my daughter, and with Mrs. Tom Granville. Coming here will not be like going among strangers. But come, let us go up and see Captain Tommy Watson," said Mr. Granville.

The merchant and his clerk went up to the City Hotel. Mr. Willard smilingly told them that Captain Watson had left word that he had gone round to the Shades in Thames street, directly in the rear of the hotel. To "the Shades" they went, and there they found the Captain with his mug of ale on the little table before him, and enjoying a cigar with great gusto. Mr. Granville and Marion took seats at the same table, and soon had their " mugs " before them. The main room was crowded with small tables, and every table had four to six persons about it. In the center of the room was a large round table which accommodated twenty persons. These were drinking, singing songs, telling stories, and enjoying themselves without limit.

"I did not know that there was such a place as this in New York," remarked Marion.

"I did," said Captain Tommy Watson. "It is the only place where you can get a good glass of beer, and a 'Welsh rabbit.' I always come here when I am in New York. Besides the good drinks and eatables, there is always lots of fun going on here, and every hour the character of the guests change. In the morning you have one class that come here to get their breakfast. Tea or coffee and a mutton-chop, or a deliciously done beef steak. Towards eleven o'clock, a class come here to get a mug of beer, some bread and cheese or a cold cut. From twelve to three, merchants—some of the best in town, come to get a regular feed—a downright dinner. Then in the evening, all the leading literary men and wits come here, and in addition, a lot of chaps who have a little spare change, come and spend it, and hear the geniuses sing and talk;" said Captain Watson

Captain Watson's description of the Shades was good a quarter of a century ago. But now, although the Shades is still in existence, and kept in the same place, yet its custom has sadly fallen off, and their character changed. Now and then a stray English actor lodges and boards there, and sometimes one of the ancient guests drop in to see how his old haunt looks. But the majority of the customers have gone up town, or to their graves, and the Shades is desolate.

The Captain and his consignee, Mr. Granville and Marion, remained until long after midnight listing to their songs, while partaking of a nice little bird supper, garnished with champagne, which Mr. Granville had ordered. The Captain contributed his quota of enjoyment by telling anecdotes of his recent voyage to and from Java.

When they parted for the night, it was with the understanding that the Captain would come up with the good ship Dorothea, and lay her along side the Rector street, as early in the morning as was practicable.

7*

CHAPTER XXIX.

Count Falsechinski Makes a Levy upon Mrs Woodruff—The Count calls in Bond street—A Palace Unsuspected of Evil—Its Gorgeousness—The Count gets a Check for a Thousand Down and Two Thousand Dollars a Year for Keeping a Secret—Accompanies the Lady to a Fashionable Party—What the Count Saw at "The Parkers"—Mr. O'Doemall and Mrs. Parker—A Scene of Excitement—Interview between Count and Mrs. Woodruff—Ten Thousand Dollars Offered for a Husband for a Young Lady of Wealth and Beauty—The Little Baby—A Horrible Outrage in High Life—The Count Falsechinski Levies Five Thousand Dollars More—His Opinion of Morality and Virtue in High Places.

When Miss Norris communicated to the Count Falsechinski the secret of Mrs. Woodruff, that noble gentleman forthwith sent a note to the Bond street lady. He received a reply the same day, requesting him to call so soon as he could make it convenient. It was not long before the Count made his appearance on the premises. He stood upon the steps and then rung the bell, but noticing that the outer door was partially opened, he passed in, and found himself in a short hall. At the end was a second mahogany door, which was fast, and another bell-handle could be seen at the side door.

There was every sign of the residence of some wealthy person, at the same time, it was evident that the arrangement of two doors was very convenient for persons who did not wish to be seen entering the house, as they would not be kept a moment on the outside of the street door. Ladies or gentlemen could run up the marble steps, push open the door, enter, and push the door to again. There they were safe from observation, and could leisurely ring the second bell. This the Count did. A colored girl soon after made her appearance.

"I wish to see madam."

"Your name, sir?"

"The Count Falsechinski."

The inner door was carefully closed by the girl, who went to seek her mistress. She returned, opened the door sufficient to allow the Count to enter, then carefully closed and locked it, and led the way to the rear parlor.

"Take a seat, Mr. Count. Missus will be down directly."

The door was partially open which connected with the next parlor. The Count entered it, and found that there was still a front parlor. Three parlors, magnificently furnished, occupied the floor. The walls were covered with paintings, and the furniture was of the most costly description. The rear parlor opened upon a balcony, which was so covered with creeping vines as almost to exclude the light, and prevented any one from looking into the yard. Between the two rear windows stood a bronze stand with a marble top. Upon it was a marble bust of Daniel Webster. One side of the room, between each recess of the fire-places, were large mahogany book-cases, with looking-glass doors. The Count tried to open some of them, but found all carefully locked. She must have a large library, thought the Count, if these splendid cases are filled with books. On the opposite side of the room was a small table, covered with a fine white cloth. Upon it, was a large quarto, bound with velvet. The Count opened the book. It was the Bible. "Queer female this," muttered the Count, and tired with looking about the room, he partly reclined upon one of the superb sofas that lined the room. Presently the lady of the house entered, and walking rapidly across the room, took the Count's hand, and bade him not rise. She seated herself by his side. The lady, who was no other than Mrs. Woodruff, was dressed in deep mourning, and also wore a widow's cap.

"Count, I received your note, and I presume you received mine, or you would not be here."

The Count bowed politely, and said he had received the note.

"Yours, Count, made me aware that you possessed a secret of mine, and that it was in your power to do me injury or "— continued Mrs. Woodruff.

"Good, as you may decide," interrupted the Count.

"I will be very frank with you, Count. If you are not disposed to injure me, you can be of essential service to me, and at the same time benefit yourself most materially; but it is necessary that we should perfectly understand each other," remarked Mrs. Woodruff.

The Count nodded his head in approbation.

"What, Count, do you require?" she asked

"Money, and I will earn it," replied the Count.

"Do you mean to have me infer that if I pay you a certain sum of money, that you will not only keep my secret, but that you will serve me in any way that I shall point out?" asked Mrs. Woodruff.

"I do," replied the Count.

"Will you take a solemn oath upon that Bible yonder that you will never, directly or indirectly, betray me or my interests?" replied the hostess.

"I will."

The lady went and got the Bible, and as she resumed her seat, placed it upon her knees, and again addressed the Count.

"What money will you require?"

"I wish the sum of one thousand dollars in cash. I then wish you to pay me five hundred dollars every three months, so long as I serve you," said the cool Count.

"Swear upon this book what I require, and I will agree to your proposition." The Count took the oath.

"Excuse me a moment." The lady left the room, but was not absent over five minutes, when she again took a seat by the Count, and placed in his hands two bank notes of five hundred dollars each. "Three months hence, Count, you will receive another note of five hundred, and so on for the year at least, or as long as our bargain holds good. Count, will you tell me by what means you discovered the character of my establishment? I do not ask you save in this regard. Will the source of your information be used again to others?" asked the lady.

"I cannot give you the name of the person who informed me as to your real pursuits, but I can and do guarantee that it shall not be repeated by that party to your injury," replied the Count.

"I am satisfied; and now let us understand each other. You move, Count, in a certain circle. You will make many valuable acquaintances. Such as you deem will be of value for me to make, I wish you to be the means of bringing us together. I want none but the highest—those who are wealthy—or hold positions of political power, or foreigners who are titled, or leading men in the professions. Do you understand me?" asked Mrs. Woodruff.

"Perfectly; and I will carry out your views in that regard. What else?" asked the Count.

"I wish you to accompany me to church, to places of public amusement, and to the select, fashionable parties among the higher classes of society," was the reply.

"What? Do I understand you to say that *you* visit in the highest circles?' asked the astonished Count.

"Did you not meet me at Mrs. Nordheim's?" she asked.

"Oh, ah, lady, yes; that was because you were a neighbor, I suppose; but there are higher classes," said the Count.

"Very well; we shall see. Read this note," replied Mrs. Woodruff, and she handed him a note.

The Count read an invitation addressed to himself from Mr. and Mrs. Parker, inviting him to a party at their house that night.

"I see, my dear Count, that you are somewhat astonished, but I have a note of invitation, and had no difficulty, I assure you, in getting one for you. Nothing will give me more pleasure than to accompany you there," smilingly observed Mrs. Woodruff.

"No. Not accompany me, but meet me there," she continued, correcting herself.

The Count soon after took his leave, but when the night came, he was at the party, and was one of the favored ones. Mrs. Woodruff was, as usual, quiet and retired, but made many acquaintances, particularly among the young married ladies. Mrs. Parker was the life and soul of her party, but the Count could not help noticing that one of her guests seemed to be an object of the deepest interest to the hostess. It was no other than Mr. John O'Doemall, the wine merchant. He was dressed superbly, and certainly far outshone the Count, who did not attempt to rival him.

"What an impudent scoundrel that O'Doemall is!" said the Count to Mrs. Woodruff, as the carriage which contained them drove off from the stately residence of the Parkers. "I had half a mind to give Mrs. Parker a warning."

"It is well you did not, Count. Mrs. Parker is one of my oldest friends and acquaintances."

The Count gave a prolonged "Whew"—"And Mr. O'Doemall also?" he asked.

"Yes; and some day I may tell you more," she replied.

The Count became a friend of Mrs. Woodruff, attended her at church, theatres, and private parties, and his salary was regularly paid, and as fast as he received it he deposited it with his Wall street bankers, adding constantly to the amount to his credit already in Prime, Ward & King's hands. So weeks and months passed on, no one suspecting or dreaming that Mrs. Woodruff was not the wealthy, pious lady that she was supposed to be. The rector of the fashionable church at which she worshipped paid her a formal visit at least once a month, and no other female member of his congregation conducted herself so unexceptionably as Mrs. Woodruff. No other made the worthy rector so many presents, and as she sent them through the hands of the sexton of that fashionable church, no one who held a seat in that church received a bow as she passed into the church, or was shown to her pew with a greater respect.

The Count had drawn his salary from Mrs. Woodruff almost a year, when one afternoon, as he was about leaving the office to go to Delmonico's to get his dinner, a note was placed in his hands by the coachman of Mrs. Woodruff.

"Carriage around the corner. Missis say you come right up," observed the coachman.

The Count read the note, and then hastily followed the colored coachman and took his seat in the carriage. It was driven rapidly to Bond street. He entered the house, and found Mrs. Woodruff in her private parlor, in a state of great excitement.

"Ah, Count, I am so glad you are come! I have had such a scene!" she exclaimed, as he entered.

"Be calm, Mrs. Woodruff; seat yourself, and tell me all about it. As I have had no dinner, will you order me something, and a bottle of champagne," remarked the Count.

The order was given, and Mrs. Woodruff resumed a seat

"Who was the scene with, my lady?" asked the Count.

"O, with those Parkers. If it were not for me, their wealth could not save them," replied the indignant Woodruff

"What is out now? Tell me all about it, and then if you want advice, I will give it," said the Count.

"Count, could you procure a husband for a young lady of high family, one of the first respectability, if ten thousand dollars were placed in her husband's hands the moment she was married?" demanded Mrs. Woodruff.

"I dare say I could do so—in fact I know I could. Ten thousand dollars? Is the lady pretty? I know fifty young fellows that would marry ten thousand dollars and take the Witch of Endor if she were alive, as the wife additional," replied the Count.

"Do not joke—I am perfectly serious; and I will tell you the young lady is Miss Julia Parker, the niece of Mr. Parker," observed Madame Woodruff.

"The devil she is! Why, my lady, what is out now? A beautiful young and virtuous girl like Julia Parker need not go begging for a husband. She can take her pick in the market," said the astonished Count.

"Yes, that is all very well; but she must be married as a widow with her child. She won't give up her child," said the lady.

"Widow—child—Miss Parker! Why, what the old Nick

is out now! Tell me all, or don't ask my aid. Where is Miss Parker?" continued the Count.

"Up stairs, and her aunt has just left. But I made her pull in her horns. I dared her to threaten me. The negro woman took away the child this morning, and the mother frets about it; but the old she devil Parker insists that she shall go to a party on next Monday night, as though nothing had happened," said Mrs. Woodruff.

"How long has Miss Parker been in this house?" asked the Count.

"About three weeks. She had a little baby about a week ago," replied Mrs. Woodruff.

"Miss Julia Parker—*leetle* baby!" repeated the Count, whose eyes actually stuck out with amazement.

"No, indeed; Madame Parker needn't put on any of her airs with me. She is a communicant at the same church—that don't matter. She has done it all. That poor girl was as innocent as a babe unborn, until the outrage was committed upon her, and why was it done? Who did it?—what for? O, Count, I could tell you such a story as would make your hair curl, without putting curling tongs anywhere near it," said Mrs. Woodruff in a very excited manner.

"Now, my lady, you have said too much, or not quite enough. I want to know more," fiercely observed the Count.

"You shall know all; and then advise me what to do. That old wretch shan't make a cat's-paw of me—not she. You know that O'Doemall—of course you do. Mrs. Parker chooses to fall in love with him. He of course agreed to it, and they met here, in this house. She wanted a handsome lover—he wanted money. Well, he got a few hundreds out of her, and it was more, more. One day, I told her not to come here any more. So they met afterwards at her own house. They got pretty bold and imprudent, and one morning Miss Julia happening to go to her aunt's apartments, she caught the naughty O'Doemall and her worthy aunt breaking Commandment No. Eight. Then there was a scene! but Mrs. Parker was equal to the emergency. She sent a note to me at once, enclosing a hundred dollar bill, and requesting a room ready in an hour. It was ready. Mrs. Parker came, and her niece was with her. The niece knew nothing of my business. She knew me as a visitor and a friend. They both took a seat in one of my parlors. Then the aunt complained of being sick, and asked me to let her lie down. The niece went up to the room with her. Then she ordered up a bottle of Madeira. The servant took it up.

O'Doemall came, and he went up of course. But really I cannot tell the rest, Count—it is too horrible," remarked the poor Mrs. Woodruff.

"You must tell it all—go on," said the Count sternly.

"Be it so. I had other matters to attend to, and my mind was not called to what Mrs. Parker was doing. The three remained in that room over two hours. Then the man O'Doemall slid out of the house. Then I went up. Julia, poor child, was acting more like a maniac than anything else. Mrs. Parker frowned, scowled, pinched her even. But still the girl sobbed in such a woeful manner that my suspicions were aroused, but I could say nothing; and shortly after Mrs. Parker took her niece and they left the house, went up the street a short distance and got into their carriage and drove home. Count, in order to keep that little girl from exposing her aunt, that fashionable lady and her lover had forced the poor girl to lose her innocence. Is not this horrible? I suspected this at the time, but it was only recently that Miss Julia told me the facts. The outrage was repeated several times, and she dared not say a word. She became pregnant, and then the aunt in alarm came to me, and to prevent disgrace I agreed to receive and take care of her through her illness, and received a thousand dollars for my trouble. She is nearly well, and Mrs. Parker, who has made her husband believe that Miss Julia is in the country, has hired a negro woman to take the child to nurse, and wants that her niece shall now return home, and take her place in the family circle. What do you think of it, Count?" asked Mrs. Woodruff.

"I think that it is in character with a good many other things. This is a funny world. It is all right. Mrs. Parker is one of the leading fashionable ladies in New York, but why does she wish to marry her niece in such a hurry? As a widow, too?" asked the cautious Count.

"Because her niece has become very fond of the child. She says she will keep the child, and that if she marries, it must be to some one who knows the facts,—that is to say, that she is the mother of the child. If any one who is respectable will marry her, the matter can be arranged, Count," observed Mrs. Woodruff.

"My lady, you are deceived. It is only to pacify the young lady that Mrs. Parker talks that way. I know better—she is not sincere. In a month, the shrewd heartless woman will wean the young one from her offspring, and she will be as fashionable a belle as ever. No one will be the wiser. So don't fret yourself at all. You have done with Mrs. Parker. She will never serve you more. You know too much. Now you must make her *pay—pay*," said the Count.

"But she has paid me," replied the lady.

"No, no. She told you she would pay ten thousand dollars to marry, eh? But it is a lie. Never mind. I will get five thousand—half for you, half for me," said the Count.

"But, my dear Count, she will not stand it. She "——

"Don't say any more. She will pay *me*. Write her a note, and say that I am the person who will marry her niece, and that you have told me *all*. Leave the rest to me."

The Count received the sort of note that he desired, and with it he proceeded to the residence of Mrs. Parker. He saw that lady, told her all that she had done, and gave her one day to raise five thousand dollars, or that he would send her and Mr. O'Doemall to the City Prison. The next day the frightened lady had raised the sum, but only about one half in cash ; the rest was in jewelry at the Count's valuation, although it had cost Mrs. Parker over six thousand dollars.

The Count made some pledges also to that lady. She continued at the head of fashion, and her niece eventually married well—the child having been disposed of in a most mysterious manner. The Count was right in his predictions. Mrs. Parker met Mrs. Woodruff at church, but their acquaintance, socially, was ended.

The twenty-five hundred dollars the Count paid over to Mrs. Woodruff, and the jewelry he made a special deposit of at his bankers. It is needless to add that the Count's faith in the genuine piety and morality of our most fashionable church goers was not visibly increased. "I will levy a tax on sin," said the honorable Count, "wherever I find it." He had done so with the Parkers to a very heavy extent.

CHAPTER XXX.

The shock to Mrs Nordheim at Mrs. Tom Granville's communication—Finds herself a rich widow and loving Marion Monck—Mr. Wilson and the Widow Nordheim—His opinion of Monck—A long conversation—Marion Monck quits the house of Mrs. Nordheim—The latter invites Mr Wilson to reside in Bond street, and to purchase another house—She offers to put him in business—A new world opened to the old bookkeeper.

THE communication which Mrs. Tom Granville made to Mrs. Nordheim was as unexpected as it was shocking. She was a true-hearted woman. She had married for reasons that have been already alluded to; but she had never loved Mr. Nordheim. The duties assumed by her were invariably faithfully and fully performed, and she would have continued to perform them until her dying day, but she was young, and of a loving disposition. It was not until after the death of Mr. Nordheim that she became aware of the nature of the feelings in her bosom towards Marion Monck. She thought she loved him as a sister. He had been something for her to love for long years. She had become bound up in all his aspirations and his hopes, and his wishes. He had become a part of herself. There was very little difference in their ages. She was a few months older than him—that was all. When Mr. Nordheim died, the reflections that crossed her mind in reference to her future were of a new and at first a startling character. Then she began to canvass Marion's conduct, and she concluded in her own mind, that he must love her or that it would soon change to love. When Mrs. Granville informed her that Marion loved and was engaged to her niece, her eyes were opened—the veil was lifted from her most secret thoughts. She knew herself, her weakness, and she determined to conquer it. She had no female friend or relative to consult—but there was one of the other sex that she respected, and felt that she could trust. It was our old friend the bookkeeper, Mr. Wilson. To him, ever since Mr. Nordheim's death, had been confided her views and wishes in reference to the settlement of the affairs of her husband. Those affairs had turned out much better than any one anticipated. It was true that Mr. Nordheim had been very extravagant, but it was no less true that the firm had been making every year a large amount. Mr. Nordheim's original capital had never been touched. On the contrary, every year when the accounts were made up, Mr. Nordheim had had a considerable sum to his credit upon the books. As soon as this was ascertained, under Mr. Wilson's advice, she had gradually withdrawn from the concern large sums at intervals, and these had been judiciously invested in real estate, and in bank stocks bought in her own name. She was independently rich. She was aware of this fact long before she became aware of Marion's ill-fated attachment to another, and it is not a cause of wonder that she sometimes dreamed that Marion Monck would share it with her. Poor Marion, little did he dream that his boyish love for Isabella Granville was to be nipped in the bud, and also to deprive him of a fond loving heart and an independent fortune.

Mrs. Nordheim had seen adversity in her early years. She

had been a wife without receiving any of those blessings of domestic life which she had heard of, and now that the hopes that were just budding in reference to Marion were so cruelly withered, her heart seemed to be crushed.

Mr. Wilson came up that evening. She was alone. "Where is Marion to-night?" he asked.

Mrs. Nordheim burst into tears, and made no reply. Honest, true-hearted Wilson sat down by her side, and tried all in his power to console her, or at least to obtain from her lips the secret of such bitter tears. As she became more composed, she felt that to have the sympathy of this cold-hearted business man was something, and her heart opened to him.

"Mr. Wilson, I am ashamed to tell you why I have wept so bitterly, but I am sure you will not betray my confidence. I have had that youth living in the house with me as a brother for so long a time. I thought I only loved him as a brother, but when my husband, whom I never loved, died, I then awoke to the real state of my feelings—I loved Marion Monck." And then she recounted to Mr. Wilson what Mrs. Tom Granville had told her.—"Can it be possible that it is not so—that he does not love Miss Granville? Tell me truly what you think. I know you will speak the truth," she observed.

"Lady, I thank you much for this confidence. It has not lessened you in my regard. On the contrary, I would do more than ever to serve you. I, too, have become very much attached to Marion. I have no body to love. I work hard for a living. I am poor, for I have saved nothing from my salary, for until within a few months I remitted all for the use of an infirm mother and a sick sister in England; who had nothing to support them except what I could send," said Mr. Wilson.

"You are a noble man, Mr. Wilson," interrupted Mrs. Nordheim.

"Death has removed my mother, but I still have to aid my sister, but having, as I said before, nothing to love, I became warmly attached to Marion. I tried all in my power to impart to him all the commercial information which I possessed. I succeeded, for he is an apt scholar. I have watched him in the office and out of it, and the more I saw of him the more I liked him. When I discovered that there was an attachment to Miss Granville, I became alarmed. He never informed me of it, but I could not be deceived. I know that Mr. Granville would not listen a moment to it. He has other views for his daughter. I know from himself what those views are, and you may believe me, Mrs. Nordheim, that I have been for months expecting an explosion. It will come sooner or later, for Mr. Granville, when he sets his mind upon any thing, will carry it through or die in the attempt. You know the history of his son's unfortunate attachment. It was to a heartless girl, but still, Walter loved her, and refused to marry Miss Benson, that his father had chosen for him. The consequence was, that he became an outcast, and is somewhere in the Pacific Ocean as a sailor before the mast, and I do not think Mr. Granville ever gives him a thought," remarked Mr. Wilson, quietly.

"But, Mr. Wilson, could nothing be done to remove Mr. Granville's objections? I would do much for Marion's happiness. Were I to agree to put a large sum at Marion's disposal to start him in business, would not that remove some of Mr. Granville's scruples? I would do any thing—make any sacrifice for him," continued Mrs. Nordheim.

"You are a loving, kind-hearted woman to say so, but it would not add a feather to Marion's chances. Nothing that you or I could do would prove of any use. Mr. Granville has made up his mind, and there it ends. Marion might run away with her, but if he did, he would have her for his pains. Granville would never forgive or see them again in life. On the contrary, he would do all in his power to ruin Marion, and plunge the married couple into deeper misery," replied Mr. Wilson.

"What a character he must be! I never heard of such a man. He does not seem to be so iron-hearted and so stern," remarked Mrs. Nordheim.

"He is even worse than I have pictured him to you. Oh, I know him well. I have known him long years. Let me offend him to-night, and although I have almost starved my life out, yet he would turn me into the street penniless, and see me starve with as little remorse as if I was a dog," said Mr. Wilson.

"My honest friend, I begin to understand you, and I like you more and more Bear this in mind. I find friends are few. You are a true friend to me, I do believe. If need be, and you want a friend, Mr. Wilson, come to me at once," and she gave him her hand, which he took, although his own trembled.

"Nothing, then, can be done in favor of Marion in that quarter?" she continued.

"Nothing. He must take his chances, and they are fearfully against him," replied Mr. Wilson.

"How is it that Mrs. Tom Granville seems to be in favor of the match? Is it not very queer?" asked Mrs. Nordheim.

"It will cost her a home; but I believe if her heart was laid bare, it would be found that she hates her proud brother-in-law so heartily that she would rather injure or thwart him in any purpose that he holds near at heart, if she sacrificed home and every thing else a woman holds dear," replied Mr. Wilson.

"Mr. Wilson, tell me what I ought to do. I cannot have Marion Monck live longer in this house."

"Is he aware, dear lady, of your secret attachment to him?" asked Mr. Wilson.

"Great God, no! I should die for shame could I think he dared dream of such a thing! No. No one but yourself knows it, and I want you to forget it, as I shall endeavor to do. I told you because I need advice. I do not know what to do. He must leave the house, but it seems cruel to tell him to go. What will he think of it? How can it be done? Oh, *do* tell me, Mr. Wilson, and I will be so grateful," continued the excited lady.

Mr. Wilson thought for several moments, but did not say a word. At last, as he noticed that Mrs. Nordheim was waiting for a reply with the greatest anxiety depicted in her face, he asked, "Do you wish him to leave immediately?"

"Oh at once—to-night if it were possible. I do not want him to remain an hour longer than is absolutely necessary. I am afraid of myself—that is, I am afraid that something might occur to Mr. Wilson that would betray my secret."

"Then you must resort to innocent deception. Do you know any place where you could go and remain two or three days?" asked Mr. Wilson.

"Oh yes, at Woodbury. I was there during the summer the cholera was here—don't you remember?"

"Certainly I do. Well, we must send you up there. As soon as Marion comes home this evening, say to him pleasantly, 'Marion, you must move to-morrow, for I am going away, and shall probably break up housekeeping.' If he asks when, or where, tell him. If he asks when you are coming back—you don't know. Let him remove to-morrow with his things. He will find some other place. Once out of the house, you will have no further trouble," was the sound advice of Mr. Wilson.

"I will take your advice, but it is hard. Still I feel myself it must be done."

"Be sure that you place his removing upon that ground

alone, that you are going away. Don't let him imagine for a moment it is for any other reason."

Soon after, Mr. Wilson took his leave. He had hardly got away from the house before Marion, using his night key, entered, and stood before Mrs. Nordheim. She received him as cordially as though nothing had happened, and it would have been hard work to have made the announcement that night. She felt that she had not the heart to do it. But he said—
"Bessy, I have got to go back to the office to-night for a short time, and shall then spend the balance of the evening at Mr. Granville's, in State street."

There was no more delicacy about telling him that she was going into the country, and that he must find another home—"at least for a while," she added, as she saw his amazed look, "although I do not think I shall keep house much longer in the city. I mean to pay a visit to Charleston."

"Can I help you in getting ready to go in the country?"

"No—you will have enough to do to get your own things ready. If I need help I will send down to Mr. Wilson."

"That is very cold language to use to me."

"Not at all. You will have enough to do, as I said before, and the sooner you get removed with your things, the sooner I shall be able to go—and now good night. I have got work to do," and she hastily left the room.

It was this communication, that he mentioned to Mr. Granville, who invited him to his house. The next day Marion went up to Bond street, and before starting ordered a cartman to meet him there, and to bring down his trunk. He found Mrs. Nordheim in the parlor. She half regretted her determination. It appeared unkind on her part, and entirely unnecessary. Probably she would have told Marion he need not go; but when he arrived, unfortunately for him, he exclaimed, "Well, Bessy, I have come for my things, and I am going with them to Mr. Granville's, in State street."

"I am very glad you have found so pleasant a place. You will find Miss Granville a much more agreeable hostess than you have found me."

"No, that cannot be. You have been very kind to me, Bessy."

"Well then, get your things in your trunk, for your cartman is at the door ready to receive them," and then she hurried to her room and locked the door.

Marion, when he had packed his trunks, tried to see her, but the girl told him her mistress had too bad a headache and could see nobody.

Mr. Wilson called that evening. She saw him, but her pale cheeks and tearful eyes betrayed that if it had not cost much trouble to get Marion out of the house, it would cost her still more to get him out of her heart.

"He has gone, has he? I am glad of it; and now will you visit the Connecticut village?"

"No, I believe not. There is no occasion for it, and I am not well."

"Should Marion call here, what then?"

"I have ordered the servants not to let him into the house, and to keep the door locked constantly so that he cannot come in as of old with the night key, and to say that I am not home, or any thing else they choose. I will not see him under any circumstances, at least for a month. By that time I shall become accustomed to his absence, and shall be able to see him without any emotion. I am very glad that he is gone. Now, Mr. Wilson, will you do me a favor?"

"I will if I can."

"Let one month go by, and then I wish you to remove to this house; will you do it?"

"If you wish it, I will."

"I do wish it."

"What will people say? I do not speak in reference to myself, dear lady, but on your account."

"Mr. Wilson, I do not care what people say. I intend to act during the remainder of my life upon my own ideas of what is right and what is wrong—following the one and avoiding the other. You have been the book-keeper of my deceased husband many years—you have acted as my agent in settling up his affairs. I still need your assistance, and shall continue to need it for a long time, perhaps. I am alone, with no male person in my house; you are living in a common lodging house. If you are sick, you have no one to see that you do not suffer. Now why should you not come and take up your residence with me? Who can or who dare object to it?"

"True, that is very true, and I feel very much flattered by your kind invitation. I will try and be of use. But I like independence, and if I come here I shall expect to pay some share—"

"Stop, sir, at once. I cannot repay you for your kindness with any thing that I can do; and if you come up here to live, I wish you to relieve me of all responsibility or anxiety about business matters. You will be made comfortable, but the word pay must never be used. You become a member of my family. Why, do you suppose that Marion ever paid for being with us ? No indeed."

" I really was not aware whether he did or not, but he rendered himself very useful to Mr. Nordheim, did he not ?"

" Once he may have done so, but you will continue useful to me. The mere fact that I have a middle-aged gentleman in my house, is full payment. I need a protector and a friend, and I shall find one. That is not all, Mr. Wilson. You have done more for me in attending to my complicated business than any paid merchant could have done. What I should have done without you, I know not. Your suggestions have been very valuable. That is not all. I do not suppose you intend to remain the slave of Mr. Granville all your life, and when you get too old to work be sent to the workhouse, if you can help it. Very well—you can help it. I say so to you now, and what I say now I will say six months or a year hence.— The moment you see an opening to go into business on your own account, and only need money, let me know, and you shall have whatever you require. You are aware that Mr. Granville promised poor Nordheim that he would take a partner whenever I requested him to do so. You can talk to Mr. Granville at your earliest convenience, and if he will take you into partnership at my request, and in compliance with his death-bed promise, then I name you, and I will furnish whatever capital he may require."

" I have no words to express my gratitude for such a liberal offer. Oh, Mrs. Nordheim, what can I do ?"

" I will tell you one thing that you can do. I have to receive in cash a sum equivalent to about twelve thousand dollars from Mr. Granville some time this month, have I not ?"

" About that amount."

" Look out for a house with a large garden in some quiet street. Buy it for me. I detest this street, the house and all its memories. As soon as you make the purchase I will remove into it with my furniture. Don't say a word more."

What curious thoughts that book-keeper had that night as he walked down to Clark & Brown's in Maiden Lane, where he had lodged for so many years. A new world was opened to him.

CHAPTER XXXI.

Struggle of Merchants to keep up—The Failure of Mac Neil & Aspinwall —Loss of Friends—The Assignment by Mac Neil & Co.—Human Feeling for those who Fail—O'Doemall's Interview with Colonel Mac Neil— The Latter begins to Dissipate—Consolation in Harrison Street with his Children—Removes from the City Hotel to Fifty Dollars a year Lodgings —His Bureau in a Centre street Grog shop—Queer Doings—A Genteel Loafer's Life—An honest Creditor gives the Colonel Eight hundred Dollars due him—The Value of a little Money.

Mac Neil & Aspinwall struggled bravely to keep on and to recover their losses, but it was all in vain. Both partners lived extravagantly, and Colonel Mac Neil was so kind-hearted that he could not say no to any request or solicitation for pecuniary aid. For some time after he had made provision for his mistress McPherson and their two children, both himself and his business partner made every effort to keep from failing, but as is usual in such cases, they made matters worse. They paid two, three, and even five per cent. a month to get their bills receivable cashed. They bought goods on time, shipped them to different parts of Europe, and received cash advances on the same, but it was of no use. Every day that this firm continued to pay their notes, their affairs became more fearfully involved. At last the day of ruin came. Colonel Mac Neil had been to his office in the morning, and although his partner tried to keep up good spirits, and speak encouragingly, Mac Neil asked him "How long is this state of things going to last?"

"O, we may get through yet. To-day will be a hard day, but Mr. Granville has promised us three thousand dollars as a loan, and with that we can keep on a week at least; before that time something will occur in our favor. Keep up good heart, Colonel."

With such consolation, the Colonel left his place of business, visited a few haunts, and then went and took dinner with Miss McPherson and his two little ones. He did not leave them until nearly five o'clock, and then he started down Broadway towards the City Hotel. He was opposite St. Paul's Church, when he met an acquaintance, a merchant whom he knew very well. He stopped, and while shaking hands with the Colonel, who was quite surprised at such an exhibition of warm feeling, expressed his regret at what had occurred.

"These accidents we are all liable to, but I hope the misfortune will be but temporary."

"Really, you must be more explicit; what misfortune do you allude to?"

Colonel Mac Neil had not the remotest idea of what was coming.

"Why, to your—failure—suspension. It is talked of in the street. The notes of your firm have been protested at the Bank to-day. Were you not aware of it, Colonel?"

"Indeed I was not. Great God! This is awful! Excuse me, but I must hurry on;" and the Colonel did hurry on. He went to his store. There was a gloomy set of clerks there, but his partner was absent. He called his chief clerk on one side.

"How is this? Have our notes been protested to-day?" asked the Colonel.

"I am sorry to say that it is too true. Mr. Aspinwall was to have received some money from Mr. Granville, but only a few moments before the Banks closed, he declined lending us the money. There was no time to remedy, and Mac Neil and Aspinwall have failed."

"Thank you. It must have happened sooner or later, and perhaps it is as well now as at a later period. Can you give me a small sum of money?' demanded the Colonel.

"O yes sir; we are not so bad off as not to have *some* money left. I drew five hundred dollars, and Mr. Aspinwall took half and told me to hand you the other half. Here it is, sir," replied the clerk.

The Colonel took the money, then proceeded to the City Hotel, and went to his room. He gave orders that he would see no one except his partner, should he call. He laid down upon his bed, but he could not sleep. He walked the room, but it brought no relief to the deep agony of his mind. He was cast down; his commercial name was blasted. "I shall never rise again."

The Colonel was an honorable man. He met his partner the next day, and they agreed to give up every thing—to assign all the property that they held jointly or individually. "Leave me only my clothes, and I shall feel happy in giving up every thing else," said the Colonel. Some of the creditors proposed giving him a release. The Colonel replied that it mattered but little, but that he should be pleased if they gave a release to his partner, who would probably endeavor to get into business again, but as for himself it mattered but little, as he should never engage in commercial pursuits any more. To his partner, Aspinwall, who asked him how he intended to get along, the Colonel replied,

"For some time, at least, I have a pretty sure source of income. I have several thousand dollars due me—debts of honor, from personal friends, to whom I have frequently loaned money. Those debts are not included or mentioned in our assignment, and the parties will only pay them to me."

"Why, Colonel," replied his more experienced partner, "have you the least idea that those friends to whom you have loaned money, now that you are a ruined man, will ever return you the money they have borrowed?"

"Of course they will, and be glad to do it, when they are informed that I need it. I did not ask them while in prosperity," replied the unsuspicious Colonel.

"Ah, my worthy partner, you have got to learn an awful lesson. Mark my words—you will never receive a dollar from those *friends*, as you call them. They will avoid you as they would poison."

"I hope not, and I know to the contrary. You regard the world as worse than it is, but we shall soon see. I hope, Aspinwall, you will not suffer much from our failure. I mean, that you will have money for your immediate wants."

"I shall, Colonel, because I shall go to work at once and earn it. I have already secured a clerk's position, with a liberal salary. Have you seen Mr. Granville since our failure, and what excuse could he make for behaving so badly to us, at the latest moment, too?" inquired Mr. Aspinwall.

"I have not seen him, and I shall not endeavor to do so. Do we owe him any thing?" asked Colonel Mac Neil.

"Not a dollar—he took good care of that. And now good-bye, Mac. God bless you! Keep a stout heart and a stiff upper lip. If I can ever serve you, let me know how," was the sincere parting words of Mr. Aspinwall.

The Colonel was deeply affected. Mr. Aspinwall had hardly left the room before Mr. O'Doemall entered.

"Ah, Colonel, I am glad to see you—indeed I am. Glad to see you looking so well. Bad business, your having to fail, but I hope you have kept back something snug, eh?" remarked O'Doemall.

"John, what do you take me for? I have given up every thing except a few debts owing to me individually by some of my friends. You, for instance, have had several accommodations from me at different times, in all I believe amounting to over five hundred dollars. Now is the time that I need it refunded, and I hope you will not be backward," observed Colonel Mac Neil.

"My dear Colonel, if you knew how I was situated. I haven't a dollar to keep myself with. I thought to get some from you, knowing that you had failed, and had no more notes to pay. I felt sure that you had plenty of money, and I was going to ask you to lend me a hundred," said O'Doemall.

"O'Doemall, I believe you are a precious rascal, and I will expose you unless you pay me some portion of what is so justly my due."

"Expose *me?* Why, Mac, you must be joking! If I owe anybody, it is your creditors. You say that you have not assigned in your schedule what I owe you, and therefore I think if you make any stir about it, you are more likely to expose yourself."

"Leave the room on the instant, or by ——. Go, go! Don't make me put my hands upon you, or it will be the worse for both of us," exclaimed the Colonel.

"Why, Mac, you are as cross as a bear; but I will leave you now, and see you some time when you are better natured," said O'Doemall.

"Scoundrel, if you ever dare to speak to me again, under any circumstances, I will break your head! Begone!" said Colonel Mac Neil, sternly.

Mr. O'Doemall was somewhat alarmed, and made a precipitate retreat.

"Perhaps Aspinwall was right, and I shall not be able to collect a dollar from my fair weather friends," thought the Colonel. Colonel Mac Neil was not to be an exception to the general rule, that when one meets with misfortune, all hope of fair weather friends is gone. He tried several of those who owed him money—honestly owed him borrowed money. Not a dollar could he get from them, and from those friends who did not owe him he was too proud to ask a favor. So days passed on, and poor Mac Neil found his position changed. He was still a gentleman—still could be amusing, and when he frequented old haunts, he met with some who at least could afford to stand a treat. There was one source of consolation yet to the broken down man, for he was completely broken down. After his failure, he began to drink to excess. His eye-sight, never good, partially gave way. This source of comfort was in the quiet two story house in Harrison street. He had provided for those three dear ones, and they could not want.

Miss McPherson tried to make the Colonel take up his home there. It was in vain. She urged her deep and tender love, and offered to place at his disposal the income which was coming in quarterly with regularity. No—he was too proud to accept that; or perhaps it was a better—a still higher motive.

"Urge me not, Jane, to any meanness of the kind. I have found by bitter experience what it is to be without money.— You nor the children shall not have such experience. Come what will, even if I die in the alms-house, I will not break for an instant upon yours and the children's means. If I thought that I could be persuaded to do so I would go to my room and blow out my brains. No, no. Let me come and see you occasionally, see the little ones happy, and that is all I wish—I shall get along somehow or other," was his reply.

His mistress knew his determined character, and that it would be useless to attempt to interfere with his determination. She was a woman of sound sense also, and loved her children. She looked to the future for them alone, and knowing that the provision the Colonel had secured to her and them would be but a drop to him with his extravagant habits, she forbore to urge his taking the income. So Colonel Mac Neil travelled the world almost alone. He was no longer invited to parties or dinners, and he withdrew from fashionable society. At last he found he could not keep a room, or board at the City Hotel. He paid his bill and removed; he told no one where he was going. He had an old-fashioned bureau that had belonged to his father—that and his trunk were all his baggage. The cartman that he employed was a strange one, and could not be found after he had removed the Colonel's things. Could one of those fashionable associates have followed Mac, or found him within a week after he left the City Hotel, it would have been in a small, badly-furnished room in a little tenement in Cross, near Pearl street. There was he and his trunks, and he had made an arrangement with the proprietor that he could have that room for a dollar a week, or fifty dollars per annum. The bureau was too large for the room, but the landlord had also a store only a few doors from his house. It was in Centre street, and extended through from Centre to Cross, only a few doors from Pearl. He had been a porter in the Colonel's store in former days, and had got up to be proprietor of a three cent grog shop. It was in the rear of this store that Mac had his bureau. Harry Mercer, the proprietor, was much grieved when Mac told him his situation, but Mac would accept no favors. He was grateful for a home where his poverty would not be exposed, and where it came within his means. Harry Mercer was glad to have Mac there. The bureau took up but little room, and was placed near the rear door. The store was always open at daylight, and Colonel Mac Neil soon after came, opened his bureau, proceeded to shave himself, and after half an hour would be ready to go to take his morning draught. Jemmy the clerk had a bottle of rather choice brandy which was kept exclusively for Mac's own use. Then he would deliberately read the paper with as much satisfaction as when he was spending twenty thousand dollars a year. His old porter respected him and his dignified appearance, for he was scrupulously neat, and his intelligent conversation made him respected by the regular customers of the store, who it is needless to say, were a new set of acquaintances.

Colonel Mac Neil was a king-pin among these new people. When he had read the morning papers, he went and procured breakfast somewhere, and then returned. At about eleven o'clock, the same hour that he used to show himself to his fashionable friends, the Colonel would go up to Washington Hall, down in Barclay street, or some other well known resort, where he could mix freely but independently with the old set. He would generally be asked to dine by some of the young bucks, who felt honored by his acceptance of the invitation. The afternoon would be spent in dining and finishing some wine. Then the Colonel would return to the store, and sit and chat with his Centre street acquaintances more sociably than with the Broadway set. They were delighted with him, and there were no end of drinks. About once a week, as it reached nine o'clock, the Colonel would say,

" Harry, let me have ten dollars."

" Certainly," would be the smiling reply of the one called Harry.

With this money placed in his pocket book he would go to some of his old gambling haunts. He rarely lost. Fortune favored him on almost every occasion. He would not abuse or tire her ladyship. He bought his chips, and calmly played them until his earnings reached twenty or sometimes fifty dollars. Then he stopped and would play no more, partake of a light supper, and go to his solitary room.

In the morning, when Mercer opened his store, Mac would hand him all, reserving ten dollars perhaps. This sum was to be used to give the Colonel the very luxury of happiness. He would forget his usual routine when such a white day chanced, and be off for a large grocery on the corner of Church and Canal streets. There he would order an old cheese, a few pounds of the best tea, a loaf of sugar, and a few choice things—as many as he could carry, and these he would carry himself to No. 27 Harrison street, and there would be a merry time of it.

How queer it is that when rich, or with plenty of money, the most sensible men have no idea how far and how much happiness a very small sum will sometimes confer. Colonel Mac Neil never spent ten thousand dollars with half the personal satisfaction to himself that these ten dollars would give. He always took care that there should be some silver left to purchase whatever the children used most to desire.

These were happy days to the Colonel. He was independent too. He was not drawing upon their little source of income.

He did not frequent the gambling saloons with any regularity. He went there for a purpose. He had lost large sums there. He went to win back—enough, as he said, to keep him afloat He played coolly and with skill. If the game was faro, he played small until all the cards were out but one. Then it was a fair bet, and his chance of winning was upon a par with the bank. If he lost his capital of ten dollars which he invariably took with him from Mercer, he played no more. Sometimes a person who had known him would give him fifty dollars to play on shares. Then the Colonel would generally win, but as soon as his share reached fifty dollars, he would play no more, but go to his little lodgings in Cross street, and the next morning add it to his pile in Wilson's hands.

There was another curious trait in Mac Neil's character.—Whenever he got a considerable sum, say a hundred dollars, in Mercer's hands, he would say,

"Harry, give me a receipt for fifty dollars for one year's lodgings."

Mercer would give it without comment, and take the fifty.

"Now that leaves fifty dollars"—or sixty, as the case might be—"in your hands; is it not so?" asked the Colonel.

"Yes, Colonel; but are you aware that you have already paid me for three years' lodging at fifty dollars a year, as we agreed?" replied Mr. Mercer.

"Oh yes, I am perfectly aware of it, and I mean to be on the safe side and be ahead for some years. You are rising in the world ; money is of use to you *now*. I look ahead, and am trying to provide good lodgings, eh ?" added the Colonel.

On other occasions when his luck would be good and he had a surplus in Mr. Wilson's hands, he would go and pay for a suit of clothes ahead. Again, he would pay for quite a bill of useful articles which he knew Mrs. McPherson or her children needed. She, poor honest woman, asked no questions, but made up her mind, that from some cause or other, the Colonel spent more money on her and her children, without an income, than he had ever done while he was rich. But Colonel Mac Neil in poverty days never got entirely broke. He always had something to fall back upon. He dressed better, seemed happier, and was more so, than in his proudest days. Sometimes a gentleman, who had means restored him, would pay back the Colonel what he owed him. On one occasion he received from such a source eight hundred dollars. He laughed in his sleeve—I don't want it now. He made Jane McPherson add it to the sum already in the Savings Bank.

Mac Neil began to feel the value of money.

CHAPTER XXXII.

The Parents of Marion Monck in South Carolina—The Count Falsechinski's Gratitude—The Count with his Bunkers, Prime. Ward & King—Old Nat Prime—His Views of Real Estate on New York Island—The Count buys One Thousand Lots—Realizes $250,000 by the operation—Miss Norris goes to Sussex and buys a Farm for her Parents, and sends her Brother and Sister to School.

Our readers may deem that we have neglected the family of Marion Monck, as rarely has an allusion been made to them. Not so, however. He was the all of his parents, and not a week passed but that he both wrote and heard from them. He was very careful to remit them all his surplus money, from month to quarter—and as he received a very liberal salary, amounting to eight hundred dollars, and his expenses being very light, his remittances during the year amounted to a considerable sum. He was devotedly attached to his parents, and he had very correct views of his relations to them. He felt that until he was of age, they had a right to what he could earn above paying his own personal expenses. These were rendered very light in consequence of the liberality of Mr. and Mrs. Nordheim, while he lived with them.

The Count Falsechinski on one occasion asked him what he did with all his money—" You can't possibly spend your money." Marion replied,

" I do not, Count, but I send it home to my parents. I do not want more than I can use."

" That is all very fine, but if you saved up your salary you could speculate a little, and add to it. What are you going to do for capital by and bye, when you want to go into business? Now I have got a pretty considerable capital in the hands of my bankers, Prime, Ward & King, and it is *growing*."

Marion said he was very glad to hear it, and added,

" But why, Count, are you so anxious to get money ?"

" Ah, Marion, you have seen me when I was very, very poor. It is bad to be poor. You have been my good angel. You brought me luck—you have made a new man of me. I will never forget you, Marion. I would die for you. I will prove my gratitude to you some day. You don't need my aid now. You will some day. I am making money. I work for it night and day. I have a fixed purpose ; never mind what it is ; and that reminds me that I have got a note from my bankers to come around there—so good bye."

The Count went to Wall street to his bankers ; when he reached there he was ushered into one of the inner offices, where he found the head of the firm.

" Count, good morning. I have sent for you to tell you that if you choose to place your money out under my direction it will pay you better than the five per cent which is all we can allow you," said old Mr. Prime, the head of the house.

"Really, Mr. Prime, you are very good. Will you point out to me a mode, and I shall follow your advice. I have found it of great service heretofore," said the Count.

" Buy real estate up town—it will advance very rapidly. It is the only certain way to make and keep money in New York. Real estate don't run away. It will always rise. It will keep going up as long as there is an acre of unoccupied ground on Manhattan island. Every dollar that a man don't require he should invest in real estate. If he does so, he will be immensely rich some day. I have heard you say that you shall not require your money in some years ; is it so ?" asked the old banker.

" You are right—it is so," replied the Count.

" Then take my advice and buy real estate. I know of some property up town that can be bought for a hundred thousand

8*

dollars. I advise you to let me order it for you," said Mr. Prime.

"But, my dear Mr. Prime, I have no such sum of money—nothing like it," replied the Count.

The banker smiled as he replied, "Nor need you to have. It only requires about twenty per cent to be paid in cash, and the rest can remain on bond and mortgage for five years. Before that time expires it may do to sell, or hold still longer—it will double in value, I have no doubt."

The Count did not hesitate a moment. He knew nothing of what he was doing, but his confidence in the stout solid old gentleman was unbounded. He requested him to order the purchase made. Mr. Prime replied,

"I will do so. You need not trouble your head. My firm will employ a lawyer to examine titles, draw up papers, and fix it all up. We will pay the twenty per cent, and charge it to your account. You will do well, Count."

The old banker was flattered by the confidence shown in him, and the promptness with which the Count agreed to take his advice—and that old man was a shrewd, wise old man in every way. He never led anybody astray. It was the time when real estate began to take that great rise which has been the means of making many immense fortunes. It was just at the commencement of that rise when nearly a thousand lots of 25×100 feet each were bought for the Count at a price inside one hundred dollars a lot.

It was but a few days after this conversation that this heavy purchase was made by order of Mr. Prime. The Count said not a word to any one except one. He had no sooner got out of the banker's office than he hurried up to Broome street to the residence of Miss Norris. She was at home, and for a wonder was alone. Tom Granville was not to be seen.

She appeared glad to see the Count, and asked him a variety of questions, to all of which he replied promptly. Then he said,

"Now Clara, I owe you a good turn. You have once placed me in the way of making money. I came up this morning to do the same for you. I can tell you how you can more than double your money, and be safe too. I know that you have saved up at least three thousand dollars."

"Four thousand, Count—four. But I have not a cent left; it is all gone," replied Miss Norris.

"Great God! Clara, I am amazed. That Tom Granville, I suppose," observed the Count.

"Why, Count Falsechinski, how perfectly horrified you do look. But I have not told you all. I have not only spent the four thousand dollars, which includes the legacy of five hundred left me by Mr. Nordheim, my lately respected friend, but I have run in debt two thousand more, which I must go to work and earn money to pay off. Tom Granville, I assure you, my dear Count, had no more to do with my wilful extravagance than you had," said Miss Norris.

"Wilful extravagance! Really, Miss Norris, I am surprised. I feel some interest in your future, and I grieve to say that I am distressed to hear you confess you have acted so imprudently. I gave you credit for a stronger mind—but it can't be helped," said the vexed Count.

"Count, you have never given me more credit than I deserve, and don't let me have your contempt for a moment. Hear me. I have parted with my money, that you know I placed in bank for safe keeping, and where it was drawing interest. Count, you know that I was sold, or sold myself to Nordheim for the sum of five hundred dollars, and that the money went to my parents. I have also a brother and sister. That money probably saved my father from a drunkard's fate, and my mother and her children from degradation or a county poorhouse. If there is any place we love it is the place where we were born—if there is any ambition in the world, it is to stand well with those among whom we are born. It don't matter where we go—what we do—how great our success may be in the wide world, we do not value our good fortune fully, unless it raises us with those in our little village, among those where we were born. Now, Count, have patience. I have not squandered *my* money, but I will tell you *what* I have done with it. For years I have been of service to my parents —since I am in New York I have helped them all I could. Last summer I was up in Sussex county, and spent a week with them in their somewhat comfortable home. I then learned that a very valuable farm, containing some three hundred acres, with good dwelling, barn, out-houses, &c. was for sale. It almost adjoined my old homestead, and was considered a great dairy farm. Luckily I met with a lawyer in that region who was always partial to me. I told him I wished to buy that farm for my father and mother to live upon. I informed him also that I had four thousand dollars in cash. The price asked was eight thousand dollars, but it was to be sold at auction in the course of a few weeks, and the terms were half cash and half in five years. I returned to New York, made my arrangements, got my money out of the Savings Bank, and took it up to Sussex, and deposited it in the Sussex Bank, and waited patiently for the day of sale. I said nothing to my parents. I instructed my lawyer what to do. The sale day came, and my lawyer, Mr. Thompson, bought the farm for six thousand dollars. I paid more than half cash, and have five years to pay the other two thousand, and an interest which only amounts to one hundred and twenty dollars. You may imagine how my parents felt. You cannot conceive my happiness, Count. It was happiness."

"You have raised yourself much in my opinion. You hold the titles of this farm in your own name?" inquired the Count.

"Entirely. My father has enough to stock it pretty well. I don't expect it to pay me an interest until it is paid for, but it will be a home for them for life, and it may be of great value to me some day. Now I shall sleep easy. The farm had been allowed to run down. It is well worth fifty dollars an acre, and can be made worth that. My father is a good farmer. In his hands he will make its value increase," replied Miss Norris.

"I hope you will succeed in all you undertake, Miss Clara; and perhaps in this matter you have done more for your interest than what I had to propose. At any rate you have shown yourself a good, amiable child, and you have made yourself happy by doing a good action. How is Master Tom?" asked the Count.

"I have not seen him, Count, since morning," replied Clara.

"Are you aware that his wife has been on to Baltimore and employed a distinguished lawyer to get a divorce for her from her husband?"

"I was not aware of it, and I do not think Tom knew any thing about it. Well, she will get the divorce without any trouble, for I believe Tom will not contest the matter. How did you hear of it?" inquired Miss Norris.

"From her brother-in-law," replied the Count.

"Why, Count, perhaps she is anxious to get a divorce from Tom to set her cap for you?" laughingly observed Miss Norris.

"My good Clara, she has got no money, and I cannot marry anybody who has not got plenty of money—money that brings in an income—property that gives such a sum every year. Then a man is a man, and can be a gentleman even in this country, if he has a fixed allowance. I want at least an income of twelve thousand dollars a year. Then I shall feel easy—

not until then. I will have it some day, Miss Clara. Nous verrons," observed the excited Count.

"Ah, Count, you have some secret that I cannot fathom; but perhaps you will tell me some day what it is," observed Miss Norris.

"I must leave you now, and I wish you a good day. The more I think of it, the more I am pleased with your purchase of that farm," said the Count.

The Count returned to his humble lodgings in John street.

It is not exactly in place to tell here the result of the real estate operations made by the Count Falsechinski, at the suggestion of old Mr. Prime, but it may be as well told here as any where else. For the moment the purchase was made, real estate began to rise rapidly. Lots sold one day at a certain price, were re-sold again the next day almost for double, and a third, fourth and fifth sales were made within a very few days at the most extravagant prices. The lots purchased by the Count Falsechinski were in about what would be now the lower part of the city. They comprised a large vegetable garden.

Not many weeks after the papers were all duly signed and the money paid, the Count was again sent for by old Mr. Prime. He went to the old banker's office. Mr. Prime said, "Count, you can get two hundred dollars a lot for your lots. Do you wish to sell?"

The Count was amazed, and he replied, perfectly cool— "What do you advise, Mr. Prime?"

"Wait. The fever has not yet got full headway."

"I will do as you advise," and the Count went back to his clerkly duties in the office of Mr. Granville, who knew no more of the Count's transaction with the banker than he did of the world of spirits. Not many weeks more elapsed before the Count received a note asking him to dine with the great banker at his country seat near Hurlgate. The Count accepted the invitation, and at three o'clock took a seat in the carriage of the banker. When they were on the way up, old Mr. Prime ordered his coachman to drive to the garden, which was, in reality, the property of the Count. He pointed out its advantages, and prophesied that ere many years it would be covered with palatial residences. The ride was a delightful one. The dinner was excellent, the Count was introduced to the banker's family, and he in his turn made himself uncommonly agreeable. That night he slept in the house of his hospitable entertainer, as it was too late to go into the city. After the breakfast was concluded the next morning, the old banker remarked, as though it was not of much consequence, "Count, your lots have gone up to three hundred dollars. You can get that for every one of them. I think the fever has reached a crisis. I advise you to sell. You can get one half cash. That is one hundred and fifty thousand dollars. You owe eighty thousand dollars mortgage. Take eighty thousand dollars out of one hundred and fifty thousand dollars, and buy the mortgage, Count. Then you will have a first mortgage for one hundred and fifty thousand dollars, bringing seven per cent. interest and seventy thousand dollars in cash. The mortgage has to run five years. Perhaps at that time it will be down, and you can foreclose and get your property back again."

It all happened as the old financier prophesied. The Count sold out his real estate, the thousand lots, paid the mortgage of eighty thousand dollars, had seventy thousand dollars in his banker's hands, and a mortgage of one hundred and fifty thousand dollars drawing seven per cent interest, and one of the best possible investments. We now return to the regular narrative and to the moment when the Count returned to his John street humble quarters.

CHAPTER XXXIII.

The "Battery" a Quarter of a Century Since—Marion Monck—Isabella Graville and Miss Benson—The Man Who Killed Mr. Nordheim—F. Gaillard! —He Accompanies Miss Benson Home from the Battery—The Accomplished Seducer—A Career of Villainy—The Due —An Anecdote of Rascality—The World's Opinion

THE old citizens of New York must well recollect what a place of resort the Battery was twenty-five years ago. Then, most of the adjoining blocks were made up of handsome dwelling-houses, and they were occupied by our wealthiest merchants and most respectable people. The hotel now on the corner of Broadway and Battery Place at that time was the city residence of old Mr. Prime, of whom we have spoken. Of an afternoon the Battery was crowded with children accompanied by their parents, or sometimes only by their nurses. Young ladies of the first respectability took their morning or afternoon walks unattended. No outrage was ever known or dreamed of. What a contrast with the dirty, filthy Battery of the present day, when it is almost as much as a man's life is worth to go upon the Battery, and a female could not walk across it without being grossly insulted. In losing the battery, New Yorkers lost one of the most invigorating and healthful promenades in the city. No uptown park or square can begin to compare with it.

It was a custom of Marion Monck, after he removed to Mr. Granville's house, to rise early in the morning and go out upon the Battery for a stroll. He was generally accompanied by Isabella Granville, and these occasions were seized upon to converse with all the sincerity of a young attachment upon their future hopes of happiness. It was a very difficult matter for Isabella to persuade Marion, who detested concealment, to keep from her parent the real state of matters. But she did succeed in doing so, and although Mr. Granville could see them walking upon the Battery from his windows, yet it never crossed his mind for a moment that there was the slightest danger to the peace of mind of his daughter from such an intercourse. One beautiful morning, while Marion and Isabella were promenading what is called the lovers' walk, they were met by Miss Benson. Isabella and the latter lady embraced each other affectionately, and Bell insisted that Margaret should join them, and then go and take a breakfast. Miss Benson agreed to promenade with them, but positively refused to go to the house afterwards. "I don't like Aunt Kate, Isabella, and my feelings are fully reciprocated, I am well aware." They then had been walking up and down several times, and finally took the outer walk nearest the water. The young ladies noticed some boat off in the river, and stopped, watching its motion; while doing so, both leaned over the wooden fence or railing. Marion stopped in his walk, and was waiting for his two companions to proceed, when a gentleman walked up to him and asked him if he was not Mr. Monck.

"I am," was the reply.

"My name, sir, is Gaillard."

In an instant Marion recognized him, for he had seen him twice at the time Mr. Nordheim was injured at the Opera House.

"I am glad to meet you, sir You have been absent from town since—since "—

"I know what you would say. Yes, sir. I have been home to South Carolina. By the way, you are from my own State. I heard of you frequently in Charleston." Marion bowed and replied,

"Yes, sir; I am also from that State."

Here the two young ladies seemed ready to walk again. Marion wished to ask Mr. Gaillard some further questions, and he at once presented him to both ladies.

"Will you walk with us, sir?" inquired Marion.

Mr. Gaillard consented willingly, and each took the outside of the two ladies, Mr. Gaillard on the side of Miss Benson. The conversation became general and very interesting. Mr. Gaillard told of many matters that had occurred in South Carolina, (for it was when nullification had a foothold in that State) which were entirely new to Marion. Finally Miss Benson, who had been looking at Mr. Gaillard very earestly, ceased walking and said. "I am sure I am not mistaken. Why, you are the gentleman that kil——that injured Mr. Nordheim."

"Mr. Gaillard bowed and said, "I am that unfortunate person."

"Unfortunate," repeated the lady. "I do not know why you should call yourself unfortunate. You acted bravely, and protected your sister from insult as a gallant gentleman should do. I like you all the better for that affair, and I assure you that I consider myself highly honored by forming your acquaintance; Marion, I am really much obliged to you. What do you say, Miss Isabella?"

"I am pleased to make Mr. Gaillard's acquaintance. I thought I had seen him before, but I could not remember when and where. You were pointed out to me that dreadful night. I almost hear the scream that Mr. Nordheim gave. But I never blamed you. Even my father, sir, said you did perfectly right."

Mr. Gaillard bowed again, and made some inquiries after Mr. Granville, whom he said he met at the hospital the day Mr. Nordheim died.

"It is about time, Miss Isabel, for us to go home to our breakfast. I see the girl is waving a handkerchief on the steps as a signal. Will you go with us, sir?"

"I must decline. I am placed rather delicately. Remember Mr. Nordheim was Mr. Granville's partner, and my presence may bring unpleasant memories to him," answered Mr. Gaillard.

"Oh," exclaimed Miss Benson; "don't decline on that account. Mr. Granville is not so excruciatingly sensitive as all that comes to. So long as you had not killed him, he don't care. I rather think he was very much obliged to you for giving Nordheim that blow."

"Miss Benson, how can you speak in that manner of my father? It is very unkind of you. Well, if you will not accompany us, Miss Benson, nor you, Mr. Gailard, we must go home without you."

"If Miss Benson will permit me to continue to be her escort, I shall be quite happy," said Mr. Gaillard.

"Very happy, indeed; and if you will escort me as far as my home, I shall be happy to have you take breakfast with my good folks. My worthy papa is rather disposed to like you, and as you are from the next State to the one in which my mother was born, she will be charmed to meet you. So good-bye, Bell. Good morning, Marion."

Mutual good-byes were exchanged, and while Marion returned to No. 9 State street with Isabella, Mr. Gaillard and Miss Benson continued on up Broadway.

"Miss Benson, I consider myself one of the most fortunate of individuals, in becoming personally acquainted with you this morning. I have desired to know you for a longer period than you are aware of. I first noticed you that night at the Opera. I have since frequently met you, and I hope you will excuse my frankness when I say that it had not been with the hope of being introduced to you, I should not have made myself known to Mr. Monck."

"Indeed," replied Miss Benson, "I feel extremely flattered. I certainly could not have supposed for a moment that Mr. Gaillard was aware such a person as Margaret Benson was in existence until this morning."

The couple continued the conversation until they reached the residence of Colonel Benson. It was with some difficulty that Miss Benson persuaded the young South Carolinian to enter her father's residence at so unusual an hour, but she succeeded, and her happy manner of making him acquainted with her parents and her brother, soon made him perfectly at his ease. Mr. Benson was glad of an opportunity to talk about the South, and the Colonel, it would almost appear, was delighted at meeting the gentleman who had so opportunely rid the world of Nordheim.

"It was really quite a godsend to Mr. Granville, I assure you. It could not have happened better, for Mr. Nordheim was a bold, bad man. He certainly cared neither for God nor the devil. If he had not died when he did, I am quite sure Mr. Granville would have been obliged to have dissolved his commercial connexion with him, and these dissolutions are always troublesome affairs. Nordheim got killed, and all difficulty was at an end. I am really quite pleased to meet with you, and I hope you will frequently visit us. We shall always be happy to see you."

The Colonel's invitation was warmly seconded by his amiable partner, and when the breakfast was over, and it was time for Mr. Gaillard to leave, he was obliged to give his address, and promise that he would call very soon again. It will be easily supposed that Frank Gaillard gave a willing promise to comply with such a pressing invitation. Mr. Gaillard gave his address as at the City Hotel. Such was not the fact however. A year previous, this gay youth had taken a house in Wooster street, not far from Canal. The rent was five hundred dollars. He had furnished it handsomely, and employed a very intelligent colored woman to keep house for him. He had arranged that his letters should be sent to the City Hotel, and every day he called there for them.

Probably one of the most accomplished seducers, and one of the most successful ones that ever visited New York, was this same Frank Gaillard. He was an only son. His father died when he was quite young, and left him a large property; but in addition to this, he inherited from an aunt a large plantation in St. John Berkley Parish, on Cooper river, a large rice plantation, and about three hundred slaves. This, when he became of age, he left under the charge of an overseer named Fredericks, who was both honest and capable of planting successfully. The young Gaillard, when in the South, resided mostly with his mother, who lived on a plantation some twenty miles distant from his own. He also owned a magnificent residence in Charleston, where his mother and sister resided a portion of the year, when the country fever prevailed on the plantations. The family also owned an upland cotton plantation near Greenville, and frequently the mother and sister passed the summer season in the up country. Not so Frank. He had been educated at the North, and graduated at Yale College, New Haven, with a fair standing. While pursuing his studies at Yale, he had frequent opportunities of visiting New York, and it was there that he acquired habits of dissipation, and a love for illicit and animal pleasures. He could gamble, but he was too cool-blooded to ever be injured by it. He could not have become a professional gambler. He was a splendid specimen of a man. Added to this, was a power of conversation beyond that of almost any man we ever met. He was perfectly irresistible when he chose to be so, and could fascinate any one, man or woman, who came within his circle. This latter power, when combined with a total want of principle, a perfect recklessness of consequences, and a courage that was unquestioned, made him, where females were concerned, a most dangerous acquaintance. He spared no pains, no money, no labor, no patience, when he undertook to ruin and seduce a young and lovely girl. Her rank or her position in society was no bar or safety guard against his designs. The poor working girl without a dollar or a friend, or the daughter of the wealthiest merchant or most powerful statesman, were equally insecure against his lustful passions. He regarded them as fair game, and while he would have scorned to have his honor questioned, or his veracity doubted, and would have fought knee deep in blood with any one who questioned either, yet when the ruin of a female was to be effected, truth, honor, all was forgotten. The basest falsehoods, the most solemn promises, the most sacred influences were brought to bear. He kept house for no other purpose than to get virtuous and respectable girls or married women to visit there. He went so far as to invite them to call and visit his mother, who, it is needless to add, never saw the inside of his residence. When once the poor victim was ensnared inside those parlors, her ruin was effected; for then, when she was startled at not meeting his mother, he would tell the poor girl that it was all a farce—that his mother was not there, but that it was a house of the worst kind, and then threaten her with exposure if she did not submit to his base purposes. After all this coaxing and threats, he laid aside all further mild measures, and resorted to force, and generally succeeded. He used wines—and if these failed he resorted to drugged wines. He boasted that no girl or married woman ever left his house in Wooster street except she left him a full conqueror.

The very intelligent reader may say that such a character could not exist in New York a day or a month, and pursue unpunished so high-handed a game. His power seemed almost miraculous in this regard; his oily tongue, when once his object had been accomplished, would seem capable of extenuating and procuring forgiveness from injured victims for the most atrocious rape; and this horrid crime, which not once, but in dozens of cases, seemed to fix permanently the attachment of the wronged one. Then he was liberal with his money, and had an abundance of it to be liberal with. Never in any one instance was the notice of the authorities called to his villainous acts. Even had it been otherwise, his money and his power of persuasion would have been placed in requisition and he would have gone scot free. Of these acts, vile as they were, he was never ashamed; but in company with male friends he would openly boast of his having seduced that young lady, or of having debauched such a married woman; would give names and dates, and all the attending circumstances.

On one occasion, at a dinner, he made use of a lady's name in such a connection. A gentleman arose, and said, "If Mr. Gaillard has told the truth, he is a scoundrel. If he has not, he is not only a scoundrel, but a vile liar to boot." Gaillard knocked him down. A challenge was the consequence, and the opponent of the renowned seducer was made a cripple for the rest of his life, for his free speech.

Mr. Gaillard made the acquaintance of Mac Neil. It was he who was relieved of some financial difficulty by the Colonel, and he repaid him when Mac needed it. He continued to meet the Colonel frequently, invited him to dine, gave him a seat in a box at the theatre often, and would have loaned the Colonel money. It was a custom of Gaillard's, when he met Colonel Mac Neil at any of the gambling saloons, to furnish him with funds to try his luck on their joint account.

This same Francis Gaillard was the Southern gentleman who had been introduced on the morning to Miss Isabella Benson, and was so cordially received by her parents. Young Benson knew nothing of his character or his antecedents. Frank Gaillard's position in society was unquestioned. He was invited to the most select parties, and associated with the highest. You may know what sort of a character he bore. On a particular occasion he was introduced to a family where there was a lovely daughter. She had a lover who knew Gaillard. With much frankness he informed Gaillard that he had told the girl in question and her parents exactly his character.

"I told them, Gaillard, that you had ruined many girls, and was the greatest libertine alive."

"Had I a design to ruin your fair flower, my dear sir, I should feel much obliged for your paving the way by giving me such a character."

"How so? What do you mean, Mr. Gaillard?"

"Simply this. Your intended is a simple-hearted, innocent girl. She believes you to be a moral and a safe man. She never thinks of you in any other light, or in connection with any unusual feeling connected with her own passions. You give me an immoral character. I meet her, for the moment; she sees me; her head is occupied with funny ideas. She is agitated. She is canvassing over the subject, wondering who the victims are—whether she knows them—what would be her fate if she too were a victim. The ice is broken—if she has one naughty thought, it will grow into fruit. Time and opportunity only is needed. She don't need me to break down the barriers by a free and unrestrained conversation upon forbidden subjects. She expects it as a matter of course, if she puts herself within my reach. I have no design upon your fair *fiancé*, but I tell you, if I had, you have paved the way for me. It is a bad policy for a young fellow to ever try to injure a rival, by telling the girl that a rival suitor is immoral and a libertine. Much better tell her that the rival is secretly a saint, and says his prayers three times a day, and reads a chapter in the New Testament when he goes to bed, and one of David's Psalms when he gets up at daylight."

Frank Gaillard in this very case forgot his resolution, for in less than three weeks he did seduce the intended bride of his friend, and she eventually became a poor miserable girl of the town.

We leave the career of this gay Southerner for a time, to begin a more interesting chapter.

CHAPTER XXXIV.

The twenty-first birth day of Marion Monck—Mr. Granville gives a grand Dinner in State street—James Gordon Bennett and the Herald—Boarding-house life in New York—A capital Story—Gaillard relates a Southern Story in reference to a Slave, who whipped his Master by his own orders, to see " how it felt"—Mr. Bennett relates an Anecdote of his first Arrival in the United States—Songs and Stories—Breaking up of the Dinner Party.

MR. GRANVILLE was so well pleased with the conduct of his chief clerk, Marion Monck, that he determined to show his appreciation of his character by giving a magnificent dinner in his honor, on his twenty-first birth-day. He announced his intention to our hero.

"Well, I really feel grateful, Mr. Granville, the more so as it is entirely unexpected on my part, and I cannot realize that I have deserved so much honor at your hands," remarked Marion in reply.

Mr. Granville gave a short happy laugh, and said, "Ah, Marion, all my dinners in your favor cannot recompense you as you deserve, but I wish to know how many friends you will invite? I have but very few to come, but I want you to make out a good long list. I am satisfied that you will invite no man to place his feet under my mahogany unless he is entitled to be there as your friend; and I am quite sure you have *no* friends who have not recommended themselves to your friendship or acquaintance by being in some way English clover at least."

"I believe my circle of acquaintances, Mr. Granville, although somewhat limited, are rather clever, and at least original. I have no particular friends except at the counting house, and from that list I shall invite but one—Mr. Wilson," Marion replied.

"Excellent—Wilson is an original in his way, and one of my oldest friends in London. I am glad you have invited him without a suggestion from me."

While Mr. Granville was speaking, Marion took a pencil from his pocket, and wrote on a piece of paper a few names. Handing it to Mr. Granville, he remarked, "Here is a full list—only a baker's dozen—including Mr. Wilson, of whom we have spoken."

"Very good. I will have invitations written in my own name, and state that the dinner is given in honor of your birth-day," said Mr. Granville.

"Thank you, Mr. Granville; and when they are ready, will you be so good as to hand them to me. Some of them it will be difficult to find without my aid;" and Marion laughed as the idea crossed his mind of what a hunt the porter of Mr. Granville would have to find some of the names on the list.

"I will do so, Marion, with pleasure. I have but four friends that I shall invite on my own account. One is Captain Marryatt, who is stopping down Broadway at Blancard's, another is an old London acquaintance who resides with his family at Staten Island, and has lately gone into business in this city, Mr. Cubson, and Colonel Benson and his daughter. The Colonel is, as you are aware, connected officially with the British Government. Besides these four and your list, my daughter and my sister-in-law will be the only ladies at the table, and they will run away early. I shall order a dinner for twenty persons, and if I am not mistaken it will be rather a choice affair," observed Mr. Granville.

"I hope it will, and be pleasant for you and agreeable to all those invited," said Marion; and with these words they parted, Marion to attend to his duties, and Mr. Granville to carry out his ideas in reference to the dinner party.

At six o'clock on the evening of December 2, 183-, the dinner given by Mr. Granville came off at his residence in State street. It was a dinner such as few could get up ; for Mr. Granville was an epicure himself, had traveled extensively, and his wines were of the very choicest quality.

The guests began to arrive before six, and were shown into the south front parlor, which overlooked the Battery. The walls were covered with really choice paintings, selected with great care by Mr. Granville, who had seen some of the best paintings in the galleries of Europe, and was not likely to be deceived in purchasing on his own account. Isabella was seated at the piano, playing " The Last Rose of Summer," very much to the enjoyment of Mr. Cubson, whose jolly red face and happy laugh made a picture of itself. Miss Benson was near the piano, listening to soft nonsense from young Gaillard of South Carolina. In a recess of the window overlooking the Battery was the brilliant Mrs. Tom Granville, and seated near her, apparently engaged in earnest but low-toned conversation, was a short thick set man, with very dark hair, and very coarse looking. It was the celebrated Captain Marryatt. Colonel Benson stood near them, watching some object upon the Battery. He was tall, slim, pale-faced, very intellectual, and a perfect gentleman in appearance, but English from top to toe. These were the friends that Mr. Granville had invited, as he remarked, "on his own hook." Scattered around the room were others, invited by Mr. Granville at the request of Marion. As they arrived, Marion introduced them to Mr. Granville, who in turn presented them to Isabella his daughter.

Distinct couples were formed all over the room. Some admired the paintings, others listened to the music, while others, who were previously acquainted, conversed together upon the various matters of the day.

The party assembled numbered twenty-one. Marion passed from one to the other, endeavoring to make each one of his own friends at home, and perfectly at his ease. He came near Mrs. Kate Granville, and she exclaimed,

" Marion, where upon this earth did you manage to pick up such a lot of funny acquaintances ? Who, in the name of all that is good-looking, are they ?"

" Friends of mine—clever people in their way, and all are men worth knowing," replied Marion.

" Do introduce me to that modest, bashful person, dressed in black, who seems afraid of his own shadow," said Mrs. Granville.

" Not now, Aunt Kate, but I will do so before dinner is

over ;" and he bent over and whispered something in her ear. She actually jumped off her chair with astonishment.

"Marion, are you in earnest? Is that so? Mr. Bennett of the Herald?" she asked earnestly.

"Precisely so," was the reply.

"And is he going to dine here?" asked Mrs. Tom Granville.

"Unquestionably he will," was the reply.

Kate Granville looked long and earnestly at him, and then remarked, "Marion, I am sure you are quizzing me. That gentlemanly, quiet person the notorious Bennett! I don't believe a word of it."

Reader, in 1834, when the Herald first started, the other papers made such unfair onslaughts on the new comer, as were perfectly terrific. It seemed as though the old sixpenny sheets had a presentiment, that unless they crushed out the Herald and Bennett, that it would be his destiny to crush them out. Some of the most worthy people in the city had made up their minds, from these attacks, that Mr. Bennett was a perfect ruffian—a blackguard in looks and actions—a man who attended balls, and sneaked into houses of ill-fame to get names of individuals to attack in his paper. They could not conceive of a more base character than he was supposed to be ; and the idea of inviting Mr. Bennett to a dinner among gentlemen and ladies, was considered a species of atrocity. But to resume our writing. It was now half past six, dinner was announced, and the entire party passed into the dining room. Mr. Granville took the seat at the head of the table, and requested Marion to do the honors at the other end. The ladies had seats near Mr. Granville, and Marion had some choice spirits of the other sex to flank him.

We have no taste for describing a dinner. Suffice it to say, that the good things were numerous, and served up in excellent style. The wines were delicious, and several healths were drank before the ladies took their departure. Then Mr. Granville opened :

"Now, gentlemen, I want every one to be at home and be happy. Get acquainted with each other the best way you can. And now let me propose a toast. It is the birth-day of that young gent at the other end of the table. He is twenty-one to-day. Here is his health—and may he and his friends be as well satisfied with him on his three-score and tenth birth-day as we are on his twenty-first."

All joined, and drank bumpers. Marion made a reply, rather confused, for he was somewhat bashful before so many, but he was let off easy.

"Mr. Bennett, shall I have the pleasure of a glass of wine with you?" asked Mr. Granville. Every eye was instantly directed to Mr. Bennett, for with the exception of Marion, he did not know a soul in the room, and not one even knew him by sight before this dinner.

"With pleasure," said Mr. Bennett, and he drank his wine and bowed to Mr. Granville.

"We all know the Herald," continued Mr. Granville, "although to most of us this is the first time we have had the pleasure of your personal acquaintance."

Mr. Bennett made a quiet reply, and conversation became general again until Mr. Cubson was called upon for a song, and he gave in the most exquisite manner, "My pretty Jane" to the great delight of all the company.

Some one else was asked, but refused, and then Mr. Granville sang a pretty air. On its conclusion he observed, "Now I have sung a song, and therefore it is perfectly proper that I should offer a resolution that every one at this table shall, in regular order, contribute something toward our spending a merry evening; if he cannot sing a song, he must give us a good sentiment or toast, or tell a good story. No one shall be let off." This proposal was acceded to at once by all, and as Captain Maryatt sat next to Mr. Granville, it was his turn next. He complied, and sang a song called "Artichokes and Cauliflowers," and his song and health being drunk, the next in order was Marion Monck.

Marion had never sang a song in his life. Speech-making was not his forte, and he had never written a line, and did not know that he had it in him, but he told a story. "I have been very lucky," said Marion, "since I came to New York to find a home, never having been but for a few days in a boarding-house, and have lived in the family of one of my employers—formerly with one now dead, and more recently with the kind friend, as well as employer, who now presides at the head of this table," and he bowed to Mr. Granville, and then continued, "but I had a friend who arrived in New York about the same time I did. He is dead now, poor fellow. Boarding-houses were too much for him. When he was on his death-bed he said to me, 'Marion, beware of boarding-houses, pious boarding-houses especially,' and he told me the fearful tale which I shall repeat as nearly as I can remember it in his words. 'My mother was a pious woman. I was an only child.

When I left home, at the tender age of fourteen, to come and try my fortune in this great metropolis of sin and commerce, she was fearful. I was born and brought up in a beautiful New England town, that contained about four hundred inhabitants and four churches or places of worship—one Episcopal, one Baptist, one Methodist, one New, and one Old School Presbyterian, and one Roman Catholic. It was a pious place. Every church had a bell, and on Sunday morning was a jingling that would astonish a small crowd. My mother was an Episcopalian, and I was brought up in that faith, but she was a good woman, and was herself inclined to think that there might be pious people even among other denominations beside her own, but she was not certain upon that point. Religion, as you see, coming from a small village with six churches, was a starting point with me in life. My mother was all anxiety to get me in a pious boarding-house. Well, I reached New York safely, and got with a pious landlady, a Mrs. Bacon. She was a sister of the Tappans. She commenced on me in a regular course. I had to be at prayers in the morning, and prayers at night, and we had to stand grace over a miserable piece of half done beef at dinner, and bean soup. Grace at tea, over dishwater, a slice of stale bread, rancid butter, and ginger-nuts of the commonest kind. The old lady bought her provisions by the cent's worth at a Dutch grocer's. I remonstrated with great benevolence—told her that by buying wholesale she could get *good* articles and at a low figure. She was grateful, said she didn't know any wholesale grocers, begged me to buy her by the quantity and she would pay me. Did so—bought eighty dollars' worth. Never got paid to this day. Insisted that I was hard-hearted; wanted me to go and hear Burchard at the Chatham street Theatre; went with old lady; cousin went with old lady's pretty daughter; Burchard went it strong; old lady got excited; rose in her seat; audience paused; begged Burchard to pray for a handsome young sinner by her side; called me by name, Harvey Foot; got up angry; begged Burchard on my own hook to pray for a swindling old lady, who had stuck me eighty-five dollars in groceries, and wouldn't pay up; audience excited; expelled by saint members, and obliged to quit pious boarding-houses. That was boarding-house No. 1.'" When Marion had reached thus far, the quaint manner in which he narrated the story—not a smile upon his countenance, not a muscle moved, the effect was richly ludicrous, and the small audience actually screamed as he continued on with Pious Boarding-House No. 2, No. 3, No. 4 and so. No one was more pleased than Mr. Bennett. He turned to a neighbor and remarked, " A man who can talk that way can write. He will make a clever editor one of these days, that Marion Monck." When Marion had finished, he proposed a toast. " Health and long life to all pious boarding-house keepers, and may they never lack stale bread or ginger cake nuts for their teas." The toast was drank with shouts of laughter. " As it is my turn, gentlemen, I call upon my neighbor here—neighbor in a double sense, as he was born in the same parish in the South as myself—Mr. Francis Gaillard." Mr. Gaillard arose, and was excusing himself from a song, when he was interrupted by Colonel Benson. " Pardon, gentlemen; I beg to ask Mr. Gaillard to tell us some story about the South—something about the slaves; these are exciting times. Horrid stories are told about the cruelty of Southern masters. Mr. Gaillard is a large slave-holder. I hope he will give us an anecdote of a different kind."

"Thank you, sir, for the suggestion. I am not certain that a little story I can tell will contain any thing interesting, or possess any especial merit. It shall have one advantage over those horrid tales of tortured and murdered slaves; it shall be true. My father, when a young man, had a favorite slave named Billy. He was coachman, and frequently travelled with my father, with or without the carriage. On one occasion they were in a boat crossing Cooper river, and it upset. My father had no more idea of swimming than he had of flying, and death by drowning seemed inevitable, but Billy was not only a splendid swimmer, but a most powerful man. He seized hold of my father, and although the tide was ebbing, yet, after almost superhuman exertions, he succeeded in getting his master and himself safe on shore. It was some time before my father came to, and he and Billy footed it to the plantation. My respected parent and Billy were nearly of the same age. The fact became known that Billy had saved my governor's life, and although it secured him a great many praises and favors from other members of our family, yet it never seemed to alter my father's course. He seemed to have forgot it, and though Billy did pretty much as he had a mind to do, I do not remember that Billy got severely whipped by my father's orders except on one occasion."

" Whip a poor negro who had saved his master's life ! That is gratitude with a vengeance," muttered the jolly Englishman Mr. Cubson.

" Let me finish, sir, if you please," continued Mr. Gaillard.

"The occasion was this. My father was somewhat eccentric, but I ever found him a very just man. He had an overseer on one of his rice plantations, a Mr. Maice, who was a great hand for whipping. My father did not exactly like it, but when he spoke to Maice, the overseer would say, very decidedly, 'It's no use to try to get along, sir, with niggers unless you give them a lashing. I never order more than twenty lashes, and it does the niggers good.' Maice took his leave, my father pondered over the matter for some time, and then called Billy.

"Billy came.

"'How d'y, Billy.'

"'How d'y, Massa Frank.'

"'Billy, go and get the overseer's whip.' Billy went and got it. 'Now help me take off all my clothes,' said my father.

"'Gor a mity, Massa Frank, what you gwine to do now?' said Billy.

"'I want you to give me twenty lashes, as hard as you can put it on, as hard as Maice whips the niggers,'' said my father.

"'Why, Massa Frank, wat de debbil you want for do now? Get dis nigger hung?' replied Billy, who was very much scared.

"'I want you to do as I say. If you don't, I'll send for Sam, and have you whipped,' said my father.

"'No; I swear God I can't lick you, Massa,' replied Billy.

"My father got in a rage, and called in Sam, who was a sort of second negro chief in the house. Sam came. 'Sam, I want you to whip Billy,' said my father.

"'Eh, Billy? What you do Massa now? Take off your coat.'

"Billy did so at once, and Sam gave him two or three good cuts, when Billy says, 'If dat is all you want, I gib dem cuts myself.'

"'Will you lick me now, Billy?' said my father.

"'O, yes, Massa. I'll lick you. Gib me de whip'—and Billy took it and gave his master two rather hard cuts.

"'Lick me harder, you rascal, or I'll have Sam lick you again,' said my father. Thus admonished, Billy put in 'de big licks,' as Sam, who was a spectator remarked, until the quantity was reached, his master counting at every stroke, one, two, up to twenty. 'There, Billy. I don't like it, and I'll be damned to hell if I'll ever have another nigger whipped on my plantation.' And he never did. He never afterwards had an overseer; and if a negro deserved punishment, he gave the very worst that can ever be given in the South—it was to transfer him from one plantation to another.

"But to return to Billy. My father died. When his will was opened, it was found to contain a clause stating that many years ago Billy Gaillard saved his life, and that he bequeathed to him, first, his freedom, second, the sum of five hundred dollars per annum, to paid quarterly at the Bank of Charleston, a house on the plantation, a horse every year, and, as he wished Billy to continue to work on the plantation, he was to receive pay for whatever he did from my father's successor, myself. There is not a more independent gentleman in the South, sir, than Billy Gaillárd. When I am at home, he is always near me—lectures and scolds me as if I were a child—has married off his family, has lots of children, and is more respected than ever was a patriarch in Bible times. He has but one weakness — when he goes to Charleston to get his quarterly dues, he generally manages to get moderately drunk. He frequently speculates, and makes more money than his income. He makes all his sons and daughters comfortable, and gives them many presents, but has never been know to even dream of buying any of them their freedom, although he has the means to do it; for he has saved and invested money for a great many years, and owns half-a-dozen valuable houses in Charleston that he rents out and receives quite an income from. Gentlemen, I hope I have contributed a little to passing away a pleasant time. I will conclude with a toast. I give—

"'The health of every Northern Abolitionist who will go South and see the Institution of Slavery as it really exists'"

. The story was warmly received, and the comical idea of the toast made all laugh. Even old Cubson growled out that he was afraid the healths of any northern gentlemen who made such an excursion would not be greatly benefitted. Mr. Gaillard called upon Mr. Bennett for his quota. Mr. Bennett very quietly remarked,

"Gentlemen, I am not much of a hand to tell a story, but I would rather be guilty of telling a stupid one than to lack the courtesy of trying to contribute my share to the general mirth and amusement. The story told about pious boarding-house keepers, but the more especially the description of the New England village of four hundred inhabitants and six distinct houses of worship, reminds me of an adventure in one of the same sort of towns, and I will try and narrate it. Some time after I had arrived in this country I found myself in Boston, and with but little to-do. I determined to travel into the interior and see if I could not pick up something. I had a good education, and I had heard that school teachers were in request. I will make my story as concise as possible, and without going into details, will mention simply that I found myself in some such place in Connecticut as Mr. Monck has described. The town was divided into three school districts, as they call them. The middle district required a "school master," that is the designation in Yankee land, and not school teacher. I offered my services to become the school master. It was necessary to see the Committee, and I applied to them for the situation. They consisted of a Presbyterian clergyman, a Squire Phelps, and Deacon Botsford. After some considerable bother, an hour was appointed when the School Committee met. I was there punctually at the time. The schoolhouse was a little one-story building, painted red outside, and the inside was covered with all sorts of drawings and ornaments made by ambitious scholars. Presently the important Committee arrived one by one. At last the solemn business was opened. Squire Phelps asked if I was the 'young man' who was anxious to take charge of that district school. I replied in the most amiable and seductive manner that I was the person. 'Deacon, we must examine whether he is capable of taking charge of our school.' The deacon grunted an affirmative—and then commenced such an examination as was never heard of before. I was asked how cheap I would act—whether I would board round among the parents of the scholars—and whether I could measure wood. I got along very well and quite satisfactorily until the clergyman asked me, 'What is your religion, Mr. Bennett?' I replied that I was a Catholic. Then the three committee men took a general stare at me, and afterwards at each other. 'Where are you from?' was the next question. I did not think, but replied simply, 'From Scotland.' 'O yes—I know where that is. It is up near Middletown, in Windham County.' There is, I have since learned, a town called New Scotland somewhere in that region. I was requested to retire. I did so, but was soon called back. 'Mr. Bennett, we have consulted together in reference to your application, and after examination, very impartially conducted, we are obliged to decline your offer, as we do not consider you competent to teach this district school.'

"Gentlemen," continued Mr. Bennett, "you may form some idea of my mortification. I assure you, I never applied since for a school teacher's berth. Yet I believe I am possessed of some ability, but it has taken a new direction. I have, as most of you are aware, started a new enterprise, and in the Herald I have had great success. I can assure you, that by the register I now circulate up in Connecticut over twenty-five hundred copies of my paper daily, and I believe I may say that that day will come, improbable as it may seem, when I will issue ten thousand copies of the daily Herald. I will give you a sentiment, 'A new era in Journalism.'"

It was drank with enthusiasm; and the idea of a man of Mr. Bennett's acknowledged cleverness to have been rejected as a Yankee schoolmaster, was perfectly rich and refreshing. Mr. Bennett hoped that Colonel Mac Neil would take his turn at the oar. The Colonel said he should not trespass long upon their time—that he was happy to meet with Mr. Bennett—that the Herald was giving new life to the community, and was making itself felt, and he hoped it would reach a circulation of ten thousand daily, but that he supposed was an utter impossibility, an extravagant idea, that Mr. Bennett could hardly expect would be realized in many years, if ever. "I cannot sing you but one song, gentlemen—I will try that;" and Mac Neil sang with good taste and feeling, "My Heart's in the Highlands."

The company had by this time become quite excited. Songs, stories and toasts followed each other in quick succession, until nearly midnight, when it was proposed that all should join in the good old song of "Good night, and God be with us all." All were in good spirits, but no one was quite intoxicated, at least to such an extent as not to be able to find his way home. When the party broke up, Marion retired to his room. A new life was before him—he was twenty-one years old.

CHAPTER XXXV.

Of age—"I am twenty-one"—Anxiety to get into Business—Monck's salary raised—Mr. Granville's Promises—Mr. Wilson to be taken as a Partner—Mrs. Tom Granville's advice to Marion Monck respecting her Niece—Marion is astonished—Concludes to make a Confidant of the Count Falsechinski.

"I AM of age." "I am twenty-one years old." "I am a man legally." "I am a citizen." What important sentences in the career of every male—what an epoch in the life of every man! Americans are not like Europeans, content to slave on for a period of years in clerkship, until the seasons of youth and middle age are passed, and old age reached without a hope or desire of bettering their condition, or of taking the chance of bettering it, by going into business upon their own account, becoming principals and employers themselves. It is a strong characteristic of the general American mind. He does not consider himself settled in life until he is in business on his own hook. He never dreams of getting married until he is his own employer. A young clerk's highest ambition is to get into business upon his own account, so soon as he is twenty-one years old. From this cause spring a thousand fearful evils in a commercial community. Half the failures that occur to persons engaged in mercantile pursuits can be traced to this going into business at an early age, before experience justifies it. Could all the young men who have gone into business upon their own account in New York city before they reached twenty-five years, be traced out, it would be found that they have failed where, had they been content to gain experience as clerks until they were thirty years of age, their after success would probably have been certain. The Jews are a sensible people in this regard. Their children don't take upon themselves the responsibilities of men until they reach thirty. Our blessed Lord and Saviour did not separate himself from parental control until he was thirty.

Marion Monck was not destined to be an exception to the general rule. He had reached twenty-one, and he began to think that it was high time to get into business. The next morning after the dinner, Mr. Granville informed him that his salary in future would be one thousand dollars per annum. "As you will continue to reside at my house without any expense to yourself, you ought to be able to lay aside some money every year, Marion. Are your parents in a situation to give you any capital to start in business, when your experience justifies such a step?"

"Indeed they are not. They might raise a small sum, but I would never consent to it. I must depend upon my own exertions," replied Marion.

"And a better reliance no man can want in this country, my boy. If you go on gaining commercial information, it will be of use to you some day. Water will find its own level, and so will business experience, capability, honesty, and activity. You possess all of the qualifications, and all you have to do is to pursue a straightforward course, and you will gain a foothold in the commercial world sooner or later. I am not justified in saying what my intentions are towards you eventually, but if you should remain with me a few years longer, and should then wish to go into business, I shall take great pleasure in forwarding your views. Very likely I shall hear of some person who has capital who would be willing to form a partnership with you, because you have such good business qualifications."

Marion had not lost a word of all this speech, which was an unusually long one for Mr. Granville to make. He was pleased with it, and yet displeased. It was cold, and strictly mercantile. It gave him no hope of the future, so far as becoming interested in the business of Mr. Granville was concerned. It seemed to remove Isabella to an immeasurable distance from his reach, but still he thanked his employer for his good intentions.

"I shall soon make a change in the style of the firm; and as I regard you as my confidential clerk, I will communicate my intentions to you. On the first of January next Mr. Wilson will be taken into the firm, which will then be Granville & Wilson."

Marion now expressed his sincere satisfaction, and asked if he might congratulate Mr. Wilson upon his good fortune, when he met him at the office. "He said nothing to me about it at dinner yesterday. In fact he never opened his lips about any thing."

"No—Wilson is not very talkative. A very excellent quality too in a man. But as he has said nothing to you, I don't think you had better say any thing to him. I suppose that you know he is living at Mrs. Nordheim's house?" observed Mr. Granville.

"I really did not know it. When did he go up there?" asked Marion.

"Very recently. I may as well inform you that I did not agree to take Mr. Wilson into the house because of his services, or of his personal importance to me. I have known him a great many years. He is a reliable, excellent man, and a most accomplished bookkeeper. He will owe his becoming my partner solely to Mrs. Nordheim. I made a promise to Mr. Nordheim that I would take into partnership any one that his wife should recommend. She has expressed her wishes decidedly in favor of Mr. Richard Wilson. She also furnishes him with a capital of fifty thousand dollars to put in the new firm. Under these circumstances Mr. Wilson will be admitted a partner. If Mrs. Nordheim had expressed the wish that you should have been associated with me, it would have given me pleasure to have taken you into partnership. I am a little surprised that she did not do so. It has appeared to me that you were a great favorite in that quarter. Had you any disagreement with her?" demanded Mr. Granville.

"None that I am aware of. She seemed anxious that I should leave her house, and appeared to act somewhat abruptly in requesting me to do so," said Marion.

"Women are very fantastic in their way of doing things, and Mrs. Nordheim does not seem to me to be an exception. What has made her take such an interest in Mr. Wilson is beyond my comprehension, but I suppose they have a secret understanding that Mr. Wilson pays her a portion of the profits he will be pretty certain to make as my partner in business," observed Mr. Granville.

This conversation made a very deep impression upon Marion's mind, in more ways than one. It set him to thinking of Mrs. Nordheim and Wilson. He wondered what could be her motive. He was not long in doubt. That same day Mrs. Tom Granville found him alone in the parlor.

"Marion, it is high time that you and me should have some understanding about Isabella. She has confided to me the secret of your mutual attachment, and I very foolishly consented to keep it from Mr. Granville; but I must tell you very candidly I think you are both young, and both particularly foolish. Mr. Granville will never consent to your marrying Isabella under present circumstances. He might do so, were you in successful business and making money. What are your future plans?" she asked.

Poor Marion, this was the extra pound that was to break his back. He did not know what to say, but he made a sort of answer, and informed Aunt Kate that he really had no definite plans for the future. "I will let things take their regular course. I am going with the current, and I cannot get out of the stream to get ashore," said he.

"I am afraid you will have to get out of the stream very soon, or you will be helped out. Have you not noticed that Colonel Benson is very regular in coming here and are you not aware that his hopeful son generally comes with his pa—and also that Mr. Granville takes Isabella and myself to the residence of Colonel Benson, and contrives that young Benson shall see Isabella home?" remarked Aunt Kate.

Marion replied that he was aware of all these facts, but requested Aunt Kate to inform him more plainly what impression she meant to convey by mentioning these circumstances.

"Why, my worthy Marion, if you don't see what it all means, I do. Middleton Benson is in love with Isabella as much as that thick-headed plodding young man can be in love with any thing, and it will not be long before he will propose for Bella, and be accepted," replied Mrs. Tom Granville.

"Accepted, Mrs. Granville! By whom, pray? Not by Isabel—she perfectly detests him, to say nothing about her affections being given to me. Pooh! pooh! You cannot frighten me with any such notion," observed Marion with some temper.

"Marion, I do not want to alarm you, nor is there the least necessity for showing to me any temper. It is all but a waste of words. I cannot alter things, but I have endeavored to kindly put you on your guard. Take it in that light," replied Mrs. Granville, with calm dignity.

"Mrs. Granville, will you answer me one question. Suppose Mr. Benson, Jr. should propose to Bella, would he be accepted?" demanded Marion.

"By Mr. Granville, do you mean? Unquestionably he would be. In fact, I think the two old heads have already arranged the matter," replied Mrs. Granville.

"No—I mean by Isabella?" anxiously inquired Marion.

"Isabel would not dare refuse him under such circumstances. She would refer him to papa, and although she would cry and take on about it in her room, yet to Mr. Granville she would appear pleased, and when the time came would marry Middleton Benson without saying a word," replied Mrs. Tom Granville.

"Great God! I can't believe it. She would never be so false to me," said poor Marion.

"False is a hard word. She is a mere child, and when you consented to being engaged to her, you have penetration enough to have formed some idea of her character. I think, Master Marion, you have behaved excessively foolish. There is no body whose advice is so good as a woman's. Before you got trammelled with such an attachment, why did you not consult Mrs. Nordheim? She always appeared to be a great friend of yours," asked Mrs. Granville.

"Because Isabella requested me not to say a word to any one about the matter," said Marion.

"When Isabel told me about it, Mr. Monck, I was extremely surprised, and I supposed, as a matter of course, that Mrs.

Nordheim knew all about it. When I told her, she was perfectly paralyzed," observed Mrs. Granville.

"In God's name, Mrs. Granville, tell me what you mean. Did you tell her? and when was it that you told her?" said Marion, excitedly.

"I did tell Mrs. Nordheim, of course, and the time was the day before you moved here. In fact, she must have requested you to move the very evening of the day that I saw her," replied Aunt Kate.

"And what, Mrs. Granville, could have been her motive for so abrupt—ay, so unkind a proceeding? Why should she be so angry at my becoming attached to Miss Granville," inquired Marion.

"You are really silly. The very best reason in the world. She did not wish to quarrel with Granville. She knew that he would not consent to your marriage with Isabel, and sensible woman that she is, determined not to be mixed up with it, by countenancing you—so she requested you to move as quick as possible, and told some foolish story about wanting to go into the country. She never did go into the country, and that is proof that it was but an excuse to get you out of the house," said Mrs. Granville.

"I see it all now," replied Marion. "My eyes are opened. What an infatuated fool I have been. She was vexed at my apparent want of confidence, and that is the secret of her cool treatment." Marion was as far from the real reason as ever.

Aunt Kate continued to pour oil upon the fire that she had kindled. "I dare say that if you had told her all about your love for Belle, she would have advised with you about it, and as she was very fond of you, it is likely that she would have backed her own advice by acts. Granville is about to take Wilson into partnership. It is all Mrs. Nordheim's doings. Had you acted right with so good a friend as that lady, she would have requested that partnership for you, and Belle's hand into the bargain. Had she done so, Mr. Granville would have consented at once. But it is too late now," was the remark of the lady.

Marion covered his face with his hands. His heart was too full to speak. At last he managed to inform Mrs. Granville that he would like to see Isabel, and have a full and complete understanding with her. Mrs. Granville replied, "It will be of no use, Marion. She will say yes to all you say. But she will not run away with you, or get married without the consent of her parent. When he puts his foot down, she will obey him, and marry the man she has chosen, and that will be the end of it. Take my advice, you would at once tell Isabel that you both have been foolish, that both had better give up all hope of the future, and forget each other," said Mrs. Granville.

"But Isabel, my dear Mrs. Granville, will not consent to any such thing. She loves me truly. Did I not think so, I would never give her another thought. She will never consent to breaking off our engagement while she is alive," said the confident Marion Monck.

"Nonsense. Try the experiment at least. It will be for your own happiness to do so, I assure you. Under different circumstances, I dare say you and Isabel might have been very happy, but not now. Good-bye. Think over what I have said, and act precisely as you deem best," said Mrs. Tom Granville.

Marion was completely paralyzed at such advice as this. He did not know which way to turn for relief. He attended to his duties the remainder of the day, and when evening came and it was about time to close the store, his mind was made up to take the advice of a third and a disinterested party. He told the Count Falsechinski that he desired particularly to see him, and asked to meet him that evening at the French coffee house in Warren street.

"I will meet you, Marion, but not there. Make it at Delmonico's, in William street. There we can have a room to ourselves, and a quiet nice dinner, or supper, if you call it so. I have an idea that I could guess the nature of your seeking a private conversation with me, but I will not do so. Be punctual to the time, which I wish you would make eight o'clock; do not be later. It is a bitter cold night, and a good cozy room with a fire, and the nice edibles and drinkables that Delmonico can get up, will enable us to pass a delightful evening," replied the Count, and the parties separated.

CHAPTER XXXVI.

The Night of the Great Fire in New York City—The Count Folsechinski and Marion Monck at Delmonico's—The Count's Opinions of Mr. Granville's Views—Marion saves the Portfolio and Papers of Mr. Granville—The Great Fire.

It was a dreadful night, that night in December, 1835, when the Great Fire occurred in New York. Marion left the store early in the evening, and as usual took the keys of the store from the porter, as he had previously taken the keys of an immense iron safe or vault, built into the solid walls of the store. He went home to tea, and after he had finished, Mr. Granville expressed a desire to have a policy of insurance, or to know if one had been taken out on property in a store on the North River side of the town.

"I shall be over in the neighborhood of our store, and it will cost me but little trouble to go in and ascertain for you," was Marion's reply.

"I wish you would do so," was the answer, and Marion left for Delmonico's, still keeping all the keys with him.

The store of Mr. Granville was on the corner of Broad and Garden street, and its rear overlooked the graveyard attached to the Reformed Church in Garden street, of which Dr. Matthews was the pastor.

Delmonico's at that time was almost as celebrated as it now is—perhaps more so, as it then had no rivals and no establishment of a similar kind could have been found in the city. It was located in William street, on the west side, about midway between Garden and Beaver streets. The eldest brother of the Delmonico Brothers was then alive. He was a fine-looking man of middle age, and his first name was John. He had another brother named Peter. Since then, several others have come to this country, while John is long since dead. He was accidentally killed while shooting over on Long Island.

When Marion reached Delmonico's it wanted but little of the hour appointed. He found the Count waiting, and soon after a servant showed them up to a nice little dining-room on the second floor, and facing the street. Soon after the dinner was served, and a bottle of wine also.

"Don't talk about any unpleasant matter until we have had our dinner," said the Count—and Marion scrupulously refrained from the least allusion to his troubles. Over an hour passed away while the Count was enjoying the meal, and then he ordered coffee and cigars.

"Now, Marion, I am ready for you. Tell me how I can serve you, and I will do so to an extent that you little dream of. Tell me all, from the beginning to the end."

Marion then related what has already been made familiar to our readers. When he had concluded, the Count remarked,

"I dare say, Marion, that you consider this unfortunate attachment as one of serious importance. Pah! if you could view such things as I do! Minds change—young men's especially. Could you jump over five years of your existence, you would laugh heartily at this boyish attachment to a pretty simpleton, for that is all that Miss Isabel amounts to under the most favorable circumstances. But I will not laugh at you, for I have been over the same road, and know just how you feel upon this occasion. Mr. Granville will not consent to your marrying Miss Isabel under any circumstances—and I would not either, if I was he. And if I was your parent, I would cut your throat before you should marry such a useless, insignificant piece of furniture. Pah again! Don't look angry, nor don't get angry with what I am going to say. You have the world before you, with health and good looks. Yes, Marion, you are a devilish good looking fellow, and when you get a trifle more manly, you will be a splendid specimen of a man. You speak several languages—you have a thorough mercantile education—and now you would throw all these advantages away, and tie yourself up with a little silly girl who has not done eating bread and butter. For shame, man! I thought you had a high ambition. If Mr. Granville would plank down a hundred thousand dollars with the young lady, it might do, but to marry her without his consent and not get a cent—Oh no, it's perfect nonsense. Don't think of such a thing—it is sheer madness," was the advice given by the experienced Count.

"But, my dear Count, although I am half persuaded that you are right, yet how can I help myself? We love each other, and we are engaged. It would not be honorable in me to break off, and I could not do it. What would she not suffer?" replied Marion.

"Not a pin's-head worth—not a particle. Try it. Go to Miss Isabel to-morrow the first thing. Tell her you are satisfied her father will never consent to your engagement, and that you cannot support a wife, and beg her to give up all thoughts of such an arrangement. Tell her that your parents won't consent to it. Tell her you have made a promise to *me* that you won't marry until you are thirty years old, and see how kindly she will take it. She won't make the slightest objection. Or if she does, your skirts are clear, and there is no occasion for you to trouble your head any further about the affair. I advise you to move out of the house of Mr. Granville also. Get some other place to live—it is more independent," continued the Count, when the alarm of fire occurred.

"Fire! Fire! Fire!" rang through the streets. The Count jumped up, and so did Marion. They flung open the blinds, and could see by the illuminated sky that it raged near them. Down stairs they rushed. The Count paid the bill, and they were soon in the street. It was nearly ten o'clock, the cold was intense, and there was a high wind. They passed rapidly into Exchange street—now Beaver, east of William—and kept on to Pearl. There were few people assembled, but one of the large dry-goods stores a few doors from Wall was in a blaze. They stopped and watched the fire for a short time, and saw it extend westward towards the Merchants' Exchange. "Count, it is very cold to be standing here. I have the keys of the store, and I am sure good coal fires are burning in both offices—if not, we can soon make one. We shall freeze if we stop here," observed Marion.

The Count agreed to the proposition, and they walked rapidly to the store of Mr. Granville. Sure enough, they found a good coal fire burning, and they lit a couple of candles and their cigars, and took seats by the fire. Some short time elapsed when they heard an unusual noise in the street, and Marion said he would go and see how the fire was getting on. He had been out but a moment, as it seemed to the Count, when he returned, his face aghast. "Count, several blocks are on fire, and so is the Merchants' Exchange. Why, our store may be in danger!" said Marion.

"Nonsense! To get at us the fire has got to burn a good sized church, and a pretty large grave-yard. However, we had better stay and see the business over or the fire out. I shall not go to look at it myself, for I am very comfortable her. Suppose you go to Delmonico's and get some cigars."

Marion started on his errand, but speedily returned: "Delmonico's is all on fire; there is no getting near the place."

"But there are no bells ringing. It is a fire without much noise," remarked the Count.

"People have too much to do to save their things. Let's both go and look at the fire," said Marion.

It was a very remarkable fact that on the occasion of the Great Fire in New York, the city bells rang but for a few moments, and while block after block was being burned, there was a fearful stillness, only interrupted by the roar of the flames. The Count and Marion got separated, and Marion was alone watching the progress of the fire. It came down Garden street like a summer whirlwind, and Marion for the first time became fully conscious that the store of Mr. Granville could not escape. He then went to work to get the books of the firm at least to a place of safety. He felt sure that the fire would not cross Broad street. Luckily, a store was open on the opposite side, and he was well acquainted with the people. He carried thither every book and paper that he regarded as of any value. When this was accomplished, he took the portfolio, which contained bills of exchange, notes, stock certificates, and other papers of value to the amount of half a million of dollars. This he carried about his person knowing that its loss could never be replaced. No one arrived to aid him. He went once more into the street: the church in the rear of Mr. Granville's store was on fire, and Marion then knew that the store was doomed. By this time the authorities had determined to blow up buildings and prevent the fire from spreading in Broad street. A store selected to be blown up was at No. 42 Garden, only opposite the corner store of Mr. Granville. From the opposite side of Broad Marion saw that blown up, and fall in one solid mass of ruins—not a brick or stone fell into the street—the store rose up and fell on the ground upon which it was built.

Shortly afterward the store of Mr. Granville caught, and Marion remained on the opposite side of the street and saw it burn and fall a mass of fire; such was the intense heat that not a brick was left standing. While watching this result, he was startled by hearing some one exclaim, "My God, I am a ruined man!" He knew the voice. It was Mr. Granville.

Marion approached him and placed his hand on his shoulder. "It is not so bad as you suppose, Mr. Granville."

"The portfolio—where is the portfolio?" inquired the merchant.

"I have it, sir, all safe. Here it is," replied Marion.

"Thank God for that. All the rest may go," was the response of the merchant.

Marion then conducted him to the spot where he had placed the books and papers. "Nothing is lost, sir, except the merchandise, and that is fully insured."

"You have done all this yourself?" asked Mr. Granville.

"Yes, sir. In a time like this aid was impossible to be had," was the modest reply of Marion.

"I owe you a debt of gratitude, my dear boy, that I can never repay. But come, let us get home," said Mr. Granville.

It was nearly daybreak when they reached State street, but the fire was burning as madly as ever, and did not stop until it had levelled every house between Broad and Wall street to the East river.

CHAPTER XXXVII.

Miss Norris Rouses the Ambition of Thomas Granville, Esq.—He Goes to Washington—General Jackson Appoints Him Consul to a Port in France—Returns to New York—Brother Advances Money—Renews Intimacy with Miss Norris—Consul Granville sails for Europe, and Miss Norris Accompanies Him—Queer Scenes in England and France—The President Removes Tom Granville from his Consulate—His Return to America, followed by Miss Norris, who has made Five Thousand Dollars by Her European Tour—The Ruin and Distress of the Ex-Consul.

THOMAS GRANVILLE seemed to have lost the esteem not only of those with whom he was connected by relationship, but also of the young woman with whom he had formed a dependent connexion. She, too, got sick of Tom, and became anxious to terminate their engagement. She was more anxious to do this, as Tom displayed no energy and no manliness of character. He was contented to remain by the side of Miss Norris at her comfortable quarters from one meal to another. At last she came to the conclusion that she would, for the welfare of Tom, rouse him out of his unmanly lethargy at any cost. About the time of the Great Fire she took Tom Granville to task.

"Is it possible that you expect to be tied to my apron-strings for ever? Have you no idea of doing anything for yourself? For shame!" she asked.

Tom replied, "I do not know what I can do. What do you wish me to do?"

"Oh, man, man, have you no energy—no self-respect left? Do? Why, rather than lead such a miserable life as you are leading, Master Tom, I would go and hire myself out as a street sweeper, carry in coal, go from house to house and offer to clear off the snow from the sidewalks, do any thing to earn my bread, were I a man, or, if like you, I pretended to be one," said the handsome Miss Norris.

Such language was calculated to arouse a new spirit in poor Tom, and it succeeded admirably.

"Do you wish to get up a quarrel with me? Is that what you are trying to do? or do you wish to separate from me? I can accommodate you in any way," replied Tom, with some spirit.

"Bravo, bravo, Tom. That is excellent. I have not seen you look so becoming in a long while. I will tell you what I want. Be a man; make yourself respected. God forgive me for ever letting you come here. Do you know that all your friends charge me with leading you astray? seducing your affections from a beloved wife? destroying her peace of mind? ruining her domestic happiness, and all such sort of stuff, which you, Tom Granville, know is as false as falsehood itself," continued Miss Norris.

"And who dares say such a thing? It is not true, and you know it all well as I do. Why, then, should you care what people say falsely? Tell me who makes those charges against you. Give me names, and if my brother or my wife even have dared to assert such atrocious slanders, I will make them contradict them," replied Tom, very bravely.

"Ah, Tom, if you would only show as much spirit in your actions as you do in your language, I should respect you much more than I do now. I do not want to make enemies, and yet I am making them every day on your account. Your wife has applied for a divorce, and she will succeed in getting it, if you do not mind, Tom," observed Miss Norris.

"I don't care a straw whether she does or not. What will it matter me?" inquired Tom.

"It matters this much, that if she succeeds in getting a divorce, it permits her to marry again, while it debars you from that privilege," remarked Miss Norris.

Tom answered that he did not care for a divorce, that he should never marry again under any circumstance, that he had had quite sufficient of married life, and wished for no more. But he continued, "I see that you wish to get rid of me. Your wishes, Clara, shall be gratified. I will leave you this very day. You shall see me no more."

"Nay, Tom," continued Miss Norris, with some feeling. "I wish to see you do something. You have cleverness, use it to some purpose, in some way, I care not how. I have no wish to get rid of you, except for your own good."

"No matter what the motive is, Clara. We won't speak of that. You *do* wish it, and it shall be done. But I have a favor to ask. I need some money for a short time. Lend it to me, and I will return it inside of a month. I am man enough for that, at any rate," said Tom.

Miss Norris went to a little portable desk, opened it, and took out a pocket-book.

"How much do you want, Tom?" she asked.

"Fifty dollars will answer my purpose," was the reply, and she at once handed him that amount.

"If it is not sufficient, tell me so, and you shall have more," added Clara, as she held out the purse.

"No. It is quite enough; and now, Clara, good-bye," said Tom.

Miss Norris wished to arouse Tom Granville to make some effort to do some thing for himself, but as she saw determination in every lineament of Tom's expressive face, she became fearful that she had overdone the matter. Perhaps Tom was going to jump off the dock, or commit suicide in some other shape. She felt that the melancholy fate of poor Nordheim, her first friend, had been tragedy enough for her lifetime, and she was not anxious to have Tom get killed, or kill himself. So she changed her battery. "Come, Tom, you need not say good-bye; or if you will do so, give me some reason for it. Tell me where are you going. What are you going to do? and if it is not an impertinent question, when am I to see your indignant lordship again?"

Not a smile appeared upon the face of Tom. He was as calm as apparent insensibility could make him. He felt indignant, but he had sense, and he had pride, and these told him that Miss Norris was acting right. It was a bitter pill to swallow, but he got it down.

"Clara, I will try and reply to your questions, or I would do so if I could, but I do not really know what I am going to do. I am going to leave New York this very evening, that I have decided upon firmly. So that my good-bye means something. I shall go to Philadelphia this afternoon. I have friends there. If nothing opens, I shall keep on to Baltimore, where I married my wife, and from thence I may go still farther south. That is all I can tell you, and once more I say good-bye."

Tom, as he said this, rose and took his hat, and walked partly to the door. Miss Norris followed him.

"Tom, I shall not say one word to prevent your going. It is necessary for your own sake. May God grant that you may find some thing to do—get into business, or get some position that will be creditable to you and to those connected with you. If you do, perhaps your wife will withdraw her application. Your brother will receive you as a brother again. I wish you well from the bottom of my heart. I am not selfish when I propose our separation. It is for your good," said Clara.

Tom replied, "So you have said, Clara, and I believe you.

One more good-bye. You shall hear from me favorably, and I thank you for having roused me from my lazy, unmanly sleep."

Miss Norris bade him an affectionate farewell, and Tom Granville left the house determined to turn over a new leaf. He did not wait for his resolves, which he felt were good ones, to cool. It was about noon when he left the residence of Miss Norris. He went from there to a quiet eating-house down in Nassau street, and got dinner. That afternoon he started for Philadelphia, and he did not halt for any time until he had gone as far south as the city of Washington.

In the chapter where we gave an account of Tom's marrying, we mentioned the conduct of General Jackson in after years, when Thomas Granville came to him in distress and in trouble. It was the present trip to which we then alluded. President Jackson took the matter in his own hands, and sent the name of Thomas Granville to the Senate for confirmation as Consul to one of the principal cities of France. He furnished Tom Granville with funds to proceed immediately to New York. Tom was delayed in Baltimore for a few days. Before he reached New York, his appointment and confirmation had been published in all the New York papers. It took all his acquaintances by surprise. "Ah, that brother of mine. He will never be taken alive," exclaimed Pitt Granville, who had a great admiration of official people, and his brother was now one, thanks to General Jackson's friendship. No sooner did Thomas Granville reach New York, than he proceeded to his brother's office. W. Pitt Granville received him kindly, and conducted him into the inner office. Before Tom left, Granville had promised to let him have all the money he needed for an outfit, and wait for it when Tom Granville should have reached France, and began to pocket the emoluments of the Consulate. It is needless to say that the mere fact of his brother's getting so honorable an appointment abroad was very gratifying to the senior Granville. A thousand or two thousand dollars to send out his brother to France, was nothing, in comparison to the gratification of his own feelings, even if Tom had never remitted back a cent.

No sooner had Tom received money from his brother, than he at once went to a hotel. There he sat down and wrote a grateful letter to General Jackson, and inclosed the thirty dollars the President had loaned him.

"Your act, General, has made me ascertain that I have more friends than I dreamed of. As you foretold, I have any quantity of friends since my appointment became public. I had no difficulty in raising money, and have sufficient not only to return you the thirty dollars which you were so good as to make me take at Washington, but enough left to procure me a handsome outfit and pay my expense to the port where I am appointed."

General Jackson was much gratified with the letter of Thomas Granville, and wrote him in reply a short but expressive letter, urging him to leave New York at the earliest moment, and giving him some good advice as to his conduct while in office.

Thomas Granville, after he had dispatched his letter to the President, found his way up to Broome street. Miss Norris was in ecstacies at his success. "I knew it was in your line, if you only exerted yourself." She then inquired what the income would be, and into various other matters. Tom said he should engage passage to Liverpool, and from thence go to Birmingham, Manchester, Leeds, and other places in England where he had relations and connexions.

"You know my wife has some very aristocratic connexions in London. One of her great aunts is the Duchess of Leeds, another is the Marchioness of Carmarthen. They were both Baltimore girls, and married well," said Tom.

"They know all about your wife, of course?" inquired Clara.

"Certainly. They know of our marriage, and both ladies wrote on letters congratulating us at the time the unfortunate affair came off," said Tom.

"Probably they have heard of your separation from your wife?" inquired Clara, anxiously.

"Not a syllable. You may bet your life that I have never uttered a word about it to those grand dames. Nothing has been said about it in the papers or in any public manner, and I am quite sure that my wife and her relations are too cursedly mortified about the affair to have written such unpleasant news," said Tom Granville.

"Thomas Granville," repeated Miss Norris, coming close to him, laying her hands upon his shoulder, and looking him full in the face, "Tom," she continued, "you have said that you loved me. Did you mean it, when you used to say it?"

"Upon my soul I did, Clara; I do love you," answered Tom Granville, returning her look.

The lady did not alter her position. "Thomas, will you prove it? Will you take me with you to France?"

"You, Clara! You! But will you go? No, no! I were mad to think of such a thing. It would d——n all my prospects forever. Great God, what a regular row it would kick up! No, Clara, it would not do. It wouldn't pay. What would Granville say?"

"Listen to me, Tom Granville. Your brother, the President, none of your friends need to know any thing of the matter. You go to work, get your outfit—uniform, letters, commission, letters of introduction. Engage passage, and do every thing that you have got to do, as though I were not going. I will secure my passage in the same ship, but under another name. When we reach Liverpool, we can then travel together, and then what a chance of your paying off your wife old scores! Take me as your wife—introduce me to the haughty dames who are her connexions, and see what glorious times we shall have. After leaving England, I can go with you to Paris—then follow you to your post—take a little cottage in the suburbs of the city. O Tom, it will be so nice—so quiet, and we can be so happy," said Miss Norris.

Ah, Tom Granville, where was your better angel when this artful syren was pouring such ideas into your confused brain? Consul Granville agreed to the entire programme as marked out by the artful Clara, and it was eventually carried out in all its details. Clara sold off all her furniture and everything of value, and placed the money in the Sussex Bank. She went up and bade her parents good-bye.

When the day for sailing came, Thomas Granville had an abundance of friends to see him off. His brother Pitt Granville and a large party went on board the ship, and came up in the steamboat. Little did any one dream that Miss Norris was on board, under an assumed name. Yet so it was, and the ship left the hook with a fair breeze for her destination.

It is not in our power to give an account of all that befell Thomas Granville during the period he was absent from the United States. He reached England, and so did Miss Norris. She travelled with him far and wide as his wife. His family received her as such, and the haughty relations, the two persons to whom we have alluded, made much of their American relations. Tom and his supposed wife were feted in the most sumptuous manner. The relatives of Mrs. Tom Granville were very much delighted with their relation, as represented by Miss Norris. But at last her intrigues became noticed, and Tom hurried her over to Paris. There they became worse, and although she kept a purse separate from Tom, before he had resided at his post a year she had coined money in abundance, while he was impoverished. She left him for London, and there her position enabled her to carry on several liasons, that brought her in enormous sums of money. She played a high game, and she won. Ere a year elapsed, she was back again in New York. She had been missed, but no one knew where she had gone.

There came letters to the Pinckney family in Baltimore from the English princesses. They had met Mrs. Tom Granville, and were delighted with her. This produced an explosion, but who was playing so impudent a part became the next question. Pitt Granville's relations also wrote to him about Mrs. Tom Granville. An explanation followed. The American minister in Paris wrote the President all about it. Tom Granville was recalled or removed just one year from the day he left New York. Miss Norris preceded him only a month. But she had a great lark, with lots of fun and frolic. She had moved in the highest circles in England and France. She had travelled all over the continent, and practiced the languages she had learned from the Count Falsechinski, and made herself perfect in all of them. During her sojourn in England, and while upon the continent of Europe, she never forgot for a single moment one purpose. As we have before stated, she was engaged in intrigues constantly, but they were not of a low character. She passed along as the beautiful and gifted wife of an American official, and she took care that under that assumed position, all those nobles and gallants who followed in her train, or who succeeded in their designs, were men that had an unlimited control of money. The costly jewelry and presents which she received were enormous. She carried over from London to Paris a sum equivalent to twenty-five hundred dollars in cash, and she had not been in Paris a week before she opened a bank account with the American Banking House of Welles & Co., and before the expiration of another week she purchased from that house a bill on New York for twenty-two hundred dollars. This she remitted to her lawyer in New Jersey, with directions to pay off the mortgage of two thousand dollars and the interest and other expenses. Then she commenced flirtation in Paris, until she made her supposed husband, Consul Granville, the laughing stock of all his friends in Paris. She then formed an intimacy with a Russian nobleman of unbounded wealth, and under his protection visited the principal capitals of Europe. She wheedled her Russian admirer out of a large sum. Soon after her return to Paris she gave him the slip, converted all her funds into a good draft on New York, went down to Havre, and took passage in the ship Erie.

On her arrival she passed from the ship to New Jersey, and at Newton deposited her money in the Bank. She stayed but a few weeks with her parents. The mortgage of two thousand dollars had been paid off, and she was the owner of a fine farm. Her father was a sober, industrious man. Her brother and sister she sent to a neighboring town to school. These duties accomplished, she soon after started for New York. Here she found Tom Granville, irretrievably ruined and disgraced. His brother Pitt Granville had had his feelings outraged, and he would no longer recognize Tom as a brother.

Poor Tom. He managed to get the address of Clara Norris, who had become more beautiful and more accomplished, but at the same time more heartless than ever. She gave him a few dollars, and at the same time announced to him that all intimacy was at an end, except she should be pleased to have him call upon her occasionally. She was residing with Mrs. Woodruff, in Bond Street. Thomas Granville asked her if she intended to keep him in money any longer?

"No Tom—not again. I am going to lead a life after my own fancy. I shall be in this house but a few days, and then I am going to follow the bent of my own inclinations. I hope you are satisfied?" she asked, in a cruel manner.

This was all the information Tom could get, except she promised that when she got settled, she would write a note to him, and she told him not to call again at Mrs. Woodruff's, but that if he wished to see or communicate with her, to send a letter addressed to her, care of Mrs. Woodruff; and he then took his leave.

We have digressed in this chapter, and brought the doings of the two principal characters in the chapter in advance of the period of our main narrative. We return to that in another chapter.

CHAPTER XXXVIII.

Destruction of Property by the Great Fire—Its amount—Mr. Granville a heavy Sufferer—Mr. Wilson becomes a Partner—The new House of Mrs. Nordheim—Marion Monck a Visitor—An interesting Courtship—The Widow Nordheim marries Richard Wilson.

THE great fire in New York was a terrific blow to its commercial prosperity, although it was not sensibly felt at the moment or for some months subsequent. Millions of property were destroyed in one night. Almost every fire insurance company was irretrievably ruined, and the merchant whose goods were fully insured, soon found that the companies where he had insured would not pay ten cents upon the dollar. The loss of Mr. Granville was very heavy. His warehouse in Broad street was filled with valuable merchandise, and he had another large store in the burnt district with an amount of almost equal value. He felt this loss very acutely. Had the fire occurred a few weeks later, it would have found Mr. Wilson a partner, and also a severe sufferer. The arrangement of having Mr. Wilson come into the firm, with a considerable cash capital, was now a matter of extensive moment to Mr. Granville. He stated frankly to the former that his losses were very heavy, and added, "I shall not insist upon your complying with the agreement we had concluded, unless you are perfectly satisfied that my losses have in no way impaired my solvency."

Mr. Wilson advised fully with Mrs. Nordheim, and then informed Mr. Granville that he should become a partner according to agreement, on the approaching first of January. When that day came, the announcements were made in the daily journals, and the firm was changed to "Granville & Wilson."

Mr. Wilson had resided some time with Mrs. Nordheim before he discovered a suitable house. He did find one, however, for sale, and it was purchased, and Mrs. Nordheim gave up her house in Bond street, and moved into her own residence. It was a three story house, not in a fashionable part of the town, but in a street running from the west end of the Military Parade Ground, now known as Washington Square. Shortly after their removal Mr. Wilson invited Marion Monck to call upon them. He did so, and was pleasantly scolded by Mrs. Nordheim for his long absence; and she pleasantly inquired after the health of his fascinating friend, Miss Isabella Granville. This was a sore subject to Marion, and he skillfully avoided it by saying that he saw so little of Isabella that he did not really know whether she was well or ill. Mrs. Nordheim then inquired particularly about old friends and acquaintances, the Count Falscchinski, Thomas Granville and Miss Norris. Marion told her that Tom had received a foreign appointment, and of Miss Norris he knew nothing. He congratulated Mrs. Nordheim upon her new residence, and with a promise to call often, took his leave. After he was gone, the beautiful widow sat and mused for a long time.

"What curious beings we are! There is that lad, Marion—I thought I loved him. Perhaps I did so—why, I cannot tell myself. Now I would no more think of making him my husband, than I would of marrying a child. I want some one that I can lean upon—some one that I can trust. This youth is as changeable and unstable as water. Had I not discovered that he loved Isabella Granville—well, it is all for the best, and I am fortunate in getting rid of my attachment, or what I thought was such, so easily;" and here the lady drew a long sigh. At this moment Mr. Wilson entered the sitting-room.

"Good evening, my old friend. I have had a visitor. I wish you could have arrived a little sooner. You would have seen how perfectly calm I received a visit from Marion Monck. Pshaw! what dupes we are to our own imaginings! I really fancied that I had a strong regard for that youth. I find he is no more to me than a hundred others," said the widow Nordheim.

"I am very happy that you are able to meet him with such composure. I feared it would be otherwise. But you have a brave heart," replied Mr. Wilson.

"And a good one, too, I hope. Have you just left the office?"

"About half an hour ago. All was going on well in that quarter. Mr. Granville has been terribly scared, and is a much more sociable sort of partner than I ever thought he would make. He consults or advises with me in reference to every matter of importance. Such a change in the tenor of any one man's life I have never heard of. From the neglected bookkeeper I am become a prominent merchant, and treated with the utmost respect by all with whom I come in contact. It is you, dear lady, that has done all this, and how can I ever repay you?" demanded Mr. Wilson. "But one thing you shall know—I fear that my residence with you exposes me to be talked about, and I would rather go and live somewhere else—on your account, lady, not on mine," continued honest Wilson.

"Who dare talk about me, Mr. Wilson, or what can any one say in reference to my conduct? Surely I am doing no harm," said the widow, with great spirit.

"I ought not to have said anything about it to worry you, but I could not help it. People joke me. Even Mr. Granville said with a sneer this morning, that as you had behaved very kind to me, that I ought to be very careful of your reputation, and that I ought not to reside in the house with you," stammered out poor Wilson.

"I begin to think they are all right, Mr. Wilson. It is curious. It must appear singular that a merchant who has been a clerk should reside alone in the house of one of his late employers. It must be remedied, Mr. Wilson—we must give no occasion to people to make severe remarks, or to talk scandal about us. What can be done, Mr. Wilson? You are older and wiser than me, and I look to you for correct advice. You are twice my own age. I am but a little girl in years," said the lively widow.

Mr. Wilson reflected a moment before he attempted to make any reply. Then he answered quietly, "Although it may put you to some inconvenience, yet I think it would be better that I should move back to my old quarters at Clarke & Brown's in Maiden Lane. I could come up here every day. Then I am sure the world could see no impropriety in you."

"That is your candid opinion, is it, Mr. Wilson? Now it is *not* mine. I have a better plan, and not half so troublesome. Come and sit down by me on the sofa, and I will tell you what my plan is," said the widow.

Mr. Wilson seated himself as requested. She reached her hand out and gently took hold of his, and continued: "I have told you that I needed a protector. Suppose, Mr. Wilson, I could find a nice, amiable, kind-hearted, middle-aged man, who would be willing to marry me. What would you think of that plan?"

Poor Wilson was aghast. "Really, Mrs. Nordheim, I—yes, perhaps it would be best. But could you love such a man as you describe? He must be a wretch if he did not love you and make you happy. It *would* be better. I know you have selected the man, or you would not talk so decidedly. Do I know him? You must confide in me, and tell me his name. I will then tell you honestly what I think of him."

Poor Wilson had made a terrible long speech, but it was an honest one. He was much too humble in his own eyes to dream for a moment of the real person that the widow had in view, and he was fearful that it was Colonel Mac Neil, or perhaps the Count Falsechinski. Had a thunderbolt fallen at his feet, he could not have been more startled than when Mrs. Nordheim replied,

"Yes, Mr. Wilson, it is right and proper that I should tell you the name of the man I intend to ask to become my husband. It is Richard Wilson," said the widow firmly.

"Me!" he exclaimed. "My God! can you be in earnest, or is this a dream? This is too much honor, too much happiness for a poor old devil like me."

"It is you, Mr. Wilson—that is if you will have me. I will

try and be a good, loving wife. I will try to make you happy;" and she gazed fondly into his face with those clear, beautiful eyes, as she said this.

"Mrs. Nordheim!" was all Wilson could say.

"Don't call me Mrs. Nordheim—call me Bessy; for you shall have that right, and no one living but you."

"I really don't know what to say. I do love you. If you wish it I will marry you—but it is not right. You are very young—gifted, beautiful, rich, and can marry any one you choose—the very pick of the land; and I am a poor old fellow, double your age, and old enough to be your father. Don't think of it—don't make such a sacrifice!" earnestly exclaimed Wilson.

"It is no sacrifice at all, Mr. Wilson. If you are old enough to be my father, then you can act father as well as husband, and I will be a dutiful daughter as well as wife. It shall be so, unless you refuse me altogether," she said smilingly.

"O no, dear Bessy! I would die for you, and would be as devoted to your interest if you had selected some one else; but if you will marry me, why you will make me the happiest man alive," said Mr. Wilson.

"Then, my dear Richard, you are satisfied. So am I. Let our marriage be as soon as you please. We will have no fuss or noise. Send for a clergyman and witnesses to-morrow—next week—or any time you choose: we will be married, and then all the notice that we will give about it to our dear friends will be when they will see the announcement in the papers. Are you satisfied, Richard?"

Poor Dick Wilson was overcome. He seized the fair widow, and pressed her to his manly bosom as though he would never release her. Then he kissed her rosy lips, but she offered no resistance to either demonstration, but returned his caresses fondly but gently.

"Bessy, I am forty years old!" he exclaimed.

"Richard, I am twenty-two years old;" and she laughed heartily. "I would not have you a year younger for anything. I respect, esteem, trust you; and, dear Richard, don't fear but that I shall learn to love you as fondly as if you were only twenty. I need one that I can rely upon in my love, and you are that one; and I shall give you all the wealth that I possess of worldly goods, but I shall give you what you will value more—all the wealth of the most devoted affection," said the widow.

Wilson embraced her again and again. His heart was too

full to speak, but he murmured, "Dear lady, you shall never regret your choice."

"I don't believe I ever shall, Richard. I will trust you with my future happiness without a doubt. Now let us talk quietly over the future."

They did so, until a late hour. Mr. Wilson urged delay in the marriage. He was anxious that she should have time to think it over. Perhaps she would change her mind. The lady was resolved.

A few days elapsed after the conversation, and then Richard Wilson and Elizabeth Nordheim went together in a carriage, one beautiful morning, to the residence of the Rev. Dr. Milner, in Beekman street. There they met Mr. Pitt Granville, Mrs. Tom and Isabella. Marion had not been invited. Mr. Wilson had two friends there. These parties were witnesses, and the venerable clergyman performed the ceremony of marriage. From the clergyman's residence the small bridal party drove directly to the house of Mr. Wilson. A table had been spread with refreshments, and all partook of them. Mr. Granville then began to make excuses, and said he must go to the office.

"Take Mr. Wilson with you, Mr. Granville. I do not want him to vary his usual habits. He has not been absent from his post for years, and I do not want to kill him on our marriage day by making him give up one of his old habits," said the fair bride.

A laugh was the consequence of this playful sally, and Mr. Wilson, after kissing his wife, joined Mr. Granville and went to the office.

The rest of the bridal party took leave of the bride, and she was left alone. "Poor dear Wilson!" she murmured, "how perfectly astonished he appears to be. I dare say he thinks it all a dream. Never mind—it shall be a happy dream, and I will begin by making him completely at his ease, and act as though nothing remarkable had happened. What a lucky thought to send him down to the store! How delighted he was to get off! I do love him. But now for dinner. I must begin to see about that, for he will be back here to dinner as punctual as the clock."

Thus commenced the wedded life of Mr. and Mrs. Wilson.

CHAPTER XXXIX.

The Marriage of Mrs. Nordheim opens the eyes of Mr. Monck—He Condoles with the Count Falsechinski—He walks upon the Battery with Isabella Granville—A very funny Love Dialogue—Appeals to Mr. Granville for his Consent to marry Isabella—The latter denies loving Marion—Mr. Granville sends Mrs. Tom Granville to Maryland—Discharges Marion Monck from his employ—Turns him out of his house—Sends for Colonel Benson—Marriage of young Benson to Isabella Granville.

WHEN Mr. Granville, accompanied by Mr. Wilson, reached the counting-room, (which was now located, after the fire, lower down Broad street, on the opposite side to where the old store stood) he announced to the Count Falsechinski and to Marion Monck and the other clerks, the event that had occurred that morning. All immediately pressed around the new married man, and offered him their sincere congratulations and good wishes. None were more sincere than the Count. Marion, without exactly knowing why, *was* embarrassed. He felt hurt that he had not been asked to the wedding. He was not conscious of feeling deeper upon the subject than this. In the course of the day he found himself alone with the Count, and he remarked to him, "Count, don't you think it very queer that Mrs. Nordheim, let alone Wilson, did not invite me to the wedding?"

"Marion," replied the Count, "allow me to say that I candidly think you are a perfect ninny—a blind male mole—an ignoramus—a jackass—and if I knew any other term to express the most consummate stupidity, I would apply it to you."

Marion sprung off his office stool.

"Count, what do you mean? Do you wish to insult me?"

"Not at all, my dear boy; but you are so queer, so extremely so, that I cannot put up with you any longer. Invite you? That would have been cool. No, no, my dear child; you were not wanted at *that* wedding. Marion, while you were making an infernal fool of yourself, and falling in love with that silly fool, Isabella Granville, Mrs. Bessy Nordheim was deeply attached to you. Mrs. Tom Granville went up and told Mrs. Nordheim that you were engaged to her niece. Mrs.

Nordheim sent you away from her house that day, for it was only on being told that you loved another, that the lovely lady discovered the nature of her feelings to you. She acted wisely, and got rid of you, determined to forget you. She is an affectionate disposition. She found sympathy in Wilson. He is a devilish good fellow. She wanted some body that she could love and respect at the same time. She put Wilson in business—took him to her home, and—to-day she has married him. She has done well, and mark my words, there will not be a happier married couple in New York than these two. I know them both. Now, are you not an idiot? Such chances—and you let them slip! Now get rid of that other affair. Get off with Miss Isabella, as I advised you the night of the fire, or you will regret that, for the moment Mr. Granville suspects *that*, he will start you out of his house and out of his employ. The girl is a heartless coquette, and she would not cross the street to pick you out of the gutter, if you happened to fall into it. What! not a word in reply?" demanded the Count.

"No, Count; I have nothing to say. I see through it all now. My eyes are opened. Why did you not tell me about Mrs. Nordheim before?" asked Marion.

"*I* tell you! That is cool. Why, my dear boy, it would have done no good. Salt could not have saved you. The moment Kate Granville informed Mrs. Nordheim about your affair with Isabella, your cake was dough. A woman that loves, when she hears that the one she loves is also in love with—another woman. Bah. It is no use talking thus. The affair is all over; but cheer up, man, the world has not come to an end, and although Mrs. Nordheim has become Mrs. Wilson, and Miss Granville will shortly become Mrs. Benson, yet there is still as good fish in the sea as ever were caught, and will be many more by the time you are thirty years old, and if you think of getting married before that period of your age, you are perfectly insane," exclaimed the Count.

Marion was in no humor to combat the Count's remarks. He felt convinced, and wanted time to think. He only replied with a few words.

"Count, if I do not say much, it is because I feel just as though I should like to go and stretch myself. That will do me good. I am going to walk for an hour with a gentleman on the Battery. Not a very agreeable companion at this moment. It is myself."

"Go along, my boy; and whatever may chance to turn up,

do not forget that Adolph Falsechinski is your friend," cheeringly said the Count.

Marion sauntered down to the Battery, and he had not walked there many minutes before he was joined by Isabella Granville.

"Why, Isabella, I thought you were up at the wedding which came off this morning," said Marion.

"So I was, dear Marion; but I have been back some time. I saw you on the Battery, and I ventured to come and take a walk with you. Was Pa at the store when you came away?" she asked.

"He was," replied Marion; "and I have no reason to suppose he will leave there until late."

"A curious wedding this morning. Were you not surprised at it, Marion? and how did it happen that you were not present?" she asked.

"I was not invited. In fact, I knew nothing about it."

"Were you not surprised at it?" asked Isabella.

"Nothing surprises me now. I should not be surprised were you to get married to some person that I never heard of before," said Marion.

"You appear quite vexed this morning. I hope you are not angry with me," softly whispered the young lady.

"No, Isabella; not with you. I am vexed with myself. I could tell you a very singular story, if I chose to do so. Isabella, you know that Mrs. Nordheim was once a friend of mine—a warm friend."

"I very much suspect, Marion, that she was once very much in love with you," replied Isabella.

"She certainly treated me with kindness until the day your Aunt Kate went up to her house, and under pretence of consulting with her, contrived to let her into our secrets, and told her that you and me were engaged. That night, Isabella, Mrs. Nordheim gave me a hint to go—no—not a hint; she told me she wished me to leave her house as speedily as possible. I did so, and since then she has exhibited no kindness to me. On the contrary, not inviting me to her wedding this morning, was in perfect keeping with her other acts," said Marion.

"And poor me is the cause of this ill-treatment, which you seem to take so much at heart. What need you care for Mrs. Nordheim, or for Mrs. Wilson as she now is? She can be nothing more to you," said Isabella.

"Indeed she cannot be. But say no more of her, but let us

speak of our own future. You love me, Isabella, do you not?" asked Marion.

"How can you doubt it, dear Marion? I have told you so a hundred times," replied Isabella.

"I did a very wrong thing, Isabella, when I consented to be engaged to you, to agree not to mention it to your father. I have felt mean ever since. I have lost my own manliness of character. I wish, dearest Isabella, you would tell me this morning, 'Go to my father. Tell him all, and when he asks me if I love you, I will say yes, and leave the consequence to Providence. We shall both feel easier. We shall have done right, and our minds will be relieved.' What do you say, Isabella? Say yes," said Marion.

The fair, but treacherous young coquette held down her head, and walked some distance before she opened her lips. Then it was to say, "But, Marion, it is perfectly useless. Pa would dismiss you from the store and from the house."

"But," pleaded Marion, "I could bear that even, provided you assure me solemnly that you will still be constant and true, and continue to love me until I am in a different situation, and that if the worst comes to the worst, that if your father cannot be persuaded to give his consent to our marrying, that you will be mine without his consent. Assure me of this, and ere I sleep to-night, your father shall know all," said Marion.

"You will do nothing of the kind if you really love me, as you say you do. Pa would kill me outright. He made me consent to marry Middleton Benson, although you know I perfectly detest that young man. But what could I do? Don't stare at me in that furious manner; you quite frighten me," exclaimed poor Isabella.

Marion had stopped suddenly in his walk when Isabella made this queer statement, and gazed fixedly into her face. At last he spoke, and it was with such concentrated bitterness that the young lady began to weep.

"Isabel, how deeply, devotedly I have loved you, God alone knows; but what are you? A trifling, silly, nonsensical doll baby, or are you a young girl of principle, character and firmness? Tell me at once, and truly, all the facts you have hinted at. Has young Benson offered his hand to you, and when?"

"Oh, some days ago. Pa told me he would do so, and that he and old Colonel Benson had arranged it all. What could I do? The young man called. He told me he loved me and all that sort of thing, and asked me if I would marry him," replied poor Isabel, crying.

"And you, Isabel," exclaimed Marion in tones somewhat agitated and rather sternly—"what did you reply?"

He took her hand in his, and led her to one of the benches. "I am very calm, Isa. Sit down quietly now, and tell me all about it. Of course you appealed to his honor—you told him that you had long loved me—that we were engaged, and—and—" said Marion.

"No, I did not do any thing of the sort," said Isabel.

"What did you say then when he asked you if you would marry him?" nervously inquired Marion.

"Why, I had to tell him *yes*, of course—what else could I say?" pleaded Isabella.

Marion dropped the pretty little hand which he had held in his, and in the most indignant manner addressed the poor silly girl—

"I am ashamed that I should ever have lost my heart to you. You profess to love me, and say *yes* to a proposal of marriage from another! Oh Isabel, had any one else told me this of you, I would have crammed the words down his throat. Do you love that young man?" asked Marion calmly.

"No, I don't," was the reply of Miss Granville.

"And yet you agree to marry him when he asks you!"

"I had to do it," said Isabella.

"And do you intend to marry him?" asked Marion.

"I suppose so: what else can I do?" replied Isabella.

"Do you mean, dear Isabel, that you would do any thing else to avoid this proposed marriage?"

"Yes, I will. I don't like young Benson, and I do love you," was her reply.

"Then, Isabel, let us walk up to the Bowling Green. There are carriages always standing there. We will enter one of them, and proceed to the same clergyman's residence who married Mrs. Nordheim this morning. He will marry *us*. As soon as the ceremony is performed I will go and tell the whole to your father; he will forgive us. Only reflect how gratefully he has expressed himself at my saving his portfolio and books from the fire. Come, Isabel, say you will consent, and I will make you the happiest little wife that ever drew breath," and again the little hand was clasped in hers, and he seated himself at her side.

"Why, Marion, what are you thinking of! I would not go in this dress, and if I was to go home and change it, Aunt Kate would smell a rat, and then there would be such a to-do. Oh no, don't think of it any more," said Isabel.

"Really, Isabel, you would tire out the patience of a saint. The dress is nothing; if you love me you will marry me, and then all will be soon settled. Your father will consent. But if you will not go now, will you make your arrangements, and run away with me the first good chance you get—say this evening?" earnestly demanded Marion.

"I can't this evening. I am going to a party at Colonel Benson's, and I would not miss going there for all the world. Why need we go and get married? Pa will kill us both if we do. Let him have his own way. It will be a great deal better," replied Isabel Granville.

"Isabel, is this trifling upon so serious a subject right? Say that you will *not* marry me, and then I shall know what to do," said Marion.

"I will marry you—that is, I like you better than that stupid Benson, if Pa will consent; but there it is again, he will not consent, and what can I do?" observed Isabella.

"If your father was to ask you, Isabel, if you loved me, what would you say, Daisy?"

"If Pa appeared to be angry when he asked me, I should say 'No.' If he appeared pleased I would say 'Yes.' It would depend altogether upon circumstances. What else could I do?" replied the fair girl.

"My poor Isabel, I pity you from the bottom of my heart, but I will not be in suspense longer. I will know my fate to-night. Come, let us walk towards the house. Take my arm," said the angry young man.

They walked to the house, and Marion bade the young lady good-bye. From the house he went directly to the office. Mr. Wilson had gone home and Mr. Granville was alone in his private office. When Marion entered the counting-room, the Count looked at him for a moment, and observed in a low tone,

"Marion, what is the matter? You seem to be very nervous and excited. Don't be rash, whatever you do."

Marion was in no humor to be pacified. At that moment it appeared to him as though the world had but one object. His marriage with Isabella Granville, his clerkship, his property, all were forgotten. He stepped hastily into Mr. Granville's private office. The old merchant raised his eyes from the letter he was writing, and without laying down his pen, asked mildly,

"Any thing particular, Marion?"

"Yes, Mr. Granville, it is very particular. I regret that I

have not told you before. I will tell you now, if you will listen to me."

The merchant quietly laid down his pen and listened to a narrative which seemed to paralyze him for a moment. Marion informed him of his long attachment—their engagement—of Isabel's anxiety to conceal it—of her repentance in reference to her promise to marry Benson, and concluded with informing Mr. Granville that he was satisfied that Isabel loved him, and that she would boldly declare it if he would not scare his daughter when he asked her the question. Mr. Granville did not interrupt the narrative except when in the relating of it Marion mentioned the name of Mrs. Tom Granville. He then simply inquired the extent of her knowledge of what was passing. It was too late for Marion to equivocate or excuse any one. He told the truth.

"Wait for a moment here," Mr. Granville coldly remarked, and then went to the cashier and received from him a roll of money. "Now, Mr. Monck, will you go with me?" politely asked Mr. Granville.

"Certainly, sir," answered Marion.

There was not another word spoken until both were inside Mr. Granville's house. The parlor was empty. He rang the bell. The servant answered it.

"Tell Miss Isabel I wish to see her," said the father.

A moment only elapsed ere the fair girl entered the room. She blushed deeply when she saw who was with her father.

"Come here, my child. This young gentleman has informed me that he has long been attached to you, and believes that you are attached to him; is it so?" kindly asked Mr. Granville.

She made no reply.

"Did you not tell young Mr. Benson that you loved him, and that you would marry him?" asked Mr. Granville.

"I did, Pa," was the child's reply.

"Have you altered your mind, my darling?"

"No, Pa," was the response, plainly spoken.

"Do you wish to marry Mr. Marion Monck?"

"No, Pa, if you do not wish me to do so."

"You can go to your room. Send down your Aunt Kate to me. Now, Mr. Monck, I presume you are satisfied," said Mr. Granville.

"I am, sir. I have been most grossly deceived, and I would not marry her, sir, if she were Queen of England," said the indignant Marion.

"I dare say you would not, nor as Miss Isabella Granville. But enough of this."

Here entered Mrs. Tom Granville.

"Did you send for me, brother Granville?" she asked.

"I did, madam, and it was to place in your hands this money," handing her a roll. "I have had evidence of how carefully you have guarded my daughter, and I wish to relieve you from all farther responsibility in the matter. Please use that money to go to Baltimore this afternoon, or so soon as you see fit. I hope to have my house relieved of your presence before night," coldly remarked the exasperated Mr. Granville.

"I shall not be here an hour longer, I can assure you, brother of mine"—and, turning to Marion—"I hope some day to thank you for your manliness in revealing secrets to Mr. Granville which, as a gentleman, you had no right to reveal. I wish you both farewell."

Aunt Kate left the room. Meanwhile Mr. Granville seized a pen and wrote a note, carefully sealing it. It was directed to the cashier of his concern. "Take this, sir," he said, addressing Marion, "and go to the office. The cashier to whom it is addressed will make up your account and give you a check for what salary is due you. I will remain here until you return. If there is not money in the office, tell him to fill up a check, and I will sign it here. Bring the cartman with you when you return. I wish you to remove from my house as speedily as possible. It is unnecessary for me to add that I shall have no further need of you in my business; in fact, I wish our acquaintance to end to-night in all ways and shapes," sternly observed the merchant.

"I can assure you that in this matter, Mr. Granville, I will be as obedient as I have ever been to your wishes," was Marion's response.

"Thank you. I regret what has occurred, but it cannot be helped. After what has passed, your own good sense will point out to you that our acquaintance is at an end," said Mr. Granville.

Marion bowed, but did not venture to reply. He carried the note to the office. The cashier made up his account, and drew a check for the balance. The Count had left the office.

"Are you going to leave us?" asked the kind-hearted cashier.

"I believe so," was the reply.

"Take the check to Mr. Granville to be signed. Here is your account, on which I have placed my initials."

Marion then found the cartman and proceeded to State street. The check was signed by Mr. Granville without a word of comment. Marion went up to his room, packed his things, and one of the servants of Mr. Granville who had gone up with him helped him to bring his trunks down stairs, and they were placed upon the cart. "Where shall I go?" asked the cartman. For a moment, Marion appeared confused. He did not know where to go. He thought of Mr. Wilson's old place, and then he told the cartman to drive to Clark & Brown's, in Maiden lane. There he went and there we will leave him.

After Marion's departure, Mr. Granville despatched a note to Col. Benson. That gentleman replied to it by calling in person. The two gentlemen were alone for a long time. Mrs. Kate Granville had been taken with her baggage to the Philadelphia train before Colonel Benson arrived. She did not bid her brother-in-law good-bye a second time, but pressed Isabella to her heart when she left her in her own room. We will not go into any unnecessary details, but will come at once to results. That evening a small party was assembled at Mr. Granville's residence. Colonel Benson, his wife, his daughter, and his son were there. A venerable clergyman was also present, and before he left, Mr. Middleton Benson became the husband of Isabella Granville.

The simple girl was very pale, but she made the responses during the ceremony with a firm voice, and it would have been difficult for a stranger to have noticed that she was dissatised in the least with her share in the proceedings. Mr. Granville appeared satisfied that he was doing a good deed, and providing well for a favorite child. Colonel Benson, also, was not displeased. His son had made what is called a good match. The settlements made by Mr. Granville were unexceptionable, and of the most liberal character. He was entirely ignorant that Isabella had any previous attachment, for Mr. Granville had considered it unnecessary to mention what he deemed a childish attachment. Middleton acted like a child who had become possessed of a pretty toy that he had admired for a long time.

It had been decided by the old people that the new married couple should continue to reside in State street, at the old mansion, and Mr. Granville was to live with them at least for a time. So closed the day, eventful by the fact of the two marriages.

CHAPTER XL.

Clark & Brown's Coffee House in Maiden Lane—Marion Monck in his new Quarters—The Count Falsechinski calls upon him with an offer of money—Meets Mr. Bennet in Nassau street, and accompanies him home—Some curious facts in reference to the Editor of the Herald—Its Early History, and the real secret character of Mr. Bennett.

Marion removed with his baggage to the coffee-house in Maiden Lane. It was a lodging house and a restaurant combined. It furnished rooms at the moderate sum of two and a half dollars a week, and the occupant had it optional with himself where to get his meals. He had to pay for what he ordered, and if he chose to live expensively and consume the choicest bits in the larder, he could do so, or he could live on a more simple fare, or he could, in case of stern necessity, live on bread and water.

When the room had been selected, his baggage carried into it, and he felt located, Marion came down into the bar-room, and ordered a glass of hot whiskey punch and a cigar. He had already learned the way to drown sorrow. He had not long been seated in the bar-room ere the Count Falsechinski entered.

"Aha, Monsieur Marion. I am seeking for you," was his first address, as he took a chair and seated himself by the side of our hero.

"I am glad to see you, Count, particularly to-night. I suppose you have heard that I am no longer one of the white slaves of Mr. Granville," observed Marion with a good deal of bitterness.

"It was the merest accident in the world. I was at the office towards night, and the cashier told me that you had been paid off, and while he was relating this to me, the cartman, Billy Christie, entered, and from him I learned that he had carted you and your baggage to this place. What led to the explosion, and your sudden dismissal, is beyond my present knowledge, and if you will favor me with all the particulars I shall feel very much obliged, and my mind will be very much relieved," replied the Count.

Marion cheerfully complied with this reasonable request, and commenced as follows:

"Count, I deemed your advice good, and I followed it to the letter. I determined to know my fate—to know the worst."

Then Marion continued, and told the Count all that our readers have been informed respecting the events of the day. The Count replied,

"Nothing but what I expected, my dear boy. I suppose you are satisfied now that what I told you is true, that you have nothing to hope for in the case of Miss Granville."

"I am satisfied that Mr. Granville is a hard-hearted, ungrateful man, and all my services to him go for nothing," said Marion.

"Of course they do. He is like all the rest of mankind—no more nor less. As long as you were of service to him, he was your friend. You cross his purpose, and you are kicked out without a word. Have you any money?" asked the Count very kindly.

"Plenty; he paid the balance of my salary, and I have a couple of hundred dollars in my pocket," said Marion.

"Two hundred dollars judiciously spent will enable you to carry on the war for some time. I was afraid you had no money, and came to request that you would make me your banker. I am a rich man, and you need but to ask me for money to obtain it in any quantity. I have had an idea of leaving the employ of Mr. Granville for some time. I shall do so at once. He has treated you so badly that it will no longer be a pleasure to remain with or be connected with him," remarked the amiable Count.

"I thank you, Count, for your generous offer—and I will add, that did I need assistance I would at once go to you for it," replied Marion.

"That is right; and now I wish to give you some advice. Don't take any situation for the present. These changes make a more sensible man. You, I dare say, Marion, think that losing your situation with Mr. Granville will be a great injury to you. No such thing. It will be of service. A young man who is in one position too long gets stereotyped. You had nothing to expect more from him. You have learned all that is to be learned in that shop. Now you must try something else. But don't be in a hurry. I have something in view for you, but my plans are not quite matured yet. As soon as they are, I shall need your services, and you will find your situation much bettered from what it was yesterday. One thing I must insist upon ; don't fall in love again with the next pretty face you meet," said the Count good-humoredly.

Here they were surprised by the entrance of a young clerk of Mr. Granville, who had been a warm friend of Marion. His eyes were sparkling with excitement, and he hastily observed,

"Well, Marion, I have got some news that I thought you would like to hear, and so I came around to tell you. I have just been to all the morning papers with an advertisement."

"What was it about, Benny ?" demanded Marion.

"It was a notice of the marriage of Miss Bell with Mr. Benson this evening ; Mr. Granville sent me with it," replied the boy named Benny.

"Oh," exclaimed the Count, I like that. That is caging the pretty bird with a vengeance. So, it is all over at last. Marion, my boy, allow me to congratulate you with all my heart. I hope you are cured now, eh ?"

Marion did not speak ; he was very pale and very angry. He walked across the room rapidly several times, ordered more punch, and then reseated himself.

"It is a bitter medicine, Count, but it is all for the best ; and as you say, I am satisfied. Thank you, Benny, for the news. Come and see me when you have a spare moment."

Benny took his leave, and soon after the Count followed his example. When Marion retired to his room that night, it was not to sleep ; his mind was too excited for that. He lay awake thinking over plans for the future ; but before any particular one to suit him had been presented to his mind's eye, he fell asleep, and it was at a late hour the next morning when he awoke. It all seemed like a dream. He hastily dressed himself, hurried down to the bar-room, snatched up a morning paper, and in it found the marriage notice alluded to by the boy Benny.

"No, no," he exclaimed, " it is no dream ; it is all true."

He read no more, but went into the dining room and ordered a cup of coffee and a light breakfast, and when he had finished this slight repast, feeling much better, he smoked a cigar, and took his way up Nassau street. Once or twice he turned about with his face towards the store. How odd it is to change our habits, and refrain from frequenting old haunts ! For years Marion's footsteps had taken him in the direction of Mr. Granville's counting room. Suddenly he found himself cut off from going there any more. He could hardly realize it, and he felt an isolation that can only be understood by those who have experienced it. He wended his way up to the Clinton Hall, in which building was the Mercantile Library Association. He had never omitted to pay his dues at that knowledge-fountain for young clerks, and had never disconnected himself from it, although for a long time he had not availed himself fully of its privileges. This morning he sauntered in, was accosted cheerfully by the librarian, and for an hour or more he amused himself by reading one of the European publications found upon its tables. Tired of this, Marion again sought the street, and passed out of the Hall by the Nassau street entrance. He halted for a moment on the step, and was accosted by a person who was passing, with a " Good morning, sir."

"Good morning," replied Marion, but at that instant he recognized the speaker, and added, " Ah, Mr. Bennett, I did not at first recognize you; how do you do, sir ?"

"Very well; and what are you doing up near little Wall street? I thought your researches did not extend above the lower Wall street," said Mr. Bennett, laughing, for he had already nicknamed Ann street, in which the Herald office was located, as ' Little Wall street.'

"I cannot say that I am connected with Wall street or Broad street any more; I am out of mercantile business," said Marion.

"Indeed! How long since ?" asked Mr. Bennett.

"Twenty-four hours," replied Marion.

Mr. Bennett added, "Then your time cannot be much occupied, and you will have leisure to go over the way to my room. Come along with me."

Marion did as Mr. Bennett desired, and went over to the editor's room. At that time, directly opposite Clinton Hall in Nassau street, there stood five brick three-story buildings, about twenty feet wide each. The lower floors were occupied as stores and the upper part as boarding houses. It was in the third building from the corner of Beckman that Mr. Bennett had his quarters Marion followed his conductor up the narrow stairs to the third floor, and into the front room overlooking Nassau street.

"This is my sanctum," said the editor, "and now take a seat and make yourself at home. I have a line to write, and then I will talk to you."

Marion glanced his eyes about the sleeping apartment of the man who was even then making himself felt in journalism. There was a maple single bedstead in one corner of the room, and between the windows was a table with but very few papers upon it; for it is a very extraordinary fact that this remarkable editor, even in after years, when an accumulation of letters and masses of manuscript read and received would have been on his hands, never appeared to have many papers about him; all were disposed of summarily and systematically, and but few papers covered his table. There were one or two books recently published, sent in to be noticed. On one corner of the table was a small pocket edition of Shakespeare, with leaves innumerable turned down as an index, and many little slips of paper markers between the leaves. The imprint was "Glasgow: 1814." The editor had now finished what he was writing, and noticing that Marion had examined the little volume, he observed, " That volume is a great favorite of mine. I value it not only as ' Shakespeare,' but as an old familiar friend. I brought it with me from Scotland. It was my only companion from Charleston here, and in many of my wanderings it has been the only book I owned, as it is now the only book I own. I would not part with it for its weight in gold.—You told me you had left commerce. How is that?"

Marion then informed him of what had passed to the extent that he had parted from Mr. Granville.

" And what do you intend to do now?" asked the editor.

" I don't exactly know. I presume I shall find some opening for me. I have served an apprenticeship of over seven years, and it would seem like folly to throw all the information I have acquired in that time away, and seek some other employment," said Marion.

" How would you like to connect yourself with newspaper life? I think you would succeed very well," observed the editor.

" Me! I never wrote a line in my life to be printed," was Marion's reply.

" It don't follow that you could *not* do it. On the contrary, I think you would write well with a little practice. Do you remember that boarding-house story you told at the dinner the day you became of age? That was very amusing. If I had it now I would publish it. If you could *write* that, precisely as you told it, it would make a capital article," said the editor.

" You flatter me, Mr. Bennett; but I am afraid I should make a poor hand at a newspaper article. I must stick to business, and I suppose I shall find something to do ere long," answered Marion.

" If you do not, come and see me," Mr. Bennett replied.

"I am rarely mistaken in my estimate of a person's ability, and I will give you a trial whenever you are so disposed. So Miss Granville is married?"

"Yes sir. She was married last night. You must have noticed it in the morning papers?" said Marion.

"I did. What passes among my friends, or my enemies, for that matter, rarely escapes my attention. I generally get hold of it early. And my white-cravated friend Wilson has also married? Why, marriage seems to be the order of the day in your quarter of the city. Bye-and-bye I suppose you will be following the example of some of these people. What has become of the Count Falsechinski? He is a very curious fellow, that," said the editor.

Marion made a reply, not noticing the marriage allusion. It was a sore subject to him; and soon after he remarked that he knew the value of an editor's time, and would not trespass longer upon it, and he took his leave. Before doing so, the editor gave him a cordial invitation to call upon him at any time he found convenient, that he should always be happy to see him. This was an invitation that Mr. Bennett gave to very few people of the tens of thousands that he came in contact with then and in after years.

That scene in a Nassau street boarding-house occurred a quarter of a century ago. That editor was as conscious of power at that time as he is now. He cared nothing for money then, save to serve the great purpose of his life, the establishment of a great independent daily journal, modelled after his own ideas of what a daily journal should be. He worked then with brain and hands—mentally and physically, to achieve success, and he succeeded. He had commenced with a partner, a stupid jackass, in Ann street. After the fire, which had burned out his establishment, Mr. Bennett started again, *alone*, with a solemn determination that for his natural life he would have no more to do with partners. He planted upon the Herald its imprint, "James Gordon Bennett, Editor and Proprietor," and it has never been changed to this day. His old partner started an opposition paper, another Herald, but that soon died out, and Mr. Bennett was in the field alone. He was not inexperienced in journalism in the city of New York, for as early as 1827 he started in Chatham Square a small daily, which he sold for one cent. It did not last long. Later he started a Sunday paper. He was for a long time connected with a paper that the celebrated Henry Eckford owned, called the National Advocate. His connection with Webb and Noah is well known. He made these men famous, and when he left the Courier and Enquirer, it was to connect himself with a daily journal in Philadelphia. From thence he came to New York, and soon after the Herald sprang into existence. Mr. Bennett was then what he has been in more mature age, quiet, reserved and thoughtful. Words may escape his memory, but *never* an idea, or a new idea. Few men can distinguish so readily the difference between mere words, however prettily expressed, and words that convey ideas. He has ever used a small memorandum book. In it he writes a catch word to a thought or an idea. This book is the key to the editorials in his paper of that or the ensuing day, or used to recall an idea, a fact, or the heading for an article weeks or months after it was noted, and eventually became the subject matter for a "leader," or a series of editorials of a thundering or startling character.

He is both shy and extremely sensitive. He admits few to any degree of intimacy with him. Those that he so selects must be original men, who are able to suggest new ideas, or strike out new and startling subjects—men who have travelled, and who can give him information upon subjects that he did not know before. All is fish that comes to his net. He values men as they contribute to the success of his journal. Personally he is as cold as an icicle. With a man of information, he will talk out an editorial in the very presence of the man who has originated the ideas or facts upon which it is based. He will enlarge upon the emanations of the minds of others so that when they read the very editorial a few days afterwards, and recognize its groundwork or base, they will be perfectly astounded at the beauty and symmetry of its appearance, its ornaments, and the genius of the entire editorial structure. If a statesman calls upon him, and he possesses genius, originality, or information of any kind, past, present or future, that is unknown to Mr. Bennett, the eyes of the latter sparkle—he moves uneasily in his chair, or rouses himself up if reclining on a sofa, and leads off in conversation until he draws his man out, and has drained him dry. Then perhaps he will talk on for his own practice, or to impress the subject more fully upon his own memory, or to shape it for an editorial. Some editors write out their thoughts—Mr. Bennett *thinks* them out, in his solitary hours, and is as ready to dictate a complete editorial from his tongue, as others were to write one. Some days a gentleman will see in the next day's Herald an analysis of his own conversation with the editor the evening previous. What he acquires from anybody goes into the editorial mind and mill, and the editorial miller grinds it and adopts it as his own, and forgets where it came from; and so completely does it become a part of himself, that he will use the identical idea or fact to the very man who gave it to him, unless perhaps he has previously used it in the Herald editorials.

Many men, or rather the vast majority of mankind who read the Herald, have no real idea of the character, mind or habits of the editor and proprietor. They regard him as a lucky individual, who as an editor has prospered in life in a financial point of view, and is enabled to cluster around him men of talent, and that these writers make the great newspaper that the Herald unquestionably is. This is true but to a very limited extent. Those men carry out ideas that originate with the proprietor. His mind is unceasing in its activity. It is never idle. He comes to his office charged with matter for his editorials. He calls in one reporter to his private sanctum. Dictating a column perhaps upon one subject, the reporter takes it down in short hand in five or ten minutes, and goes out to his desk to write it out. Another reporter succeeds him. Mr. Bennett is perhaps ten minutes more in dictating another column, upon another subject. So it goes on for an hour, until editorial articles of the highest importance are dictated. The reporters write out these articles. They are sent up to the printing office, and all the force is put on them. Mr. Bennett, if he chooses, can read the corrected proof, and yet not be detained more than an hour at the office from the time he arrived. Such are the inner workings of the Herald office.

Money, this singular man regards as dross, except so far as it contributes to the increase of his paper. Show Mr. Bennett a mode by which he could make a million certain in a speculation, and he would laugh at the proposal, but decline to have anything to do with the affair. This can be said of him with truth, that he never speculated to the extent of a dollar in his life, and never prostituted or used the columns of his paper to forward the speculations or private objects of others knowingly. Show him a working plan of type and press that would strike off a million of copies an hour, and he would buy it, if it cost a million, and would not give a penny more for it, were he guaranteed the exclusive use of it. He wants the best of everything that increases the power of the Herald, but he cares not a fig if the rival papers have the same facilities. He wants the machinery of the Herald equal to any other paper. He don't want any to exceed him, but he cares not how near

they approach him, if they have the genius and means to do so
The Herald is himself—he knows no other joy or pleasure
compared with it. It is his god—his idol—his all; and every
thing else falls below it in his mind. His is a terrible power,
and he knows it. He is conscious that every line tells upon
thousands of the human race.

He has the giant's power, but does not use it like a giant.
If Mr. Bennett had malice, he could dictate an editorial that
would set New York by the ears, and have mobs and riots
every week of his life. But no—that he does not regard as
the proper vocation of a great newspaper conductor.

We are somewhat in advance of our story, but the author
has written of a man who twenty-five years ago was what he is
now, save success—which he had not then reached. People
have an idea that the Herald twenty-five years ago was a horrible paper. It was not so, and would not appear so if the old
files were re-published to-day. When Mr. Bennett started
the Herald he published every thing that occurred or that was
talked about in the street. At that time it was an innovation
upon the old established newspaper custom, and the Herald
was regarded as an immoral publication. Now the same things
are published daily, only a hundred times worse, by every
daily paper, but nothing is thought of it.

CHAPTER XLI.

Mr. Wilson demands explanations of Mr Granville, his Partner, in respect to the discharge of Marion Monck—Mr. Granville gives them—Wilson invites Marion to his house to dine—Cordial reception by Mrs. Wilson—The bad success of Marion's friends in procuring him another clerkship—Marian becomes dissipated—Gets acquainted with Theatrical Managers and Actors—Gives suppers and dines in restaurants—The Count Fulsechinski wakes him up to a higher course.

THE sensation created upon the minds of Mr and Mrs. Wilson at their breakfast the morning after their own marriage, when they read in the morning papers of another marriage, that of young Benson with Isabella Granville, can be better imagined than described.

"Impossible! What can it mean, Richard!" exclaimed Mrs. Wilson.

Each offered half a dozen supposable cases, but none were satisfactory. At last Mr. Wilson remarked, "It is beyond my ability to solve the riddle. I know of but one way to ascertain the facts, and, my dear, as you appear to be so anxious about the matter, I will go at once and find out all about it. When I come home to dinner you shall know all."

With this understanding Mr. Wilson left home, and proceeded down town. At the head of Wall street, opposite Trinity Church, he met the Count Falsechinski. The Count immediately told Mr. Wilson all he knew about the matter. Mr. Wilson asked, " Do you mean to say that Marion Monck has been discharged from our employ by Mr. Granville?"

" In the most peremptory manner. Paid off, too. I met him at his new lodging place, for he left the house of Mr. Granville last night, bag and baggage, and took up his quarters at your old place in Maiden Lane. I think he has the identical room that you occupied when you boarded in that house," remarked the Count.

" I must see about this. It is rather a high-handed proceeding, I think, on the part of Mr. Granville, to discharge that young man and not say a word to me. I thank you, Count, for your information. We shall meet soon at the office. In the meantime, good-bye," said Mr. Wilson, and passed onward to the counting-room.

Mr. Granville had just arrived. When Mr. Wilson entered the office, he walked up to his partner and congratulated him upon the marriage of his daughter, adding, " It seems to have happened in a hurry, or I presume you would have informed me that so important an event was to take place in your family."

Mr. Granville replied, " Yes, Wilson, it was a marriage got up somewhat hastily, but I had my reasons. Walk in the private office, and I will tell you all about it."

Both partners remained closeted together for some time, and when Mr. Wilson re-appeared, he seemed worried, and not at all satisfied. He took his hat, and left the office for Maiden Lane. At the coffee-house of Clark & Brown he found Marion, who had just returned from his visit to Mr. Bennett. He put out his hand in the most cordial manner, and observed, " I hope, Marion, you do not think that I have had any hand in your abrupt dismissal from our employment."

" No indeed, sir," replied Marion. " I know to whom I am indebted, and it could not well have happened otherwise. I blame no one. Not even Mr. Granville. He has acted in the matter as he deemed would most conduce to his own happiness, and I have not a word to say. I trust it will prove for the best."

"I am rejoiced to find you take it so coolly, and like a philosopher. But what are you going to do now? You must not remain idle," said Mr. Wilson.

"I have not settled upon any definite plan. I shall be forced to remain idle for a short time at least, although I hope it will not be long, for mine is not a disposition to keep quiet. I must find some thing to do, or I shall die," replied Marion.

Mr. Wilson rejoined, "Come with me this afternoon to dinner. I will take no excuse. Mrs. Nordheim—I mean my wife—will be pleased to see you. I will not take 'No' for an answer. Go you must."

Thus invited, Marion, accompanied by Mr. Wilson, walked up town to the residence of that gentleman. Mrs. Wilson welcomed Marion cordially. Dinner was not quite ready, and Mr. Wilson unfolded his budget of news. He informed his wife of all the reasons that Mr. Granville had given for his urging on the marriage of his daughter, and for discharging Marion.

"Well, Marion, you must not let it break down your spirits. There is no remedy for you that I see. Isabella has married, Mr. Granville has discharged you from his employ, and now we must put our heads together and see if we cannot do some thing to remedy your loss of a situation. What do you say, Mr. Wilson?" asked his wife, as she made these practical observations to the discharged clerk.

Mr. Wilson replied that undoubtedly a better situation even could be obtained for Marion, but that it would take time, that he would use his utmost exertions to get him as good a situation as he had lost.

Here the servant came in to say that dinner was served, and the parties went to the table. Dinner occupied a long hour, and Mrs. Wilson did all in her power to cheer up Marion's spirits. She so far succeeded that when Marion left the house, towards evening, he promised to return again soon, and walked to his lodgings with a higher ambition to succeed in New York than he had felt for a long time.

"This trouble is only a trial of my strength of mind, perhaps, and now I can show that I am as capable of bearing adversity as prosperity," was his thought, and when he reached his lodgings he had reasoned himself into the belief that his discharge and the marriage of Isabella were two things that had occurred for his particular benefit, instead of to his injury.

Marion continued to look about him for a situation for some weeks, but without any success. He was aided by Mr. Wilson, and also by the Count Falsechinski, but the efforts of the three amounted to nothing. Marion seemed destined to remain idle. For the first time in his life, he indulged freely in all the pleasures to be derived from visiting places of amusement in New York. The place in which he lodged was frequently visited by English actors and their friends, who could there order an English beefsteak. One of those visitors, whose name was Adam Close, although an American, was an intimate friend of Brough, the English singer, who was then engaged at the Park Theatre in connection with the Woods, singing in the operas of "La Sonambula" and "Amelia." Mr. Close was also a friend of Mr. Simpson and Mr. Barry, and he introduced Marion into the interior of the old Park Theatre. In the green room he made many acquaintances. Mrs. Vernon was then in her prime. John Kemble Mason, who afterwards married the daughter of worthy old Cram, the distiller, was one of the stock actors, and an intimacy sprang up between him and Marion which continued many years afterward. Not a night passed that Marion did not attend the Theatre, both before and behind the curtain, and hardly a night passed that he did not invite some of his new species of acquaintances to a supper with him, either at "Windust's" cellar, near the Theatre, or at Salum & Suscombe's famous restaurant, which many of our readers will well remember.

Not alone did he limit his patronage to the Park Theatre. The Bowery was just then in its glory, under the regime of the renowned Hamblim. Miss Waring was the star of that establishment, and the gorgeous plays enacted at that popular haunt were a source of great attraction. Marion became well acquainted with all the popular actors and actresses on those boards, and even with the immortal Hamblin himself.

The Franklin Theatre in Chatham square was then in full blast, with William Seften as the Golden Farmer and John Seften as Jemmy Twitcher. The Olympic, with Mitchell as manager, had just commenced its career of success. A very few months of idleness made Marion well posted in the theatrical business of the town. He had acquired, in addition, another habit, that seemed to grow with what it fed on. Marion had always been abstemious in his habits so far as drinking spiritous liquors or wines was concerned. A few glasses of wine at most, would, at an earlier period, have completely upset his equilibrium, but after a few months had been spent in giving suppers and drinking parties, a few bottles would hardly disturb his nerves; and a habit of drinking was growing upon him every day. He seemed to have forgotten his old associations, or his business hopes. But this was not to last forever. He had not been forgotten by others, and one morning he was astonished by the entrance of the Count Falsechinski.

"Come, Marion, rouse up. I have work for you to do. A new chapter in life for you to open."

But before we continue this narrative, we must preface it by a history of the Count's personal operations during a period of some months. To do this, we will commence a new chapter.

CHAPTER XLII.

The Count Falsechinski's Fortunes—An Interview with old Nat Prime—The Russian Minister, Mr. Bodisco—The Count a real Count—His Narrative of Family Affairs in Poland and Russia—Confides to Mr. Prime that he loves Miss Grasper—The old banker negotiates the matter with old Mr. Grasper successfully—Astonishment of Mr. Granville when the Count leaves his employ—Draws his balance of salary and gives it to Marion Monck—The latter hires a room in the house where Mr. Bennett lodges—Visits Colonel Mac Neil at 46 Centre street—A bird's eye of the characters found there.

WE must now return to the Count Falsechinski and his success in real estate speculations. The Count had fairly gained the entire confidence of the old Wall street broker, Nat Prime. He called upon him frequently, and was always well received. Some time previous to the result of the real estate operation being known the Count asked to see Mr. Prime alone. The former had in his hands a bundle of papers and letters. When he was closeted with old Nat, and when they were not likely to be interrupted, the Count asked, "Mr. Prime, do you believe that I am a Count?"

Mr. Prime gave a sort of laugh, and answered the question by saying, "I never troubled my head much about the matter, Count, for I did not care whether you were or not. It made no difference to me."

"For that reason, my dear sir, and because you have not seemed to care, but have treated me in the most cordial manner as a *man*, without knowing any thing of my antecedents, I feel happy to be able to show you authentic documents proving who and what I am. I could not do so until this morning, when the mail brought me a letter from Mr. Bodisco, the Russian Minister at Washington. Will you read this letter?" asked the Count, as he passed a letter to the old man.

Mr. Prime received it into his hands, looked it over a moment, and observed, "Count, this is all, Greek to me. I can't read Russian, Polish, or whatever language this letter is written in. You must translate it for me."

"I forgot, Mr. Prime. The letter from Mr. Bodisco is written in the French language. I will translate it for you."

"Do so, and it will answer all necessary purposes," was the reply of Mr. Prime.

The Count continued: "Before I do this, Mr. Prime, I must mention some facts connected with my family interest. I am a younger brother of one of the oldest families in poor Poland. My brother Stanislaus took an active part in a rising against Russia some years ago. He was seized, and exiled to Siberia. I was a mere lad at the time, and perhaps might have shared his fate, had not a friend of my father at some risk to himself protected and educated me. I was forgotten until I had grown to be a young man, when accident revealed to the authorities at Warsaw who I really was. I barely escaped with my life, and reached England safely. I soon after came to this country, and then I swore a solemn oath that I would not eat, drink, or do any thing that involved expense, except to barely keep life in my body until I acquired sufficient funds to pay whatever fines the Russian government might inflict upon me, in order that I might then be restored to my position in society, and be enabled to return to my own country without danger to my life or to my liberty. My brother had no children; but as there was no pardon for him, no hope of clemency from the emperor in his behalf, it perhaps was lucky for me that his death, which became known at St. Petersburg about eighteen months ago, placed me at the head of my family, and enabled me to treat for restoration to my own rights. A powerful friend of mine in the Russian capital went to work faithfully for my interest. Letters upon letters have passed. I have given the most solemn assurance to the Russian government of my devotion. The result of all this is that I am fully restored to my true rank, or the rank that my brother held before his unfortunate patriotic failure, and without any conditions except the payment of a fine which amounts to about twenty-two thousand dollars of your money, which has been imposed upon me. The matter is now in the hands of the Russian Minister at Washington. I have to arrange the financial part with him, and he will send the same to the European Government. In less than a year all obstacles will be removed. I shall be once more upon a good footing with the Government—the head of my own family, and be the manager of the family estate in Poland of the Falsechinski's This is the purport of the Ambassador's letter, dated at Washington."

"What is the income of the estates of your family, Count?" asked the banker.

The Count replied, "Before they were confiscated and my brother exiled, the revenue was almost princely—I believe as high as twenty-five thousand pounds sterling. But I have no idea that they can now be anything like that amount, even under the most favorable circumstances. Be these revenues small or great, is not the question. I want to be a man once more in the land of my birth, instead of a wanderer; I wish to hold my true rank and position, even if the revenue were not one cent," said the Count.

"Right, perfectly right, Count; you are a man, every inch of you, and I am glad you have told me this. What can I do to aid you?" asked Mr. Prime.

"You can draw a check to the order of M. Bodisco, and I will remit it to him. This check will be returned to you after it has been paid at the bank, will it not?" asked the Count.

"Aha! my Count. I see what you are driving at. It will be evidence that you have paid the money, in case the Russian Minister proves tricky, eh?" said Mr. Prime.

"He may not acknowledge receipt of the money, and as you say, Mr. Prime, the check with his endorsement would be pretty conclusive evidence that he had got it, but I hope there will never be any necessity to use it against him," was the remark of the Count.

"There is nothing like being on the safe side with those diplomatic chaps. They are an uncertain set. More so than common counts and humbugs. Excuse me, Count; I did not mean you. But to tell you the truth, Count, I have always regarded you as a sharp, shrewd, intelligent man. I always liked you, but until this morning I fancied that so far as your Countship was concerned, that it was all humbug. But I did not like you the worse for it, and I can't say that I shall like you any better for knowing that you are a real, instead of a sham Count," said Mr. Prime.

The Count bowed, but did not make a reply. He knew that he had raised himself full one hundred per cent. in the banker's estimation by what he had stated, for the old gentleman was a real admirer of aristocracy, let it belong to what country it might. The Count had not done yet.

"Mr. Prime," he asked, "how does my account stand with you since the sale of the real estate?"

The banker made no reply, but rose and walked to the door. He opened it and called "Mr. Christmas," and then reseated himself. A moment elapsed, and the employee answering to the name of Christmas made his appearance.

"What balance has the Count in our hands in cash, and what securities also?" asked the banker.

"Shall I make out his account with the interest added to his credit?" asked the bookkeeper.

"No, no. Simply the balance, without interest. That can be made up at any time, and, by the way, draw a check for twenty-two thousand dollars to the order of Mr. Bodisco, the Russian Minister at Washington," ordered the banker.

"Make it twenty-five thousand dollars," remarked the Count, and turning to Mr. Prime, he added, "It is better to make it somewhat larger than the exact amount. It will do no harm. Although a minister cannot be bribed, yet it don't do any harm to have two or three thousand dollars in his hands. He may have expenses to incur, eh, Mr. Prime?" quietly observed the Count.

Both laughed heartily, and the expression of their faces would seem to imply that they had no idea that the Russian Minister would ever return any change on the twenty-five thousand dollar check. Presently the bookkeeper returned and stated, "The Count has a cash balance to his credit on our books of one hundred and six thousand dollars; less this check of twenty-five thousand dollars, it is eighty-one thousand dollars. We also hold bond a mortgage for one hundred and fifty thousand dollars, bearing interest at seven per cent., payable semi-annually."

"Thank you. That is all, Mr. Christmas," said Mr. Prime, and the bookkeeper returned, and the old banker turned to the Count. "Pretty snug, that, Count. Eighty-one thousand at four per cent. is three thousand two hundred and forty dollars, and seven per cent. on one hundred and fifty thousand dollars, is ten thousand five hundred dollars. Total, thirteen thousand seven hundred and forty dollars. Nearly fourteen thousand per annum, Count, is a nice little income for any single man, and can be increased still more. Count, when you go back to Europe, I suppose you will be marrying some of those blooded dames, eh?"

"Really, Mr. Prime, I cannot say; but you will laugh at me if I confide a little secret to you," replied the Count.

"Not a bit—not a bit of it. Tell me your secret. Some love scrape, eh? Some pretty girl in your eye, eh?" and the old banker rubbed his hands with delight.

The Count saw his advantage at once, and he had a plan fully matured in his own mind. He needed the assistance of Mr. Prime to carry it out to a successful conclusion.

"Ah, Mr. Prime, you have guessed my secret. I am in love with a beautiful young lady, but I have no hopes. She is not within my reach," said the Count, in a very humble tone.

"Not within your reach? How the d—l is that? You have a capital of nearly two hundred and fifty thousand dollars, that I know. You are a Count. You are very good looking. You are intelligent, and how is she not within your reach? Perhaps the lady is already married," said the banker.

"Oh, no, sir. She is single, and her father is a particular friend of yours," replied the Count.

"Indeed. Who is she? Tell me her father's name. Perhaps I can give you a helping hand in the matter, eh? Do you know her well? How long have you been acquainted with her?" hurriedly asked the banker, who was now fully interested in the affair.

"I am not even acquainted with the lady to speak to her. I have met her on one occasion, but she was so far above me that I did not dream of ever being able to aspire to her hand. With your aid, Mr. Prime, the case is different. Her name is Irene Grasper, and she is the daughter of your friend Mr. Grasper. There, the secret is out, and I hope safe in your keeping," said the Count.

"Safe, my dear boy, as a rat in a trap. Above you, man alive! No such thing. She shall be yours. I will make it my business to see her father. You are no humbug. You have got the tin, the solid rocks, and he must pint, too, if you marry his daughter," said the banker.

"My dear sir, I do not mean to marry for money. Never dreamed of such a thing," and the Count could hardly keep his countenance, for it *was* the money that the Count had in view. He had a list of all the young ladies of property in New York. He had corrected and altered it for three years according to circumstances. He had made up his mind to marry a fortune, and to go through with the entire list, one by one, until he married the richest that he could get out of the lot. Miss Grasper was A No. 1 on the list. The old man was reputed to be worth a million, and this was an only daughter. To the Count's reply that he never dreamed of such a thing as marrying for money, the old banker remarked that he was a fool if he did not.

"I'll tell you what it is, Count—that is all very fine on your part, but you have consulted me in this matter, and I am your banker. I will not permit you to be imposed on. You have, as I said before, a title and the hard stuff. If you marry my old friend's daughter, he shall come down handsomely. He shall put up the solid. I think he ought to give his daughter as much as you can show. Leave that all to me. Do you secure the girl, I will arrange the matter with my old crony. You have got nearly two hundred and fifty thousand dollars that I can vouch for, Count. Suppose old John don't or won't agree to plank down for his daughter that sum. What shall I do then?" asked Mr. Prime.

"Excuse me, Mr. Prime, but the idea of mixing up money matters in an affair of the heart really shocks me, but if you insist upon my saying some thing, I will only say I leave it entirely in your hands. I think if he gives any thing to his daughter, he ought to secure her one hundred and fifty thousand dollars in your hands the moment she is married to me. You arrange it for her secretly. I don't want the money—don't need it," said the Count.

"Say no more, Count He shall do it. You are as liberal as a prince, and I will see that you are not imposed upon, and now I am going to bid you good-morning, Count, come down to No. 1 Broadway to-morrow and dine with me. I don't *say*, but I think you will find some body there that you will be pleased to see," said the banker.

The Count Falsechinski took his hat, and left the banker's office, after having politely accepted the invitation to dine. When he was clear of the premises, he walked down to Delmonico's and ordered a cup of coffee and a cigar, and while sipping the one and puffing the other, his reflections were of a very pleasant character. Occasionally he rubbed his hands and shrugged his shoulders as he counted up the success of his plans. "The remittance to the Minister will place my affair right in Russia. So much for *that* business. I will make love to Miss Grasper. Her papa, under Mr. Prime's tuition, will settle one hundred and fifty thousand dollars, or about ten thousand dollars a year on her. My own income will make it up to twenty-five thousand dollars. With that and my affair all arranged, I will return to Poland, and there I will live like a prince, I will be somebody. The income of my own hereditary property—bah! I am afraid that my titles would be a poor concern, if they depended upon the income of my Polish property, without other sources of income. But now I must finish up my career mercantile at once—bring it to an end to-day. It may excite wonder in old European minds why I am a clerk; and until my object is achieved in that quarter, I will end it." These were the unspoken thoughts of the worthy Count. When he had finished his coffee and cigar, he went around to the office of Granville & Wilson, in Broad street. The two partners were conversing together when the Count approached them.

"Gentlemen," said he, "I have to thank you for all your kindness to me while in your employ: and I am grieved to say that I must leave your employment to-day."

Both partners stood in amazement. The Count continued:

"I am restored to my rank and position in Poland by the act of His Imperial Majesty, who imposes upon me a small fine of twenty-five thousand dollars, which I have just received from my bankers, Prime, Ward & King, and which I must to-day send to the Russian Ambassador at Washington."

Here the Count carelessly displayed the check, and Mr. Granville took it into his hands; and after gazing at it in stupid silence, passed it over to Mr. Wilson.

"I have in my banker's hands, in cash and good securities, about two hundred and fifty thousand dollars—so you see that I can get along very well. I would remain with you longer, but I must make my preparations to go to Russia and take my place—my real position—and manage my estates, which have been very long neglected. Will you give me a check for what may be due me—it is not much," added the Count.

The conversation of the Count was like the shock of an electric battery. Mr. Granville was astonished;—Mr. Wilson was less so, and coolly made up the account of the Count, and drew a check for three hundred and twenty dollars.

"That is the amount due you, Count," remarked Mr. Wilson; "will you sign a receipt for it?"

Meanwhile Mr. Granville recovered his speech, and listened to further explanations about the Count's affairs. When the receipt was signed, the Count again thanked the two partners, and took his departure. They looked at each other for some time in silence.

"That is a rum chicken, that Count, but I can hardly believe that he is humbugging us. That check at least was genuine. Two hundred and fifty thousand dollars in Prime & Co.'s hands! Impossible! Good God, if I had but known that!" exclaimed Mr. Granville.

Mr. Wilson did not seem at all surprised, and when Mr. Granville observed that he meant to see one of the firm that day, and ask if what the Count had stated was true, Mr. Wilson remarked that it was useless—that he knew he had money there. This did not discourage Mr. Granville, for ere two hours had passed, he had ascertained from Mr. King that the Count Falsechinski had kept an account there for years, and that he had over two hundred thousand dollars in their hands; and Mr. King added, that if Mr. Granville thought of having any financial transactions with the Count, he would find him perfectly safe to an unlimited amount.

Mr. Granville returned to his own office mortified to a degree that he could hardly have believed. "I did not believe, Wilson, that the man had five hundred cents;" and then he muttered something about locking the stable door after the horse was stolen, implying that he had had it in his power to have made a warm friend of the Count, but had neglected to do so, until the time had arrived when the Count was in such a pleasant position that he needed no friends. "What a most consummate ass I have been," was the only consolation that Mr. Granville could find for what he deemed the most stupid stupidity. It was too late, however, to mend matters fully, but Mr. Granville resolved to do the best that he could under the circumstances, which was to be extremely civil to the Count, and trust to chance for the result.

The Count, when he left the office of Mr. Granville, proceeded directly to Clark & Brown's, in Maiden Lane. As we have related, there he found Marion, somewhat depressed in spirits, and he addressed him in a cheerful manner.

"Cheer up, my boy, and open a new chapter. Have you a pen and ink handy?"

Marion procured him one from a little desk in one corner of the room. The Count seated himself at the table, and took out the check for three hundred and twenty dollars that he had received from Granville & Wilson. He indorsed it, for it was drawn to order, and passed it over to Marion, saying pleasantly,

"Will you go and get that money, Marion?"

"Certainly. Shall I bring it back to you? Will you wait?" replied Marion.

"No—I have not time," said the Count.

"What shall I do with the money, then?"

"Put it in your pocket, my dear boy, for it is yours. Don't

bother me. Spend it, and when you want more, let me know. I have got work for you to do, but not quite yet. You must get out of this hole. I don't like it. Can't you find no other place to live in except this?" asked the Count.

Marion replied that he could and would that day. "Count, you do not know how you have relieved my mind. I have no money left. I could not have paid the very trifling amount I owe here, but for your kindness. How shall I repay it?" asked Marion, feelingly.

"It has already been paid to me in advance, Marion, by you. Now I will repay you some part of the large debt which I owe you. I am not quite ready yet. When you have selected a new place, write me a line to that effect, and leave it at Prime, Ward & King's. I have left Granville & Co. That check was for a balance due me, and closed my account there forever. God bless you, my boy—take care of yourself! You will be all right before long;" and with these hopeful words, the Count left.

"I have one friend left, and I will do at once what he recommends—but first to draw the money," said Marion to himself. He went at once, and received the money for the check. Then it occurred to him, that when long previous he had called upon Mr. Bennett at his room in Nassau street, he had noticed a bill upon the house, with "Rooms to let." He hurried up there. First, he inquired for Mr. Bennett. He was still residing in the house, but was at his office. Then he engaged the back room on the same floor, and paid a month's board in advance. This done, he proceeded to Clark & Brown's, paid his bill, got a cartman, and took his baggage to his new quarters. The next step was to write a note to the Count, informing him of his new location, and this he took to Prime & Co.'s office, and left it.

It was late in the afternoon before Marion had concluded his work. He went at once to No. 46 Centre street. There he found Colonel Mac Neil, with whom he had retained an intimacy during all this period. Mac Neil had been a true friend; and the young clerk had the good sense to respect him more in his fallen fortunes, than when he knew him prosperous and successful. A man of the world like Colonel Mac Neil had it in his power to give many instructive examples to a youth like Marion, and he had not failed to do so upon every occasion. At this visit, however, Marion seemed possessed of the attributes of manhood. He shook hands with the Colonel. There were many in that room, for it was the holiday season, and Marion asked all hands up to drink, and then he sat down by Mac Neil

"Colonel, this is a funny world, is it not? Queer changes occur;" he remarked.

"Just found it out?" abruptly asked the Colonel.

"This morning I was dead broke—not a red. Owed Clark & Brown nineteen dollars. Look here;" and Marion, as he spoke, exhibited a roll of money.

"Put that up at once," said Mac Neil, sternly. "You do not know who may notice it. Never show money—no gentleman does so. Besides, in such a place as this it is dangerous. It might cost you the loss of the money and a broken skull. There are men in this room at this moment who would not hesitate to give you a clip over the head for the sake of a five dollar gold piece; but tell me all about this sudden change of fortune."

Marion related all to him. He only replied, "That Count is a deep one. I never could make him out satisfactorily to myself. I ever believed him to be a sharper and a sham. I may be mistaken. That three hundred and twenty dollar check would lead me to a different conclusion."

"Colonel, will you not be angry with me if I presume to do something?" asked Marion, in a very apologetic voice.

"I am not apt to get angry with you, my boy," replied Colonel Mac Neil.

"I want you to take fifty dollars of this money. I counted it out before I came in here, and I have placed it in my side pocket—here it is;" and as he spoke he poured the money into the hands of the Colonel. The tears started in the old man of the world's eyes as he received the money.

"What do you wish me to do with it?" he asked.

"Keep it, to be sure. I thought it might serve you, and I might throw it away. If I should need it, I will come to you," observed Marion, delicately.

"Upon such conditions then I accept it. Wait a moment." The Colonel passed to the bar, and spoke a few words to Henry, the proprietor, and handed him the money. Then he returned to the side of Marion. The latter remarked,

"Colonel, you seem to know this crowd, or they all know you. Who are they?"

"I will ask them all up to take another drink, and then I will tell you," replied the Colonel.

This was accordingly done, and the Colonel continued:

"Notice that stout man who is seated upon a barrel, talking

so loudly. That is fighting Charley—one of the worst men in the Sixth Ward. He has been engaged in several prize fights. The one talking to him is Parson Charley. He is so nicknamed because his brother is one of the most famous assistant rectors of Trinity Church in this city. That red-faced seedy-looking young man is Theodore Van Ness—one of the richest young men at twenty-one years old in Dutchess county. He is now a beggar. That crazy, wild-looking genius, who has a torn blue coat with brass buttons, was in the Tombs all last night. His father once commanded a ship out of this port. She was chartered to take out provisions to the Greek patriots in 1828. His uncle owns the Waverley House down Broadway, and is one of the richest men in town. He has a firm called Fitch Brothers & Co. in Marseilles, France. The uncle's name is Asa Fitch."

"Who is the venerable old man with gray hair who is talking to him, Colonel?" asked Marion.

"That is Pop Junk. He keeps a junk shop down near the Five Points. He has been in the State Prison for ten years, but is now rich. Curious characters come here," continued Mac Neil, "but they are hardly worth knowing, except to one who is old and experienced enough not to be injured by coming in contact with such people."

Marion remained with the Colonel until evening, and then bade him good night and went to his new boarding-house.

CHAPTER XLIII.

Old Mr. Prime and Mr. Grasper—The Count to marry Irene Grasper—The Dinner at Mr. Prime's—Satisfaction all around.

No sooner had the Count Falsechinki left the banking house of Prime, Ward & King, than the senior partner of that great firm took his hat, and soon after could have been found in the directors' room of one of the principal city banks. He was one of the directors of the institution, and Mr. John Grasper was another. Soon after the latter arrived, and the two old millionaires were engaged in a very earnest conversation. Now and then a sudden but very emphatic exclamation could have been heard from Grasper.

"What! a real Count? None of those impostors!—are you sure of it?"

Then Mr. Prime's low tones assured his friend that of this there was not a shadow of a doubt. Again Grasper would open his lips—

"Income of his estate twenty-five thousand pounds sterling —impossible!"

But when he was again assured that whatever might be the income of the Count's estates in Poland, there was no mistake in the fact that the firm held cash and securities to the extent of a quarter of million of dollars, his astonishment seemed to have reached a climax, for he was perfectly silent. There was no occasion for expressing incredulity in a financial matter, when Mr. Nat Prime stood ready to guarantee it.

It was some moments before the parties opened their mouths again, when the celebrated banker continued the conversation—

"Yes, Grasper, my old friend, the best you can do. You say your daughter has no previous attachment."

"None that I know of. In fact I am quite sure not, and I have no particular objection that it shall be a match if all that you say of this Count proves true," said Grasper, in a very quiet manner.

"If!" exclaimed Mr. Prime with some spirit—"do you doubt my word, old friend?"

"Not in the least, but it is a large sum, a very large sum. A quarter of a million! And suppose these two young people should become attached, what would I be expected to do?—that is, what sum would I have to settle on my daughter?" asked his companion.

"Now you begin to talk up to the mark; why, I suppose the advantage of noble blood and all that sort of thing, you ought to put down as much cash on the nail as your future son-in-law can show, eh?" said the banker.

"I shall do nothing of the kind, but I will do this; if you will satisfy me that this Count *has* all you say, *is* all you say, I will put down as the portion of my daughter one hundred and fifty thousand dollars when the parties are married," said the other.

"Do I understand you to mean that you will give it to her, out and out?" demanded the banker.

"Not exactly. I will place that sum in the hands of your house to be invested in a manner most satisfactory to the Count. The property or the income to be used by the married couple, and to go to any children that my daughter may have by the Count," said Mr. Grasper.

"No, no, that won't do. It is not fair for the Count; give it out and out to your daughter when she marries him: I will see that it is properly invested. Don't tie them up. If the Count were a beggar it would be different, but he is not. He is amply provided for, worth all or more than I tell you, and the amount that you give to your daughter under the existing circumstances should not be encumbered with conditions. You are not going to live forever, and you will have a nice sum to leave somebody when you die. Use your judgment when you come to making your will. Then you can settle upon your daughter what you think fit," shrewdly observed the banker.

"Right, old friend. I am satisfied that your advice is good. Now when shall I see my future son-in-law?" asked the old man.

"I will have him on the course to-morrow, and you can trot out your filly at the same time—that is to say, come and dine with me to-morrow, and bring Irene with you; I will have the Count there," was the answer.

"I will come; and now let us shake hands upon our agreement; I am much obliged to you for proposing it," observed Mr Grasper.

"Wait a while until you see how the new team work in harness. Then thank me if you are satisfied with the match."

The two worthies parted mutually satisfied. Mr. Prime sometimes talked "stable." Some people made the assertion that before he entered into the brokerage and banking business, that he had been hostler to old Billy Grey, a quiet merchant in Boston; whether true or not is no affair of ours. He did frequently use language that smacked of the stable; and upon one occasion, when a friend asked kindly after one of his own family who had been sick, Mr. Prime replied, "She is better, thank you, but she has not come to her feed yet." Mr. Prime also prided himself upon his knowledge of horse-flesh, but he did not boast of it much after a terrific sell was perpetrated upon him. He was shown a white horse, beautifully variegated with coal-black spots, and his owner called him the "leopard horse." He sold him to the old gentleman at an enormous price—some say two thousand dollars. After a while Mr. Prime began to believe that the Bible, when it asked if the leopard could change his spots, implying that he could not do it, was sadly mistaken—for his leopard horse did change his spots, or rather all the beautiful spots washed off, and the horse was nothing more nor less than a plain white one. But the banker was a good old soul after all, and did many a kind act equal in benevolence to his friendship for the Count.

The succeeding day the Count Falsechinski met at the dinner table of the old banker, Mr. Grasper and his daughter. The fair Irene was even more stately beautiful than when we described her appearance at a party given by Mrs. Nordheim.— She was accomplished in almost every variety of the so-called female accomplishments. She spoke Italian and French equally well, and much to the delight of her parent, she maintained a long and animated conversation with the Count in both of these languages. After dinner was finished, while the two old fogies remained at their wine, the Count excused himself and joined Miss Irene at the piano. There was a guitar by the side of the piano, which the Count took in charge, and played with exquisite taste and feeling, while he sang several charming odes. They were much pleased with each other, and the old people noticed this fact with great pleasure.

When Mr. Grasper and his daughter got ready to leave, the Count asked permission to accompany them, and it was readily granted, and on the arrival of the party at the father's splendid residence, the Count received an invitation to enter, and spend the remainder of the evening. The Count wondered whether his intentions were known to the fair damsel. Mr. Prime had taken him aside at his residence and informed him that he had come to an understanding with Mr. Grasper, and that if the Count succeeded in obtaining the consent of the daughter, that the father would give his child one hundred and fifty thousand dollars. This was very gratifying news to the Count, and it gave an impetus to his attentions to Miss Irene Irene Grasper, which bid fair to win success. The Count need have had no fear that old Mr. Grasper had communicated any part of what he had heard from Mr. Prime to any member of his family. He was too much a man of the world, and knew human character too well to be guilty of any such gross act. He knew his child possessed an independent spirit, and he left the Count to conquer it, and to win the young lady's affections by his own merits.

When the Count left that evening he was well pleased with his day's work, but he added, " I am really in love myself.— She is just the tall, stately woman I have always had in view as my Countess whenever I married. What a sensation she will create in Paris, Warsaw, or even St. Petersburgh. I am a lucky dog if I win her, even had I not the assurance of the trifling sum that will become hers whenever our nuptials are celebrated."

He dreamed of Irene Grasper that night when he went to sleep.

CHAPTER XLIV.

Mrs. Woodruff—Her House—Her great Game in New York Life—Modes of Capture—Miss Norris a great Card—Jane Graham Weston—A Horrid Story—Her Death, leaving Sixty Thousand Dollars—Mrs. Miller, the Mother of Miss Josephine Clifton—The study of Character and Life, by Miss Norris.

MRS. WOODRUFF pursued the even tenor of her way in Bond street, respected by all in her church, and all those with whom she came in contact who did not know her real character, or that she was a "whited sepulchre." She had long since quarrelled with the Count Falsechinski, or rather that noble individual, after the Parker affair, consulted his prudence and cut the good lady's acquaintance. Such sort of proceedings as those connected with Mrs. Parker and her daughter, assisted by Mr. O'Doemall, the Count deemed extremely dangerous; and after levying what he thought a fair tax upon such fair sinners, he withdrew from the connexion.

But the business of Mrs. Woodruff did not diminish. Her horses pranced more proudly than ever as they whirled her carriage down Broadway, or out upon the avenues. No grander equipage rested for its mistress at the portals of God's fashionable sanctuary, Grace Church, than the widow's. A coat-of-arms was neatly emblazoned upon the panels of the carriage, and her coachman and footman both wore costly liveries.

Her visitors increased. Ladies from the South, accompanied by their husbands, and who stopped at the leading hotels, left their cards at Mrs. Woodruff's, and frequently called. Such ladies as were disposed to criminal indulgence, either to gratify their passions or to increase their pecuniary resources, found a friend in Mrs. Woodruff. Her correspondence was extensive. Her acquaintance with the old roués and men of wealth seemed almost incredible.

One of the most gifted, beautiful and fascinating ladies on Mrs. Woodruff's list was Clara Norris. To her gentlemen customers pious Mrs. Woodruff represented Clara as one of the most fashionable and virtuous young married ladies in the city. She was the beautiful "Mrs. Sinclair," the accomplished "Mrs. Percy," or the wealthy "Mrs. Jones,". as occasion served. When Mrs. Woodruff wished to make a deep impression, and had a wealthy man in tow, she would promise to introduce "Mrs. Sinclair" to the party. "But you had better see her first. I will get her to take a seat in my pew at Grace Church next Sunday." Then the rich fool who was to be victimized would watch the descent of the widow and Clara at the church door next Sunday. He would see a young, and as he supposed married lady, glowing with beauty, meekly entering a church to pay her morning devotions. He could hardly believe it possible that his good fortune was so great as to be able to secure so much beauty; and when he went to Mrs Woodruff to make his financial arrangements, the worthy would name as the price of the interview, in consequence of the great risk, or the difficulty of approaching the lady, who had plenty of money, or some other cause, the sum of five hundred dollars for an interview of an hour. She never named less than one hundred dollars—and whether the sum was the larger or the smaller amount, or an intervening sum, the honest woman divided it fairly with Clara Norris.

Clara was a great card for the widow, and the game between them was played for a long time with such success, that Clara would have been a constant visitor at the house, had not the parties limited her acquaintance within bounds. Some of those gentlemen who made her acquaintance wished it continued from day to day, at even *such* enormous prices, but the prudent and pious widow was made of sterner stuff—her rule was made, and it was as unalterable as the laws of the Medes and Persians, which her minister read about—and even the five hundred dollar customer considered himself fortunate if he succeeded in seeing the fascinating syren more than once in a fortnight. This game would have continued for years, had not Clara herself finished it, by becoming a frequenter of houses of ill-fame of the first class down town.

In Duane street, No. 106, resided for a great many years a most extraordinary female, of the name of Jane Graham, alias Jane Graham West. It was the misfortune of Miss Norris to become acquainted with this lady, whose memoirs would fill a book. At that time, her house was the first in New York. It was visited by the most aristocratic, old and young, citizen or stranger. The house is still standing—a three story house, not far from Broadway, on the North river side. In this den, in one of the largest and most splendidly furnished apartments in the house, was Clara Norris induced to take up her abode for a long time. Her fame soon spread, and hundreds, yea thousands visited the house for the purpose of seeing the accomplished and widely talked of Clara Norris.

The keeper of the house could play no tricks upon Clara—she was as shrewd as Jane Graham herself. She paid for her board twenty-five dollars per week—and the harvest left to Mrs. Graham was the immense quantities of wines sold to the visitors brought to the house to see Clara—and the sums she herself received were enormous. It was a gay life, and she liked it; and although she remained at the head of the first-class ladies of Mrs. Woodruff's house, she did not like that mode of life as well as the one she led with Mrs. Graham. Clara Norris liked the society of the house where she lived. She reigned a queen, and all bowed to her supremacy. She thought that such a life would last forever—but after six months' residence in that establishment, she had a quarrel with Mrs. Graham and left her. She then visited for a few days her parents' home, and carried up with her savings bank credits for a very large sum of money, obtained in the residence of Mrs. Graham, and from her occasional visits to Mrs. Woodruff. She cleared in this business in the space of nine months over ten thousand dollars, and presents of jewelry that almost equalled that amount. She never varied from one purpose. However careless or dissipated, she did not neglect visits to the savings bank once a week, and the sums she deposited were never equalled by any woman of her class. She invariably visited the bank alone, and kept her bank book from all eyes but her own. When she visited her father she showed it to him, and sometimes would say, "Father, if ever I should die, look out for this bank book, and claim it on call at the bank, and claim it as my heir." Her prudent lawyer in Newton was informed of the amount she had in bank. He explained to her how much better it was to have it in a safer way. She paid his expenses, and he came to New York. Under his direction, she became the owner of two small brick houses in one of the cross streets below Canal, that ran from Broadway to the North river.

When the purchase of the houses had been completed, and the deeds taken out in her name had been recorded, he took them with him to Sussex, and deposited them in his iron safe. The rents from these two houses was nine hundred dollars.

The worthy Jane Graham was very loth to part with Miss

Norris. "Better stay, Clara; you are the best card I ever had in my house. I am rich—I will leave you my business, and if I die, as I have no heirs, you shall be my heiress."

Clara turned a deaf ear to these proposals. Yet Jane Graham West could have made all good. She owned at that time fifty thousand dollars in United States Bank stock, and was worth an equal sum in other property. She made it in that business, and although she held on to her United States Bank stock until it was worthless, yet she seemed no poorer. She fell in love with a young mate of one of the Havre packet ships, named Frederick Hewitt. He promised the old dame marriage, and she bought him one-half of the ship Manhattan, and made him captain of her. He refused to marry her after he became a commander, and married a young lady in Mobile. Jane Graham sued him for a breach of promise of marriage, and one of the most ridiculous law trials took place between these parties that ever occurred in any country. The lady recovered six cents damages, and the captain a ridiculous notoriety that followed him to the grave. He did not live long afterwards, and the lady, Jane Graham, after the loss of her United States Bank stock, took it into her head that she was *beggared*, and never held up her head more. She was abandoned by all of her girls, and left alone in that large house, her only companion being a negro hag.

Jenny Graham was found strangled one morning. It was a question whether the deed was done by the negro woman or by Jenny herself; but as the latter had frequently threatened to put an end to her own life, the negress got the benefit of it. Her two nephews turned up, and although they came into possession of over sixty thousand dollars each, from Jenny's death, and were miserably poor before it happened, yet the ungrateful wretches boxed her up in a wooden coffin, and sent her without expense to Potter's Field. Such was the end of a remarkable woman, who for many years was a warm friend and a great admirer of Clara Norris.

When Miss Norris returned from her home, after her quarrel with Jane Graham, she made a short stay at the palace of Mrs. Woodruff. But it was too gloomy for her—more especially as she had now got a taste for a free and easy life.

"I must follow the bent of my inclinations, and I cannot help it, good woman," was her reply to Mrs. Woodruff, who in vain remonstrated with Clara Norris against her becoming a public character.

"You will ruin yourself, body and soul. You will spoil

your market, my beauty, and that will be the upshot of this business," observed Mrs. Woodruff.

"Can't help it—can't help it, if I die for it.

"'There is a destiny that shapes our ends,
Rough hew them as we will,'

as Shakespeare says, and mine is fixed, Mrs. Woodruff. I must pursue my own career."

And true enough, a few days after this conversation Miss Norris was a resident in a house of a lower grade than that of Jane Graham. She went to reside with Mrs. Miller, one of the most extraordinaay women of her class in New York. When Miss Norris went with her, the age of the old lady was fast verging upon seventy years.

About this time Clara met the Count Falsechinski in the street. He stopped, and politely accosted her. She gave him her address—"Mrs. Miller, No. 114 Church street." The Count looked at it a moment.

"Good God, Miss Norris! Are you in that house from necessity, or to please yourself?" he asked.

"To gratify my own curiosity, Count," she replied. "I want to get acquainted with this woman. She is a study to me. Do you know, Count, that she is the mother of Josephine Clifton, the great actress? Do you know, also, that she is the mother of Miss Missouri, that Hamlin is just bringing out, and who promises to be equal in genius and talent to her splendid sister, Josephine?"

"Indeed, Miss Clara, I did not know it. But I must say good-bye—I will call and see you ere long;" and the Count passed on.

"Afraid to be seen speaking to me in the street," remarked Miss Norris, after the Count's sudden departure. "Well, it is the way of the world. I ought not to have expected different treatment."

For some months Miss Norris was a resident of Mrs. Miller's, but she found the old lady a miserly old woman, without one redeeming feature. She became acquainted with one of her sons named Nelson Miller, on whom the old woman lavished her affections and her money. Clara became disgusted with the old woman, and again made a removal, but this time it was back to Mrs. Woodruff's, where we shall for the present leave her.

CHAPTER XLV.

Home of Mr. Granville—Happiness of the Young Couple. Mr. and Mrs. Benson—Young Benson Goes into Business—Depressed State of Mind of Miss Margaret Benson.

The marriage of Middleton Benson to Isabella Granville, although a very sudden affair, seemed to give the fathers of the young couple the most unbounded satisfaction. Mr. Granville gave up his house to the young people, and even went so far as to deed to them all the costly furniture that it contained. Colonel Benson was not behind hand. He made the bride the most costly presents, and so far as household furniture was concerned, he purchased a sufficient quantity to have started a dozen new married couples in all necessary articles for housekeeping. Spacious and roomy as was the old State street mansion, yet every room was crowded with furniture, and presented an odd mixture of old and new fashions.

The young couple appeared very happy. Isabella did not seem to have lost any portion of her gaiety, and her laugh was as merry and cheering as of old. Their appearance seemed to confirm the father in his belief that all he had done had been for the best. Middleton Benson, his son-in-law, had been admitted a partner into the commercial firm where he had been so long a clerk, and his father retired from it, giving to his son the interest and the capital that belonged to him as a partner. Every few evenings the two fathers would meet, and over a bottle or two of choice wine would congratulate themselves upon the happy results of their proceedings. From Mrs. Thomas Granville they had not heard except indirectly. She was living with her aged grandmother, and long since had succeeded in obtaining from the Maryland Legislature an act which divorced her from her husband, but the departure of Mrs. Granville had not altered Mr. Pitt Granville's domestic arrangements. He never spoke of her to his daughter—never missed her. She had attempted to interfere with his domestic purposes, and to use his own expressive sentence to Colonel Benson, "I kicked her out of the house, and that is the end of her so far as I am concerned."

There was one chosen old friend that Mr. Granville missed sadly. It was Colonel Mac Neil. He even went so far as to send a note to the Colonel, inviting him to renew his intimacy. The Colonel was poor, but he was a proud man. He could not get over the fact that in the dire extremity to which his firm was reduced, Granville, his *friend*, had refused relief, and at a moment so late that his failure was the consequence.

"It might have happened later," would the Colonel reason, "but then, that probability ought not to weigh in favor of Granville's course. He did refuse me a small loan which he had promised, and even if he had lost it all, what was that to him?"

The Colonel sternly resisted all overtures, and took no notice of Mr. Granville's note, except to exhibit it to every mutual friend that he met. Not only did Colonel Mac Neil refuse to associate with Mr. Granville, but he also dropped all acquaintance with Colonel Benson and his family, where he had been a great favorite. His place, however, as a visitor at the residence of Colonel Benson, was fully supplied by Frank Gaillard. He was a regular and a constant visitor, and Miss Margaret rarely went out without being accompanied by her lover, as he styled himself. The poor girl was completely fascinated with this arch deceiver. She loved him with her whole soul, and it was noticed by her mother, that from being a lively and gay girl, she was frequently much depressed in spirits and often found in tears. In vain did her mother seek her confidence, and endeavor to fathom the cause of her wo. Did she ask if Mr. Gaillard had told her that he loved her? Margaret replied with the simple word "Yes."

"Has he proposed to marry you?"

The reply of the poor girl, with a deep drawn sigh, was "No."

That was all that could be obtained from Margaret. The mother felt that there was some thing wrong, and mentioned the facts to her husband. The Colonel laughed at her. Called her a silly, anxious old woman, and then forgot all about it. That Frank Gaillard or any other white man alive, dared to dream of doing him or any member of his family a deep wrong, never entered into his brain. He conceived such a thing impossible. Meanwhile, time passed along, and while poor Margaret Benson drooped more and more, the young Southerner, Francis Gaillard, became less and less devoted to the sweet girl. From being a daily visitor, he ceased to call but once a week. Then once in two weeks, and at last his visits suddenly ceased, and the poor but proud spirited girl bent to the rod when she learned that Mr. Gaillard had left New York for his home in the South. She read his name among the passengers by a vessel that had sailed for Charleston. Still, she spoke not to her parents of the intense agony that his departure had caused. She seemed stupified, and a few days after his departure she called at the office of Mr. Granville, and asked to see him alone.

"Certainly, my dear young lady, come at once in my private office, and tell me what I can do for you. Some thing is on your mind," kindly remarked Mr. Granville.

Miss Benson followed him into the inner office, and when she was seated she asked if he would confer a favor upon her for a few days.

"And not mention it to my father, or any one of the family?" she imploringly inquired.

"If you do not wish me to do so," was the reply of her father's friend Granville.

"I wish to borrow of you fifty dollars," said Miss Benson.

Mr. Granville replied, "With pleasure, immediately," and walked into the front office and procured the money from the cashier. He was frightened, and yet he did not know what to say or what to do. Some thing was wrong. What could it be? Why did she not go to her father, mother, brother? Why come to him? As he handed her the money, he pleasantly observed, "Really "——but she shook her finger.

"No questions are to be asked, and more than that, not a word is to be said to my parents or any of my relations. I shall see you this evening at our house, shall I not?"

Mr. Granville bowed, and followed her to the door. When she had left him, he sat down for several minutes to try and fathom the mystery. The young lady went directly from Mr. Granville's office to that of George Sutton, the agent of the packet line that plied between New York and Charleston. There she inquired when the first vessel sailed for Charleston. She was told that a ship would sail the next day, and she instantly paid for the passage of a lady, and this accomplished, and obtaining the exact hour when the ship would sail, she wended her way home. That evening she was the gayest of the gay. Early the next morning she sent a carpet bag to a store in Broadway by a servant, saying that it was goods she had purchased, but wished to return. About noon she dressed herself as if for a walk—went to the store, and took the carpet bag. In the street she hired a porter, who took it on board the ship, and she went on board and retired to her state-room. That afternoon the vessel went down with the tide and a fair breeze and passed the Narrows.

When dinner time came Miss Benson was missed, but no alarm was exerted in the minds of any of her relations. The tea hour came, but no Margaret, and then the mother became somewhat alarmed, but not seriously. So she sent a message to Mr. Granville's house to have Miss Margaret come home. Then her brother, Middleton Benson, came, and when he said his sister had not been there that day, the whole house was alarmed, and the utmost confusion prevailed. The male members of the family started in different directions, but up to a late hour that night no clue could be obtained of the missing one. The next day the search was renewed, but with no more success than had been obtained the previous day. When Margaret was first missed, suspicion was attached to Francis Gaillard, but his having departed for Charleston cleared him in their minds. Mr. Granville did not mention for some time the circumstance of her borrowing the fifty dollars. No sooner had he mentioned this than the mother exclaimed, "Is it possible that she can have used that money to follow Gaillard to Charleston?" This started the pursuit on a new track. At the office they found that a young lady had taken a passage in the ship that had sailed for Charleston three days previous The description answered to Margaret. "I will follow my child in the next ship," exclaimed the agonized father—and he did so.

CHAPTER XLVI.

The Rascalities of Mr. O'Doemall—His Experiences among Boarding House Keepers.

Soon after the Count Falsecbinski had quarrelled with Madame Woodruff, that worthy lady turned her attentions toward Mr. O'Doemall. She had seen that gentleman frequently in company with Mrs. Parker, and admired his unparalleled impudence. She invited him to escort her to church on Sunday morning, and used him occasionally as a decoy. But the fact was, she was afraid of him, for O'Doemall was boisterous—a loud talker and a great boaster. Mrs. Woodruff, on the contrary, was as secret as the grave in all her transactions—and if she could have prevented her right hand from knowing what the left hand was doing, would have done it. It can easily be imagined that an alliance between two such opposite characters would not last long.

Mr. O'Doemall was a great spendthrift, and when he could no longer obtain funds from Mrs. Parker, and was thrown upon his own resources, he became very short of cash. Mrs. Woodruff furnished him with an outfit, and Mr. O'Doemall could again promenade Broadway the well-dressed gentleman, and the observed of all Broadway observers. Mr. O'Doemall was one of the most accomplished scamps that ever floated on the fashionable scum in New York. A large portion of his time was occupied in prowling about New York, seeking female victims. He had a keen eye, and could tell at a glance such as would suit his purpose. He watched for them early in the morning, and half the afternoon. Sometimes upon the Battery, and oftener in St. John's Park, and the parks and squares and places up town.

On one occasion he met a young and pretty girl in St. John's Park. O'Doemall had procured a key that would open the gates. He made bold to accost her, and discovered that she was of English stock—and while he apologized in the most humble manner for his boldness in addressing her, yet he managed to throw in the announcement that he was an English Captain, nephew to some English Peer, and that he was passing through the city on his way to join his regiment in Canada. The young lady allowed him to escort her home, and then introduced him to her father, who really was a half-pay officer in the English service. Luckily for O'Doemall he was well posted in the locality of the English regiments, and the names of their officers, and for a long time was not detected. He even went so far as to borrow a hundred dollars from the father.

He made rapid advances in the affections of the young lady, and the night rambles in St. John's Park, (one of the worst assignation-places and where more loveliness has been wrecked than in any house of ill-fame in the city.) soon completed her ruin. He then promised to marry her if she would leave home and go with him to a small town on the New Jersey coast. She consented, and the father became a broken-hearted man. He followed the seducer to Canada, where he supposed he had gone, and there met the real officer, whose name O'Doemall had taken, and whose rank he had assumed, and learned how grossly he had been deceived. But he could get no clue to

O'Doemall, and he went back to England. The instant O'Doemall became aware of the fact, he brought his victim to New York, placed her in a brothel, and then abandoned her forever. She of course became a girl of the town at once, for she had no other resource left.

It was not unfrequently that Mr. O'Doemall was turned out of his hotel. He had used himself up in every prominent one in the city. There was not one that he had not swindled. Blancard once said that it was really a pleasure to be victimized by him, as his explanation and apologies were "so very funny and interesting." He managed to pay the rent of his office in New street, so that if he was turned out of a hotel, he could rally at his office. He would go there when thus turned out, pack up two or more large trunks with bricks, boards, and rubbish, hire a cartman, and tell him to drive to some private boarding house. He had a list, and would select one where it was not probable that he could be known. Once in the house, he would select the most extravagant apartments to be had, find fault with every thing, and play the rich Southerner, or any other character which he had adopted.

A glance at the parties assembled around the dining-room table would serve to convey to O'Doemall the peculiarities of any person present. His conversation, dress, and impudence, would sweep down all opposition. Then he would, before twenty-four hours had passed, ingratiate himself fully with the landlady, and if she had one or two daughters his game was secure. He would notice that one daughter was receiving the attentions of a young man boarding in the house. O'Doemall would boldly say to the young lady, "Miss, I am astonished that you associate with or permit the attentions of that young man. I tell you this in confidence, for I am a warm friend of your mother; but this young man—(he must have been drunk, I think)—told me in confidence last night that he had no idea of marrying you, because he slept with you frequently, without any such ceremony." To the youth in question, O'Doemall had previously told him that the landlady saw through him, and had said that he "was trying to marry her daughter in order to sponge out his board bill."

These barefaced assertions would quickly make Pandemonium of the most pious boarding houses in the city—and if Mr. O'Doemall was ever called upon for any explanation, he would face the music, and declare the assertions had been made to him by the parties themselves. If he accidentally met the wife of any rather weak-minded boarder in the street alone,

O'Doemall would hurry down to the gentleman's place of business, beg him not to get angry, as he only wished to say that he saw his wife entering such a house with such a clergyman, (if there was one boarding in the house,) and that he the husband had better look into the matter. The house would be some private assignation house, and O'Doemall knew every one in the city.

A month would generally raise particular Ned in the boarding house, if it had not nearly ruined it, and the mischief-maker would be the powerful adviser of all the belligerents, and the particular friend of the landlady. If he was called upon for money, he had a hundred excuses ready, but he generally contrived to make such a scene of confusion in the house, that money was unthought of. When his game was nearly played out, after living on the fat of the land for four or six months, and landlady and boarders were loud in their execrations, and anxious to get rid of him at any price, O'Doemall would determine to leave a sting behind which should prove a deadly one. If it was at dinner, he would rise and say, " Ladies and gentlemen, I am forced to leave this house. It is extremely unpleasant for me to remain here longer. The pious landlady has made a statement that I am in arrears for board. What will you think when I tell you that I have let her have ten, twenty, and fifty dollars at a time ? She has come to my bed night after night for months, and now she says that she is in a delicate situation—that I am the author of her misfortune, and wants me to marry her. Of course I shall do nothing of the kind—I will leave the house first."

The landlady would generally faint at such an infamous charge, and the daughters would scream. The boarders would be perfectly aghast, and some believe it, and the lying scoundrel would walk out in triumph. No one would take it up. The very enormity of the charge would make the innocent objects of it quail, and exhibit all the terror of real guilt. Or perhaps it would be a landlady who in a moment of weakness had become a victim to this arch deceiver ; he would then live on her for weeks and months, borrow all her earnings, and not leave until he had ruined and broken up her establishment.

Mr. O'Doemall in a quiet boarding house could only be represented by a fierce, unrelenting hawk, quartered in a barnyard surrounded by a peaceful lot of roosters, hens, and different sized chickens. It was all one side ; the poor domestic fowls stood no sort of chance.

In his business, no one could get any hold of him. His office or store rent was cheap, and that he paid promptly. He had a handsome business card, and he paid two dollars and a half a thousand for them. These alone gave him respectability and position with strangers, for who could gainsay it? He could be found at his store; and many a tailor, shoemaker, dry goods dealer, and tradesman, was victimized to a greater or less extent. He owed all. But those who sued, made costs for themselves. His very furniture in the office could not be disturbed, for it was mortgaged to the landlord. The only way for his victim was to laugh, for O'Doemall did find associates with gentlemen, and particularly among English noblemen or gentry, and he would take these persons to shops that he knew, and owed money to.

His malice was intense and fearful. He made a purchase of some wine of one of the most sturdy merchants in the city. This man was a member of Dr. Spring's church. He refused to let him have the wine until he paid for it. The swindler swore vengeance. Unluckily the merchant left New York on a visit of some weeks' duration. O'Doemall managed to put himself in the way of all this merchant's acquaintance, and as if by accident, mentioned his regret that so fine an old merchant should be so sorely afflicted—that he visited him once a month in the Bloomingdale asylum, where he was confined as a madman.

No matter who starts such a story as this, where there is a shadow of foundation, it runs like Greek fire, and is very speedily so extensively spread, that in a large city it cannot be traced to the real author. O'Doemall was revenged—the story flew among the business acquaintances of the merchant, and he was ruined. When he returned, he did not know what had hurt him, for few like to tell a supposed madman that they are aware of his having been in a mad-house.

This bad man, as bold as he was wicked, had, as our readers will remember, formed an early intimacy with most of those who were connected with the firm of Granville and Nordheim. He knew Marion Monck, but that young man had cut his acquaintance after the shirt story affair. But O'Doemall was not one to be easily cut, and no insult could prevent his recognizing one he had once known.

He ascertained that Marion was sick and confined to his room in Nassau street where Mr. Bennett lodged; he called, was admitted, and presented himself in Marion's room, where he was lying upon a sick man's bed.

"How d'ye do?—heard you were ill. Come to see you, and if I can be of any service to you," said he.

Marion replied that he was glad to see him. So he was, and so he would have been to have seen any one who could relieve and pass away the weary sick hours. O'Doemall continued to be a frequent visitor at the sick room. Once or twice he watched all night. Other friends called—Colonel Mac Neil was among the number, and when he learned that O'Doemall had been so kind, even he was disposed to overlook his owing him money, and renewed the acquaintance.

No one knew the extent of O'Doemall's rascality. All believed him a bad fellow, but perhaps not worse than many others: and when he himself related some of his most villanous stories, his hearers had the charity to believe he was lying, and only told such tales to please the company. Such was not the fact.

The effect of renewing his acquaintance with O'Doemall, both upon Marion and Mac Neil, will form matter for another chapter.

CHAPTER XLVII.

Miss Benson arrives safely in Charleston—Calls on Madame Gaillard, the Mother of Frank, her Lover—Tells her Story—The Mother conveys Miss Benson to her Plantation at St. John's—Young Gaillard is Sick—His Marriage with Miss Benson—The Arrival of Colonel Benson—His Satisfaction, and Departure—Birth of a Son—Death of Francis Gaillard.

THE passage of the ship that conveyed Miss Benson to Charleston was a remarkably short and pleasant one. To say that the fair traveller did not undergo the usual tax of sea-sickness, would be untrue. She suffered greatly, but her stern and determined purpose kept up her spirits, and when she reached port, she was ready to go on shore the moment the vessel in which she had been a passenger reached the dock or wharf. She was astonished at her own coolness and courage, for she was not aware that she possessed these qualities. Her baggage was easily carried, and she hired one of the sailors to carry her carpet bag, and to conduct her to the Planters' Hotel. As soon as she found herself settled, she sent for the landlord, and begged him to ascertain whether Mrs. Gaillard was in town, and if not, whether she was at one of her plantations, and which one. The answer was favorable. Mrs. Gaillard was in town. Miss Benson at once ordered a carriage, and in it proceeded to the town residence of the mother of her lover.

Her visit occasioned some surprise; but when she stated her parentage, the circumstances under which she left New York, her attachment to young Gaillard, and at last informed her of the deep wrong her son had done her, and that she was soon to become a mother, and that her long journey had been undertaken in order to save the honor of her unborn child—*his* child, all the good in that mother's nature was thoroughly roused. She placed her in a room—sent to the hotel, paid the bill, and had the carpet bag brought to her own house.

"I believe all that you have stated—every word of it. My son shall do you justice, and that too immediately, or I am no longer his mother. We will start for the plantation this very afternoon. Frank is sick, and I feel alarmed about him. Now lie down, and make yourself perfectly at ease. You require rest and quiet, and I will soon send my daughter to you," said the mother.

Miss Benson was overcome, and she flung herself upon her knees by the bedside, and poured forth sincere thanks to God for his kindness and care. Then she laid down upon the bed, and soon fell asleep.

In the mean time, Mrs. Gaillard had informed her daughter who the visitor was, and her purpose in coming to Charleston. The young lady was prepared to receive her as a sister.

"What a cruel wrong Frank has done to her! O mother, who could have thought that my brother would have been guilty of such an infamous thing? I never will forgive him until he makes wrong right, by marrying this sweet girl. Will he do it, Mamma, dear, do you think?"

There was a stern contraction of the haughty brow of that stately mother, and a quivering of the lips, as she replied,

"He will, darling, or"—— but the threat remained unspoken, and she continued. "Go, my child, to the apartment of Miss Benson. If she is asleep do not wake her to misery. Remain by her bedside, and comfort her when she awakes."

The Southern beauty did as her mother directed, and when Margaret Benson woke from a short sleep, and exclaimed "Where am I?" her hands were seized by the affectionate Miss Gaillard, and she pressed her lips, as she exclaimed,

"With those who will love you for your own sake, and who will try and make that naughty brother of mine give you a legal title to our love. Now try and sleep again."

The next day after Miss Benson found a home in the residence of Mrs. Gaillard, that lady, her daughter, and the New York arrival were packed in a travelling carriage and on their way to the plantation. They arrived about the middle of the afternoon, and as the carriage turned off from the State road into a long avenue, each side of which was ornamented by a row of stately live oaks, Miss Benson almost fainted. How was she to be received by her lover? At last the carriage drove up in front of the old stone mansion. Troops of negroes of all sizes and ages poured out to meet "Ole Missus."

"Where is your master, Tommy?" demanded Mrs. Gaillard of an aged gray-headed negro.

"Massa Frank gone down to de creek fishin'," was the reply.

"That is all. I am very glad of that," said Mrs. Gaillard, addressing those in the carriage. "I shall have time to converse with him before he is aware of the arrival of Miss Benson."

The occupants of the carriage entered the mansion, and Miss Benson was speedily shown to a room. Miss Gaillard accompanied her thither, and as she assisted her to change her dress, she endeavored to soothe the agitation of the stranger, and to give her every encouragement.

"You must not leave your room, dear Miss Margaret, until Mamma has had a serious talk with our gay deceiver of a brother. I have never seen Mamma so decided and so angry," said Miss Gaillard.

"O, I hope, dear Miss Gaillard, that my arrival will not be the means of causing discord in your peaceful family. If I thought so, I should wish I had never left New York," replied Miss Benson.

"Give yourself no uneasiness. If there is a storm it will soon be over, and a clear sky will follow. I pray God that my brother will be convinced by Mamma of the necessity of doing what is right in this unhappy affair," replied Miss Gaillard.

"Amen," was all the reply that Miss Benson could make.

A few moments only elapsed, when Mr. Francis Gaillard was seen coming up the long avenue through which the carriage had just passed. He was extremely pale, walked very slow, and had every appearance of suffering from severe illness. His mother went out upon the piazza, and when he entered, cordially embraced him.

"Are you better, my son?"

"I really do not know. I think I am stronger, but at times, Mother, I get discouraged, and feel that I shall never be any better. But what has brought you back from Charleston in such a hurry ?" he asked.

"That, my dear son, I will tell you presently. Meanwhile, come into the sitting-room," she said kindly.

Young Gaillard followed his mother, and they were alone. Mrs. Gaillard spoke.

"Francis, will you come and sit down by me ?"

He complied.

"Now inform me, my son, of every fact connected with your acquaintance and conduct to a young lady in New York, whose name is Margaret Benson."

"Mother, what do you know about her, and why do you ask me for information ?" asked Francis, excitedly.

"My son, answer my questions as if you were in the presence of your God. But for her attachment to you, was this young lady a virtuous girl ?"

"As the fallen snow. I only led her into sin," was the honest reply.

"Are her parents of respectability ?" asked the mother.

"Unquestioned. Equal to my parents in every regard," replied the son.

"Then how could you be so base as to ruin her ?"

"I, Mother? But why should I deceive you, Mother? I have acted like a rascal. How you came to know anything about the matter I will not stop to ask. I feel the deepest remorse in reference to that young lady. If ever woman loved man, she loved me," was the truthful reply of the son.

"And yet you could deliberately abandon her in the delicate situation to which you had brought her ?"

"I, my mother ? What do you mean ?" he asked.

"She is shortly to become a mother—a mother to your child! O Frank, Frank!" said the mother.

"Mother, I will return to New York, and do her full justice. I will marry her, if she will consent to marry such a wretch as me," said Francis.

"My son, she is here—in this house. She has alone followed you on from New York, for the sake of her child."

"Not a word more, mother. I will see her at once ;" and before Mrs. Gaillard could arrest his speech, Francis Gaillard found his way to the apartment of Miss Benson. The meeting between the two young persons was affecting in the highest degree. Poor Margaret, when she listened to the first bursts of repentant words from Frank, was overwhelmed with happiness. It was long ere she could find words to reply to his extravagant fondness. "Thank God that you had the nerve to come South, dear Margaret! You shall not regret it. I will marry you without any delay, and at least the little one promised to us shall make its advent under more auspicious circumstances than I deserve. Cheer up! I go to hold counsel with my good-hearted old mother," exclaimed the lover.

Frank Gaillard went to the mother, and told her all his plans. She listened quietly, and finally replied,

"My son, I am rejoiced at discovering a disposition on your part to repair the wrong that you have committed against the peace of a young lady of such respectability; but the matter must be settled quietly, and without any noise. I can arrange your marriage so that no question will ever be raised in regard to the legitimacy of your child."

The old lady sent a note to Dr. Wallace, the rector of the Episcopal Church, within a few miles of their residence. The ceremony of the marriage was performed that evening. A certificate of the marriage was given, and a corresponding entry made in the record book of the Parish Church. What mattered that it was dated six months earlier than the day when the marriage rites were celebrated? It ought to have been celebrated six months earlier, and who should ever study for proof to the contrary? The good doctor believed he was doing right, and when asked for a duplicate certificate, he willingly gave it.

This duplicate Francis Gaillard intended to send to Colonel Benson with an explanatory letter, but he delayed writing it until he himself should go to Charleston. Meanwhile, the fair Miss Benson was presented to all as Mrs. Francis Gaillard. The marriage was kept a profound secret; no one of the domestics dreamed of such a thing. The only witnesses to the ceremony were the mother and the sister.

Before a week elapsed, the family was startled by another arrival. They were just sitting down to dinner when a carriage drove up the Live Oak Avenue. It contained Colonel Benson. He sprang out of the carriage, and had reached the top of the steps leading to the mansion, when his daughter flung herself into his arms.

"Oh, dear Papa, how glad I am to see you, and so will my husband be."

"Husband!" and he held her at arm's length while he repeated that single word "Husband!"

"Yes, dear Papa. Husband; for Mr. Gaillard is my husband, and I will tell you all about it, Papa, but not now. Here is Frank."

Mr. Gaillard offered his hand to Colonel Benson. It was barely touched by the latter.

"When I hear all, perhaps I shall be more cordial," he observed, coldly.

He followed his daughter and her husband, and then was introduced to Madame Gaillard. If the latter was pleased at meeting the stately and gentlemanly father of her daughter-in-law, the Colonel was no less pleased with the magnificent old lady, the mother of his daughter's husband.

"You have arrived just in time for dinner, Colonel Benson. I need not add how welcome you are," she observed.

"Many thanks, dear madam, but I am afraid that my presence here has occasioned you some surprise. I confess that I arrived here with far different purposes than to eat a friendly dinner," said Colonel Benson.

"No one could be more welcome than the father of my son's wife. I hope we shall be able to make your visit a most agreeable one," said Mr. Gaillard.

"The first words spoken by my child have relieved my mind of a load of agony and anxiety," replied the Colonel.

An excellent dinner was partaken of, and when it was finished Madame Gaillard advised the young couple to go and walk. Then she dismissed the servants in attendance. When she was alone with the Colonel, she deliberately requested him to listen to her explanations. She informed him of the arrival of his daughter in Charleston, and her surprise and anxiety of her bringing his daughter home and the marriage. When she spoke of the maternal situation of his daughter, the Colonel was dumbfounded. Then she told him of the delicate manner in which the marriage had been managed, and handed him the marriage certificate.

"It will probably be some two or three months before my daughter-in-law's confinement. Then if God wills that no accident happens, there never can arise cavil or flaw in the proceedings. Bear in mind, Colonel Benson, that we had to make a wrong right, and out of evil to get good. I, too, am more interested in having our large possessions go to an unquestioned legal descendant, than you possibly can be. Now, are you satisfied?"

"Madam, I have no words to express my gratitude. If I had a hundred lives, they should all be yours. You have indeed acted nobly, generously, and how can I repay it?" said Colonel Benson, warmly.

"Simply, Colonel, by treating your son-in-law and your daughter as though nothing irregular had happened—make no allusion to it. The parish record and the marriage certificate, and the entry of the birth of the first born child will tell all the story in future times, should it ever need to be told. Introduce the bride as an old married lady, or at least as having been married so many months ago as to have ceased being a novelty to talk about, and the world, that is so fond of scandal, need have nothing to say. We have only to keep our own counsel. The members of my family will keep theirs. When you get to New York, an equally prudent course on your part will be productive of equally happy results," replied Madame Gaillard.

"You are a lady of a thousand. I agree with every word you have uttered. As soon as I reach New York, I will give out that your son was privately married to my daughter before her family knew any thing about it, and that the young lady followed her husband to the South, where she now is."

"And where, Colonel Benson, she must remain for one or two years. I say this for the sake of the child that I hope will prove a grandson, and be a blessing to my old age. When the babe reaches a few months old, then my daughter-in-law can visit the North with safety, so far as important questions are concerned."

"Again you are right, lady," observed Colonel Benson. "And I must add that few parents will enjoy a sounder and more refreshing sleep than I shall to-night. My mind is completely at ease. I have been extremely worried for many days."

"I can readily understand that, sir, but you will have no further cause of embarrassment. My son is rich, and Margaret has made a good match, so far as wealth is concerned. My son has been wild, but I hope *that* will pass away, and that he will be a good, kind husband. I regret to say that his health is far from good since his return from the North, and there are moments when my fears get the better of me. We must hope for the best," said the mother.

This was news to Colonel Benson, but when he closely examined the countenance of his son-in-law, and contrasted his present feeble appearance with what he had know him in New York, he, too, partook of the alarm, and suggested to the elder Mrs. Gaillard, as his opinion, that medical advice of a high character be resorted to at once. Colonel Benson wrote that evening to his wife in New York. He simply informed her that he was well, and that Magaret had been secretly married to Mr. Gaillard, and that she was quite an old married dame when he reached her. He cautioned his wife against saying much about the matter until his return to New York. After despatching this, the Colonel felt completely happy, and gave himself up fully to his enjoyment. He fished, hunted, and rode about the neighborhood, making the acquaintance of the principal planters in that vicinity. After a fortnight spent in this manner, he could not be contented to remain longer, but took his departure for Charleston, and from thence sailed for New York.

After the departure of her father, the young wife devoted herself to her husband. His health failed daily, but still, he was not regarded as in great danger. It was resolved that he should take a voyage to the West Indies, but the interesting situation of his lovely wife prevented. Weeks passed away, and then she gave birth to a child. It was a boy, and was christened Francis Benson Gaillard. When Mrs. Gaillard had recovered sufficient strength, after her confinement, to travel, it was discovered that Francis could not make a journey, and he made up his mind to remain at home and abide the fate, which was now evident.

He lived but a few weeks after the birth of his son, and then his spirit went to another world, and his wife was a young widow.

CHAPTER XLVIII.

Editor Bennett of the Herald—Marion Monck falls in love—A boat upsets—He saves his own life, and the lives of his companions by swimming ashore—The Herald's account of the affair—Mr. Jones, the Father, declines all further acquaintance with Mr. Monck.

It would seem almost an impossibility for Marion Monck to be on the same floor with the editor of the Herald, and in the habit of meeting and conversing with him every day, without imbibing a certain quantity of the spirit that animated the editor in a new era in journalism.

On one occasion he had been traversing an upper street of the city when he found himself in the midst of a riot. He saw the whole of it. A man was killed. Marion went home, and, as it was a matter of news of some moment, he went into Mr Bennett's room and narrated the whole of it to him. "Excellent," said the editor. "I am really much obliged to you. Add to the favor by writing down what you have already told me, and I will publish it in the morning's issue. It will make a capital article, and you have related it in excellent style."

Marion took a pen, and after some hesitation wrote an account of the affair. Mr. Bennett read it and then exclaimed, "Bah, what trash!"

"Why, what is the matter with it, Mr. Bennett?"

"The matter is that you have not written it at all as you told it. You have attempted to improve upon it, and bungled it all up. You have got the cart before the horse. As you related it to me it was excellent. This writing of yours is nonsense. I shall have to write it all over again from my own recollection of what you have told me, in order to make a readable article. There is not one person in five hundred of those who claim to be editors or writers, that can write an editorial as it should be written. An editorial, Master Marion, should have a beginning, a middle, and an end. An editorial should have an object—a point. If a man happened to fall into a sink because there was no cover to it, and an editor wanted to call the attention of the authorities to the neglect, and consequent injury, the occurrence of the man falling should be related plainly, and as it occurred; then state the danger to others from this neglect; and lastly, point out the way to mend all further accidents by covering the hole up with a stone or a piece of marble or an iron top. It is a common simile, but it answers as well as a better one. You write what a shame it is that rows are allowed to occur, and then tell that a row has occurred, and a man has been killed. But don't get discouraged; you may not think so, but one day you will be able to write a clever editorial, which is the highest style of composition known," said Mr. Bennett, encouragingly.

Such conversations frequently occurred between the editor and Marion Monck. But such was the low estimate that Marion had at that time of the destiny of the Herald, that though he had not a cent, if Mr. Bennett had offered him an equal partnership, he would have declined the offer. Marion, however, did not underrate the ability of the editor. He discovered then that clear-headed ability, that careful thought, vivid imagination and ready wit which has since been developed, but which great body of his readers have never given Mr. Bennett credit for. He possessed a winning way with young people, and had a happy faculty of drawing them out. Marion was somewhat susceptible in love matters. He had not suffered quite enough with the affair of Miss Isabella Granville, but some months after became violently in love with a rich banker's daughter. The name of the father was Jones. Marion got introduced to her, and accompanied her to church on one or two occasions. The father was excessively pious, and so was the daughter. The old Jones abominated theatres, and considered a Sabbath-breaker as out of the pale of any sort of salvation. Marion was on the free list of almost every theatre, and was check by jowl with every actor and actress of any note upon the New York boards. In regard to the Sabbath, after the acquaintance commenced with Miss Euphenia Jones, he was very regular in his attendance at the same church where she worshipped. Unfortunately, on one occasion three young gentlemen persuaded him to accompany them in a White Hall boat to a place in the lower bay. It was Sunday. All went on very well until they attempted to return to the city in the afternoon. The wind came out from the north-west, and blew a stiff breeze. It was night before they beat up to within some distance of the Narrows. The tide was at ebb. A sudden flow of wind capsized their frail boat, and they were all immersed into the water. All succeeded in getting upon the keel of the boat, and their united weights sunk down the boat so low that the water nearly reached the necks of these young men. Upon comparing notes it was found that but one could swim. That one was Marion. They were a mile or two from the shore, and floating out rapidly to sea. There was but little chance of being picked up by inward bound vessels, for the wind was ahead, and all such, of course, would come to an anchor. Under these appalling circumstances, Marion, with great gallantry, offered to swim ashore and get aid. One of the young men was an acquaintance of Marion's new flame. His name was Robert Knight, and his uncle was governor of the little State of Rhode Island. Marion stripped off every rag of clothes, and after he had bade all good-bye, he said to young Knight, "Bob, dear Bob, should I be drowned, remember me, for God's sake, to Pheeney Jones."

After a terrible time, Marion succeeded in reaching the Long Island shore. He ran up directly to a private residence situated high up on the shore. He forgot his nude state, and rushed into the parlor, where the family were congregated, and among them a number of young ladies. Their screams were fearful, but nothing daunted, Marion seized a candle-stick and rushed back to the shore. He had told his story, and luckily a negro overheard and understood it. He asked Marion for particulars, and without a word went down to a boat belonging to the house, and rowed off to rescue the sufferers. He was just in time, and he succeeded in getting all into the boat, bringing them ashore and conveying them to his own humble cottage. Then commenced a search for Marion. They found him senseless at the foot of a cliff, with the candle and candlestick beside him. He had fallen through a tree which grew at the foot of the rock, and this had saved his life. The negro furnished the party with old clothes, and at midnight they left him and walked to New York. It was near daylight when they crossed the Fulton ferry. That day three of the party took a carriage and went down to the spot. They found the negro, and made him a present of a hundred dollars in silver. Marion contributed his share, but he was too ill to go with his companions. He lay upon his bed, and a medical man was called in. The affair got wind, and the afternoon papers of that day had a long article upon the matter. They gave credit to Marion for his gallantry in saving the lives of his companions, but one of the Journals, the " Commercial Advertiser," stated that it was " Sunday," and that God would have acted perfectly right if he had drowned the whole party. That evening Mr. Bennett called in to see his sick friend Marion, and he, too, congratulated him upon the gallant act.

" Curse that commercial newspaper. They take that paper. Sunday. My cake is all dough now," exclaimed Marion, very petulantly.

" What is the matter? Tell me all about it. I will put it straight in my paper in the morning. Let me have all the facts," said the editor.

Marion narrated them, and added, " Of course it was very natural, that with a good show for being drowned, I sent a message by Bob, in case he got picked up, to Miss Jones."

" She ought to be obliged to you, very much so," said the editor.

The next morning Marion sent out early to get a Herald. When he opened it, there was the article headed " Narrow Escape from Drowning. Gallant Behavior of Marion Monck." Marion read on—all pleasant—praised him up—told the whole thing pretty fairly, but all at once his face became a foot and a half long, and he rushed into Mr. Bennett's room.

" Why, what is the matter?" exclaimed the editor.

" You have ruined me. I am a dead man. Look here :"

and he read, "' *Bob, dear Bob, should I be drowned, remember me, for God's sake, to Phecney Jones.*' That is my death-warrant."

"But Marion, you don't mean to say that Jones, Phœney Jones, is the real name of your flame?"

"Of course it is. Old Jones the banker's daughter. One of the vestry of Trinity Church. Sunday, too! You also say that I was '*engaged and shortly to be married to that young female to whom he sent a dying message.*' It is no such thing. O, it will play Ned with me!"

"On the contrary, my dear boy, you are not responsible for what appears in the Herald. *You* don't say that you were engaged, it is the Herald that says so. Throw the blame upon the Herald. As for Miss Jones, I will print another edition, and say it was Miss Smith, and you can send her a copy; although I think she ought to be extremely flattered that a talented fellow, a gallant chap like you should think of her, when he expects to be drowned shortly, eh? Look at it in that way."

"O, that is all very fine, Mr. Bennett, to talk. No matter what she thinks. If it had been any other day than Sunday, it would have been all right. But her father—Jehu! Sunday, eh! I'll go up to the house of Mr. Jones this evening, and know the worst."

Evening came, and Marion did as he stated he would do. He went around to Ann street to the Herald office. When he saw Mr. Bennett, the latter observed,

"Well; Marion, what success?"

"I could not get in. The servant, a grinning negro, handed me this note. Just read it."

"*Tuesday Evening.*

"SIR—I have to beg that you will no longer consider yourself an acquaintance of mine or of my family, and I have given orders that you never be admitted inside my doors. My daughter Euphenia joins me in these sentiments. We both regard you as a Sabbath-breaker of the worst kind. The Lord evidently kept you from being drowned in order that you may repent. Hoping you may do so

I am, respectfully, PETER JONES."

"Of course you will publish it. Give him as good as he sends. Let me write an article about it. He will regret the longest day he lives that he ever sent you that note," exclaimed Mr. Bennett, reaching out his hand for the note.

"O Lord, no! I could not think of such a thing. It would ruin me with the girl."

"You have nothing more to hope for in that quarter, if you put up with such a thing. It is a shame—but never mind—if you don't choose to take my advice, you are no worse off for my having offered it," said Mr. Bennett.

It was in those days actually considered a horrible matter to get into a newspaper. Marion so regarded it. Not so Mr. Bennett. He regarded those matters which became talked of among a set or circle, as legitimate articles for a newspaper. So they were; and now, that the ice is broken, half the people in the land are only too anxious to get their names into the newspapers, attached to anything. All seek notoriety.

CHAPTER XLIX.

Mrs. Wilson has a Son—Walter Granville returns from Sea as a Sailor—Visits a House of Bad Repute, and meets Miss Norris—Walter has a friend, a Sailor, son of a Bank Presid'nt, in his Company—He meets Rose Barker—A Rich Scene—Robinson takes her out of the House—Walter and Clara aid in their escape.

Mr. and Mrs. Wilson after their marriage continued to reside in the house purchased for Mrs. Nordheim in West Washington Place. Mr. Wilson was a kind, careful, parental sort of husband, and every day's experience convinced the wife that she had acted most wisely and well when she gave her hand to the worthy book-keeper. Nearly a year elapsed after the marriage, when Mrs. Wilson presented her husband with a charming boy. The birth of this little fellow opened a new source of happiness to the parents—he was a new bond of attachment, and bound their hearts together closer than ever. When the little fellow was about two months old, and the strength and health of the mother was fully restored, Mr. Wilson asked his beautiful wife if she would be pleased if he gave up business altogether. She laid her babe in the wicker cradle, and gazing at her husband a moment, said,

"Ah, Wilson, you cannot deceive me. You have a motive for asking that question, but I will answer it plainly. I wish you would give up business, or if you wish to do business to employ your time, do it in a prudent manner and in your own name."

"That, wife, is precisely what I am coming at. But it will be necessary to get off with the old love before I get on with the new. Things are prosperous now. The house of Granville & Wilson have made money, and I have contrived under various pretences to withdraw from the concern a considerable amount and invest it in securities in my own name. I think there will be a crash in the commercial world before long, but by submitting to some extortion I think I can get out of the concern now, with the capital which you placed in it and about half as much more as I am entitled to for my share of the profits. I can also make Granville cancel or secure me for all outstanding liabilities," observed the prudent Wilson.

"Then, my dear, do so as speedily as possible. I am a great believer in luck, and there is none where Mr. Granville is concerned," said the wife.

In pursuance of this understanding between the husband and wife, Mr. Wilson proposed to Mr. Granville a dissolution. He made it in such a way, and it appeared so much to the advantage of Mr. Granville, that he instantly acceded to it—and thanks to the good financial management of Mr. Wilson, the firm were in a situation to give him back in cash all that he had put in, and twenty-five thousand dollars for his share of the profits.

Granville knew that the apparent profits were four times that amount. Mr. Wilson calculated that the losses for the next year, under more unfavorable circumstances, would eat up all the profits. Mr. Granville also was able to give security for the outstanding liabilities of the concern, and Mr. Wilson signed the dissolution, giving the closing up of the affairs to Mr. Granville.

Thirty days made Mr. Wilson free from all further responsibilities, and he retired on his laurels, and devoted his whole time to the wife and child. The cash that he received he invested in real estate, and placed it in the name of his wife. She was a woman who could appreciate a delicacy like this, but she made no comment upon it.

From the very day that Mr. Wilson withdrew from the concern it seemed as though the prosperity of Mr. Granville declined. He met all his liabilities and engagements promptly, both for the old house and the new, and every month Mr. Wilson re-transferred to his old partner stocks and other securities.

Then a commercial crisis followed. Mr. Granville seemed to lose money by every operation. He had done a very heavy commission business, and held a large amount of business paper, a large portion of which was protested as it become due. His losses were tremendous, but he bore up stoutly under them; and although he lived higher, drank a great deal more than usual, and relaxed much in his strict business habits, yet he appeared to hold his own, and his commercial credit stood unimpaired, although it had a terrible shaking. He felt that he had consented to a dissolution too hastily. But he kept a brave heart, and was not a man to be moved by trifles. He became a grandfather too of a fine boy about the time that Mr. Wilson had a son. This son of his daughter Isabel was a new source of pride to the old merchant.

He regretted that the grandson was not Walter's child, so that it could bear his own honored name of Granville. Then the proud father wondered what had become of his son—whether he was dead, or would ever turn up again. His wonderment was destined to be solved, but in a manner that was almost a deathblow to the aristocratic parent. The events that led to this discovery we will narrate as briefly as possible.

It was at a late hour one Saturday night that two young men applied for admittance to a celebrated house of ill-fame in Church street. In the centre of the door were some iron blinds about the size of an ordinary window glass. Through these blinds the person who came to the inside surveyed the applicants for admission.

"Who do you wish to see?" was the query of the female doorkeeper.

"Some of the young ladies," was the reply, in a manly tone of voice.

"Are you acquainted with any of them?" was asked.

"No, madam, we are strangers; we know no one in the house, and have just arrived," was the reply.

"You are not rowdies anyhow, and I will let you in."

The parties entered, and the door was again closed, locked, bolted, and securely chained, as is the ordinary but prudent custom of such houses.

The girl took a good look at the two persons she admitted. They were both draped in the garb of the better class of sailors, yet they appeared to be gentlemen. Probably they had disguised themselves in this manner for a lark, thought the girl—and her survey being satisfactory, she observed,

"Both of the parlors are occupied. I shall be obliged to show you into Miss Clara's parlor, and then I will send some of the young ladies into you."

"Thank you," replied one of the persons. He was much stouter than his companion, who addressed him as "Walt." His countenance was large and open; his teeth when he laughed were exposed, and white as ivory. His laugh was merry and hearty, and the smile which accompanied it would have won any woman's heart. He appeared to have been a sailor. His face was bronzed, evidently from exposure, and his dark hair, which hung long about his face, appeared not to have been cut in a long while. He was very stoutly built, broad across the shoulders and chest, and he looked like a youth that it would not be safe to trifle with. The younger of the two was called Harry Robinson; he was not so stout as his companion, but evidently was not a common sailor; his language was equally correct as his friend Walter.

The girl conducted the new comers into a small but exquisitely furnished parlor. There was a piano in it, and also a guitar. Several choice paintings adorned the walls, and an elegant sofa was in one corner; there was a door which opened to a room in the rear. Harry, as he was called, tried to open it, to see where it led to; it was fast. Both persons took off their hats, placed them upon the centre table near a superb astral, when they entered the room.

The guitar seemed to attract the attention of the one called "Walt."

He took it up and struck a few notes.

"The best guitar I have touched in a long while—I wonder who plays it," he asked as the girl who opened the door to admit them entered the room.

"That belongs to Miss Clara," replied the girl.

"Shall we have the pleasure of seeing Miss Clara?" asked Walter.

"No, sir, Miss Clara does not see company. She has this parlor and the sleeping room attached, and is a private boarder," said the girl.

Walter had commenced playing while the girl was talking—and when she had finished he sung a Spanish love song, accompanied by the guitar.

The girl stopped and listened. Walter finished, and then ordered a bottle of champagne, adding,

"Where is this Miss Clara, into whose parlor we have been intruding?"

The girl replied that Miss Clara was in one of the main parlors, amusing herself.

She was interrupted by a sweet musical voice—

"Miss Clara is here to speak for herself, and to ask who is playing her guitar with such unusual good taste," and at the same time one of the most beautiful visions burst into the parlor that Walter had seen in many months. Her long auburn tresses fell in ringlets that reached behind her waist. She was dressed in white, and not a single ornament of jewelry was about her. Her face was beautiful, and her figure perfect. Both of the young men arose and uttered exclamations of delight. She noticed but one of them. From the moment she entered the room her gaze was fixed upon Walter.

"Fair lady," he observed, "we owe you an apology for thus intruding into your apartments, and I for touching this private property—but the girl is to blame for showing us in here, and I must apologize for touching the guitar," observed Walter respectfully.

The lady gazed at him, but for some moments did not reply a word, but took a seat on the sofa. Walter then resumed his seat, and she took his hand, and still continued to examine his features. At last she appeared to be satisfied with her close examination, and a peculiar smile played for a moment upon her fascinating mouth.

"Miss Clara, I hope you will know me again when you see me," said Walter.

"I know you now, if I am not mistaken," said Clara.

"Indeed I do not remember having ever had the pleasure of seeing you before," replied Walter—"in fact I have been away from New York some years," he continued.

At this moment the girl entered and announced that one of the parlors was empty, and that Miss Brown wished the party to adjourn to the principal parlor.

"I have taken the wine there," said the girl.

"That is perfectly right," Clara replied. "Show that gentleman (pointing to Harry) into the parlor. I will follow with one who plays the guitar. I want to ask him one or two questions. Go at once."

The girl left the room with the young man, and as soon as they were gone and she was alone with Walter, she locked the door of the parlor, then passed to the other door, and took a key from the pocket of her dress, and opened it.

"Look in here, Master Sailor," she added.

Walter came to her side as she stood in the open door, and there he discovered a sleeping apartment fitted up equal to any room in a palace. The bed was a lofty one, with fine carved posts, and was one that a king would have been satisfied with.

Walter glanced over the apartment, remarking as he did so,

"I have never seen an apartment for sleeping more exquisitely furnished."

He looked for a moment at the loveliness by his side, and sighed.

"What is that sigh for, and what is your name?"

"Walter—and I drew a sigh thinking what a happy man he would be who could occupy that apartment, and have as a companion its beautiful owner," was the gallant answer.

"Indeed! Do you know, Mr. Walter, that I am not one of the girls belonging to this house?" asked Clara.

"I am perfectly aware of it—and don't suppose that I, a poor devil of a sailor just off from four years' cruising at sea, had formed any idea that I could have so much happiness," said Walter.

"Answer me some questions. You came here to-night, you and your friend, to see each a young lady?"

"I confess we did," was the reply.

"This is a somewhat expensive establishment—are you aware of it?" asked Miss Norris.

"I am; but we are not without some funds. We were paid off to-day, and what we order we can pay for," said Walter, with some pride.

"Now, Master Walter, let me say to you that your friend, or you, if you had a thousand dollars, could not enter these private apartments of mine, but "——

"I am aware of it—perfectly aware of it. Let us go into the parlor," said Walter.

"In one moment. Look at me, Walter. We will go into the parlor. You shall see all the young ladies in the house—some are exquisitely beautiful. If you do not see any that you can admire or desire for a companion until to-morrow morning, then, on one condition, I, my poor humble self, will be your slave. You shall be lord and master of the apartments and my person at your disposal on *one* condition," and as she said this, she, like a true Oriental, flung herself upon her knees, and took Walter's hand and kissed it reverently.

"Why, I should be the happiest, luckiest dog in existence. But you can't mean it, and what is the condition?" asked Walter.

"That the word money is not used between us. You shall not even pay for the bottle of wine that you have ordered, nor for others that I shall order. You shall go into the parlor, see all the beauties of the establishment—play—sing—dance, and amuse yourself until you are tired; then, when you whisper that to me, I will leave the room and have you conducted in here. We will pass the night as pleasantly as we can. We will have a choice breakfast ready in my parlor when we get up, and after you have partaken of that with me, then you shall go wherever you please; but the word money—or pay—or compensation, is not to be used by you. If you forget your promise, I will leave you in an instant," said Clara Norris.

"Am I awake? or do I dream? Lady, I accept the condition," said Walter.

Clara flung herself upon his manly breast, and he was not backward in holding her tightly in his powerful embrace, while he feasted upon her soft, dewy lips. He was losing all control of himself, when she, with her face crimsoned with blushes, broke away from him laughing, and as she unlocked and flung open her parlor door, said, "Come, my lord and master, I cannot permit you to be naughty. You have a long night before you, and you must see all the beauties of this house before you will be able to decide whether you will accept my offer. Not a word more."

They entered one of the main parlors arm in arm, and Clara crossed the room and presented Master Walter to Mrs. Julia Brown, the proprietor of the establishment. Walter bowed to a magnificent woman, who was "fair, fat and forty." He then seated himself, and for a moment was lost in amazement. In different parts of the room were eight or more of the most exquisitely beautiful girls he had ever laid his eyes upon. Some were not over fifteen, or at most seventeen years of age. One was presiding at the piano, playing a waltz, while two others were waltzing with grace and elegance. All were dressed costly, but with exquisite taste. Walter had read of Turkish harems and voluptuous Circassian and Georgian beauties, but here he fancied that it was realized. The wine was passing freely, and Walter noticed that his friend had made no special acquaintance. He went up and spoke a few words to him. Henry made no reply except "Is is possible?" and then looked at Clara, who, amid all this galaxy of beauty, was partly reclining upon the sofa, the most beautiful among the beautiful. Her eye met Walter's and it seemed to say, "Are you satisfied that I am peerless here?"

Henry asked Walter a question, and directed his attention to a young and lovely creature that scarcely seemed to be twelve years old. Her cheeks were like roses, and her hair, which was in long clustering curls, seemed to cover her little figure as a black cloud. Walter went and spoke to Clara, who, laughing, said, "Oh, that is my sweet rose. I am very glad that your friend has made so good a choice. I will introduce him."

She went across the room to the young girl, brushed away the dark masses of hair from her face, talked with her a little while, and then beckoned to Henry Robinson. He crossed the room directly. "Henry, this is Rose, a little rose that was plucked away down in the State of Maine, at a place called Bangor, not many months ago. She has a loving heart, and is not very well suited for this house. She is very low spirited to-night. You must be responsible for her cheerfulness," and addressing Rose, "In the morning, you and Mr. Henry come and get breakfast in my parlor. Then the two friends can leave together."

Rose raised her beautiful gazelle eyes. "You, Miss Clara—you—you—his friend—why, I thought you never "———

Clara placed her finger on the Maine girl's lips. "Yes Rose, I am in love with his friend. I, the haughty Clara. Now don't say any more. Good-night, both of you," and she crossed to the sofa, and Walter took a seat by her side.

"Don't you think that Rose is exquisitely beautiful, Walter?" asked Clara.

"I don't think—look—or care for but one in this room. I believe I am getting crazy. That is you, Clara,"—and as he pressed his arm around her small waist, her exquisitely shaped head fell upon his breast. For some time they sat and listened to the music. Meanwhile, Rose and Henry had left the parlor, the former crossing and wishing his companion good-night. When they reached the sleeping-room of Rose, Henry found a large room, luxuriously furnished, and a sofa, upon which Rose flung herself.

"Lock the door and come and tell me all about yourself—where you have been, who you are, what brought you here to-night. What magic your friend Walter has, to be accepted by Clara, who never sees company, except it be some very rich, private friend, although she frequently goes into the parlor. Tell me every thing, and perhaps I will love you, if you will," exclaimed Rose, in almost the accents of a little school-girl.

Henry took her up in his arms as if she had been a child, and then related to her that he and Walter had been sent off on a whaling voyage, that both their fathers were gentlemen, that flung together in this way they had become very fondly attached, and that four years had elapsed since they went away.

"How Walter has fascinated Clara, I don't know. We only

landed to-day, and after getting some thing to eat, we came here. That is all, my little rose-bud, that I can tell you."

"Harry is not a pretty name. Henry is better. How I do hate this house! I wish I never had entered it. But—heigho—it can't be helped. You are the first person that has ever entered my room that I did not detest in five minutes," said Rose.

"Why, how is that?" asked Harry.

"You have treated me as if I were a young lady. You held me in your arms as my brothers once used to do, and you have not once taken advantage of my position. I feel very different to you from what I ever have done to visitors at this house."

Rose had met one who had sisters of his own equally beautiful as she. The next morning, when she and Harry Robinson entered the parlor to take breakfast, she blushed like a young bride who receives congratulations the morning after her wedding night. She attracted the attention of Clara, who exclaimed, "Why, you little silly chit. Take care you and Master Harry don't get in love, or you will have Mistress Brown about your ears. She has no objection to her girls making money, but she don't like to have them fall in love. Take care,"—and she shook her head menacingly.

Harry Robinson then observed, "Miss Clara, we wish you to be our friend. I want to take Rose out of this sort of business. She wants to leave it, too."

"Treason, treason to good Julia Brown. Why, you foolish child, where will you go?"

"I will fix that somehow, if I can only get her out of this. I have got a pocket-book pretty well lined, ain't it, Walter? She says she owes Julia Brown some money," remarked Robinson.

"How much, Rose dear?" demanded Clara.

"She told me thirty dollars last night, when I refused to talk with that drunken gambler, and she scolded me until I cried," replied Rose.

"She shall go with you if I have to have a quarrel with her. Take the poor child out of the house, Harry, and you will never regret so good a deed. Ask her out to walk when you go. Then take her to a hotel in the Bowery, called the North American. Go boldly in, and enter your names as man and wife. Walter will go and see you to-morrow night, and when Mrs. Brown finds that you have escaped her clutches, she will be very glad to give me your wearing apparel and trunks, and I will pay her all of her demands. Now eat your breakfasts, and then you, Rose, go and get on such clothes as will answer your purpose until to-morrow. Make up a small bundle of your night-clothes, and carry them in your hand. Mrs. Brown will not be up for two hours. I will let you out of the house, and Robinson, may God curse you if you ever desert that little thing, or allow her ever to get into a house of this kind again," exclaimed Clara Norris, earnestly.

"She never shall, if I can help it," and the young sailor meant what he said.

The breakfast was finished somewhat hurriedly, for Rose was somewhat anxious. Then she got ready. Clara walked to the door, and quietly undid the fastenings. Henry Robinson and Rose Banker followed, and in a moment were outside—free in the street. Clara carefully fastened the street door, and returned to her own apartments.

"Who knows, Walter, but that a human soul is saved? What a time I shall have with Madame Julia! Now, dear Walter, have you thought over what I have proposed? And have you made up your mind, after the most mature deliberation, to accept my proposition?" exclaimed Clara.

Before I give the replies of Walter to these questions, I must make a few explanations. Clara Norris had often seen Walter Granville, and knew his features well at the time she was the mistress of Mr. Nordheim. She had seen him at the theatre, had seen him with Miss Madison Pinckney; and although he had grown older and more manly in appearance, yet there was no very great change in the young boy she had known, and the young man she found in her parlor on the night that Walter came off from the ship. She knew him at once. Walter did not know her—did not know her name even. Of course, his female relations never allowed it to pass their lips, and his father or his father's friends and clerks were not likely to talk with him upon such a subject—one which affected the moral character of his father's partner. Consequently when he met Clara Norris in her parlor, he was ignorant of her person or of her name and antecedents. He was extremely flattered to find in an expensive house of its kind a beautiful woman, evidently flattered with his appearance—the more flattered, as she was of a higher grade than the regular residents of the mansion, and not dependent upon prostituting her person for a livelihood. She was beautiful—far more charming than any of the others, and placed herself at his disposal for love—certainly it was not for money, for she made it a condition of her love and favor that money should not be offered her.

Walter was vain at heart, and not supposing Clara knew anything about him or his family-friends, he came to the conclusion that she loved him, and he entered the luxurious trap without a thought of danger, and supposed that when breakfast was over in the morning he would probably never see her again.

But what were the thoughts of the gifted syren, who had so adroitly flung her auburn meshes around young Walter? Love! She had no more love, than would naturally arise towards a handsome, vigorous youth, who had been absent on a long voyage, and who had found in her the first female who was to respond to his caresses. But she had deeper and more dangerous designs; and she no sooner was satisfied that the runaway son of Pitt Granville was before her, than her mind was decided to have him at all costs and at all sacrifices. The first step was to place him under obligations to her.

When Henry Robinson and Rose had left the parlor, Clara waited a short time, and then whispered to Walter,

"Do you see any that you can love better than me?"

A loving kiss, and a whispered "No," was the reply.

"Follow me then;" and she sprang up and went to her parlor. Walter entered with her, and fastened the door.

"O, what will become of me, dear Walter? I am madly in love with you! I feared that you might see some one that you would like better than me, and I have been dreadfully alarmed;" and she flung her arms around him. "I am fainting—undress me and lay me on the sofa! What can you think of me?"

Walter was flattered in the worst manner. He did help her to undress, and there was revealed to him charms that would have tempted Saint Anthony. He was frenzied; but the artful girl was perfectly herself. She had her purpose.

"How dare you attempt such liberties!" and she assumed a sterner air. "I *do* love you, but I know nothing of you. I am a fool! Here you are, a strange sailor in my room, and I almost naked! What is there about you that has so fascinated me? Don't dare to take a liberty with me! Now tell me all about yourself. Who are you? Where do you belong? If you will tell me the truth, that moment I will let you carry me in yonder;" and she pointed to the sleeping apartment, the door of which was opened. "If you do not, you shall go. You are dressed, and I will open that door and call help, but you shall leave me. Now kneel down by me, and tell me all."

Walter was nearly mad—frantic with the arts of this syren.

He commenced and gave her his name, his history, the name of his father, in fact everything that he knew. Clara listened attentively. She knew it all before. She knew more than Walter did, for there were many things about his own family that he did not know. She did not offer to tell him these, but said,

"Dear Walter, I am not such a mad fool as I thought I was. You are a gentleman, and that is why I loved you from the first. Now I am yours—do what you please with me."

Her object was achieved, and she gave way to all her fiery and fierce passions, which had been so thoroughly aroused by the young sailor. As he lay clasped in her arms, could he have known her secret thoughts—her feelings of gratified revenge! There was a light in her sleeping apartment.

"O," thought Clara Norris, "could old Granville only know this! His son—my partner! It is a sweet revenge! Tom, too, who has abused me so—where is his loved nephew? Here in my arms—the abused, neglected, insulted Clara Norris—whom I am binding to me by chains stronger than those of father, sister, uncle or friend. Beautiful Isabel, that has insulted me wherever we have met, where is that manly, loving brother, that you would give almost your life to see once more! Where is he?—here in my arms—pillowed on the bosom of Clara Norris! O, this is delicious, exquisite revenge!" And with such feelings in her bosom—her worst passions, lust, hate and revenge all being gratified, she passed a sleepless night.

The next morning she met, as we have related, Henry and Rose. She had done apparently a good act, but it was to bind the friend of Walter to her more closely, that she had assisted in his running off Rose.

When they had departed, Walter spoke of leaving.

"Indeed, sir, you shall do no such thing. You are my prisoner. You shall not leave this house nor this room this day of our Lord. It is Sunday, and you shall worship here. Besides, you have told me your history, and now you shall follow my advice before you see any of your friends or your parent. I have no doubt I can help you to be reconciled with your father. You are independent. You need ask no favors. See here."

She showed him a large amount of gold, and bank bills of a large denomination.

"That is all yours, my dear Walter, if you need it. I don't love by halves, and I don't know but that I shall invite you to go up in the country, where I own a farm, and spend a week there. What do you think of it, dear Walter?"

"I will go anywhere with you—to the devil, if you say the word," replied Walter.

"We will see your friend and Rose settled, and then we will go," observed Clara.

"Will you see Harry all snug with his woman?"

"What is his name?" asked Clara.

"Henry Robinson," was the reply.

"Is his father the rich judge of that name?"

The same. That is his father is Chancellor of the State," replied Walter.

Walter remained all day in that house.

CHAPTER L.

Pledging a Watch—Simpson of Chatham street—Colonel Mac Neil pledges his duelling pistols—A scene at 43 Centre street—Marion gets scared—Finds the Count Falsechinski—He gives the Colonel one hundred dollars—O Doenvill watches the loan, and follows the Colonel to Harrison street.

MARION had a beautiful gold watch, which he had purchased of Allen in Wall street. It was a good watch—solid gold, lots of jewels—and cost one hundred dollars. The chain and other outrigging cost thirty dollars more. About once a month some stern necessity would compel him to part with this costly affair temporarily. He detested borrowing when he was short. It is a horrible degradation to an independent mind. When Mr. Monck had occasion for a small sum he would go openly to Mr. Simpson, in Chatham street, who ought to be regarded as an institution of New York. He is supposed to work for a large per centage. Grant it. He ought to get a much larger one. Who earns it so dearly? Simpson ought to charge more—he would do so, did he not find a large reward—

> In his calm and manly breast,
> In his blessed daily task
> Of pledging the distressed,
> Raising up the *broken* ones,
> Short as pie-crust now;
> *Bleeding* drops of deep remorse
> From an anguished brow.

His frequent visits attracted the attention of the elder Simpson, and on one occasion he observed to Marion Monck, "Do you give your real name when you pledge your watch?"

"I do, sir. I am not ashamed of it. Why do you ask?"

"Mere curiosity. Nothing more, I assure you," replied the pawnbroker. "Most people sneak in here as though they had been robbing a hen-roost, and felt mean. I am not ashamed of my business; and I like a customer who comes openly to me and says what he wants; and if I can let him what he needs I do it without any chaffing. Now I've given you twenty-five dollars on that watch. If you had wanted fifty dollars you should have had it," said the pawnbroker.

"You are a man of business, Mr. Simpson. Egad, you must see a good deal of the under-current of life. I would like to be hired by you for six months, just for the sake of studying human character. But don't you get taken in sometimes?" asked Marion.

"Indeed we do. It requires one to keep his eyes open to do this business and make any thing by it. We have so many rogues to deal with that we regard every man as a rogue until we are taught better by experience. We hear some sad stories—some heart-rending stories. We don't know whether they are true or not. Some doubtless are, but 'we have no time to examine,'" replied the pawnbroker.

"Those who love to relieve suffering would find lots of opportunities, Mr. Simpson, if they would watch those who came in here for relief," said Marion.

"Indeed you never spoke a truer word. Did you notice a very beautiful girl, who went out just as you came in? Neatly but poorly dressed? She pledged two sheets for twenty-five cents. She wanted fifty. Said it was to get food for a sick mother until she got her pay next Saturday night, when she would return the money. She is a book-folder. Her mother and she can sleep between blankets—do without sheets—can't do without food. I am a blessing to that girl. But for me, where would she go to keep her mother from starving? On the town!—where else?" emphatically demanded Mr. Simpson.

"You are a philosopher. I wish I had known how she was situated. She should not have wanted a few dollars to help her along in her dreary walk," said Marion, kindly.

"Oh, yes! I dare say—and you would have wanted something else before you finished with her. Young men are young men. I make it a point never to speak of what I know in reference to young females who come to my shop. Were I to do so, I should be the cause of the ruin of a great many. Now I know that young girl's address. She gave it true. It is on the duplicate ticket for the two sheets. You seem to be a little better than these seducers about town; but do you suppose I would put you in the way of temptation, and, having told you how destitute that girl is, tell you also where you could find her? No, sir. You would go, relieve her, get her gratitude, talk marriage and honor, and all that sort of lying nonsense, and—probably I should not see her again until bye-and-bye, after the lapse of a year, she would come here, rouged like the red sides of a peach, to make a raise on a gold watch or a silk dress to pay room rent to some boss prostitute. No, sir. I don't do business that way. I don't trust such secrets to any body," said the conscientious broker.

"But, my dear sir, you don't suppose I am such a sort of person, or that I would use information so obtained to debauch a young and beautiful girl?" replied Marion, a little angered and mortified.

"I do not know what you might do. I do know that you will not get any information from me about it. Poverty to a young and attractive girl is a fearful thing any how; but it is her defensive armor only so long as prowlers don't know it. When a bad man is aware that a girl and her poor mother are in a state of starvation, he has the game in his own hands, if he chooses to run it down," said the pawnbroker.

In the pawnbroker's shop of the worthy Simpson there is a long counter, but at the extreme end there are some three or four cubby-houses, opened to the counter, but with high sides; and when the door of this little pigeon-house is closed, it can be locked inside, and the party occupying it can keep partially concealed. Just as the pawnbroker had finished about the girl, a person entered hurriedly, and passed into one of the boxes. Marion was startled—he thought he had recognized the person, although he had but a glimpse of him as he passed. The party handed to the pawnbroker a dark-colored mahogany box, saying,

"How much can you let me have on these?"

Simpson opened the box, for the key was in it.

"They are hair-trigger duelling pistols," said the applicant.

"Old-fashioned affairs—out of date. Wouldn't sell for much," replied the pawnbroker.

"They have been used on two melancholy occasions with deadly effect," observed the applicant.

"Have a sort of historical value, have they? But it don't count much with us," said Mr. Simpson.

"That identical pair of pistols, sir, was used in the duel between Burr and Hamilton, and more recently in a duel between Colonel Graham and Mr. Barton," observed the applicant.

"You are Mr. Barton, I suppose," asked the pawnbroker.

"I am not, sir, but I was a second to that gentleman when his opponent was killed," replied the applicant.

"Indeed! How much do you want on them? If they had been used to murder all creation, it wouldn't make 'em worth a mite more in this shop," said Simpson, very coolly.

"I dare say it would not; but those pistols must have cost over eighty guineas," urged the applicant, and added, "I want twenty dollars upon them."

"Can't do it—will give you ten, if that will do;" and the pawnbroker turned to another customer.

"Give it to me, then, and take them," said the applicant.

"Your name and residence, sir," asked the pawnbroker.

"Smith—43 Centre street," was the reply.

"First name?" asked the pawnbroker.

"William," was the reply.

The tickets were arranged, and the applicant took his departure.

"Good-bye, Mr. Simpson," said Marion Monck.

"Good-bye, sir. Come in again—glad to see you," replied Mr. Simpson.

No sooner was Marion Monck out in the street, than he addressed himself thus: "Poor Mac! This will never do. I am hard up, but he is worse off, or he would never have pledged those redoubtable duelling-pistols of his, which he exhibits with so much reverence. What can have happened?"

He hurried up to Centre street, and there he found the Colonel sipping a glass of liquor, as though nothing had happened.

"Egad, I will not mortify him so much as to tell him I am aware of his visit to the pawnbroker's," thought Marion; and as he approached Colonel Mac Neil, who was so short-sighted that he could not distinguish a face before he heard the voice, he exclaimed, "Good morning, Colonel; how do you feel this morning? Anything new? I will join you in a drink. I collected some money this morning, and am quite flush."

Saying this, he pulled out a roll, and without waiting for a reply to his first salutation, gaily remarked, "If you want some, Colonel, help yourself—but I know you never want money."

"My dear boy, you were never more mistaken in your life. I do want money—I want just twenty dollars. I have ten—

see it—and—I will help myself to a ten from your pile—if you can spare it, that is?"

"Easily, my dear Colonel, and as long as you want it," added Marion.

"No, I don't want it very long. The fact is, Marion," and here the Colonel lowered his voice to a whisper, "I have had a hard time of it lately. Things have all gone wrong. I am getting quite discouraged. I have a home with the proprietor of this store—old porter of mine when I was rich, you know. Always kept some cash in his hands, and I hate to borrow without being able to repay, eh? Safe rule that, eh? Keep one horse saddled and one in the stable, eh?" said the poor Colonel.

There was an unusual wildness about Colonel Mac Neil as he said this, which Marion was very sorry to perceive. He discovered that the Colonel had been drinking very freely the day before, and he was so nervous that he was obliged to take three stiff drinks while Marion was with him, to steady his nerves. Marion felt inclined to give the Colonel a few words of friendly advice, and to caution him against excessive drink; but he had hardly spoken a word respecting it, when Mac Neil uttered the sentence, "Boy, stop! Not a word more, or never dare speak to me again!"

Marion was silenced. He was awed by this wreck of humanity, who was so much older, and who had seen so many vicissitudes in life; and he mentally resolved never to open his lips again upon the subject, no matter what occurred. He felt it to be useless. For a proud man, who has become addicted to drink, and continues it to excess, is the last man in the world to permit old friends to discuss such a subject, or to give him any advice. He regards it as a wanton insult, and would affront the only remaining friend he had on earth to resent such interference.

There were in that place other persons well known to Colonel Mac Neil, and also to Marion. One of these, whom we have alluded to as Charley, the clergyman's brother, was a very sensible and a very practical man. Loss of business, of property, and utter hopelessness, had led him to abandon himself to drink to drown sorrow, but he had a limit which he never exceeded. He never went to bed sober, but he managed to eat his meals regularly, and this gave the rum he drank something to feed on. Mr. Charles addressed Marion, and requested to speak with him alone. Marion retired to the back of the store, and both took seats upon a pipe of mixed gin.

"Mr. Monck, I want to tell you that our friend the Colonel is going it *too* strong. He can't stand it. If he don't let up a little he is a croaker. His constitution is cracked."

Marion asked in some alarm if anything of importance had recently happened.

"O no, except the Colonel has been keeping up a tremendous head of steam, and until a very late hour. I heard him say this morning, when he came down, that he had had no sleep for forty-eight hours. When he took his first drink this morning, I had to help him steady his glass to get it to his lips. He was very shaky, I assure you. It can't last long," observed the good-natured Mr. Charles.

"Good God, I should think not! But what can be done? I don't like to say anything. I did speak to him just now, and he gave me a reprimand that I shall not forget in a hurry. I will do anything that I can do. Tell me what I can do?" said Marion.

"He ought to be placed under some restraint, sir. He can't control himself. Has he no friends that would pay for placing him in the Hospital? It is only twelve dollars. They cure him for that, and keep him from drink while he is there. If he is fool enough to drink when he comes out, and rush it again, why he must take the consequences," observed the prudent Charles.

"The money," replied Marion, "is of no consequence. That is easily raised. But who will broach the subject to the Colonel? If he don't see the necessity of going to the hospital he will not go, and there is an end of it."

"True, very true. But he is getting worse every day. If he don't see the necessity to-day, he may to-morrow. I will try and see what I can do. He may listen to me, as I am nearly of his age. He will not to you—that is certain. I will talk to you again to-morrow;" and with this benevolent sentiment Mr. Charles put an end to the conversation by reporting himself in person to an invitation to take a drink.

Marion began to sicken of the scene. He saw Colonel Mac Neil again going up to the bar for another drink. He saw even the proprietor shake his head reprovingly to the Colonel. Then Marion made his escape from the premises by a rear door. He was very anxious about the Colonel. He had received twenty-five dollars, and he had let the Colonel have ten. He went at once to his landlady, and gave her the remaining fifteen dollars. He now determined to see the Count Falsechinski. He knew that at that hour the Count would be at Delmonico's in Beaver street. He hurried down there, and luckily found him. The Count received him very cordially, but scolded him for not coming oftener to see him.

"I have sought you this morning, Count, to tell you about poor Colonel Mac Neil. You know I like him. I this morning gave him ten dollars."

"Where did you get the money to spend on him?"

Marion's blood rushed to his checks, and he took out his pawn ticket.

"There, sir. I pledged my watch to get twenty-five dollars, and ten dollars I gave poor Mac, and fifteen dollars I paid my landlady," said Marion.

"Pshaw, my boy—don't get vexed with me! I have a fixed purpose for you. It is only fair that I should pay your expenses until my plans are ripe. Here is money. Don't turn an angry look at me—I will not see it. Here are two bills of one hundred dollars each—make them go as far as they will. This money is for yourself—not for Colonel Mac Neil. Still, Marion, as the Colonel was the means of making you and I acquainted, I will do anything for him that you desire. Where can I find him? I will go with you now," said the Count.

Marion was surprised at the alacrity of the Count. He received and pocketed the two hundred dollars without any remark. The two started for Centre street. While on the way the Count was pleasant and communicative, and talked upon a variety of topics. At last he said,

"Upon second thoughts, I do not wish you to go with me to see Colonel Mac Neil. Tell me where he is to be found, and I will find him. Now go and get your watch and join me at the Colonel's."

Marion complied with the wish of the Count's. As he entered Simpson's the second time that day, he handed him the ticket and a hundred dollar bill. Mr. Simpson received it, gave the change, and ordered a boy to go get the watch. He made no comment. Most men would have said something, as, "O, you are in luck;" "Have you been robbing anybody?" or "Found a gold mine?" but such a man was not Mr. Simpson. Commenting was not in his line. There was some little delay attending the delivery of the watch, and when Marion reached No. 43 Centre street, where he was to meet Count Falsechinski, he found that gentleman engaged in earnest conversation with Colonel Mac Neil. Marion did not interrupt their conversation, but he was surprised. He had never noticed the Colonel in such glorious spirits. He seemed to be a new man, and perfectly sober. He remarked this fact to Mr. Charles. The latter was an old soldier. He observed in reply, "That is all false. He is drinking upon dead liquor in his system. A gallon of rum would not have made him drunk this morning. But to-morrow—wait until to-morrow! See him in the morning! It will be dreadful, and it will be worse every succeeding day, until the Colonel has the delirium tremens. I know just how it works—you can't tell me anything about that matter. Colonel Mac Neil don't eat anything—he don't sleep, and he drinks like a fish. Of course such a bad state of things cannot last long. There will be a pull up some time or another."

Having delivered these brief philosophical observations, the brother of the Trinity Church clergyman went to take another drink to his own cheek.

Marion approached the Count and Colonel Mac Neil. The latter spoke in a stern voice, "No, sir. No, sir. Not as a favor. Not as a loan from you, sir. I am a gentleman, sir. I am of the race of Mac Neil. I accept the hundred dollars you are so kind as to loan me, provided you, sir, accept this ridiculous pawn-ticket for a petty ten dollars for pistols that have killed a Hamilton and a Graham."

The Count took the ticket at once, for he was afraid of a scene. "That is right, sir. We are now equals. It is a regular business transaction. You have collateral security of at least two hundred and fifty dollars for a loan of one hundred dollars. Now let us take a drink. What will you have, Count Falsechinski?" Colonel Mac Neil continued.

The Count pleasantly named his drink to the bar-tender.

"Count," continued the Colonel, "did you ever see in me, sir, any thing incompatible with the character of a gentleman? One of the race of Mac Neil. The best blood in the Highlands in olden times, and I am proud of it, sir. You are a blooded masculine, if Poles can have blood, Count, eh? Excuse the pun, but you are a Pole, are you not? A noble Pole. Well, success to you. Here is your very good health."

The Count replied in courteous terms, and began to look at the door, and seemed uneasy. Just at that moment Marion noticed Mr. O'Doemall seated near the chairs recently occupied by the Colonel and the Count. O'Doemall had evidently been a witness to the money scene between the two parties. As soon as he perceived that he was noticed by Marion, he came forward in his bold, daring way, said "How d'y?" to Marion, and addressed both the Count and Colonel. The former bowed, but the latter treated Mr. O'Doemall with coldness, and made an excuse to leave. O'Doemall then ordered a drink for himself, and began to converse with the Colonel. Marion no sooner observed the departure of the Count than he followed him into the street, but he lost him, and concluded not to return to the drinking saloon.

The artful O'Doemall had it all his own way with Colonel Mac Neil after the departure of the Count Falsechinski and Marion Monck. He flattered his vanity, and the Colonel was fast getting too intoxicated to notice the hollowness of praise coming from such foul lips, and he also forgot the character of the man with whom he was associating.

Finally, the Colonel expressed his intention of going and spending an evening with his family.

" Family !" interrupted O'Doemall, " I did not know that you had a family. Where do they live ?"

This question for a moment sobered the Colonel, who felt that he had said too much, and with a scowl at his impudent companion, remarked, " You are a rascal. Clear out at once, or I will order you to be put out."

Mr. O'Doemall went out at once, but his departure was not noticed by the Colonel. Unluckily for him that this artful scamp had again been permitted to renew an acquaintance which had ended for ever, but for his kindness to Marion Monck when sick. Mr. O'Doemall had seen the Count hand Colonel Mac Neil money. He had tried to get into Mac Neil's good graces, but had failed. He now determined to watch him. Shortly after Colonel Mac Neil left 43 Centre street, and passed over to the west side of Broadway. At several stores he stopped and made purchases. Some of the smaller articles so purchased he carried on himself. The others he ordered sent to the address he left with the different store keepers. When he had satisfied himself, he continued on his way to 27 Harrison street, and entered the house. No sooner had the door closed than O'Doemall, who had been following him, crossed the street to the house, and after having carefully noticed the number, he passed down the street to the dock.

" I have housed my game, and I will try and amuse myself for a short time, or until he comes out," was his soliloquy.

CHAPTER LI.

The Plans of Walter Granville and Miss Norris—Julia Brown—The Departure of Rose—Miss Norris leaves Miss Brown's Residence.

If Walter Granville had returned like the Prodigal Son in the year 18— or thereabouts, no doubt old Granville would have bid him welcome, got up a great dinner, and celebrated the event with considerable rejoicings; but young Granville came back after years of absence with no repentant feelings. His father had kicked him out, and Walter felt much obliged to him that he had done so. It had made a man of him—made a free man. He had returned to this city because the vessel in which he had been cruising was ordered to New York. He had landed without intending to call upon his father, friends, or any body else. As a rover he had called at No. 100 Church street, because he had known in earlier years that the house at that number was kept for pleasure purposes. He had money to spend, and he intended to spend some of it there, and the meeting with Miss Norris was entirely accidental. He regarded it as a piece of good fortune. Her curious conduct had saved him money, and he felt obliged.

When Clara proposed to Walter Granville to remain there that Sunday, and to go up in the country with her, he consented at once, because he had nothing to do on board the vessel, and nothing in town that he was aware of. His sea chest was where he could get it at any moment, and he had no alarm about that.

Neither Clara Norris nor Walter Granville had any idea of what a storm was brewing in Church street, to be shortly poured out upon their devoted heads by the worthy Mrs. Julia Brown. That lady was not a woman to be robbed of one of her most beautiful night birds without fluttering her motherly wings.

This lady deserves more than a passing notice. Previous to the date of our Chapter, Julia Brown kept a two-story house of ill-fame in Leonard street. It was pulled down in 1837 to make room for the new Italian Opera House. Thence Madam moved to 100 Church street, and after residing there for some years, she returned to Leonard street, and in one of the most magnificent Palaces of Sin ever built in New York, continued business for a long time. This house was next door to the Italian Opera House. When that edifice was burnt, Julia's house was consumed also. It was in this fire that the celebrated Mr. G., who was sleeping with the noted courtesan Mary Moore, the female partner in London of Colonel Monroe Edwards. G. barely escaped in his shirt from being burned to death.

Miss Julia Brown made a large fortune in this business.— She was a beautiful woman, but not immoral herself. She was married to a fancy man named Jack Harris. For a long time he was her fancy man, but when a daughter was born, he became her husband.

This Jack Harris was also a character in his day. He was a sporting man, drank hard, lived high, made bets on every thing—and in a word was a thorough-bred gambler. He was also a great politician, and in those days ruled the Fifth Ward Democratic politics, and presided at the primary meeting that first elected Fernando Wood to a seat as a member of the Young Men's Committee at Tammany Hall.

Jack Harris had a friend named Allen who would lend him a thousand dollars whenever he needed it, and for a week's use of this sum would charge Jack one hundred. Miss Julia Brown, though conducting a business for the public down town, had her own magnificent residence in Fourth street, up town. At this house lived her daughter, who probably never was inside of her mother's " place of business." The daughter was not pretty, but intelligent and virtuous. While living in Fourth street, which house she owned, Julia came down in her carriage to her business in the morning, and retired at night, leaving in charge for the later hours, a housekeeper.

All of a sudden, from being a pretty sinner, Miss Julia Brown became a violent saint. Her first appearance in this character was at a sale of pews in a Universalist church in her neighborhood. She bought a pew half way up the middle aisle, and paid for it one hundred and seventy dollars. She attended this church, occupying her own seat, for several Sundays, accompanied by her daughter. No one knew her—but on the sixth Sunday, a gentleman in the adjoining seat became aware of the proximity of his old acquaintance Julia Brown, and he mentioned the circumstance to his wife, who was a member of the church. She told it to a dozen other female members, and it kicked up a delight for the devil in that congregation. A large majority were for putting Julia out of the synagogue without a word of explanation. More peaceable measures were recommended by the clergyman, and it was decided that he should call upon the frail but somewhat notorious sinner at her own domicile.

He did so. Julia was a good actor. She spread herself at once: confessed that she had been bad—very bad, but that she had repented, was living in private—had married Jack—was bringing up her daughter right, and had hopes that she should be enabled to convert Jack Harris, and get him all straight. The clergyman felt bad. It was a mighty hard case. He preached a sermon about Mary Magdalen—the congregation sympathized—and the upshot was that Julia continued in favor, and eventually became a religious lioness in that church, and visited freely with the different families of that congregation—and among others, that of Mr. Allen.

Meanwhile Julia did sell out her establishment down town —or pretended that she had done so. Her daughter had grown up to be a fine young girl. She was courted by several young men. One of them was Mr. F. E., one of the handsomest men in the City, or that could be found in the State. Mr. E. was accepted, and the parties were married, with the full consent and approval of both Julia Brown and Mr. Harris.

Not long after the marriage was solemnized, Julia, who was posted in all the wickedness of the world in general, and of mankind in particular, discovered that her son-in-law had become the fancy man of one Ellen McVean, a handsome courtezan that resided with Cinderella Marshall in Leonard street, opposite Julia's old house. The mother went to work and procured a divorce for her daughter. Not long after, another suitor appeared. He was a lawyer, named McM. He married the divorced Mrs. E. Then Julia Brown died, leaving a very large property to this daughter, and left Allen (Jack's friend) executor. Then Jack died, and he also left his property to this daughter, and also made Allen his executor. The daughter of Julia was now rich in her own right. She owned a large tract on the Fifth avenue. Then she built a house and moved into it with her husband. The lady believed that money was the *sesame* that opened all doors. She had money, and she desired to shine in the Fifth avenue. But powerful as is money, it failed to place Mrs. McM. at the head of the sett about her. One's grandmother may have been a washerwoman, or never have had any existence. But when one's mother is notorious for having made the money we are inclined to spend off the souls and bodies of human beings by keeping a house of ill-fame, it brings things too near home. It is coming it too strong. So thought some of Mrs. McM.'s neighbors, and they "cut her."

Disappointed as was Mrs. McM. in such a result, she was not dispirited or disheartened. She determined to command success—to shine as a star somewhere. Her mother was a woman whose fame was a public one, why should not the daughter appeal to the public for favor, although in a different way, and under somewhat different auspices? This decided her, so she took to Shakespeare and the stage, and made her first appearance in Buffalo. She came to New York, and hired the Academy of Music for one night. Not satisfied with these appearances, she determined to try another feat. She became manager of a theatre in Chambers street, and we hope she will carve her way to a niche in the temple of fame.

This digression is not out of place. It is an episode that could not be left out; and having followed in brief the fortunes of the mother to her death, and the daughter to her becoming a public character, we now return to Julia Brown when she was in her glory at No. 100 Church street, coining money as if she were owner of a mint.

We left Walter Granville and Clara waiting in the parlor appropriated to Clara. It was near midday before Mrs. Brown made her appearance. It was then reported to her that Rose had not been down. Mrs. Brown sent at once to Clara Norris to ask if she knew anything about Rose. Clara made no reply, but went to Mrs. Brown herself.

"Rose is not in my room, Mrs. Brown," said Clara.

"Did not she and her companion of last night get breakfast with you?" asked Mrs. Brown, who was getting warm.

"They did," replied Miss Norris.

"Then where is Rose?" again demanded Mrs. Brown.

"To tell you the truth, Mrs. Julia Brown, I think Rose has gone for good. She was but a child, and the person who was with her last night took her off," was the reply of Miss Norris.

"Why in h—ll did you not stop it? Why did you not rouse the house—rouse me? I had rather have lost five hundred dollars than that girl!" exclaimed Julia.

"I was not aware of that. I let her out myself," innocently observed Miss Norris.

"You, Clara Norris! Do you dare to tell me this!" and

she seized an iron bar that fastened one of the windows, and approached her as if to strike.

"Have a care, Mrs. Brown. One step nearer, and you will go to h—ll before your time;" and Clara drew from her bosom a small dagger. She held it so close to Mrs. Julia, that the latter dropped the bar, and putting on one of her sweetest smiles, exclaimed,

"Why, Clara, dear, what is the matter? I was only joking."

Clara replied, calmly, "Take care, Julia, that you don't try such jokes on me once too often. Have a care."

It was now Julia's turn to be calm. She asked who was to pay a debt that Rose owed her?

"Come, Julia," said Clara. "If you will send all Rose's things to my room, I will pay you out of my own purse. You shall not lose by my carelessness. Really, had I known that Rose was such a valuable little package, I should have been more careful. Now be a good woman, and go get Rose's things packed. How much is her debt?"

"Forty dollars," replied the somewhat mollified Brown.

"I will pay it when I have her trunks; and now I think of it, I will go and see Rose's things picked up and packed, and have her trunks placed in my room;" and she tripped out of the room. Could she have heard the curses hurled at her by Julia when she had left the room, she would have hugged her small dagger more closely.

The trunks of Rose were packed and placed in Clara's parlor. Then she sent for a carriage to be at No. 100 after dinner. She and Walter dined together, and then had the trunks of Rose placed in the carriage. The driver had his instructions, and the couple entered and were driven to the North American Hotel, in the Bowery.

They found Mr. and Mrs. Robinson's names on the book, and were shown to their room. Rose was very grateful, and ordered up her trunks. Walter and Henry Robinson left the ladies together, and went down into the sitting-room, and had a cosy chat about matters.

"I hope, Robinson," said Henry, "that I shall soon see some opening in New York. I will never go to sea any more."

"Indeed, and by the way, what are you going to do with that little girl Rose," asked Walter.

"Save her from destruction, if I can, and become steady myself. And you, Walter, what are you going to do with Clara?" replied Henry.

"Probably she will send me to destruction. I do not know.

I shall take my chances. Where will I find you if you leave her?" asked Walter.

"I will always leave my address at the hotel for you," replied Robinson.

Soon after Clara and Walter returned to Julia Brown's. That lady was ripe for a row. She had heard of Clara's proceedings, and the course she had pursued with the sailor Walter was perfectly disgusting to the landlady.

"I wish you to quit these premises, Miss Clara, as soon as you find it convenient. I won't have such carryings on. You put yourself up—you make out yourself a lady, and put on airs. Hoity-toity, what a long tail our pussy cat has got! Get out!" exclaimed Mrs. Brown, choking with indignation.

"Leave my room, madam, instantly!" said Clara, for it was in her parlor that this scene occurred.

"I will leave your parlor—*my* parlor, that is. I don't associate with picked up common sailors, I don't," replied the indignant Brown.

A decanter hurled by Walter at the head of the saucy landlady, and which dashed to pieces against the wall, brought the dialogue to an end, and Mrs. Brown made good her retreat, threatening police, and all sorts of vengeance.

Clara rang the bell. It was answered, and she a second time ordered a carriage, and then told the messenger to say to Mrs. Brown that Miss Norris would leave as soon as the carriage was ready. Again Mrs. Brown came, and this time it was to try to make up.

"Be it so—I have nothing against you. Hand me fifty, Julia, and we are quits."

The money was paid. It took some time to pack up all the articles of apparel belonging to Miss Clara, but at last it was completed, with Walter's assistance. The baggage almost loaded down the coach, and when Clara and Walter entered it, they had barely room to seat themselves.

"Where now?" asked the driver.

Clara replied "Bond street," and gave him a card.

Walter made no observation until the carriage stopped at an elegant house in Bond street.

"We will not go into the country for some days, Walter, and I have brought you to a friend's residence, where we will stay a short time," said Clara.

"Is she one of the *other* sort?" asked Walter.

"No. She is a pious lady—keeps her own carriage," replied Clara.

Mrs. Woodruff was really glad to see Clara, and when she introduced Walter Granville by his own name, she regarded Clara with astonishment.

"Is he the son of Pitt Granville?"

"Yes, Mrs. Woodruff; and you must make him at home for his father's sake," replied Miss Norris.

Tea was soon after served, and Walter was more amazed and more mystified than ever. The pious Mrs. Woodruff and her palace and its solitude he could not pretend to fathom, and did not try to do it.

CHAPTER LII.

Colonel Mac Neil's Last Night with His Family—He has a Presentiment of His Fate, and Prepares for it—He is Knocked Down, Robbed, and Badly Hurt in Franklin street—Gets to 40 Centre street About Daybreak—He Dreads Delirium Tremens, and is Persuaded to go to the City Hospital—Marion Monck goes up with him.

COLONEL MAC NEIL's appearance in 27 Harrison street, under any circumstances, was a welcome apparition. He carried thither sunshine and happiness. His two children were delighted, and a calm peace diffused itself through the bosom of that mother. Miss Jane McPherson was an extraordinary woman. She was Scotch, had many of the prejudices and opinions of the Scotch people; she worshipped Mac Neil, and regarded his proud family and his descent as some thing so superior to her own, that she never blamed him for not marrying her, but framed excuses in her own heart for his conduct. Her soul was given to him and his children. If she sometimes prayed that he might marry her, it was not from selfish considerations, or from the thought that her position would be more respectable. It was because, in her simple way of thinking, if the Colonel was her husband, he would live in the house with her and the children, and she would be able to nurse, tend, and care for him in sickness.

To the children he was affectionate and tender, and showed more marked kindness than if they had been legitimate. Both were attending the free school in North Moore street, and were making rapid progress in their studies. In these studies the Colonel took a deep interest, and encouraged them to be pursued on every visit. He never failed to bring them presents of any thing that he thought they would like, and scarcely a week passed that he did not send them a sufficiency of the best of provisions for their maintenance. He would not suffer Jane to broach the subject of money. He had not drawn a dollar from their little fund since he made the settlement upon her. On the contrary, he had added to it, at one time eight hundred dollars, and in small sums to the extent of two hundred dollars more. On the occasion of this visit, Colonel Mac Neil was unusually kind and affectionate. He kissed the young people fondly, and to Miss Jane he seemed perfectly devoted. The good woman set out the table, and prepared a pleasant spread for him. Soon after the Colonel made his appearance, different porters arrived with things he had bought that he was unable to bring himself. All seemed happy, but Miss Jane felt a gloom that she could not account for. She had a presentiment of evil, and it was increased when the tea was over, and the Colonel handed her a package.

"Jane," said the Colonel, "we are all liable to die, and I have thought it best to write out an order for my few things in case of any accident ever happening to me. I have a valuable bureau—old family papers in it—that some day I want my son to have. It is in the rear of No. 46 Centre street. The owner of that store has rooms in his house to rent. I occupy a small one, and in it are personal matters that I want to become my son's. I have written all about these matters in the letter I now give you. Should I die, I think it would be better that you move out of New York. It is a bad place. You do not know who to trust, and a lone, unprotected woman has a hard time of it—or if you do not choose to do that, send for your father to come to New York. The old man would not refuse to do so when I am dead and out of the way. But mind, I do not wish to advise you against your own good common sense."

While the Colonel was delivering this melancholy address, Miss Jane placed both hands to her face and wept.

The Colonel kindly observed, "Don't be so foolish, Jane. I have got to die some day, and I say these unpleasant things now, for they have got to be said some day, and it may as well be done first as last. With my letter to you and to the children in your possession, I feel relieved. I am rid of an unpleasant duty," and as if to confirm his words, the Colonel began to be quite merry. He told anecdotes, sang a few songs, and when he said he must go, it seemed as though the children would not let him do so. Poor Colonel Mac Neil. He kissed them all affectionately, and left the house. It was near eleven o'clock, and he hurried onward as fast as possible, hoping to get as far as 46 Centre street before Harry closed up for the night. He knew what time it was, for at the moment of leaving his children he took a gold repeater from his pocket and looked at the hour. Then he looked at the massive chain and the seal. He had frequently explained to his son that the seal bore upon it the coat of arms of his family. He gave the watch to his son, telling him he might wear it if he would be careful of it. Then he added, playfully, "As you are going to sport a gold watch, you ought to have corresponding clothes. Let me see if I have got any money about me." He took from his vest pocket a roll of money, and counted out fifty dollars. "There, sir, that must do for you; and you, Sissy," for so he called his daughter, "you must have some, too,"—and he handed her an equal sum.

"But Popsy, you have none left for yourself," exclaimed Willy.

"Yes, I have over twenty dollars, and that is all I need to-day, and if I get short to-morrow I will come and borrow of you rich folks, eh?" replied the father

This had occurred before he left 27 Harrison street, and as we mentioned before, when he got into the street, the Colonel knew that it was nearly eleven o'clock. He walked up to Franklin street, and stopped for a moment to get a glass of brandy in at Thomas Riley's Fifth Ward Hotel. Then he passed across to Centre street, walking on the north side of Franklin. Little did poor Mac fear that there was an enemy on his track, watching every movement, and all for the purpose of securing his watch and the money he was supposed to have about his person. But the Colonel's thoughts were of the scene he had left, of the dear spot where he had spent the evening. He passed Elm street, and was opposite the Tombs, on the side where the arsenal yard then stood. He felt a blow, and stars sparkled in his eyes, and he remembered no more. The first recollection after this was of partly lying on a wet sidewalk close to the board fence. The rain was pouring in torrents. It was pitch dark. The Tombs loomed up opposite to him, and he only recognized that massive Egyptian architecture by the light of the lamp over the Franklin street entrance. The Colonel was amazed. He remained still for some time, and tried to recollect what had happened. "I must have fallen down; but it did not rain when I was walking. It is very queer. I certainly was not drunk; and where is my hat? It must be after eleven o'clock. I will hurry on to Harry's place. He may not have shut up yet."

These were his thoughts. With great difficulty he stood upon his feet. He could not find his hat. This annoyed him. The idea of Colonel Mac Neil doing such a shocking thing as to walk through the street without his hat worried him extremely. He had never had such a disrespectable affair occur during a long life. He felt confident of one thing; he had not been so drunk as not to know what he was about. Then he kept on to Centre street. He walked—walked—and turned and looked about him. Not a store was open, not a light visible, save the lamps of the street. His head felt queer, but he kept on. Again and again did he stop and look about him. Not a place, or corner, or house could he recognize. At last he came to an open spot. It still rained, but as it poured upon his head, the Colonel seemed relieved. Then he found himself close to an iron railing, and he sat down upon the stone foundation. "I ought to know this spot," he exclaimed, aloud. Just then, directly over his head, pealed out the deep tones of a bell. "One," "two," "three," "four," "five," he counted, and the bell ceased to strike, and its dying notes vibrated off into the upper air. "As I live, that is St. John's Church. This is the park, and it is five o'clock. Great God! what is the matter with me? This is the most singular thing that ever happened to me in my life. I will go to some hotel, for I feel weak." He arose with difficulty, and tottered towards Hudson street. Here he recognized his whereabouts, and he turned down town. When he reached Harrison street, he recognized that street "Ah! there are my loved ones. I will go there; but no, I won't do it, either, poor things." Even in that hour of distress, sick, wet to the skin, without a hat, he preferred to suffer himself rather than discompose Jane or disturb the rest of his children. He turned up Chambers street, and walked slowly across to Centre street. It was becoming lighter every moment, and as he reached the store No. 46 Centre street, Jemmy, the clerk, was opening the front door. The Colonel got inside and grasped a chair.

"What do you want?" exclaimed Jemmy.

"My God, Jemmy, it is me, Colonel Mac Neil."

In a moment Jemmy closed the door and lit one of the gaslights, and then as he gazed at the hatless Colonel, he exclaimed, "Gracious Heaven, Colonel, what has happened?"

"Really, Jemmy, nothing particular. I've lost my hat somehow," replied the Colonel.

"Why, you are covered with blood. You lip is cut open, and your hair, Colonel, is filled with blood."

"I am faint, Jemmy. Give me a glass of spirits—any thing," said the exhausted man.

In a moment it was procured and drank.

"Examine me, Jemmy, and see what is the matter."

Jemmy examined his head. In the back were two deep cuts, from which the Colonel must have bled freely. Three front teeth had been knocked out, and the under lip was laid open, and fell down almost to the chin. Jemmy told him all this, and went and procured a glass, in which the Colonel could see reflected his ghastly, bloody appearance.

"I have had a severe fall."

"Fall, Colonel! You have been knocked down. Where is your money?"

The Colonel attempted to put his hands in his vest pockets. They were turned inside out. Not a cent was about him.

"I have been robbed," he exclaimed. "Knocked down and robbed. That is it, is it not, Jemmy? Well, I am thankful that I have not brought myself into such a disrespectable position by being drunk."

"Had you much money about you, Colonel?" asked Jemmy, who exhibited the deepest sympathy for the Colonel's misfortunes, and who had ever treated him with the greatest respect.

"I had, Jemmy, over a hundred and twenty dollars and my gold watch and chain last night."

"And all is gone, Colonel?" exclaimed Jemmy.

"No. Hang the rascal or rascals, they got bit, Jemmy. I left my watch with some dear friends, and a hundred dollars of my money also, so that I have only been robbed of about twenty dollars. Curse them," said the Colonel, who seemed pleased that he had done the pickpockets out of some plunder.

"Do you suspect any one, Colonel?" asked Jemmy.

"I? not one. No body that I know would rob me."

"Who was with you last yesterday, in this place?"

"The Count Falsechinski, Monck and O'Doemall."

"Did any one of them know that you had money, Colonel? asked Jemmy.

"To be sure they did. Two of them gave me what I had and they certainly would not rob me of it," said Mac Neil.

"Not likely; and the third one, Colonel, was Mr. O'Doemall You yourself called him a scamp yesterday, and ordered him out of the store. He saw that Count hand you the money. I will bet all the money I have in the world, that Mr. O'Doemall was the man who knocked you down and robbed you," exclaimed Jemmy.

"Pooh! pooh! Jemmy. That can't be. John O'Doemall is a hard case, but he would not commit a robbery. Besides, how could he know where I was to be found last night at eleven o'clock?" exclaimed Colonel Mac Neil.

"Well, Colonel, there is no proof of it, but my opinion cannot be easily shaken, that the fellow O'Doemall robbed you last night; but I must open and put the store to rights," said Jemmy.

"And I, Jemmy, will go and change my dirty linen and wash up."

When the Colonel got back to his bureau and the glass, he discovered that he was severely hurt, and the wounds pained him extremely. He washed, changed his linen, arranged his hair, and even while performing these operations, he called to Jemmy to bring him a glass of brandy and sugar.

It had now become broad daylight. The rain had cleared off, and the sun was up. It was a beautiful day. Presently Harry, the proprietor, entered the store. He was the Colonel's old porter, and he was much attached to him. He heard the Colonel relate what had happened, and his sympathy was so much excited that he went at once to a physician and brought him to the store. The doctor sewed up the lip with a single stitch. He dressed the wounds in the back of the Colonel's head, but the Colonel continued to grow worse, and he felt very weak. He drank again, and then Harry called his attention to the fact in this manner.

"Colonel, we are old friends, and I advise you to let up a little. You have received two or three very ugly wounds, you have a great deal of liquor in your system, and I afraid that you will bring on inflammation of the brain or some other thing, unless you give way a little."

The Colonel for once was cowed. He was not himself, and was frightened.

"I know, Harry, all you would say. I feel as though I shall have a fit of the horrors. I want to stop drinking, God knows, but I can't. I must drink this morning. See how my very hand shakes; and yet I have drank four glasses of brandy this morning. Try and get me some thing that will lie on my stomach. Make me an egg nogg, and put three raw eggs in it. Don't be alarmed, Harry. I have drank so much recently, that all I can get down now will not make me intoxicated. It only brings me up to an even keel. I am drinking up on dead liquor. If I were to knock off suddenly, I should die," said the Colonel.

Harry went and procured the egg nogg, and Mac Neil got it down.

"Now Mac Neil," said the good-natured rumseller, "don't drink any more for some time."

"I will not—indeed I will not; I will keep quiet," said the Colonel—and he honestly intended to do so.

It was nearly nine o'clock before Marion Monck arrived. He too had drank to excess the evening previous, and went at once to the bar to procure 'a hair of the dog that had bitten him'—in other words, to get a mint julep. He had just finished drinking it when Jemmy pointed out the Colonel in the rear of the store, and told him what had happened. Marion was shocked, and went at once to the Colonel, who appeared very glad to see him.

"I am very ill, Marion," said he, in a low tone of voice. "I feel I am getting worse every hour."

"Any thing that I can do to relieve you, Colonel Mac Neil, I will do cheerfully and willingly. Here comes Mr. Charles."

The latter approached, and after expressing his sympathy, exclaimed,

"Colonel, you must be attended to without delay. You are in a bad state; why not allow us to take you to the hospital?"

"The hospital!—why, my dear fellow, I have a horror of that place; but perhaps you are right. Can I have a room there?" asked the Colonel.

"Certingly. Good physician, good nurse, and all that sort of thing. It will only cost twelve dollars to enter, and I don't think you will be there a week. A few days' nursing will bring you around all right," replied Charley.

"But the money, man! I was robbed last night, and have none left."

"Not a word about that. I have plenty, and will go at once to the hospital and make arrangements for your reception. I know them all up there, and it will be all right," exclaimed Marion.

"Good boy—fine boy. Do as you please; and Charley, you will remain with me; don't leave me till I go up there, eh?" was the Colonel's request.

"No, old fellow, I will stay by you; never say die. You are worth a dozen dead men yet," said Charles.

"Charles, you are experienced. I have a dread of having the delirium tremens—a horrible dread of it Now if I go to the hospital, and they cut me off short with tod, God knows what will become of me. If they let me taper off—give me a little now and then, to keep the nerves braced, I think I shall get over it, eh ?" pleadingly put in poor Mac, who was awfully scared, and well he might be.

"They know just what to do up at the hospital ; have no fear, Colonel. But here comes Marion. Well, what success ?" asked Charles.

"I have paid the twelve dollars, informed Mr. Roberts about you, and at any moment when you are ready to go, we will accompany you. You need not take any things, for I will come and see you every day," replied Marion.

The Colonel drew a long sigh, then cast a look at the bureau, and exclaimed, "Good bye, old mahogany. I don't know that I am doing right. I feel bad, and sadly perplexed. I have an idea that I shall never see this place or my old bureau again. I will die game, though, if I am to die—but I must have a drink before I start. Jemmy, make a stiff glass of old brandy and sugar. Suppose you all join me—who knows but it may be my last drink ?"

The drinks were taken all round. Harry the proprietor approved highly of the course that the Colonel had determined to pursue. He was afraid that he should have trouble, and he had no idea but that the hospital was the best place for the Colonel under the circumstances. All hands talked cheeringly to the desponding Colonel, until at last he felt cheered up himself. He shook hands with all except Marion and Mr. Charles, who were to accompany him to the hospital, see him safe inside his room, and then return.

They reached the open gate on Broadway, and the Colonel halted for a moment, and looked up and down the street as though he expected to see some one. Then as he passed the inner gate where the gate-keeper's house is, Mac observed, "I hope my case in entering this gate is not like one of those where 'he who enters here leaves hope behind,' eh ? . I hope I am not in that category, Marion ?"

Marion replied soothingly—and yet he felt embarrassed. He did not know that he was doing right, and he could not make up his mind that he was doing wrong. If, for a moment, the least idea had flashed across his mind, he would have faced about and taken the Colonel back to 46 Centre street. The party reached the office, and directions were given to conduct Colonel Mac Neil to a certain ward. A nurse was sent for, and he led the way, followed by the three persons. When they reached the right ward the nurse opened the door, and all entered. The door closed, and Marion noticed that it locked itself.

The Colonel, as soon as he saw where he was, exclaimed, "Why, this is not a single room! I am not going to remain here!"

The nurse replied readily, "Oh, certainly not. We will have a room ready for the gentleman presently. He can remain here for the present, and he had better lie down for a moment." This was said kindly, and the Colonel; who was completely exhausted, observed,

"Well, I will lay down a moment. Marion, Charles, you need not remain. I may sleep a moment. Come back to-morrow, Marion—hear?"

Marion said he would do so. The nurse applied a key to the door, opened it, and as the two passed into the hall the door closed and locked again. "I am not exactly pleased with all this business. Why is not the Colonel's room ready?" asked Marion.

"Nonsense. He will have no room except that or the inner lock-up. Why, that is the delirium tremens ward, and there Mac will be kept until he dies or gets over it," coolly replied Mr. Charles.

"Good God. You don't mean to say there is any danger of his dying of delirium?" asked Marion.

"He is pretty near it. He will have the delirium tremens most certainly. He may die. He may not. But he may as well die in that room as in the street. Besides, with all the rum he has got in his blood, and the bad cuts upon his head, he will have a bad time of it," said Mr. Charles.

When the two reached Broadway, they separated.

CHAPTER LIII.

Thomas Granville—A Genteel Loafer's Daily Record—Cheap Lodging Houses—The Liberal Stranger—Tom in Funds once more—The Stranger Walter Granville places Him at the Hotel de Paris—Dialogue Between Walter Granville and Miss Norris About Tom.

AFTER the return of Thomas Granville from Europe, his fortunes became desperate. He seemed past hope. He had been down upon the ground. The human car was off the track. The President of the United States—stern old Hickory—had picked him up, placed him on solid ground, and started him a new man. He went out Consul to a city in France, and could have restored himself to position, wealth and influence. Under the sad guidance of Clara Norris, he had ruined his reputation, squandered his property, and completely used up those friends who had re-rallied about him. He had not been in the city of New York many days before he fully realized the contrast between holding an official position, having plenty of money, and recognized by respectable relatives, and the loss of all these advantages. How he lived, no man but himself ever knew. He managed sometimes to make a few shillings by singing at a garden concert, or a free concert in some by street. He went to such places and performed under an assumed name. He might have used his real one; no one would have troubled his head about him. Sometimes Tom was almost in despair, for he really suffered. He went to haunts frequented by old friends and acquaintances. There he could always obtain a drink, and nibble a cracker and cheese. As days passed on, matters grew worse, instead of better. It was rare that Tom Granville had over a quarter. He had no regular place to sleep, but found a bed in some lodging. If he had three shillings, he went to Tammany Hall. If only a quarter, to a neat lodging-house in Pearl street, near Broadway. If only a shilling, Tom went to a lodging-house in Chatham street, near Duane. There he got a bed in a room where several others slept, and Tom had to be satisfied. It was better than sleeping in the Park, or walking the streets in a cold winter night. Sometimes Tom would be the delight of an audience in a low bar-room where liquor was sold for three cents a glass, and his droll stories in a dark room in a lodging-house to the other queer lodgers in the various beds, would make the occupants scream with laughter, and their first questions at daybreak would be for the funny man who had told stories or sang songs in the dark the night previous. What a happy disposition, that amid scenes like these, and hardships even worse than we have narrated, could keep up and lose none of its elasticity.

There was scarcely a low priced lodging-house in the lower part of New York that had not had the honor of having, as a lodger, Thomas Granville. Occasionally, there would be adventures connected with them of a very ludicrous character.

Late at night, on one occasion, Tom found that he had a solitary shilling left. He wanted a drink badly. The place in which he found himself was a three cent shop in Cross street,

kept by Peter Melville. There were several loafers around
the stove, for it was a bitter cold night. Tom knew them all,
but not one had a cent, and business was at a dead stand. The
excellent Melville showed symptoms of closing up. Tom was
dry. He was as dry as a pump is said to be when there is not
a drop of water in it. He determined to have one more drink,
anyhow. The landlord looked untrusting. Tom drew near the
bar.

"My lord Melville, will you give me a glass of your most
excellent, I might say exquisite whiskey?"

"Have you got the money to pay for it, Tom?" asked the
proprietor.

"Excellent Melville, I regret to say I have not, but assuredly, if you will trust me until this hour to-morrow, by Hercules, the three cents shall be in your hands," said Tom.

"I won't do it," replied Melville.

"Inexorable Melville, say not so. Remember, worthy son
of the land where Wallace bled, that ' 'Tis a little thing to give
a glass of Scotch whiskey. But its draught of warm refreshment, drained by chilled lips, will give a shock of pleasure to
the frame more exquisite than when wine its nectarine riches
pours.' Ah, stern man, pour out one glass, for poor Tom's
a-cold."

The comic look which Tom gave the keeper, as he pronounced these words, upset the Scotchman's gravity. He
handed over the decanter to Tom, and told him to help himself.
"But no more, Tom, to-night," he added. Tom drank off the
wine, and then continued, "' 'Tis a little thing to speak a word
of kindness, but falling upon the ear of him who thought to die
unmourned, it sounds like gentlest music.' You have spoken
that word to me, my Melville, and I thank you. Good night,"
—and Tom felt in his pocket to see that his shilling was safe
to pay for his lodging, and then hurried out into the cold air to
go and seek his lodging-house. He paid his shilling and hastened up to the room, where he found a dozen men in different
beds. He selected one that was unoccupied, and was soon fast
asleep. In the morning, he was up by daylight, for he was
almost crazy to get a drink of water—grog—any thing. He
hastened down stairs. There was a bar in the room, and pie
was kept upon a plate at one end of it. The boy was dressing
when Tom came down.

"I'll let you out in a moment, Mister," he said.

"Hurry, then," replied Tom, and he put his hand in his coat
pocket.

The boy had his eye upon him.

"None of that. I saw you. Put that back again," said the boy, as he approached Tom, angrily.

"What do you mean? What are you talking about?" said the unconscious Tom.

"You just put that piece of mince pie back on the plate, or pay me two cents for it," said the boy, in a very determined manner."

Tom began to understand. "Why, you impudent son of a gun, do you mean to insinuate that I have taken any of your nasty pie?" exclaimed Tom, indignantly.

"I know you put it in your pocket. I saw you when you did it. Fork over," said the boy, or rather the young man, for he was full grown.

This was too much for our philosopher Tom. The young man seized him, and Tom then gave him a blow which sent him reeling. In a moment he had unlocked and opened the door, and was in Chatham street, and he ran as if for life. He felt how ridiculous it would be to be arrested for knocking the fellow down, and to be charged, too, with stealing two cents' worth of mince pie. He—Thomas Granville—ex-Consul to a city in France! He ran the faster as he thought of all these things, and never stopped until he was near Melville's, where he had spent the previous evening. Melville's place was not open, but a few doors below there was a grog-shop opened. In his emergency, Tom entered that, approached the stove, and took a seat. How the slightest circumstance will sometimes effect a change in one's whole life. Jemmy, the bar-keeper of Harry, had just opened and fixed up the place. He made an observation to Tom that it was a cold morning. Tom replied, and then roared with laughter. Jemmy was not exactly pleased, and Tom good-naturedly related the pie story and his narrow escape. The comic manner in which Tom related it was inimitable, and Jemmy joined in as chorus. Jemmy then invited Tom Granville to take a drink. The invitation was most cheerfully accepted. Jemmy was pleased. He also took a drink. It was cold outside, and they were seated by a warm fire. Its genial influence warmed out Tom, and in less than an hour he had Jemmy so completely fascinated that Tom could have been treated with the whole shop.

Tom had no coat, and his clothes were seedy. His boots were nearly gone, and his shirt, it had not been changed for a month or more. His hat shone bright, but it was napless, and yet Tom was as merry this cold morning as if he had the wealth of Astor. Later that morning customers began to arrive, and Jemmy had to go behind the bar, leaving Tom puffing a cigar at the stove, and seemingly quite happy. Just then a customer of a different character entered the place, approached the bar, and ordered a drink. He wore a fur cap and a bearskin overcoat. He had partly finished the drink he had ordered when his eyes rested upon the pleasant face of Tom.

"Great God! it cannot be possible!" he exclaimed, and then, with the glass in his hand, went and sat himself in a chair next to Tom Granville. "Excuse me, sir, but is not your name Thomas Granville?" asked the stranger.

"I was once Sir Thomas Granville, Esquire. I am now Tom Granville, or plain Tom, at your service,"—and a comic smile played over his expressive features.

"When have you seen your brother Pitt Granville?" the stranger asked.

"Pitt—yes—my brother Pitt. Oh, it is a long time since I have seen Pitt, but it is much longer since *he* has *seen* me," said Tom, with feeling.

"Then you and your brother have quarrelled, eh?"

"No, sir. I never quarrel with my brother. He has, for good reasons, I dare say, done with me. That is his business; not ours, sir," said Tom.

"Suppose you join me in a drink, Mr. Granville."

"Mr. Granville! Certingly, with pleasure. Jemmy—a glass of hot toddy—my private bottle, you understand. I am much obliged to you, sir," said Tom.

"You once had a nephew, Walter Granville, what has become of him?" the stranger continued.

"Ah, there you touch me. A fine boy—a noble boy—gone to sea. Unheard of for years. Dead probably. The good aye die young. A family affair, sir. Here is to your very good health," said Tom. Had he noticed the stranger, he would have observed that he appeared to be very much affected.

"Your own wife, Mr. Granville, where is she?" asked the stranger.

"In Baltimore, living with her grandmother. She is divorced from me," replied Tom.

"So I have heard. What ever became of one of her sisters?" asked the stranger.

"Which one? She had several," asked Tom.

"Madison Pinckney," said the stranger, with feeling.

"Oh; she married a young fellow named Charles Wharton,

and has moved to Columbus, Ohio. A very good match, I am told. Have you got any more questions to ask? If you have, propel ahead. I am ready to answer to the best of my ability," observed Tom.

"No; I have no more to ask about your family. I have one to ask about yourself. Suppose, Mr. Granville, that I, a stranger, should say to you, 'Mr. Granville, go with me to different stores. Buy an overcoat, a coat, a vest, a pair of pantaloons, a pair of boots, a new hat, shirts, underclothes, socks, a necktie, and any thing else that a gentleman needs, and I will pay for them,' what would you reply? and what would you think of me when I, as I do now, make you such an offer?" said the stranger.

"I should say *yes*, and I should think that you were a particular d——d fool," replied honest Tom.

"Perhaps I should be; but why do you think so, Mr. Granville?" pleasantly asked the stranger.

"Because, sir, I am poor. I am dead broke. I don't have food half of the time. How long do you think, under such circumstances, I should keep my good clothes? Why sir, in less than a week, or a month at most, those articles would all go to a pawnbroker, and I should fall back upon the old rags, sir. That is truth—don't you think it is, Jemmy?" said Tom, as he aprealed to Jem, who had been an attentive listener for some moments.

"It may be, but if the gentleman makes you the offer I would accept it. It won't do you any harm to do so," said Jemmy.

The stranger rose. "Come, Mr. Granville, and go with me. When you have all these things I have named, then we must try and get some money, or food, or a place to board. One thing at a time. Will you go?" he asked.

"I will—but first let me ask who you are?" said Tom.

"Call me Smith, until we are better acquainted," replied the stranger.

"Well Smith, you are a devilish good-looking young fellow, but decidedly mad. I will go with you."

The parties left the place, and left a wondering set of people in it. Jemmy the bar-keeper was the most astonished of all. He could not make it out.

It was near midday before Tom Granville and his friend Smith returned to 46 Centre street. Thomas Granville was a different person. He was dressed like a gentleman, and his actions did not belie his dress. Every article was new, and of the finest quality. The stranger evidently did not do things by halves. He ordered drinks for all in the room. When they had been taken, he said to Thomas Granville, "Now sir, I will bid you good-bye; but I will meet you at your hotel this evening at precisely seven o'clock. Remember what you have promised, and don't break it. Good-bye."

Tom shook his head, and after he had left, he observed to Jemmy, "That chap is mad—quite mad."

"What did he mean by your hotel, eh?" asked Jemmy.

"Mean? Why I am stopping at a hotel. It is Vigin's French Hotel de Paris, corner of Reade street and Broadway, No. 34—best room in the house. Paid my board one month in advance, thirty-two dollars—eight dollars a week, eh? See the receipt. What do you think of that, Jemmy?" said the delighted Tom.

"Who can he be? What was the promise?" asked Jemmy.

"Smith is his name—I promised not to get *very* drunk, but to be sober at seven o'clock this evening. Bless your heart, I will be as sober as a judge!" exclaimed the enthusiastic Tom.

"He is a good friend," observed Jemmy.

"He gave me ten dollars, and advised me to pay what I owed here, or any where else in a small way. How much do I owe you, Jemmy?" asked Tom.

"Not a red cent, Mr. Granville. You are perfectly welcome to what you have had," replied Jemmy.

"Thank you, Jemmy. But what a breakfast we had at that French hotel! O my! That Smith understands good living. He is a perfect prince," exclaimed Tom.

We must now follow the stranger. He had no sooner parted from Thomas Granville, than he turned his course to Bond street, and entered the house of Mrs. Woodruff. He walked up stairs, and entered the front room on the second floor. There was a lady in the room, who rose as he entered. He gave her an affectionate kiss, and observed,

"A thousand thanks, dear Clara, for enabling me to do a good deed. O, if you knew how far that hundred dollars has gone! But sit down, and let me tell you all about poor Tom."

She listened, and he related the particulars of the interview which our readers are aware of. She wept, and at last observed,

"If it will only do any good, I shall be glad. I do it and will do more—but mind me, Walter, it is for you, not for Tom. I have come to hate him—to *hate* him," she repeated, emphatically.

"Never mind your motive, dear Clara. You have enabled

me to benefit my uncle, and I thank you for so doing," said Walter Granville, for he was the stranger that had so electrified the crowd at No. 46 Centre street.

"And will Tom come up here to-night with you?" she asked.

"He will, and then I will tell him who I am, and that I should not have been able to do what I have but for you. Now let us go and walk. Are you ready?" said Walter.

"I will be in half an hour—remain quiet until then." And she left the room.

CHAPTER LIV.

The New York City Hospital—A sad Chapter—Colonel Mac Neil in the Delirium Tremens Ward—Stern Treatment of Patients in that Ward—The attack of the Maniac upon the Resident Physician—The Colonel chained—His Death—The body in the Dead House—The horror of Marion Monck—Distress in Harrison street—The Body of the Colonel taken to his Home.

Those who pass up and down Broadway in the great city, must have noticed on its west side the dark, gloomy building known as the "New York Hospital." Seen from the street, it looks like some gloomy old castle, with its iron railing, the green lawn, the venerable elms, and the gate-keeper's lodge. It is a pleasant place to look at from the outside, and but few are aware of the horrors that are daily witnessed inside. The stabbed, the accidentally injured, the suicide who has only partly done his work, the almost maniac, on the eve of delirium tremens, pass inside those iron gates without notice or comment. Sailors who have paid United States Hospital money, no matter what may be their disease, are entitled to be received into that hospital free of charge, to the extent of one hundred at a time. The sick or wounded man who can raise twelve dollars to pay the admission fee, can find a home and medical attendance until he is cured by medicine or death. In either case he pays no more than the twelve dollars.

In the basement floor of what is called the North building is one large room, capable of holding five or six small iron bedsteads. The door has a strong spring lock, and fastens of itself. The large window to this room is strongly barred with great stout iron bars, that no human strength can wrench or tear asunder. There are three doors that lead out of this room. One opens into a cell, where there is no window. Nothing but four solid walls, and an iron bedstead. Not an article of furniture else is in this room. Another door leads to a bath room. Here too the windows are barred with iron staunchions. Another opens into the nurse's room, and this door also closes with a spring lock, and like the main door, has to be opened with a key. This room or ward is called the *delirium tremens* ward of the Hospital. Into this are thrust those patients who are brought to the hospital laboring under this fearful malady, or when it is suspected that it will break out, from the fact that the patient has been drinking freely, and has suffered or is suffering from want of sleep. This is the most fearful ward in the Hospital, and the nurse, as a matter of self-preservation for his own life, and the lives of those entrusted to his care, is a man of experience, and perfectly hardhearted. He knows no feeling, until actual observation has convinced him of the danger or absence of it, in a new patient. No mildness, no manner or language of a perfect gentleman, no money can disarm for a moment the fear of the nurse for a new comer. The moment a patient is committed to his ward, he is aware that madness is the main complaint, and he is on the watch for its appearance in any shape or at any moment. His doors are locked. His eyes are as watchful as a cat's. He orders a new patient to undress and go to bed. Frequently the patient refuses. Force is at once used, and he is placed on the iron bedstead, and every particle of clothing is removed to the nurse's own room. If the patient becomes more obstreperous, he is at once pinioned to the bed, or a straight jacket put upon him, and a hand chained to each side of the bed. This confinement of itself would almost drive a sane man mad. If the patient becomes raving, then the scene is changed. He is passed into the dark cell, where the solitary iron bedstead is, and where no article of furniture can be found to aid him in self-destruction. Then the patient may yell with horror, or utter screams that thrill the stoutest nerves, or die in madness. The door is strong—the walls are thick, and but little is heard by others, however fearful the agony. Sometimes the patient tires out the patience of the nurse, and then he forgets the rules, and beats his patient into submission until death takes up the cudgels, and finishes what the indignant nurse had only begun.

The regular house physician, or the visiting surgeon, never enter this ward without fear, and a full appreciation of the danger. As a consequence, when a patient is placed in this ward, the very circumstances attending his being there, or the mere fact that he is there, shuts him out from all human sympathy and kindness. The poor inebriate who is suffering the horrors of abstinence from drink, who needs kind words, and encouragement, and soothing, gets none in this ward. He sees others chained down to the iron beds—he hears the horrid screams of the one in the dungeon—he sees them die in beds alongside of his own—he hears the fearful screams until death seals the lips. If he had not the seeds of delirium already in his blood, all these things, and such horrid surroundings would make him mad. Many hundreds of worthy men, who have died unlamented in the delirium tremens ward of the Hospital, might now have been alive and well, had the friends or relations who placed them there have exercised a little forbearance and a little kindness. That treatment of a man who has been drinking until his nerves are burning wires, who cannot sleep, which suddenly cuts off the spirit which has caused the difficulty and the danger, and leaves the shattered nerves to sustain the additional horrors of confinement among madmen, is murder—and such is the practice hourly in the delirium tremens ward of the New York Hospital.

Blessed be those gallant, glorious men who have inaugurated a new era in this matter—who have started into existence the "Inebriate Asylum."

When Colonel Mac Neil was placed in the ward we have been describing, and left there by Marion Monck and Mr. Charles, he laid down upon one of the iron bedsteads. He dozed for a few moments, and then rose up.

"Lie down," said the nurse Patrick.

"Who are you addressing—me ? Where is my room, sir ? I will not remain here any longer," said the indignant Colonel; and he marched proudly to the door. Of course he found it fastened. "Open the door, sir," he continued.

Nurse Patrick went to another door, and called to a sort of assistant. The other man came.

"Look here, Colonel, you must take off your clothes and go to bed. We are not going to have none of your nonsense here," said Patrick.

"Where is my room, sir ?" asked the Colonel.

"O, blast you and your room ! This is all the room you will have in this building. Come, strip, or I'll do it for you," said the nurse, and he approached the Colonel, who stood near the door.

"Stand off, I say ! or if you touch me I will make you suffer for it. I have never heard of such impudence !"

The Colonel, as he said this, placed himself in an attitude of defence.

"Help me, Bill," exclaimed Nurse Patrick; and at the same moment he suddenly jumped upon the astonished Colonel. He was overpowered in a twinkling, and the nurse and his assistant flung him on his back upon the vacant bed.

"This is outrageous!—infamous!—where is the Superintendent? I am a gentleman; what do you mean? Are you going to kill me?" muttered poor Mac Neil. But it was of no use; in a moment he was stripped to his shirt; and then his clothes, hat, boots, and all of his apparel was taken to another room.

"Now get into bed and keep quiet, or it will be worse for you," said the nurse Patrick.

The Colonel saw that resistance was useless; he made no further efforts, but determined to complain to the doctor when he saw him. There were other patients in the room, but Mac Neil did not notice them. He lay awake, and moments seemed hours, but at last the visiting doctors came—one old man and two young ones. They sat by the bed, and the eldest kept examining Mac's wounds. The Colonel began to tell who he was, and to complain of the treatment.

"You have been drinking, sir, and you are placed here to be cured, and we will try and cure you; when that is done we shall listen to your complaints. Meantime you must try and get some sleep. Your condition, without you get sleep, will be a critical one," said the elder doctor.

The Colonel began to realize his position: he asked the doctor if he thought he was really very unwell.

"Yes; you will probably be delirious unless you get sleep. I will order some medicine that will give you sleep probably. It may not. How long since you have had any sleep?"

The Colonel replied that he had not slept well for several nights.

"I am very nervous now. Could I not have a glass of brandy and water?"

The old doctor smiled, and so did his two assistants, and they passed on to the next patient. Soon after they left the ward; and the nurse, who had received some directions, came to the bedside of the Colonel.

"How do you feel now?" he asked in a kinder tone than usual.

"Very bad indeed. I am really sick. I would like to get up and put on my clothes," said the Colonel.

"Can't be allowed. You must get some sleep before you are allowed to sit up," replied the nurse.

"Then I will try and get some sleep," said poor Mac Neil. He did try, but there was a fire in his veins that would not let him sleep. Tea came; he tried to swallow it, but his nerves were so unstrung that he could not hold the cup to his mouth, and he fell back upon the bed. Then came the long hours of that night. Moments only passed, and yet the Colonel dreamed of horrid matters and doings that would have taken hours to perform. He would start up in his bed, and a cold sweat poured from his brow. The building seemed to totter; the room turned round; the sickly lamp seemed to be glowing meteors. He would satisfy his mind that all was imagination, and then the horrid thought would cross his mind that he was going mad. In a moment more he would doze, and then he would be with his darling children. Oh what happiness! the loved mother was there. Then snakes would come among them —hateful, venomous reptiles, with unheard of forms, and his children would be snatched away, and he would raise himself in bed. "Lie down," the nurse would sing out. All his dreams had been but a moment transpiring.

By and bye the nurse would come again. "Take this—the doctor ordered it." The Colonel hesisated, but took the teaspoon in his hand, and swallowed the contents. "Two hours hence you are to take another one," said the nurse. "Now lie down and try to sleep—it is all that you can do, or that any body can do for you; it is sleep or die." The Colonel would lie down again. In a moment he saw the doctor slyly enter, and pass to the nurse's room; he heard them whisper softly to each other. One said, "Yes, I have given him the dose. It will kill him; then we will take his body up stairs, and nobody will know it; he will make a good subject." The other replied, "I must not be known in the matter. He is Colonel Mac Neil. His friends don't care about him while he is alive, but when he is dead they may ask about him."

Mac heard all this dreadful conspiracy. He sat up in the bed, but there was no one in the room. "Aha! kill me, will they?" He jumped out of bed and seized a wooden bench. 'I will not die without a struggle."

The doctor *had* passed through the room, but it was to take a bath; the nurse was in his own room, occupied with some business, but the poor victim, (for Mac was now delirious,) thought he had heard all this talk, and he was ready.

The doctor came out of the bath room. No sooner did Mac

see him, than elevating the stool he exclaimed, "Poison me, you d——d doctor, will you?" and made a blow with the bench at his head. Had it hit him, he never would have prescribed for any more patients. The doctor dodged it, but fell. In a moment the Colonel was upon him. The nurse, hearing the struggle, came in, and at once fastened upon the Colonel, and choked him until he released the doctor. Then more help came, and at last they got the raving man upon the bed, and then passing a chain over him, fastened his hands and legs so that he could not move. "He is safe now, doctor," said the nurse. "You had a narrow escape, doctor: lucky I came in. I thought we should have trouble with him; he has been a hard drinker."

"Yes, Patrick, don't let him loose again until I see you; he is very dangerous. I don't think he will get over it, though he may if he gets sleep to-night," and with these remarks the doctor passed out and got a good night's sleep, leaving orders to keep poor Mac chained until morning.

The struggles of the Colonel when he found himself made fast, were fearful. Sometimes it seemed as though he would either break the chain and fastenings, or wrench off his wrists. His torrents of curses and reproaches were horrible. The other patients who had gone through the ordeal and were getting well, could not sleep, but they sat up in their beds and watched the rum maniac. "For the love of God, take those snakes off my hand!" "Oh Graham, you deserved a better fate." "Poor Will! my bright, beautiful boy." "There! there! what a horrid snake!" "Water! give me water!" these expressions and a thousand others, gave a key to the thoughts which were passing in the poor maniac's mind. Sometimes he would utter scream after scream of agonized horror; then he would weep as though his heart would break: and so he continued all that night. Towards morning he seemed to be getting quiet.

"I am glad of that," said the nurse to his companion.

"I thought, Bill, we would have to lock him up. But he is pretty quiet now, and I am going to have a snooze."

"Day broke, and soon after the light came through the large window, and fell upon the chained man's countenance. The patient in the next bed appeared to notice something unusual. He observed to another patient, "I believe that man is dying. It is enough to kill any one to be treated so—chained down all night. What a perfect gentleman he is, too!"

The other patient added, "He don't make no noise now. Is he asleep? Take a look."

The other did look, and placed his hand upon the forehead of Colonel Mac Neil. "My God, he is dead. Let us call the nurse."

"Don't call him—let him find it out. He knows he will get the gentleman's clothes, and that is all he cares about," said the other patient.

The Colonel lay thus cold and unconscious, and the other patients soon went to sleep. Later the nurse Patrick entered, and went to the bedside of Mac Neil. "Dead, eh?" and then he opened the door and went to the office to report. Such things are very common in that old building. The nurse was gone a few moments. When he returned, he was followed by two other men. They all then assisted to place the body upon a sort of bier, and carried it out of the ward down to the dead house, and then placed it upon the table to await further orders. There was no noise and no fuss at such a melancholy termination to a man's life in the hospital, as there would have been in a private mansion. No message was sent out to any body, for that is not the business of people in the hospital. People go to the hospital with one of two objects to accomplish—to get well or to die. Colonel Mac Neil was dead, and if his friends discovered it well and good; if not, his body would be taken from the dead house in the hospital yard to the Potter's Field. About ten o'clock that same day, Marion Monck, agreeably to the promise he had made to the Colonel the day previous went from 46 Centre street to see him. He passed through the gate, and went directly to the ward in the North building. The door was not fast, but stood partly open. The nurse was not there. Marion gazed around the room, expecting to see the Colonel—but he was not there. He turned towards a patient who occupied a bed near the door: "I came here with a friend yesterday. He was placed upon that bed. Can you tell me where he has gone to?"

The man looked at Marion a moment: "Yes, I remember you. They have removed your friend—Colonel you called him—to the dead house."

"Dead house! Why, what should he be removed there for?" asked Marion, horrified.

"What for? Why, because he is dead," replied the man.

"Dead. Colonel Mac Neil dead. Impossible. Why, I left him here yesterday. Dead!" Marion exclaimed, and seemed to be paralyzed at the information. Another patient joined him, who seemed to be a little more human. He related all that had occurred, and that the Colonel had died soon after daylight. Marion cried like a child. The nurse came in, and Marion heard what he had to say. He then went to the office and obtained permission to go to the dead house and see the body. The dead house man opened the door. There was no mistake now. There lay Colonel Mac Neil, cold, stiff and insensible to all affairs of earth. Marion was too shocked to oped his mouth. He hurried out of the building—out of the grounds, and never halted until he reached No. 46 Centre street. Mr. Charles was reading the newspaper. Marion hastily told the story, namely, that Colonel Mac Neil was dead. Mr. Charles said he expected as much. Harry, the proprietor, at once took an interest in the matter, and advised Marion to go to No. 27 Harrison street and communicate the awful intelligence to Miss Jane. He went over at once. He found that lady just sitting down to dinner with her children. He asked to see her alone. Half reluctantly she came out into the hall. He told her what had happened. One shriek rang out, and he fell senseless on the floor. But there was no time for delay. "You are Marion Monck, I am certain. Go and make arrangements that his body shall be brought here. Poor William, he shall have no burial from a public hospital." The parties in house were spoken to, and they advised Miss McPherson to pursue that course. The children of the Colonel were very much affected. When the mother told them what had happened, they sobbed as if their little hearts would break. They did love that poor father who loved them so truly.

Marion left them to weep at their great loss, and went to an undertaker and gave orders to him to take a shell and convey the body of the Colonel to Harrison street, and then to take measures for a handsome coffin and a respectable private burial. He accompanied the undertaker to the hospital. Permission to remove the body was at once obtained, and the unconscious Colonel was with those who loved him that same evening of the day he died. The notice of the death of Colonel Mac Neil appeared in the papers next morning, and the funeral was announced to take place that afternoon.

CHAPTER LV.

The House of John Grasper, in Broadway—The Wedding—Count Falsechinski is Married to the Rich Irene Grasper—A Startling Contrast—The Brilliant Marriage of one Lover, and the Melancholy Funeral of the Other.

In that brown granite building up Broadway, the residence of John Grasper, Esq., there was a grand gathering of all the elite of New York city one night late in the month of September. The Count Falsechinski had that day led to the altar Irene, the handsome daughter of the rich old banker. She was now a Countess. The bride and the bridegroom were both present at this party given by the parents of the bride to celebrate the nuptials. Music, the rarest and best that could be procured, added liveliness to the scene. What a contrast to the scene that same night in the humble dwelling-house in Harrison street! Could the fair bride, whose brow was undimmed by even a passing sorrow cloud, have realized that her admirer—her lover, and the one she loved in other days—the gay and fashionable Colonel Mac Neil, had died that morning in a public ward in the hospital, manacled, uncared for, and unknown, and that at that moment, when her father's mansion was illuminated with light and with beauty, and crowds were offering incense at her shrine, he, the poor lover, was lying dead in a small room, and by his lifeless body knelt a woman and his two children? What would have been the bride's sensations? We will not stop to inquire. Such was the fact, however, and it was known to the Count that Colonel Mac Neil was dead, for he had met Marion Monck, who informed him of it as an excuse why he should be absent from the wedding party, to which the Count had given him a cordial invitation. To the credit of the Count, we will say that he not only bade Marion God speed in his work of kindness in assisting the widow and the fatherless, but he insisted that he should receive from him, the Count, a sufficient sum of money to liquidate all expenses connected with the funeral of Colonel Mac Neil.

Old Mr. Prime, the banker and the friend of the Count, was at the wedding party, and as merry as every old gentleman ought to be. He considered this wedding as partly got up by his individual action. He had satisfied Mr. Grasper, and Mr. Grasper had paid into the banking house of Prime, Ward & King the dower agreed upon, namely, one hundred and fifty thousand dollars. The settlements had been made to the entire satisfaction of all parties.

Among the guests was the Russian Ambassador, who had undertaken to arrange the Count's affairs at the Court of St. Petersburg. He had succeeded, and his presence was a full indorsement of the Count's claim to his title, had any one chosen to dispute or to doubt the matter. Mr and Mrs. Wilson were invited, and were present. So were Colonel Benson, his son and Isabella Benson, his son's wife, and her father, Pitt Granville. The latter was an unhappy, miserable man. He had made a grand mistake in the Count. He had always supposed he was a nobody—an adventurer. He had had him as a clerk, and had treated him as a clerk, and now to find that this *ci devant* clerk was a real count—a nobleman, with a princely income and a large cash capital, and about to carry off a bride with a hundred and fifty thousand dollars more, was too bad. He might have had the Count for his own daughter, if he had awoke a little sooner, and then, as he contrasted the elegant, well-dressed, accomplished Count, passing from one to another of the guests, an object of universal admiration, and winning smiles from the most beautiful by his wit and brilliant conversation, and then turned his eyes to his own son-in-law, who sat in one corner, looking sheepish and stupid, no one appearing to be aware that such a person was in existence, he felt mortified and vexed at his own past folly and stupidity.

All the friends and connexions of the Graspers were present in full force. The bride radiated among them, dressed in spotless white and sparkling with jewels. She was proud of her husband, and well she might be, for the Count could shine any where, and he appeared devoted to his wife.

It had been arranged that the bridal pair should start the next morning on an excursion, which was expected to occupy some weeks.

The Count approached Mr. and Mrs. Wilson, who were quietly enjoying the gay scene. He shook hands with them cordially, and they congratulated him upon his brilliant marriage. The Count replied with deep fervor to Mrs. Wilson, "Ah, dear madam; I can never forget you. That first night, when I was so poor, and when Marion, God bless him, carried me to his room. Oh, you have brought me good luck. It started me anew, and you, Mr. Wilson, how kind you ever were to me, I shall never forget."

Mrs. Wilson replied, "Poor Marion. I am told that he is not doing very well, Don't forget him, Count, for if you do owe any one for your success, it was Marion."

"May my head perish when I forget it. No, Mrs. Wilson, I have a place on my hands for the good of Marion. He shall be in business before I leave this land for my own country, and with plenty of means. You have heard of that dreadful event this morning, Wilson?" he inquired, in a low voice. Both husband and wife started, and asked to what he alluded.

"Don't mention it here to-night, but Colonel Mac Neil died of delirium tremens in one of the wards of the hospital this morning about daybreak. Marion Monck has removed the dead body to residence of Miss McPherson and Mac's children. Is it not shocking? I must leave you now. Do not forget me,"—and with these words the Count passed on to greet other guests.

Wilson gazed into the face of his wife. Neither could speak for some moments. Both knew the history of Colonel Mac Neil. Both knew that he was once a favored lover of her who was now the Countess Falsechinski. At last Mr. Wilson spoke.

"Darling, I am sick of stopping here. Can't we contrive to go? Poor Mac Neil; what a sad fate. I shall go to his funeral, wife. I wish I could have done more. What a blow it would be to the gay bride, if the truth could reach her to-night, eh?"

"I hope it may not, Richard. She could not have helped the matter—and only think of that poor woman and her two children. Well—well—as people sow, so must they reap. What a contrast between the melancholy death of one lover and the gay bridal of another, and yet the one who has died a horrid death, I first met the courted and caressed by all the wealth and fashion of the city. The other, who is now surrouded by wealth, admiring friends, a title, a rich bride, came to my house in the dead of winter, and without food or scarcely any clothes. But for the kindness of Marion Monck might have perished in the streets that night. Does it not make you shudder to think of such changes in life, husband?" asked the wife.

"Thank God, and you, my darling Bessy, I am too comfortable to dread them. We must stay until supper is over. I will go and tell Mr. Granville about Mac Neil's death."

He left his wife to do as he stated. He was absent but a moment, and when he returned he observed, "I have done a very foolish thing. I never saw a man so horrified as Granville appears to be. I am sorry I told him any thing about the matter."

Mrs. Isabella Benson was at this wedding party, and her beauty attracted a great deal of admiration. Many solicited an introduction to her, but her conversational powers were not sufficient to retain by her side those that her pretty features attracted thither.

The supper was a superb affair, and no pains or expense were spared to make it excel all suppers that ever came off before in a private house. Old Mr. Prime declared that he had never been at such a supper, and his indorsement was always a good one for a note or a supper.

It was at a very late hour when the party broke up. All the guests were pleased, and went to their homes envying both bride and bridegroom. Such is life.

The next morning all the gay guests at that wedding read the notice of Colonel Mac Neil's death, and that his funeral would take place that afternoon from 27 Harrison street.

When the appointed hour arrived, there was a large crowd gathered. It hardly seemed possible that the Colonel had so many friends, or even acquaintances. Mr. Granville was there. So was Colonel Benson and Mr. Wilson and many others. The body was to be conveyed to Greenwood Cemetery. The widow and the children were in a carriage by themselves, where they followed the corpse until it was placed beneath the sod. Then Marion Monck got into the carriage, and returned with the three weepers. As the little party crossed the ferry, Miss McPherson spoke. "Mr. Monck, you have been a true friend to us in our need, and God will bless you for it. Out of all the Colonel's friends, you alone seem to have been a true one. I want you to do one thing more. Get all his things from the place that he frequented, and bring them to me. I will give you his own authority for their removal." She then told Marion about the last day he had spent with his little family. "He had a presentiment that he was to die, and it came true."

The day following that of the funeral, Marion caused the bureau and other effects of the late Colonel to be removed to the residence of his widow, as he called her, and by which title she was ever after recognized by those who valued Mac Neil's memory.

Soon after the Colonel's death, the widow wrote to her father in Canada. He came to New York. Mrs. Mac Neil appointed a trusting agent to manage her property in the city, and as soon as those matters were arranged, she and her two children returned to Canada with their relative.

CHAPTER LVI.

Walter Granville and Clara Norris—Their Marriage—The Hotel de Paris, and Tom Granville—Curious Speech of Clara Norris to Henry Robinson—The latter's Marriage with Rose Barker at Mrs. Woodruff's residence—Mar on Monck—His Poem, "The Outcast"—Tom Granville's degradation, and Reflections at Clara's Wedding with his Nephew.

SOME weeks had passed after the arrival in the city of young Walter Granville before he made himself known to his uncle Tom. The time had been devoted to Miss Norris, who had continued to reside at Mrs. Woodruff's, and where she had a full opportunity to exert her extraordinary powers of fascination upon the young sailor. Never had she appeared so young and so lovely. She accompanied him to every place of public amusement, rode out with him, walked with him, delicately furnished him with a stream of money, and bestowed upon him presents of value and of utility. She had a purpose in all this. She made up her mind to succeed, and success seemed almost within her grasp. She determined to injure the elder Granville, and she saw no surer method than by plunging his only son into a vortex from which there was no escape.

She had proposed to Walter that he should marry her. She explained to him that she was comparatively independent—satisfied him that he had gained her affections, and that her whole soul was his. He certainly was leading a pleasant life. He had no idea but that his father had closed his heart and his doors upon him forever. Clara had behaved nobly to him, as he thought, for she had not only made him comfortable, but she had advanced Henry Robinson a considerable sum, to enable him to support the expense of Rose and himself at a second-rate hotel. Yet Walter hesitated. He had not made up his mind fully in the matter until the morning of his interview with his uncle Tom. The night previous he and Clara had conversed together upon the subject of marriage. He had asked means to give a helping hand to his relative, and she had agreed to it at once. At the same time she told Walter that they were both doing very wrong in living together in the manner they were doing without being married, and that much as she loved him, it should not continue another day.

"It will break my heart, Walter, to part with you, but it must be done. You have one advantage over me, Walter. When we are married, if you do not continue to love me, or get tired, you can run away and go to sea again."

The hint was not lost upon Walter, and that morning, when he went out to find Thomas Granville, he said, "Clara, I will marry you as soon as you please, but let it all be done quietly."

"Then suppose it be this evening, in presence of only one or two witnesses. You promise to bring up your uncle, and I will go out and invite your friend Robinson," said Clara.

"The clergyman—who will you get to perform that ceremony?" asked Walter.

"Leave all that to me, dear Walter, and don't worry yourself about the matter. It shall all be regular, and with no noise," replied Clara.

With this understanding the parties separated. Walter went in search of his uncle Tom, and Clara Norris to make her arrangements.

Walter found his relative in the destitute state we have described. He left him well provided for, and it did Walter's heart good, for with all his faults he loved his uncle Tom, and sympathized with his misfortune. After leaving Mr. Thomas Granville in the manner we have described, he returned to Bond street. There he found his friend Henry Robinson and the lovely little Rose. He was still more gratified when he found that the two friends were invited to stay and dine.

"So, Walter, you are going to marry Miss Norris," exclaimed Henry Robinson.

"Yes—that is my intention. Have you any thing to say against it?" replied Walter.

"Not a word, my dear boy. I am not so certain but that I shall follow your example one of these days. I shall if I ever see my way clear to support my little Rose; but hang it, man, I am afraid that had it not been for your intended, Rose and me would have had to part company before this. Money was getting very scarce when Miss Clara came to our relief," remarked Robinson.

The opinion of his friend and companion for years, had its weight with Walter Granville, and confirmed him in his intentions. Rose timidly asked if his father, meaning the elder Granville, was pleased with the proposed match. Walter gave her a stern look, and then perceiving that she did not notice it, added,

"My pretty Rose, my father troubles his head very little about my affairs, and I presume does not care whom I marry. He must have heard that I am in the city, but not a word of kindness or a message of any kind have I received from him or any other of my family. They may go to the old Harry for all that I care. But come, dinner is ready, and we ought to be thankful that we can get a good dinner. We have not always been so lucky, have we, Harry?"

The dinner was a choice affair, and the hostess, Mrs. Woodruff, graced the head of the table and did the honors.

"My beautiful landlady," exclaimed Walter, "you are the prettiest of the three ladies now at this table. You actually look younger than any of them, and if my hand was not already disposed of, I would certainly offer a share of my hard fortunes to you."

"Thank you, sir. I am exceedingly flattered, but Miss Norris has taken the matter in hand, and I am too late. I must say, however, that if I envied any lady it would be Clara. I think you are one of a thousand, and she is an extremely fortunate young lady."

"Thank you, madam, for both of us," replied Clara.

Dinner was over, and evening approached, when Miss Norris went to her room to commence dressing for the important ceremony, which it was arranged should come off in the front parlor. Rose accompanied Clara, and Harry joined Walter, who left Bond street to walk as far as the Hotel de Paris, where he had agreed to meet Thomas Granville. They found Tom deeply engrossed in a game of dominoes with old James Gemmel, the Broadway watchmaker, who owned the building occupied as the Hotel de Paris.

"Excuse me one moment," exclaimed Tom, when he saw Walter, "I have only got twelve to go to beat this gentleman, and then I am at your service."

Walter took a seat at one of the small marble-top tables, and motioning Henry to a seat opposite, he ordered two cups of coffee. The *garcon* brought the cups, and Walter lit a cigar.

"Harry, did you notice that gentleman that I spoke to?" he asked.

"I did. Pray who is he?" asked Henry.

"He is mine uncle Tom, that you have so often heard me chat about, during our watches at sea in the good old whale ship," replied Walter.

"The deuce he is! Well, I like his looks very much. Will he be at your wedding?" asked Robinson.

"Yes. But I don't exactly know how he will take it. He must know Clara. But I will find out presently," said Walter.

At this moment they were joined by Thomas Granville. He rubbed his hands, and exclaimed with delight, "Aha! I am conqueror. I have beat old Mr. Gemmel, and he is considered the crack player in this house."

"Sit down, sir. One would think you had won a second battle of Waterloo, or some other equally important affair. Allow me to introduce to you my friend Henry Robinson," said Walter.

"I am most happy to meet Mr. Robinson, or any other friend of yours, my excellent Smith. Gents, will you join me in a drink?" inquired Tom.

It was quite evident to Walter that his worthy uncle had already drank quite sufficient, and he suggested in place of a drink, that he should join them in a cup of coffee.

"Very well—I think I will do as you suggest. I have been drinking considerable wine to-day," said Tom.

"I should judge so. The coffee will sober you, and I want you to be perfectly cool to-night, for I am to be married this evening, and you are to be at the wedding," said Walter.

"The devil I am! And is that what all these new clothes are for—hem—I beg your pardon, sir." And Tom addressed Robinson. He had forgot himself.

"Never mind, Mr. Granville. You will be welcome to my wedding in any dress. And now I perceive that you have been getting a new rig—out of compliment to me, I presume. Really, I am under obligations to you. Come, suppose, we pay our shot, and then leave—what say you, gentlemen?" asked Walter.

All agreed, and soon after the trio left the Hotel de Paris, and proceeded up Broadway to Bond street. When the party reached the house of Mrs. Woodruff, Tom remarked that his brother's old partner, Mr. Nordheim, used to reside next door.

"I am well aware of that," quietly observed Walter. "Come in, gentlemen," he continued; and then led the way into the front parlor. No one was there. "Excuse me, Mr. Granville. Come, Harry," said Walter Granville, and with his companion he passed up to the room occupied by Clara.

"May I come in with my friend Harry?" demanded Walter.

"Yes, come in, we are almost dressed—but we don't mind you. Look at Rose, Harry. How do you like her?"

Harry did look. The beautiful girl was dressed in a robe of white satin, and her dark hair, parted upon her forehead, and divided to the back of her head, fell in two distinct masses down her back, and the end of each was tied with a white ribbon. Her lover flung his arms about her, and said,

"Thank you, dear Miss Norris. Rose was always lovely, but I have never seen her look so superb as she does to-day. What do we not owe you?"

"Harry Robinson, let me tell you one thing, and God knows it is true. The talk of men, when it concerns women, is as light and evanescent as a summer cloud. Under certain influences men agree to do any and every thing for a woman—a young and pretty woman. They will marry—do this, or do that, or the other. In an hour—a week—a month, all this is changed. They will see the Magdalen they have made despised, trampled upon, stoned even—and that same deceiving man will cast the additional stone that crushes the poor outcast. She who has believed these promises dies a slow death from poisonous disease in the almshouse, and finds an unknown grave in the Potter's Field. Young man, you have a proud, rich father. He would see you wed with wealth and respectability, with a girl who has read all sorts of vile trash—who has never known sorrow, who has drank wine daily at her father's table, and nursed her luscious imagination with a thousand corrupting thoughts until her soul was polluted. But she is virtuous! Nay, the very girl your father would wish you to marry, from the rich, the fashionable, and the pious circles of high society, ninety-nine chances in one hundred, is a prostitute at heart, and when once your wife, as the fountain is already poisoned, so the rivulet will be, and she will become a prostitute in body the first chance she gets. Now look at that vision of loveliness, gazing with her big black eyes at me while I speak. She was made a prostitute in body while her mind was as pure from stain as the white satin that now adorns her person. Her body was polluted, but her soul never entered into the act. She loved you with her mind the first time she saw you. She loved you with her soul. You are her god. With you she leaves the den of infamy as gladly as the wild bird leaves the wiry cage where it was confined. Take her now to the altar, and let her become your wife, and she, that little one, so beautiful, would cling to you till death, true as steel, and as impervious to vice or vicious influences as the flint stone. She would never be unfaithful—never untrue. She would guard your honor as her life, as the very jewel of her existence; for her virtue lies in that particle of Deity—her soul. That has never been polluted or soiled. The world judges differently, but I speak what I know. Marry Rose, dear Harry, and if you live on bread and water, sweep streets for a living, while she acts as washerwoman for your mutual livelihood, as long as you are true to each other, you will know a happiness that wealth cannot give."

While Clara Norris was giving vent to these expressions, Walter Granville was looking at her in amazement. While she was speaking a pin falling would have been heard.

He then added, "Clara, have you spoken for yourself?"

"God knows I have spoken for Rose, for she has a pure, loving, innocent heart, that a few weeks' residence in a brothel has not soiled or tarnished. As for me, I have been a worldling deeply—perhaps damnably. The Great Judge only knows. I do not know my own heart, Walter. Did you bring up Thomas Granville with you?" she asked.

"I did. Left him down stairs, Clara," said Walter.

"Go down at once and apologize. Tell him you will be back presently," said Clara.

Walter descended to the parlor, but returned almost instantly, and addressing Clara, said, "Uncle Tom is fast asleep upon one of Mrs. Woodruff's exquisite sofas."

"Well, let him sleep there until we are ready to descend—and now what was I saying? Oh, about the vice of the body and the vice of the mind, so far as us poor women are concerned. Never mind. I don't think, Walter, that my heart is corrupted, and I am sure that of Rose is not. To-night I become your wife, and wild and wayward as has been my career, dear Walter, I will be true to you while I live. So help me, Heaven. Henry, you do not need to be told what Rose will do. You can read all that is passing in her heart in her sweet, heavenly face. Walter, will you forgive me for one act I have done to-day?" asked Miss Norris.

"Tell me what it is, Clara. If it is not the unpardonable sin, I think I can forgive you," replied Walter.

"I have invited Marion Monck, once a favorite clerk of your father's—once a favored suitor of your sister Isabella, to be present to-night," said Miss Norris.

"You are a strange creature, Clara. Why invite him? What have I, or you, for that matter in common, with him? What is he to us now?" haughtily demanded Walter.

"More than ever he was in what the world calls his prosperous days. He was once kind to me, but he is now writing for a living—depending upon his brains for his bread and water. Mr. Bennett, of the Herald, has taken him up, and—don't laugh—he writes poetry. He has not spoken to me for some time, but last St. Valentine's Day I received from him this precious valentine." Here Clara went to a small desk and took an envelope from it, and the enclosure she handed to Walter. "Read that."

Walter drew near the lamp. He looked at the hand-writing a moment. "How well I remember that writing," he exclaimed. "It is indeed written by Marion, but no signature is attached. How did you recognize it, Clara?"

"Pooh! pooh! I have seen his hand-writing a hundred times in the days of Mr. Nordheim. I knew it at once, but read it." Walter read the poetry. It was as follows:—

THE OUTCAST.

I look upon that face, but while
  It seems so passing fair,
I ask me if that sunny smile
  Is wont to linger there;
I ask me if that bosom's heave
  Hides not a heart that's doomed to grieve
And wither in despair;
I ask if joy or peace can be
With one so desolate as thee.

I knew thee not, thou fallen flower,
  When virtue marked thy growth,
I knew thee not in thy bright hour
  Of purity and truth.
I knew thee not till treacherous ways
  Had dimmed the sunshine of thy days,
The freshness of thy youth;
And then I knew thee in thy shame
Without a friend—without a name.

An outcast from thy father's home,
  A blighted, joyless thing;
Thy journey onward to the tomb,
  A rayless wandering.
Uncheered by hope thy bosom heaves
  Yet like the rose's scattered leaves,
Some sweets yet round thee cling;
And dimly round thy ruin shine
Like ivy on the shattered pine.

There's beauty still upon thy brow,
  And kindness in thy heart,
A smile is with thee even now,
  All hopeless as thou art.
But sorrow's wave too soon will chase
  The light of beauty from thy face,

And thou wilt then depart;
As bends the lily to the blast
Unknown, unloved, thou'll sink at last.

God cheer thee on that awful day,
  For none will watch thy bed,
None sigh to see thee pass away,
  Or grieve for thee when dead;
None seek the silent, lonely spot,
  Where, cold, forsaken and forgot,
Reclines thy lovely head:
The turf, alas, will soon be green,
And few will know that thou hast been.

"Yes, dear Walter, I want that young man who could address me such lines, to see me married—yes, *married.* I should die were he not here to-night, for that poetry has weighed like lead upon my heart. But as your wife, the spell will be removed," exclaimed the excited Miss Norris.

"I am very glad, then, Clara, that you have invited him. But come, you are all dressed. Holloa, what is the matter with you, my beautiful Rose?"

Rose was weeping as though her heart would break. The few lines, as read by Walter in his deep-toned voice, touched a chord that had vibrated through her bosom. She made no reply to Walter, but fell upon her knees before Henry Robinson.

"Oh, dear Henry, save me from such a fate as that of the poor outcast," she exclaimed.

"It shall be, Rose—it shall be. My mind is made up. Dear Miss Norris, may I ask one favor? After the clergyman has made you and Walter one, let him do the same for us two—make Rose my wife. Come what will, I will be her legal protector; her husband."

"God bless you, Harry," was all the reply that Rose could make.

"I will see to it," said the majestic Clara.

A slight tap at the door interrupted the conversation.

"Who is there?" asked Walter.

"Me—Mrs. Woodruff. There are some guests in the parlor. Are you not most ready?" she asked.

The reply was in the affirmative, and in a moment the door was opened and the party followed Mrs. Woodruff down stairs. As they entered the parlor a singular sight was presented—Thomas Granville lay asleep, and was snoring upon the sofa. There was a clergyman in his robes, evidently of the Episcopal order, for he wore a white surplice, and held in his hand the Book of Common Prayer of the Church of England.

In one corner of the room was Marion Monck. It was the lady-like duty of Miss Norris to place these people at their ease. She walked to Marion.

"Old friend, have you forgotten one known to you many years ago? This is Walter Granville.

Simple as the words were, they electrified Marion. Walter was his old employer's son—the brother of her he remembered with such tender recollections.

"Walter, why when did you come? I am glad to see you," was all Marion could say, and it was enough.

Walter said some kind words, and sat down by him. Clara proceeded to the clergyman.

"Venerable sir, in a moment we will be ready for you to proceed. When you have married me to Mr. Granville, will you marry these two to each other?" and she pointed to Henry and Rose.

The clergyman bowed, and replied, "Most certainly, if there are no objections."

"None in the wide world," said Clara, and she passed to the sofa where Thomas Granville was lying. She placed her hand heavily upon him, and in a deep voice pronounced the single word "Tom!"

In a moment he aroused himself, rubbed his eyes, looked up in her face, and replied,

"Holloa! what's out now? Clara, is that you? Where did you come from?"

She made no reply. Then he sat up and looked about the room, recognizing Marion, and also the man he knew as Smith. He repeated, "Marion and Smith here? That is all right."

"Tom!" Clara repeated again.

"Well, what is it?" asked Tom.

"You are invited here to be present at a wedding. Are you sufficiently awake to be a witness?"

"Certainly. Of course. Go ahead. I am all right," said Tom.

Clara turned about and walked to the clergyman.

"We are ready now, sir. Please proceed with the solemn ceremony."

She was joined by Walter, and the clergyman opened his book and performed the ceremony of marriage according to the Ritual. When it was finished, and the reverend man of God pronounced them man and wife, Walter kissed Clara affectionately, and then Henry Robinson and Rose were made "one flesh." Clara then approached the clergyman and placed a bill in his hand.

"Allow me," said she, "to settle the fees for myself and for the other couple."

The clergyman, perhaps without meaning to do so, glanced at the denomination of the bill.

"Really, madam," he suddenly exclaimed, "there is some mistake; this note is for one hundred dollars."

"So I supposed. Keep it. If it is unusual, use it to make others as happy as I trust you have made several in the room this evening," quietly observed Mrs. Walter Granville.

"Where can I find pen and paper?" asked the clergyman.

"That lady," pointing to Mrs. Woodruff, "will show you," and she whispered to the clergyman, "May I ask that you will give them certificates for each marriage, if not too much trouble? You have the names."

"Certainly," said the minister, and he left the room.

Marion Monck had seen so many astonishing things in an experience of some years, that he had long ago arrived at the conclusion that he would never more be astonished at any thing which might occur in New York; still he was surprised, to say the least of it, at the marriage of the somewhat celebrated Miss Norris to the runaway son of his old employer. He offered his congratulations to the lady now Mrs. Granville and to her husband. The former requested to speak with Marion for a moment alone.

When she found herself thus with him, she observed, "Marion, we have known each other a long time, through some strange vicissitudes, eh? Is it not a strange world?"

"Rather so," replied Marion in a very laconic manner.

"Will you take back your poetry about 'the OUTCAST?' I am now a married woman—married to a man whose father is an eminent merchant, eh?"

"Exactly, dear lady; I understand perfectly well your sarcasm, but it don't apply; I don't take it. I wrote 'the Outcast' when it did apply. You were at old Mother Miller's, you know. Don't be angry; I will write another piece which you will like better when I have leisure, and call it 'The Wife,' eh?"

"Now stop all foolishness. Here is five dollars: take it," said Clara Granville.

"What is out now? Do you mean to insult me?"

"No, Marion, far from it; but I want this notice copied,

and to appear in all the daily papers to-morrow morning: will you attend to it? I know you will. Say nothing. I must speak to Mr. Thomas Granville," said Mrs. Granville.

Marion read the note. It was as follows:

"Married—On Tuesday evening, the 29th instant, by the Rev. Samuel Fuller, Walter Granville, Esq., son of W. Pitt Granville, of this city, to Miss Clara Norris, formerly of New Jersey."

It is needless to say that this notice appeared in all the journals the next day.

Clara approached Tom Granville. She seated herself by his side. This gentleman had listened to all that was going on. He was perfectly conscious that people had been married—he knew that Clara Norris had married his friend Smith, and he had made up his mind that Smith was "sold," according to his ideas of how the world ought to wag on; but he had caught no other name, or if he had, it had not fastened itself upon his mind. But he was soon to be enlightened. Clara had him alone, and she commenced.

"Tom Granville, do you remember how you treated me in France? Your heartlessness, your villany—selling me to make an income for you to spend upon other women? Hear me, and don't say a word. You know this is true. Grant that I in many things did wrong. Does that justify what you have done?"

"Oh Clara, don't let us bring up old sores. Let byegones be byegones. You have married Smith. Nice man, I dare say. Respectable man, evidently. I'm mum. I'll not say a word. Do you understand?"

"Tom, do you recollect how your brother humbled me when I was kept by Nordheim? Do you know the exertions that he used to deprive me of what I received from Mr. Nordheim? He called me harlot, prostitute, vile wretch, and a few other names that a woman never forgives nor forgets," said Clara.

"Well, what of it? It don't amount to anything now," replied Tom.

"Your wife, your niece—how did they treat me?" asked the now excited Clara.

"Oh, what matters all such stuff—what is the use of bringing it up now? This is your wedding night, old gal. You have married Smith, let's all be jolly, eh?" said Tom, who was still under the influence of liquor although he had had a good nap upon the sofa.

"Tom, now listen to me. I want to give you an introduction to my husband. Walter, come here," said Clara.

Walter approached the sofa.

"Mr. Thomas Granville, allow me to introduce to you my husband, Mr. Walter Granville. If I am not mistaken, he is also your nephew;" and when she had said this, she gave one loud scream of hysterical laughter, and then sat down. Tom could not join in it; he was sobered, and asked,

"Walter, is this so?"

"It is, uncle Tom. Did you not know me?"

"And are you the husband of this lady?" pointing to Clara, who was watching this conversation.

"I believe that there is no mistake about that," replied the other.

"Then may God have mercy upon the Granville family; we are a doomed race," said Tom solemnly.

"Why, uncle Tom, cheer up; don't you get down-hearted. You at least know how I am situated—a cast-off. I found a true friend in Miss Clara when I had no other friends," observed Walter.

"I am a broken-hearted man, nephew—crushed. I have no hope except to get a bed at night, an occasional meal of victuals, and drink and clothes. You have helped me along on my rough bye path, and I thank you for it. I do not know how you came by the means to do so. But what matters it, Clara? God bless you. You are my niece now. What you are driving at is beyond my ken. Never mind; play out the game your own way. You hold ace, king, queen and jack of the Granville family in your own hands, and your suit is trumps. It is the winning hand. Heaven send queen to Pitt Granville. When will he hear the news?" continued Tom.

Clara and Walter had listened attentively to the abrupt language of uncle Tom. Both knew that in other days, when his proud spirit was dominant, such a marriage would have been repudiated on the instant if it had cost him his life blood. But they knew that stern poverty will humble the haughtiest heart. He who lacks food for months, he who stoops to almost beg from friends a shilling for a night's lodging; he who is ragged, shirtless, and wants the ordinary comforts of even a wash-bowl and towel, soon comes down to that low level, that were his wife, sister, or even mother, placed in affluence at the price of her virtue, would receive a portion of the wages of vice, and be thankful for it. Pride of birth or anything else vanishes into thin air, when placed in contact with the silent degradation of poverty. Marion had left for down town.

Mrs. Woodruff had left for her apartments, and Henry, with the happy Mrs. Robinson, had gone to the nuptial couch. The clergyman had also taken his leave, and man and wife, with that worldly uncle, were alone. At last he bade them good night. Walter did not rise. Clara followed him out of the room. As they stood in the hall, she said:

"Tom Granville, I know what you would say. This will be a fearful thing for Pitt. He will see it in the morning papers. Will he die?"

"No. It will make him mad—stark, raving mad."

"Tom, you may need money. Take this roll—take it kindly. I don't know how much there is—two or three hundred. You are a man of the world—use it wisely, Tom. Good night."

Thomas Granville, late United States Consul in the second city of France, was in the street. The moon was shining brightly over his head, and he had more money in his pocket than had been there for many long months. As he passed down Broadway, he soliloquized,

"Last night I had no bread—I had no money. I had barely a few dirty coppers to keep me from sleeping in the streets—no clothes—no decent boots—no hat—no cravat—no nothing. To-night I have as much as I need. A hotel—a room to go to, and money in my pocket. How did I get it all? Least said is soonest mended. From this day forth I will never be without money. Gold is all.

> 'That yellow slave
> Will knit and break religions; bless the accursed;
> Make the hoar leprosy adored, place thieves,
> And give them title, knee and approbation
> With senators on the bench.'

Whatever else I lose, I will never be again without gold."

Thomas Granville reached his hotel. A silver shilling amply rewarded the porter for opening the door, and he went to his room.

CHAPTER LVII.

Perils of Youth in New York—Tammany Hall Committee—Marion Monck's first Article in the Herald—The Spanish Boarding House, and the two Peruvian Girls.

THERE are few situations of more intense peril in human life than to be in a large city, needing money for the ordinary necessaries of existence, or without any regular source of income. The man who works from six in the morning until dark at night, even if he only gets a dollar a day, is comparatively independent, and is not exposed to temptation. His wages are small, but he makes his expenses bear a fair proportion to his income. If he earns but six dollars a week, his board costs him but two—his clothes do not cost him fifty cents a week, and his other expenses, for pipes and tobacco, and his glass of beer or gin, may make a dollar more per week, and he actually can lay up two and a half dollars per week. Women, wine and cards are beyond his wishes. His income would go but a little way for the indulgence of either, and he never gives them even a passing thought. If he gets out of employ as a day laborer, it is not a source of much anxiety, for as he has no pride to get over, but is content to take up with whatever turns up, he soon finds something to do, and he is at his ease once more.

This is not the case with the young man who has been a clerk in a store. He considers a clerkship an honorable employment. He engages in it, hoping one day to become an employer, a merchant on his own hook. From a hundred dollars a year his salary is increased to a thousand, but extravagant habits have increased with it. His board alone costs him two hundred to four hundred dollars a year. His clothes are two hundred more. He visits bad houses two or three times a week, adding two hundred dollars for this tax; and he smokes cigars, drinks occasionally, goes to the theatre and other places of amusement—and these last inconsiderable expenses count up easily two dollars a day; the sum per year is about seven hundred dollars. Add it to the eight hundred dollars already enumerated, and our clerk is living at the rate of fifteen hundred dollars, when he only gets one thousand. This discrepancy of five hundred dollars must come out of somebody. As a general rule, a portion falls on the place where he boards—his tailor, his bootmaker, and a few others who have trusted him, share the deficiency among them. It is bad enough when the salary continues steady; but when a young man who has been living at this rate, gets out of a situation, and out of money, in a place like New York, the chances are fearfully against him. Temptations surround him on all sides. If he stays in New York, his fall is certain—his degradation sure. He begs and borrows to the full extent of his tether. These sources used up, he has nothing left but to steal. If he is an American, he will not turn to manual labor, and he will not take menial service. Who ever heard of an American *servant*, and how far will one travel in New York before he finds an American day laborer?

Marion Monck was out of a situation, yet he had hopes ahead. Hopes, however, although very flattering stock in one's imagination, will not pay a board bill, obtain a decent suit of clothes, a pair of boots or a hat. The young fellow had a proud spirit. He would not beg if he could help it—he would not have written home to his parents for aid. He would have cut his right hand off first. The Count occasionally let him have money, and had made Marion promise that he would come to him (the Count,) before he borrowed money, or before he took any new situation. Consequently Marion was resting upon his oars. The Count Falsechinski had married, and was spending several weeks out of town with his bride. Marion did not know where he was.

He had boarded in the house in Nassau street for many months. As we have said before, his room was the rear one on the third floor, that of the editor was in the front. Sometimes they talked together, but Marion was very shy of any overtures. He had no confidence in his own ability to write, and even if he had succeeded as a writer, his prejudices were altogether in favor of success as a merchant—he considered it more reputable than success as an editor. In after life his views underwent a great change. He learned to do full justice to the power and the respectability of the pen.

Soon after the marriage of the Count Falsechinski with Miss Grasper, Marion Monck settled his bill with the landlady in Nassau street, and removed to a Spanish boarding-house in Fulton street near Cliff. It was kept by a Spaniard named Alfayez, who agreed to give Marion a good room and a seat at the table for a moderate sum per week. Marion was a good Spanish scholar, but he wanted practice in speaking it. This was a good opportunity, and he availed himself of it. We have somewhere mentioned that Marion Monck had a great inkling for politics. His sympathies were with the Democratic party, owing probably to the fact that when a clerk with Mr. Granville, who was a Whig, he became a Democrat from the mere love of opposition. At that time there were two Committees that regulated Tammany Hall; one was called the "Old Men's General Committee," and the other the "Young Men's General Democratic Committee." These Committees were elected once a year. Marion had always been elected to the latter Committee from the ward in which he lived, and as he was ready with the pen, extremely willing to work, and had no game to play, or spoils to seek after, he was generally selected as one of the secretaries of the "Young Men's Committee," and the work fell upon him, as it always does upon the free horse, his colleague being contented to sign anything that Marion had drawn up or engrossed.

On one occasion the Committee had a very exciting debate. A procession was to be got up in reference to a political victory in Maine or some other State. In this victorious procession several very distinguished military men had volunteered to act as Marshals, but they refused to do so unless all the other marshals were military men.

"Very well," said the chairman of the Committee. "That matter can be easily arranged. There are to be three marshals from each ward—make 'em all military men;" and as each name of a marshal was proposed and accepted, the chairman observed, "Make 'Bill Gage' a general."

"Enoch Camp."—"Make him a major."

"Nick Dimond, first ward."—"Make Nick a general."

"Bill Dennis," said the Secretary.

"Make Bill a major," said the chairman.

"Joe Sweet," called out the Secretary.

"Make Joe Sweet a Colonel," dictated the chairman.

"Thomas McSpeddon," said the Secretary.

"Put General to Tom's name."

"William Shaler, sixth ward."

"Make Bill Shaler a Colonel—he has been in the wars;" and in this ludicrous way the list, which was to be published, was made out, amidst the screams and shouts of the Tammany Hall Committee. When the list was fairly completed, word was sent to the *real* Generals, Morris, Ward, Stryker,

Arcularius, and others, that the Committee had placed none but *military* men on the list of marshals from the different wards.

It was late when the Committee adjourned. It was also Saturday evening. Marion passed down Nassau street, and into the Herald publication office. Somewhat unusual it would be now, but at that hour in those days Mr. Bennett was still in the office. The two commenced a conversation, and in the course of it Marion Monck related the ludicrous debate that had occurred that evening in the committee room in Tammany Hall. It appeared very droll to the editor, and irresistibly comic. He actually held his sides while he roared with laughter. Marion did not laugh at all.

"I am going home—good night," said the editor.

Marion returned his "Good night," and passed to his Spanish boarding-house.

On his way down, it occurred to him that his month was up, and that he owed the Spaniard twenty dollars that very day.

"I am dead broke! Suppose he was to ask me for it? I have not got five dollars in the world, and the Count is off somewhere. When he will be back, Heaven only knows!"

These were the thoughts of Marion Monck as he reached the door in Fulton street. He rang the bell. Alfayez, the proprietor, opened it himself. It was an unusual thing for him to do, and Marion expected to be dunned for his bill.

He was not doomed to be disappointed. "You no pay me my money to-day?" exclaimed the Spaniard in English. "I want him. You got him now, eh?"

"Sorry to say I have not, Senor Alfayez, but I suppose a few days hence will answer all purposes," asked Marion Monck.

"No, Senor, he no do two tree days—bym-bye. I want de money. *Ahora*, what you call *now*? No do two three days. Hab got him?" demanded the Spaniard, who had admitted Marion into the hotel, but seemed disposed to bar his progress to his room.

"Really, Mr. Alfayez, I have not got the money to-night. You are in no danger of losing the amount, although I am comparatively a stranger to you. My trunks are worth more than ten times your bill. However, to satisfy you, to-morrow you shall have the twenty dollars," said Marion.

"Bueno. Manana, Senor. Buenos noches,"—and after this parting salutation, which means "Good. To-morrow morning. Good night," Marion went up to his room. Where to get the money on Sunday morning was not so clear, and it was a long time before he could get asleep. The next morning Marion Monck rose very early. At the breakfast table he met two sisters, very sweet girls, who spoke Spanish to him upon every occasion. They were lovely creatures from the city of Lima, in Peru, and their father, a grey bearded old Peruvian, was their protector. He, of course, was stopping in the house. These pretty senoritas were aged thirteen and fifteen, extremely anxious to learn English. Marion Monck had already made a bargain with them that he should teach them English while they kept him in practice with his Spanish. Very probably Marion felt anxiety to end the financial war between the Spanish proprietor Alfayez and himself as much on account of these two extremely beautiful pupils as for any other reason. At any rate, no sooner had he finished his breakfast and smoked a cigar, than he hurried up to the office of the New York Herald. He inquired for Mr. Bennett.

"In his private office," was the reply, and thither went Marion Monck.

"Good morning," said the editor, and then continued making some memorandum in a small book. One of the most prominent traits in the character of Mr. Bennett, and which is only known to those who know him as well as he knows himself, is his perfect editorial closeness. He does not let his left hand know what his right hand writes. He will appear to be communicative and frank, and yet what he says is the very frankness of hypocrisy. His hearer gains nothing, obtains nothing from him. He will listen unmoved to what he knew before, but the teller will not discover any sign of impatience or any indication that Mr. Bennett is already aware of what he is telling him.

No man in the city of New York is better posted in reference to the affairs of the city, the prominent men in it, or in its various wards than Mr. Bennett. Consequently, when Marion Monck related to him the scene at Tammany Hall, which to a man not familiar with the prominent military and political men of the day, it would have been dry and uninteresting, to Mr. Bennett, who knew the name and character of every man, it was uncontrollably comic and ludicrous.

When he had finished his work, he turned to Marion Monck.

"Well, Marion, what have you got new this morning?"

"Nothing, sir. I have called here this morning for a very particular purpose," said Marion.

"Indeed. It is raining in torrents, is it not? What can I do for you?" Mr. Bennett asked kindly.

Marion hesitated a moment. He had never, since he had known Mr. Bennett, asked him for a loan of money in any shape, but this morning he felt that he had no other resource, and so he replied, "Yes, sir, it is indeed raining very hard, but the fact is, I am in a tight place. You know I am down at that Spanish boarding-house. My month was up yesterday, and unless I get twenty dollars this morning I do believe the old Spaniard will turn me out of his house to-day. I could get the money if it was any other day but Sunday. As it is, if you will lend me the twenty to-day, I will return it to you to-morrow,"—and Marion felt relieved, that the application was made, whatever might be its fate.

"No; I never lend money," was the abrupt reply.

"Oh, well, never mind. There has been no harm done by my asking you. I hated to do it, but I must have money, and stand up to the rack, fodder or no fodder. As it is '*no fodder*,' I must try somewhere else," said Marion Monck.

"There is no harm in your applying to me," observed Mr. Bennett, who wrote some thing on a small piece of paper. Marion rose to go. Mr. Bennett held up the paper and observed, "Wait a moment. Here is an order for the exact sum you wish to borrow. I will not lend it to you. You must earn it."

"Earn it! Earn twenty dollars. How in the world am I to do that?" demanded Marion.

"Last night you told me a very interesting story of some doings in Tammany Hall in reference to a Democratic victorious procession that is soon to come off. You made me almost go into convulsions with laughter by the funny way in which you told it," continued the editor.

"Well," said Marion.

"Now, here is my order, for which you can get twenty dollars when you go down stairs. There, on that table, is foolscap paper, and pen, and ink. Write out what you told me, and the order is yours," coolly remarked the editor.

"It will take me all day to do it, and I don't think it will be fit to read then," said Marion.

"Never mind that. Do as I say, and do it as near as possible to what you told me, and I shall be satisfied," said the editor.

Marion took a seat and went to work. In less than two hours he had filled ten sides of foolscap paper. He handed it to Mr. Bennett, who did not even pay him the compliment of reading it, but laid it aside, at the same time handing Marion the order for twenty. He took his leave, and down stairs he received the money.

"I suppose he made me write out all that stuff for the purpose of affording him an excuse to lend me twenty," thought Marion.

The next morning, however, when he opened the Herald, he found his article. It made two and a half columns on the outside of the Herald. It was extremely ludicrous. It was a *point*. One of Mr. Bennett's frequent great points, and when his sagacity as an editor was never at fault, either in the subject or manner of handling it, no matter how incapable the pen he made use of. There were tens of thousands of military men in New York. There were an equal number of Democrats. Such an article, naming the principal leaders in both the political and military ranks, and making them figure in a ludicrous manner, would soon find its way through the streets. At ten o'clock that day as high as a dollar was paid for a Herald. There were none to be had at any price. It was one of those millions of original articles that in a great many years had made the Herald talked about. Mr. Bennett is the most suggestive mind in the United States. He could keep a hundred papers filled with original matter if he had the mechanical minds and hands to work under him in sufficient force.

The appearance of this article was a matter of astonishment to Marion Monck. It was the first newspaper article he ever wrote. He did not believe that he could write one. Mr. Bennett had told him that he could. He had made him do it. The article was written. It appeared in the Herald. Marion read it and could not doubt that he had written it. "It was an accident," he said to himself. "I succeeded by Mr. Bennett telling me how to do it. I doubt whether I could do it again." With the twenty dollars he hurried from the Herald office out into the rain and down to the Spanish boarding-house. He called for Alfayez, handed him the twenty, the Spaniard gave him a receipt, and a friendship commenced which lasted many years. After paying his bill, Marion passed up stairs to the parlor occupied by the family of the Peruvian. He found the two senoritas pouting because he had not arrived sooner to give them their lesson. The father was in his own room, and the old duenna was in another part of the house. The charming pupils, with their long dark locks floating loose over their white and almost naked shoulders and bosoms, sat upon the sofa with Marion between them. For some time the studies went on very smoothly. Marion had procured a book with Spanish and English conversation upon each page. From this he taught his pupils and they taught him to pronounce Spanish. Marion finally passed an arm around each of their waists. The youngest, Inez, sprang up and locked the door, saying, "What would the senora say, if she came in and caught us?" and then resumed her seat. Marion tried the lips of the sister who had fastened the door, and she returned kiss for kiss with an ardor that surprised him. Then the elder sister, Isabel, got up and poutingly observed that Marion did not care for her, or he would kiss her as well as Inez. This invitation was not lost, and the book was soon laid aside, while Marion gave way to the loving kisses and caresses of the two beautiful sisters. They were innocent, and so was he. What a strange contrast between American and Spanish girls. Two Americans might be alone with a young man, and their conduct would be the same as if their parents were present—they are accustomed to depend on their own self-respect—they are to be trusted, and their conduct would be modest and prudent, without being afraid of the opinion of their parents. Not so Spanish girls. They are watched. They are shown early that they cannot be trusted. They are not allowed to associate with the young of the other sex. Hence, when a chance occurs like that with Marion, they only regard the danger of being found out. They fondled their teacher as if he had been a young kitten, and he returned their innocent embraces and kisses. Then they finished their lessons, and he retired to his own room.

CHAPTER LVIII.

Pitt Granville reads the notice of his son's marriage—Seeks out his Brother Tom at 43 Centre street—Thomas Granville believes in luck—Buys a Lottery Ticket.

WHEN Pitt Granville opened his morning paper, and his eye fell upon the few lines which informed him that his son— his only son, had married 'Clara Norris,' the paper fell from his hands, and a few moments after, when one of his clerks entered the office, he found him lying senseless upon the floor. A physician was sent for at once: he bled the old gentleman, and then recommended that a carriage should be sent for, and that he should be conveyed to his home as speedily as possible, and there be kept perfectly quiet. No one present had the slightest idea of the real cause of this sudden illness; the doctor pronounced it a fit of apoplexy.

When the unhappy father reached home he refused to go to bed, but sent every one out of the room except his daughter. He informed Isabella of what had occurred.

"Bell, my heart is broken; I shall never hold up my head more. If he had died I should have mourned for him, for he was my son, although a disobedient one; but to bring disgrace upon us all, to marry one of the most notorious courtezans in New York, the very one that ruined my poor brother Tom—Oh, this is dreadful, and I feel as if my senses were leaving me."

Isabella was deeply affected, and endeavored to soothe her father, and prevent if possible another fit, for she had been told by the physician that any violent agitation would induce a relapse. She sent a note to Colonel Benson, and ere an hour the cool old Englishman was with them. He was more shocked at what he called Walter's mad infatuation than even the father, whom he advised to break it up. "Get the parties divorced, or buy the lady off with a sum of money." To all of these suggestions the humbled father turned a deaf ear. "No, Colonel; as he has made his bed, let him lie on it; I will not interfere—no, not to save his life; it is too late now. He must have been in New York sometime without my knowledge; had he come to me at once—had he—but what am I talking about? He is ruined, body and soul, and our name is the laughing stock of all the good and the respectable in New York. If my business was only closed up, I would sell every thing and go back to England," said poor Mr. Granville.

Colonel Benson urged it upon Mr. Granville that he must not take the matter too much to heart. "Bear in mind," he added, "that you have another child and a grandchild—a glorious fellow too, who must take your son Walter's place. For their sakes, don't give up."

"I will not. I will try not to do so. I will try and forget my unworthy son. But, Colonel, where is my brother Thomas? I must try and find him out. He too is unworthy of a thought—but, poor devil, he is a fool. He does the best he can, but he is half imbecile, and don't know wrong from right. He must not starve. That affair of our old friend Mac Neil—was it not dreadful, to die all alone in the hospital! Poor Tom, I am afraid he is following in the same direction. I have not heard from him for a long time. He must be seen before it is too late. I have heard that he can be found at a place No. 46 Centre street. I will go there at once. I feel much better: will you go with me, Colonel?" asked Granville.

It was in vain that Colonel Benson remonstrated, and tried to persuade his friend that such a course would be worse than useless. He was not to be persuaded, and when the Colonel, hoping that his refusal to go would prevent Mr. Granville from doing so foolish a thing, refused to accompany him, Mr. Granville rose and said,

"Well then, Colonel, I will go alone, and perhaps it is better that you should not go."

Isabel tried to dissuade her father from going out, but his mind was fully made up. Colonel Benson accompanied him as far as the corner of Broadway and Chambers street, and there they shook hands and parted, the haughty British Colonel wishing his friend success in his present attempt.

When the latter reached Centre street, he commenced examining the numbers in order to ascertain whereabouts No. 46 was located. He was in a quarter of the city with which he was no more acquainted than with the localities in the neighborhood of the North Pole. He kept up Centre street on the right hand side. At last he found the right number, and entered. His striking appearance attracted Jemmy's attention the moment he entered the door. There was indeed a strong resemblance between the brothers. There were in the store the usual quantity of loafers, and the visitor, after passing his eyes over them, took a seat. Jemmy the bar-keeper had not had his eyes off the new-comer for a moment. As he entered he was serving a customer, but when he had finished that duty and placed the money in the drawer, he crossed towards where the merchant had seated himself.

"Can I serve to you anything, sir?" asked Jemmy.

The merchant laid down the paper.

"Yes, if you have any good brandy I would like some in water. I want good—no trash; here is a dollar. If you have no good brandy here, send out for some"

"I have some in a demijohn of the very choicest kind. It was selected by Colonel Mac Neil, and kept exclusively for his use: he was a judge of that article, but since his death; no one has used any of it."

How long Jemmy would have gone on it is impossible to say, but no sooner had the name of Colonel Mac Neil caught the ear of the old gentleman than he interrupted him.

"Who did you say—Colonel Mac Neil? what did he do

here, or what do you know about him?" asked Mr. Granville, hastily.

Jemmy was now on his hobby. He informed his listener that Colonel Mac Neil kept a room for fifty dollars a year; that his old bureau had stood in the rear of that very store until recently, when it was removed to his widow's house. He told him how the Colonel got hurt, and of the money which the Count Falsechinski had given him; of Mr. O'Doemall, who was last seen to converse with the Colonel—of Marion Monck —of the pledging of the pistols, and of his opening the store the next morning, and of finding Mac Neil all bloody; of his being taken to the hospital by young Marion Monck, and how surprised every body about the place was to hear next day that the Colonel was dead.

"Not a word more; I cannot bear it, it is too frightful. I knew the Colonel well. Here, my lad. I know you were very kind to poor Mac; he was a friend of mine, and a hard fate he had! Take this and put it in your pocket. I give it to you out of regard to his memory," and at the same time he took from from his pocket a roll of money, from which he selected a ten dollar bill. Presenting it to Jemmy, who thanked him very warmly, the young man resumed attending to the customers who were cursing at his absence.

Mr. Granville continued buried in deep thought. Occasionally his eyes would glance over the casks and barrels of liquor, but his thoughts were of a most melancholy character. A thousand traits of the amiable disposition of his friend flashed across his memory, and he soliloquized "Here he kept out of the gay world and his former associates for years; he too, the gallant, wealthy, successful and envied favorite of fashionable society, was reduced to this haunt, and to a room at a dollar a week in the neighborhood. Good God! what may we not all expect? what may not the most powerful and wealthy be reduced to! Perhaps it will be my fate: who knows? Here too is a favorite haunt of my poor brother Thomas; well, I am glad I have come here. I see things as they are and as they have been. I am learning a lesson in life which I should be long in learning in my own handsome mansion in State street." He looked at the different persons in the place. "All of them I suppose have seen better days." While he was thus reflecting, a hand was quietly placed upon his shoulder—it was his brother.

He could not speak. Not so, however, Tom; he took a seat and commenced,

"Well, Pitt, how goes the world with you?"

"So-so, Tom: but you are looking better than I expected. I had heard—but no matter. You are looking well.".

Tom replied,

"Indeed! No thanks to you, though, brother Pitt. I should have looked bad enough had I been dependent on you; but I am glad to see you—heard of your son's marriage?" asked Tom.

Pitt Granville winced as he replied,

"Yes, I have heard it, and it pained me much; it is a very disgraceful affair."

"Could he do any thing else? he had no money, and I suppose he might have starved if that girl had not taken him up. It is to him I owe my present respectable appearance; had I applied to you, I presume I might have starved, eh?" said Tom.

"No, Tom, no; I came here to-day on purpose to afford you relief if you needed it."

"Needed it? I do need it—need money."

Tom said this, for he had become heartless, and had determined to adhere to his plan of getting gold whenever he could—he felt that something had shaken or softened his brother's feelings, and he was now anxious to know to what extent he could venture a financial demand.

"How much do you want, Tom, to make you comfortable?" asked the brother.

"All that you can spare. I want a home, with some money in my pocket besides that which I want to return to Miss Norris, which I borrowed of her."

Tom lied when he added this last.

"How much do you owe Miss Norris?" asked the merchant anxiously and quickly.

"What is the use of asking such a foolish question? Let me have some money, if you intend to do so, and I will then go and pay her," said Tom.

The elder Granville took out his pocket book, and handed his brother two hundred and fifty dollars.

"Take that, Tom. Make it go as far as you can. Above all, pay Miss Norris what you owe her. When you need more you can send to me or call upon me. Find some respectable boarding-house, and get settled in it," said Pitt Granville.

Thomas Granville placed the money in his pocket, and then his mouth was opened. He informed his brother that he had been present at the wedding of his nephew without being aware of it, until the clergyman had made the parties man and wife. Pitt Granville groaned in agony as he listened to the narrative. Tom did not spare his brother from reproaches. He told him that he had driven Walter from his home, and how severely he had been punished for it. He then related his own hardships, his want of food, of sleep, of ordinary comforts. But he added, "I thank you, brother, that even now your heart has relented. It has done me good to see and feel some of the hardships of life, and if I live, they shall not have happened to me in vain. I will never be in such desperate want again." The elder Granville listened, but could say nothing in reply but to beg his brother to come and see him at his house in State street as though nothing unpleasant had ever occurred. He shook him cordially by the hand, and remonstrated kindly at his not having a more respectable haunt. When he had gone Tom exclaimed, "Well, I am in luck. Who would have dreamed that I, a poor devil two days since, that lacked a meal of victuals, wanted a shilling to get a night's lodging, charged with prigging two cents' worth of pie, should now be worth—let me count my fortune. My gold, my yellow slave—five hundred and odd dollars. Well—

"'There is a tide in the affairs of men,
Which, taken at the flood, leads on to fortune.'

"It is ebb with me. Maybe, whatever I do will turn out lucky. What are my lucky numbers? This is 46. I came here, met my nephew, got clothes, home and board. Good—46 is a lucky number. Then I went up to that she devil's in Bond street, No. 32. I came away with a pocket full of money. Two hundred and sixty dollars in good city bills. 32 is a lucky number. Now, to-day my brother Pitt wakes up, and comes from a sick bed in No. 9 State street to give me two hundred and fifty dollars. No. 9 is a lucky number. 9, 32, 46. If I could get a ticket with those three numbers upon it, wouldn't it win? Of course it would. I'll go and try. If I can't get a ticket with those numbers upon it in the very next lottery, I will go for once into the policy business, and gig those numbers for five hundred dollars. Jemmy, give me a mild drink. Make it merciful.

"'The quality of mercy is not strained;
It droppeth, as the gentle rain from heaven
Upon the place beneath: it is twice blessed;
It blesseth him that gives and him that takes.'

"James, take a drink with me. It will do you good. I am going to seek for money. James, when you are poor, never try to borrow. No one will lend a poor man. Get ten dollars, and if you want to borrow a ten, go to your friend and show him *that* ten, and tell him you have to make up twenty dollars. He will lend you ten. With the twenty dollars go to a second friend, show him the twenty dollars, and repeat the story, but make the amount you have to make up fifty, and borrow thirty dollars. No. 2 will lend you it. With a fifty you can raise up fast. Show it to your No. 3 friend. 'Charley, I have to lend Bill Astor's nephew a hundred this morning. Count that pile and see how much I lack, and then lend it to me like a good fellow.' Ah! Jemmy, you find Charley counts it, and lends you the lacking fifty with pleasure. He would have seen you damned before he would have lent you fifty cents, if he thought you really needed it and had not got it. Jemmy, you have now a hundred. Get it all in small bills, except one of fifty, and put that on top. Now go to No. 4 friend. Tell him you have to buy a draft to remit three hundred dollars to your brother in Philadelphia, and only need a hundred. 'Hand over, old fellow.' No. 4 is not going to count your pile. He sees the fifty dollar bill and a pile. He lends you the money without a word. You have now got two hundred. Take an old bank book and go to some friend who has plenty of money, but who is always on the borrow. Put in your two hundred dollars, and then say to him that you are short to make up a thousand, and if he will let you have three hundred dollars he will oblige you, and you will do as much for him next week. With the three hundred you can travel. Then return the one hundred and ninety dollars that you have borrowed respectively from No. 1, ten dollars; No. 2, thirty dollars; No. 3, fifty dollars; and No. 4, one hundred dollars. Return all these loans, exhibiting your full stock as you do so. With the three hundred dollars in hand, you can borrow three times that amount from your Nos. 1 to 4 friends, with whom you have established a credit. You can travel on this credit. You can victimize one of them occasionally, or increase your list to ten or twenty friends, of whom, at any time, you can borrow easily three hundreds, but of whom you could never borrow three cents if you needed it. Jemmy, I am going to try my luck. I have five hundred dollars. I will double my money to-night. I am in luck. See if it is not so. Your very good health." Thomas Granville finished his glass and left No. 46 Centre street.

At that time, and until within a very few years, there was a young man named Clark who kept an exchange office on the north-west corner of Duane and Chatham streets, where Sweeney's hotel now stands. In the front office Mr. Clark did an exchange business. In the rear, partly divided by a low wooden partition, he kept and sold lottery tickets. There was an entrance to this rear office from Duane street. Into this little cubby place came Tom Granville. He asked to see some tickets, and they were shown him. He examined wholes, halves, quarters, eighths, in the Pokomoke Lottery, but upon no ticket could he find his combination of 9, 32, and 46. He was then shown the Delaware Lottery. Upon a half ticket, true enough, he found 9, 32, 46. He bought the half ticket at once, and paid for it five dollars, and left the place. For luck, he placed his half ticket among his roll of bills, and then went up to the "Hotel de Paris," entered his room, and laid down to take a nap. When he awoke the light from a street lamp was streaming into his room. He descended to take a cup of coffee, and then carelessly approached Madame Vigne, the landlady.

"Madam, I have more money about me than I care to carry. Will you keep it for me?" asked Tom.

"Certainly, with pleasure. How much have you?" she asked.

"About five hundred dollars, I believe,"—and Tom handed her the roll.

"Five hundred!" repeated the landlady, who, from Tom's looks, supposed his deposite might reach about twenty. She counted it, and it overran about twenty dollars.

"Give me that for spending money," said Tom, and he received and placed it in his pocket.

Thomas Granville had travelled. He knew that there was no safer banker in the world than a careful, prudent French landlady. His money he knew was as safe in Mrs. Vigne's hands as in those of the wealthiest banker of New York. Tom drank his coffee.

"It is a long time since I have played. I will go and try my luck to-night,"—and so saying he buttoned up his overcoat and went out into Broadway. He soon found himself in a large gambling establishment in Barclay street. Tom was in luck. When he entered the room the deal was almost out. Without looking at the state of the game, he put all his money in a roll. He placed it upon the "queen." "My luck is in a lady," was his only observation. The queen won. The amount was counted and paid. Tom left it lying on the queen. The queen won again. The sum was paid.

"There is another 'queen' in the box yet," said some one.

"Then I will leave it all upon my friend the queen," said Tom, dryly. The queen won a third time, and Tom placed in his pocket a hundred and sixty dollars, adding, "Now I will get me some supper." He drank sparingly of a bottle of wine, tasted a choice bit of game, and returned to the table, and bought a hundred dollars' worth of red chips. Then he played cautiously, and only one or two, until of some particular card, three had been dealt out, and one remained in the box. Then Tom played fifty dollars on a "bet." He won until he had two hundred and fifty dollars bet on different cards. When the deal was over, he was a winner of over four hundred and fifty dollars. He had sixty in his pocket. He returned to the hotel, and handing another roll to Madame Vigne, he said, "Here, madam, add this to my sum in your hands." She took the money, but made no comment, and Tom joined old Mr. Gemmel in a game of dominoes. He was perfectly self-possessed—not elated—and when midnight came went quietly to bed.

Towards evening the next day he went to Clark's exchange office. Mr. Clark recognized him.

"You had 9, 32 and 46—half ticket in the Delaware, had you not?" he asked.

"I believe I have that ticket," replied Tom.

"Allow me to congratulate you, sir," said the broker. "It has drawn two thousand five hundred dollars. The half is one thousand two hundred and fifty dollars, gross. Discount off will be one thousand and thirty-one dollars and twenty-five cents. Call here to-morrow, and I will cash the prize and pay you one thousand and thirty-one dollars and twenty-five cents."

Thomas Granville went around to 46 Centre street. Jemmy asked him what his luck had been. "I made over a thousand, Jemmy,"—and he told him the particulars. Tom did not drink as freely as usual. The next day he received the money from the ticket. He went to Madame Vigne, showed it to her, and received the sum she had on deposit, amounting to over a thousand dollars. Then Tom took two thousand dollars and went down to the savings bank and deposited it to his own credit and received a bank book.

CHAPTER LIX.

Marion Monck and the Harpers—Publishes a Book—Virgil Maxcy and John C. Calhoun—James Harper and the Temperance Societies—Tom Flynn as a Lecturer—Mr. Monck writes him a Lecture on Temperance—Its delivery at the Tabernacle—Tom a Delinquent—The Dinner ordered by Mr. Flynn and paid for by Mr. Monck—End of Thomas Flynn, Comedian, in the Almshouse.

MARION MONCK felt quite elated with the first money he earned with his pen, and it was but the commencement of another task. Marion had a friend in Maryland whose name was Virgil Maxcy. This gentleman was a statesman and a scholar. His melancholy fate a few years after the date of this chapter is fresh in the memory of thousands. He was an invited guest on board the steamship Princeton, when a cannon burst, and killed Mr. Maxcy and several others.

This gentleman had prepared a work for the press. It was the life of a friend—the great southern statesman, Calhoun; and he wrote to Marion Monck, requesting him to publish it at the establishment of Harper & Brothers, and to superintend the publication. Marion accepted the trust, and forthwith made an agreement with the Harpers to publish this Life at a stipulated price, the copyright to belong to Marion Monck. This was the wish of Mr. Maxcy, and it was his desire that the profits of the publication should accrue to Marion, for the trouble it would occasion him to attend to the business, read the proofs, etc.

Not long after he commenced the work, he received a package of speeches from Mr. Calhoun himself, with a request that he would also superintend the publication of a volume of speeches. This Marion readily undertook; and in the performance of the duties, it required him to be a frequent, in fact an almost daily visitor at the establishment of the Messrs. Harpers. One afternoon, as he was about to leave for his boarding-house, he was stopped by one of the brothers.

"Have you an engagement to-night?" he asked

It was James Harper.

"None in particular," was the reply. "Why do you ask me?"

"Because if you have not, I should like to have you spend the evening with me," said James Harper.

"Nothing that you could propose would give me greater pleasure," replied Marion.

"Then come with me, for I am going home," said Mr. Harper.

The two started for Mr. Harper's residence, which was at no great distance from the publishing building. He then resided in Rose street, next door to the Quaker Church. Marion knew the house well, for in the abolition riots, some years before, he had seen the mob enter that identical two story brick house, then occupied by Lewis Tappan, and plunder it of its furniture, which they burned in the street before the door. When they were inside the house, Mr. Harper ordered tea, remarking that Mrs. Harper would not be present, as she was very ill—in fact, dangerously so. She died not many days after. After tea was finished, Mr. Harper remarked,

"A carriage will be here presently, to take me where I can fulfil an engagement. I want you to go with me."

The carriage came. Both entered it, and continued talking until it stopped before the doors of a church in Forsyth street.

"We get out here," said James Harper. "Follow me."

Marion did so, into the church, up to the pulpit. Mr. Harper opened a pew door near the altar, and when Marion had passed in and taken a seat, he shut the door and passed to the pulpit, and took the principal seat. Marion then noticed that the church was crowded with people, called together for some sort of purpose, and that Mr. Harper was to be the chairman of the meeting.

The exercises soon commenced, and then Marion discovered that it was the anniversary of a Temperance Society. Prayer was made, a hymn was sung, then a clergyman made a speech, another hymn, another address and another hymn. Then there was a pause. The chairman then arose, and with great seriousness announced that the Rev. Doctor Tyng was expected to make an address that evening, and added, "But illness in his family will prevent him. This would be a great disappointment under ordinary circumstances, but I am happy to inform the meeting, that I have secured the services of a young gentleman, who I am sure will favor us with a short address, that can fill up the gap caused by the non-appearance of Dr. Tyng. He is extremely clever, and has written a book that my firm have published. I am not aware that he has ever joined any temperance society—very likely he may do so to-night. Allow me to introduce to this audience Marion Monck."

Marion had followed Mr. Harper's language, wondering what he was driving at; but when he pounced down upon him by name, and pointed at the seat where he was sitting, he was completely thunderstruck. Had the steeple tumbled in upon the crowd, it would not have astonished him half so much. He was so vexed with James Harper, that it gave him the confidence necessary to make an address, and he did astonish that crowd for half an hour. He was really eloquent upon the temperance topic, and his address was received with great applause. The services were soon after over, and he again got into the carriage with James Harper, intending to blow him up for placing him in such a false position. It was of no use. Mr. Harper laughed at him, and when they parted that night, Marion observed, "Have a care, Mr. Harper; this is the last time you will ever bring me in for a temperance address."

The next day, when Marion made his appearance in Cliff street, the other brothers had a hearty laugh at his expense, and at the "sell" so successfully made by "Brother James." Marion received it all in good part, and enjoyed the joke as well as any of them.

The Harpers were always interested in the Temperance reformation. They upheld the "Washingtonian Parent Society" in the good old times, when that Society counted upon its books the names of over ten thousand reformed drunkards, and were not sparing in their aid to the Society and its various branches, or to individual members.

When the excitement that this Society caused, and which would crowd their weekly meetings with two and three thousand people, had died away, it was followed and replaced by a new order of things, called the Sons of Temperance. Then the Daughters of Temperance. In these movements the Harpers engaged earnestly, and none more so than Brother James. He was active in all of them, and presided frequently at the annual meetings of these societies. Then came the Rechabites. In the latter James Harper was a principal leader.

To his credit be it said, he was extremely liberal to those who were without means, but who were willing to aid in the Temperance movement. Gough, Wallace, and many others were indebted for means to be useful to Mr. Harper. When Brother James found a person in any particular profession who was likely to be useful in making converts from that profession, he encouraged him to become a speaker and leader in the great Temperance movement.

Not long after the appearance of Marion Monck in the

Chrystic street church, he was engaged in reading some proofs at his own room, when a visitor was announced. He was shown up. This visitor was a stout, thick-set, full-faced individual, and he brought a note from Mr. James Harper, introducing him to Marion Monck.

"Sit down, sir," said Marion.

"Certainly—with pleasure. That note is from Mr. Harper—my very particular friend, James Harper. He is to assist me in giving a lecture at the Tabernacle, and he told me to come and see you," said the fussy individual.

"I do not see how I can aid you in the matter," replied Marion.

"Indeed, but I do. I told Mrs. Flynn this morning, and she is extremely well aware of the fact, that I could and should deliver an extremely interesting lecture, if I had it written for me. There is money to be made in it. Thousands, sir, will crowd to hear Tom Flynn deliver a lecture at the Tabernacle. The house will be a perfect jam, sir. Mr. Harper advances the money. I shall be a great card, sir—an immense card to the cause of Temperance," said Mr. Flynn.

"How long since you joined the movement?" inquired Marion.

"Over a week, sir—nearly two. Now, sir, I am an actor. I am not good at an off-hand speech or lecture, unless I have it all *pat* beforehand. Now you write out the lecture for me—that's a dear good fellow. Mr. Harper said you were just the chap to do it, and I know you will. I can learn it by heart in a very short time after it is written—*that* is in my line. I shall reform the whole theatrical profession—make 'em all join. My lecture will be perfectly overwhelming. When will you go to work? I want it done at once," said Flynn.

Marion took a good look at his customer. There was something so jolly about Tom Flynn, that no one could help admiring him, until they had become well acquainted with the man. Then admiration generally ceased.

"Well, Mr. Flynn, suppose I write this lecture. You will make money by it. What am I to get for writing it?" asked Marion.

"O, anything you please—we won't stand upon trifles. Money to be paid over after the lecture," said Tom Flynn.

"I would like to have it understood now how much I am to get. Will twenty dollars be too much?"

"Not half enough, my dear boy. It will be a magnificent hit. I'll bring down the house. Bless your heart! I shall want you to write fifty—a hundred lectures. Harper says I must visit every city in the United States, and deliver my lectures, and then go to Europe. Star it on Temperance all through England, Ireland, Scotland and Wales. I will keep you with me, my boy—eh? How do you like that?"

Marion was in a hearty good humor with the illustrious Tom, and agreed to go at once into the matter. To do this, it was necessary that he should go to Tom's apartments. These, Tom said, were at the Shakespeare Hotel, corner of Duane and William street. Accompanied by Marion, Tom wended his way from Fulton street to the Shakespeare. This was kept at that time by a man named Pierrers, now steward of the St. Nicholas Hotel. Tom Flynn's apartment was on the fourth floor; and into his room, for he had but one, he ushered Marion Monck. There was a lady seated there, and the new comer was introduced with much ceremony to the celebrated and extremely clever Mrs. Flynn.

She received Marion with much amiability, and listened to her husband's extravagant ideas of his success in temperance matters with a smile of incredulity. At that time Mrs. Flynn was a woman of great beauty, and her success as an actress had been long gained. Tom Flynn was doing nothing at all, and the means of support were earned by Mrs. Flynn at the theatre in Chatham street.

It was a long time before Marion could get Tom down to common affairs, or the practical business in hand. He had no more idea of a temperance lecture, than he had of Mahomet's Koran; and would relate theatrical anecdotes, and his own experience, that had no more connection with temperance than with algebra; and Marion, with a powerful imagination, could not torture or twist any of Tom's stories into the skeleton ideas for a lecture. At last he gave up in despair, and went to his room. There the thought crossed him to write a lecture without the slightest reference to Tom Flynn. He did so. All the experience in it, and thrilling scenes, were purely imaginative—none of Tom's, at least. When it was finished, Marion carried the lecture to Tom's quarters at the Shakespeare. It was read in presence of both Mr. and Mrs. Tom Flynn. The latter approved it, and flattered Marion by telling him that his performance was a most creditable one. Tom undertook to learn it at once.

Some days passed, and the eventful night came, when the Tabernacle doors were opened to admit the celebrated Thomas Flynn to deliver a temperance lecture—"tickets twenty-five cents." There *was* a crowd, and notwithstanding an enormous quantity of "dead-heads," the lecture was a money-making affair. Tom hired some person to act as treasurer, and when the lecture was finished, he grabbed the proceeds.

Marion Monck went into the gallery to hear his own original lecture delivered. It certainly made a sensation, and was cheered tremendously. There was no humbug about that. Marion felt convinced of one thing. The lecture had some points in it that told well on an audience. Tom delivered it well. He had learned it by heart, as though it had been a part of a farce, and it appeared to the audience as though it was extemporized. So far so good.

Marion tried to get a sight of Tom Flynn after the lecture was delivered, but Thomas, with seventy or eighty dollars in his pocket, was not to be seen. The next day the chase continued, and he found the lecturer about three o'clock in a drinking saloon. Thomas was not exactly sober, nor was he very drunk. It was a sort of maudlin medium.

"My dear boy, where have you kept yourself? I have been hunting for you all day. Ask Thomas Shortland if I have not. Come now, let us go and have a nice, quiet, old-fashioned dinner. I have ordered one for us both, and let us go to the place at once," said Tom Flynn, and he appeared extremely anxious to get to the dinner. It was an enormous fib, but never mind that. The author and the actor wended their way over into a Broadway restaurant. The proprietor placed them in a small room by themselves. When they were fairly seated, and the dinner had been ordered, Mr. Monck boned Tom about the twenty dollars.

"Bless your heart, my dear boy, I had to pay out every cent. You have no idea what a time I have had! Wasn't it a capital house? How they did cheer! My fortune is made. I've struck a vein. Harper says he never saw anything like it. Mr. Harper advanced the rent of the building, but I had so many demands made upon me for money to-day, that I cannot refund him his advance. It is a hard case, ain't it? But those Harpers are rich—he won't feel it. When will you commence another lecture for me, Mr. Monck?" said Tom.

Marion Monck was really indignant; and he replied angrily, "I'll tell you what it is, Mr. Flynn, I don't consider this fair treatment. I wrote your lecture for you. You have made money, and I expected to have received the twenty dollars at once."

"You are perfectly right, my boy. I don't blame you—not

a bit of it. I'd feel just the same, if a man had used me as shabbily as I have you. I know it is outrageous. You ought to have had the money. But what am I to do? You see how I am placed. Dead broke—but never mind, we will have a good dinner, any how. I expect it will be a magnificent dinner. Do you know I like good dinners? What do you say to a bottle of Champagne, eh?"

"I am agreed," replied Marion; "but what would your temperance friends say if they were to drop in upon you—James Harper, for instance?"

"O, he be blamed. It will not do for me to break off so sudden from *all* stimulants. It must be done by degrees," replied the actor.

The wine was ordered—not one bottle but two was placed upon the table. A splendid dinner was served up, for Tom Flynn knew how to order a good dinner. It was well cooked. It was a dinner that any gentleman in the land might have been proud to have partaken of. Under its genial influence Marion became reconciled to the disappointment connected with the twenty dollars. Tom promised faithfully that he should have it in less than twenty-four hours. Still Marion refused to write a second lecture until he received pay for number one, and he added, "Flynn, you can make money as a temperance lecturer, if you will deliver twenty lectures written by me, and do as you have done this one, by each *new* one. Learn it by heart. By the time you have committed twenty lectures to heart and can deliver one on call, you can then practice on all, and really you will have matter enough to deliver an extempore lecture apparently, merely throwing in a few local facts or matters whenever you deliver a lecture at a new place. You will succeed, and you will be a popular lecturer, but you must pay *me* honest, every time I write you a lecture. It was very wrong in you to 'do' Mr. Harper out of the Tabernacle rent," said Marion.

"It was bad—very bad—a d—— shame. But it can't be helped now, and I dare say Mr. Harper won't mind it. What a glorious dinner we have made, eh? Is there any thing else you will have? Order whatever you have a fancy for—wines, cigars, coffee—d—— the expense. One may as well be in for a sheep as a lamb," said Tom.

Here the landlord came in, and was very polite to Marion. He asked if there was any thing else he could put upon the table. "Nothing more," was the joint reply. When the proprietor of the restaurant passed out from the little room where the author and actor had dined, Tom Flynn followed him, and, after an absence of a quarter of an hour (during which time Marion was extremely anxious, for he had no money, and he feared Tom had departed, leaving him in a strange place to foot the bill), he returned rubbing his hands in great glee, and exclaimed, "Lord love your soul, my boy. It is *all* right. I told him who you were, and he said you could pay the bill whenever it suited your convenience. It takes me, don't it?"

Marion was indignant, and at first could not comprehend what Tom Flynn was driving at. "I! Satisfied with me? What the devil have I got to do with it? It is your dinner. You ordered it," said Marion.

"That is true. But keep perfectly calm—what difference does it make? I have no money—not a dollar. The bill is twelve dollars twenty-five cents. He wouldn't trust me twelve cents. I have satisfied him that you are as good as the Bank of France; that James Harper, or all the Harpers, would be responsible for fifty dinners; and that you were short to-day for a wonder, but would call back to-morrow and order a dozen dinners. He is perfectly satisfied, and will let us go out without the money. Don't be afraid," continued Tom Flynn, consolingly.

"Hang your infernal impudence! You told him the Harpers would pay my bill! that I was short—that—that——O, the devil! You have played Ned with me. It is bad enough to stick me for the lecture, but then to stick me for a dinner that I never ordered, and tell a parcel of lies in order to induce the proprietor not to have us arrested, or kick us out of doors, is too bad. Tom Flynn, I will never forgive you—never," said Marion.

"Nonsense, my boy. We are all right. I've fixed it with the proprietor. Says you can pay it any time you like. What else can I do?" asked Tom.

"Else can you do? You had no business to come here, or induce me to come here, unless you could pay for what you ordered. But I have done with you—mark that!" Marion indignantly left the room, and went to the proprietor and told him how he had been stuck for the dinner. The landlord enjoyed the joke, and the next day Marion paid the bill.

To return to Tom Flynn. He delivered his lecture several times—once in Jersey City. He did well, but he could not keep from drink. It eventually *fetched* him, as it has millions of good fellows, and Thomas Flynn died in the Almshouse of New York city.

CHAPTER LX.

Reformation of Thomas Granville—The Hotel de Paris—The Domino Club—Bruce—Trinity Church Anecdote—The Beautiful French Girl Clotilde—Tom's Second Marriage—His Death at the Staten Island Small Pox Hospital.

ALAS, alas! poor Tom Granville! gifted with genius, with kindness of heart, with every thing which could make thee a worthy member of society, what a melancholy fate was thine! Why was this? He had thoroughly reformed, and changed his habits from being a careless spendthrift into becoming a miser, and he counted every cent he expended, and incurred no outlay that he could do without.

In a former Chapter we have related the manner in which he had accumulated the sum of two thousand dollars. This was deposited in the Savings Bank, and the bank-book, as evidence of its being his property, he carried about with him at all times, and not a day passed that he did not take it out and gaze earnestly at the items inside of it. He dressed neatly, and continued to board at the 'Hotel de Paris,' in Broadway. Unexceptionable in his conduct, he foreswore houses of ill-fame, gambling, and excessive drinking; he had his bottle of claret daily at dinner, and drank sparingly even of that. As he dined with his brother every Sunday, during the week he would occasionally call in State street and invite his niece to promenade with him upon the Battery. If she did not go herself, she permitted one of her children, for she had now three fine boys to go with 'Uncle Tom.' Such conduct won upon Pitt Granville, and he no longer hesitated about giving Tom money, nor even wait to be asked, but would frequently say,

"Well Tom, how do you fight your men? Have you any ammunition left?"

Tom never replied in the affirmative; but always laughed and plead poverty.

"I am about broke, but luckily my expenses are not much."

To such a hint there was but one reply—

"Take this, Tom; perhaps you can spend it," and Tom would get a twenty or fifty dollar bill. After such financial successes, Tom would go to his hotel, and make a special deposite with his landlady, keeping in his own pocket a few shillings for his wants.

Thomas Granville visited almost every place of amusement, but he was on the free list, and did so without expense. He neither courted nor avoided the society of those with whom he had been formerly intimate in his prosperous days, and consequently they once more sought his society—for he dressed with care and taste, and his social habits made him always an agreeable companion. But on such occasions he never spent a fraction upon them; if he dined or drank with them, it was at their expense, not his own.

After being present at the wedding of his nephew with Miss Norris, he avoided them as he would poison. He however changed his deportment toward Marion Monck—he not only treated him kindly, but sought his society, and many an hour the two passed together in playing dominoes at the 'Hotel de Paris,' where Tom originated a Dominoe Club. Besides themselves, there were men of some note that belonged to that club. Mr. Bruce, for many years the confidential clerk of old John Jacob Astor, and after his death holding the same position with his son, William B., was of this club.

Mr. Bruce was a character in his way. No man knew New York for forty years better than he did—he knew every house and building below Houston street, and was a man who solved a difficulty in an unequalled manner. Upon one very extraordinary emergency, Mr. Bruce was called upon by a vestryman of Trinity Church.

"Bruce, the Corporation intend to open Pine street through to Albany street, and it will cut through our graveyard; what can be done to prevent it? Suggest something."

Mr. Bruce thought for a few moments, and then replied,

"Trinity is rich, and don't mind spending money. Go to work at once and put up in the graveyard opposite Pine street where the proposed cut will go through, a costly monument to the memory of the American Patriots who fell or died at Wallabout Bay. Give out that the bones of these Revolutionary heroes were buried under the monument. Do that, and you will have no further bother. The Corporation are not bold enough to dig up the bones of Revolutionary heroes."

The vestrymen of old Trinity saw the wisdom of the hint.— At their next meeting the monument was decided upon, and workmen commenced their labors at the head of Pine street. Bruce was right—there stands the monument, and no street has yet disturbed it, or the bones of the Wallabout heroes, which probably repose some four miles off.

But to return to Mr. Bruce. He was posted upon every subject, and to an editor of a daily paper would have made a valuable assistant as a suggestive editor.

Another member of this club was Aaron Turner, one of the most remarkable men in New York. He was nicknamed " the Doctor," from his unvarying attention to any of his friends who became sick. One of the club was once confined to his room for thirty days—the " Doc" never left him. When the regular physician had given the patient over to death, Doctor Turner interfered, and by feeding the dying man upon rare, half-raw beefsteak and old port wine, brought him around again, and he is still a member of the Dominoe Club.

The Doctor had an income of two thousand dollars a year. Half he spent on himself, and religiously devoted the other half to the relief of suffering humanity. No man knows how the Doctor lives, nor where he lives, and no man ever saw him do any regular business—and yet he is a master of all trades and all sciences. He can paint a picture, or he can set up thirty thousand ems of type a week with ease. He once navigated a schooner from Chagres to New York, and not many months afterwards, when a passenger on the Erie railroad, and the engineer and fireman were both killed, he mounted the engine and ran her and the train eighteen miles to Port Jervis.

Old James Gemmel, the rich watchmaker in Broadway, was a member of the club for many years. He is dead now, and has gone to a better world, where dominoes are not permitted. There were others of the Dominoe Club. Some are now living, and some are dead, but we omit mention of the former because they are cashiers in bank or Judges upon the bench, and those who are dead are of no account in the ' game.'

Tom Granville was a great admirer of the game of dominoes and of the society which it brought nightly around him

One evening he came into the room where his friends were playing, and there he found Marion Monck; he seated himself at the centre table and called for a cup of coffee, observing,

" Gentlemen, I will take a hand in the next game with you. I have seen a leper to-day."

" A leper !" was repeated by a dozen members of the club.

" Yes, gentlemen, I have seen and conversed with a genuine leper to-day—no mistake about it. I myself had doubts about there being any lepers in this country, but I was mistaken. Listen to me, incredulous ones, and believe me. I was turning up into the Bowery from Chatham Square, on the left hand side as you go up, and at Pell street—a little bit of a street which empties into the Bowery near Chatham, I was detained a moment. I there saw a man surrounded by a lot of curious boys; he was seated upon the ground, and his face was like a leper. I started the boys off, and then cross-questioned the individual. I gave him a quarter, and suggested that his face was covered with leprosy. He confessed it at once—what do you think of it, eh?" asked Tom triumphantly.

"Is leprosy catching?" inquired Mr. Gemmel.

"Pooh, pooh, no. It is nasty, but not catching, replied Tom.

Marion Monck had listened attentively, and when the story about the leprosy was finished, said,

"Mr. Granville, did you ever see a man with the small pox?"

"No, I never did—and what is more, I never wish to, for I have never had it myself; but what the devil do you ask such a disagreeable question for—who is talking about small pox, and what has that got to do with my leper that I was telling you about?"

All the company shuddered at the suggestion. Marion replied calmly,

"I asked if you had ever seen a case of the small pox, because I have been informed that before it breaks out, the appearance of the face of the person who is infected bears very much the appearance of him who in Eastern climes is affected with the leprosy—that is all."

"Indeed! Come, don't let us say anything more about small pox or leprosy, it makes me nervous," replied Tom. So the subject was dropped, and just at that moment Madame Vigne came to the table and requested Tom to accompany her to the supper room. Supper was on the table, but there were no guests partaking of it, and Madame and Tom were engaged in earnest conversation. Of the nature of that conversation we will give an idea before finishing this chapter.

Not a week had passed after Tom became a permanent occupant of this hotel, before a creature made her appearance behind the bar whose beauty was of a kind that startled as well as captivated at first sight. Granville had risen very early that morning and descended the stairs; he went to the bar to address Madame Vigne, but the face that beamed upon him made him exclaim, "Good heavens, who are you?" The person thus addressed was a girl evidently not over fifteen years old, and girlish in every action. Her hair was jet black, and combed back from a large alabaster forehead and gathered up in a close knot that was as large as one third of the girl's magnificent head. Her skin was perfectly transparent, and the clear white and red were only visible. She had a Grecian cast of features, and her smile exhibiting a pair of delicate red lips and snow white teeth, was irresistible. Her form was beautifully proportioned—a full bosom and small waist, and her movements were grace itself. She walked with that lithe and limping air, which in a young and beautiful girl has a powerful charm. She did not understand a word of English, but Tom spoke French as well as English.

They were alone in the room, and when Tom questioned her closely, she informed him that she had come from France not many months previous with her mother. She was from the very province in France of which Lyons is the capital. She had been frequently a visitor to that city. Tom could describe every building in it, and this at once was an interesting topic of conversation between them. Her name was Clotilde. She informed Tom Granville that her mother had recently died, and that "Madame," so she called Mrs. Vigne, had agreed to support her, and she, in return, was to tend the bar and wait on such customers as called for coffee. Tom became really eloquent to the beautiful Clotilde. He told her of the dangers —of the attractions of her beauty—of the insults she would receive, and finally asked her if he, Tom, would get Mrs. Vigne to give up the idea of her tending bar, whether she would agree to it.

"I have money, and I will pay Madame Vigne your board, rather than you should be exposed to be gazed at and insulted," said Tom.

The honest, heart-felt interest Tom expressed had its effect. The poor girl's eyes opened to the widest extent as she regarded Tom's speaking features. She was interested, and months of ordinary intercourse could not have made Clotilde so deeply grateful as that morning's conversation. Tom told her where his room was, and added, "For your own sake, I shall avoid conversing much with you while you are behind the bar. When you receive a signal from me, make your escape and come to my room." The girl agreed to do so. That day Tom remonstrated with the Madame against employing the girl in the bar-room, but it made no impression upon her mind. He offered to pay her board. That Madame listened to. The beautiful girl was employed as bar-tender for several days, but her ignorance of money and the trouble her presence occasioned among the boarders, who all became in love with her, made the Madame anxious to withdraw her from such services. She talked with Tom Granville about it, and he again repeated his offer to pay her board.

"Very well, Mr. Granville, I agree to it on one condition. You shall tell me why you do this—why you care about her—and what are your intentions. I have a right to ask these questions, for the *leetle* girl is under my charge."

"Certainly you have, and as my intentions are not wrong, I will tell you. You know that I have money. Very well. If you will keep this girl in the house, and let her go to school, I will pay all her expenses. When I find that she likes me, I will marry her. Is that enough?" asked Tom.

It was more than enough. Madame at once summoned the fair object of so much trouble, and informed her of what Tom had proposed.

"I love Monsieur Granville now with all my heart and soul," was the frank respose of the girl. In fact, not a day had passed that she had not been to Tom's room and held a conversation with him. Not a hand or a finger had Tom placed upon her. Not a single caress at their interviews, and the young French girl who had expected, and was prepared to repel them, was agreeably disappointed, and these facts combined with Tom's fascinating manners, had won her heart. When other boarders had been civil to her, or made love to her, she had repelled them with as much scorn as if some great wrong had been proposed to Tom. When Tom had the conversation with Madame, and she agreed to his proposition, Clotilde was at once taken out of the bar. She became a sort of companion to the Madame, and Tom, with her sanction, went out with Clotilde about every night, and visited some place of amusement. She was delighted. Tom told her to regard herself as his wife, and to ask for money, and he proffered all she needed from week to week. One night he had been with her at the opera, where her extreme beauty had attracted the attention of all in the vicinity. As they were returning home, linked arm in arm, Tom asked her if she would marry him. Clotilde replied at once. She would do so then or at any time. Tom Granville pressed the white hand that reposed in his own, and begged her to listen to his story. He then told her of his wife —gave the entire history, and again asked the sweet French girl if she would marry him.

"I love you more than ever, because you have been so badly treated by that proud woman," replied Clotilde.

Tom was delighted, but honest. He then informed Clotilde that his wife had procured the divorce, that she could marry again, but that he could not, and explained the divorce laws to the best of his ability. He told her that were he to go and marry her, he would be liable to be punished for bigamy. The wild girl replied,

"Then, Monsieur Thomas, do not marry me, but I will be your wife, and you shall be my husband. I love you. I am yours, and death only shall separate us."

When they reached the hotel, Tom proposed that they should confide in Madam, and to her Tom told his history.

"Then I will marry you," said the sympathising landlady. "Do you write a paper solemnly promising that you will take Clotilde, support, live with, and be a father to her children, if she has any, and that your will give her all your money if you die, and swear to it on the Holy Evangile, and put in it that you would marry her in church but for the reasons you have told me you cannot? Clotilde shall write another paper, and sign it, and promise to be your faithful, good wife. You also make a will before a lawyer, that if you die you leave all you have to Clotilde, and when you have both done this, then you shall leave these papers in my hands, and I will pronounce you to be man and wife, and then you and she can do what you like and amuse yourselves as you please."

All went to bed that night pleased. The next day Tom religiously executed the papers, and so did Clotilde. Madame changed Clotilde from her old room to one that adjoined Tom's, and which communicated by a door, the two rooms having been occupied formerly as a parlor and a bed-room. No noise was made. All was done quietly, and not a soul was the wiser of these matters but Madame herself, and Tom Granville found himself the actual possessor of one of the loveliest girls that France had ever sent to these shores. Tom admired his new wife. He found her as charming in mind as she was in person, and she returned his love with ardor, for it was her first love, and she worshipped him. A few days after their occupying the same apartments, Tom playfully told her that she was a perfect copy, made by Nature of the "Venus de Medicis," and added, "I want to see your hair fall as Nature made it." She undid the fastening, flung it loose, and the dark masses, when she leaned slightly backward when standing, swept the floor. Tom caressed her, and while playing and tangling it, observed,

"Dear Clotilde, I was not deceived. The first time I met you, I was attached to you by your *hair*."

"But, Tom, it was all done up in a tight knot. How could you tell whether it was long or short, thick or thin?" she asked.

"My eyes could not deceive me in the beautiful ornament, my dear Clotilde," replied Tom.

Tom became really happy. He had some thing to love, and some thing to love him. His stern economy can now be accounted for. The extra expense incurred by his beautiful companion was nothing. The Madame merely added a few dollars to his monthly board, and Clotilde Granville was her companion when Tom was out, or when engaged in the dominoe-room. At the table she ate her meals with Madame and her husband, and Tom continued to take his at the same time. Thomas Granville had been thus pleasantly situated for some weeks when the occurrence took place in reference to the lesson which we have narrated at the beginning of this chapter. The pleasant arrangement between Thomas Granville and Clotilde had some drawbacks. Tom accompanied her whenever she went out, and her beauty attracted great attention. Tom's friends made many inquiries as to who she was. His roué acquaintances tried hard to get an introduction. It was all in vain.

Early one morning Tom, accompanied by Clotilde, was sauntering upon the Battery. He had pointed out to his companion the house occupied by his brother, when that same brother stood suddenly before them. Tom was not often taken by surprise, and without a moment's hesitation he introduced Clotilde as Madame Michel. Never did a more perfect lady stand upon the Battery, and Pitt Granville was sensibly aware of it. He was a gentleman when he chose to be so, and immediately offered his arm. Tom explained that Madame Michel had but recently arrived to look after some property of her husband, who had died in Martinique, where the widow was bound; that he knew her in France, and was agreeably surprised to meet her here at the Hotel de Paris, where she was stopping. Clotilde had learned English from Tom to an extent that enabled her to express a few words very prettily in English, and Pitt Granville talked on as though she understood all he was saying. At last he invited them over to breakfast. This Tom explained to the lady, but prudently declined, giving a satisfactory excuse. Before Pitt Granville parted from them, he placed some money in Tom's hands, and after his departure Tom handed it to Clotilde, and then returned up Broadway to the hotel. Clotilde could not conceal her satisfaction at having met with Tom's brother.

"What shall I do with so much money as you give me? Every week it is a great deal. All you have given to Madame she has given to me. I pay all our bills. I pay for nice dresses for myself, and yet we have plenty left. I have more than four hundred dollars in my pocket-book."

Tom found that his brother Pitt had given him a hundred; and the next day he took Clotilde to the Savings Bank, and had four hundred more passed to his credit. The teller also, at Tom's request, gave a new book, placing all Tom's money, amounting to about twenty-four hundred dollars, in such a manner that Clotilde Michel or himself could either of them draw the money on presenting the book. He explained the matter fully to Clotilde after they left the bank. She was amazed.

"Do you mean to say that in case I should take that little book, and go to that bank without you, that they would pay me all that money—twenty-four hundred dollars?" asked Clotilde.

"Every cent of it, pet, and ask you no questions. It has been placed to your credit as well as to mine. So we must take good care of the book," said Tom.

The French girl was very much affected. Such generosity surprised her. "Why have you done this?" she asked.

"To make you comfortable in case of my death. I know you would never rob me of it, or abuse my confidence in your integrity and virtue. Clotilde, I want to see you placed above want, in case of accident to me. You love me, and you make me very happy. What is a few hundred dollars with what you are to me—a fond, loving friend?" said Tom, earnestly.

The French girl wept. She fully comprehended Tom, and she determined that she would make him happy as long as she lived, and she did.

There are many of the then boarders at the Hotel de Paris who are now living, and who will well remember a tragedy that occurred in that hotel, and which originated with this fair French girl. A young Frenchman came out from France, and stopped at the Hotel de Paris. He had a room on the same floor with Tom, and directly opposite Tom's room. He had seen this young girl, as he supposed, and fell madly in love with her—regular French frenzy love. He offered money to Clotilde to marry him. Of course, her mind was filled with Tom Granville, and she rejected all overtures from the young Frenchman with scorn. He knew nothing of Tom Granville, and he consulted Madame Vigne. She told young Paris to keep quiet, and assured him that he had not a show to gain the affections of her young countrywoman.

On Sunday morning the young Frenchman wrote a letter to Clotilde. She at once handed it to Tom. The letter was returned to young France. Soon after Tom descended to the bar-room, and was in the act of lighting his cigar, when one of the waiters rushed down stairs and said that young France had blown his brains out. Tom and Madame Vigne hurried up stairs to the suicide's room. He had strength enough to say that he had been despised by Clotilde, and life was no longer valuable.

"Poor devil, what a melancholy fool!" quietly observed Tom, as he went to Clotilde's and his own room, and they locked themselves in, while he explained the tragedy. A coroner's jury was called; and as the young man had in his trunk over a thousand francs in gold pieces, he had a superb funeral. The jury rendered a verdict in accordance with the circumstances, without the slightest idea of the real state of the case. Thomas reflected upon the matter like a philosopher, but Clotilde scouted the idea of such foolishness as any man killing himself on her account.

This tragedy decided Tom to move his quarters; and to take Clotilde with him. The very day he met the "Leper" man he had been looking for a part of a house in the eastern part of the town. Some days passed, and meanwhile Clotilde went with him to look at the house he proposed renting, when an event occurred that destroyed all housekeeping projects.

Tom complained of being ill, and kept himself in his room for a day or more. Marion Monck called, and Tom ordered the servant to bring him up stairs to his apartment. Clotilde was with him, and refused to leave the room. When Marion entered, Tom received him cordially, and after a short conversation, made him take a seat closer to him.

"Marion, do you know that I have fretted myself about that 'Leper' I told you of. I am satisfied that the man has the small pox."

The last words he whispered in Marion's ear.

"Good God! You don't think so, really?"

"I do—and what is more, I have caught it."

"Nonsense;" replied Marion. "But I will go and bring you a doctor."

"That you may do; and mind, if I have it, will you see me conveyed to the Staten Island Small Pox Hospital? I don't want to go to the Almshouse, and I know I must leave this hotel. Not a word to a soul, remember."

Marion promised, and then left the room, and immediately went for Doctor Carnochan, a physician as well known to Tom as himself. The doctor came, and pronounced upon the case at once. It was the small pox. And now shone out the worth and the devotion of a true-hearted woman. It was decided that Tom should be taken at once to Staten Island. Clotilde refused to leave him. Marion went down to the Island and made all the necessary arrangements, and that very afternoon Tom was conveyed to the Staten Island Hospital, and Clotilde was by his side as his nurse. She did not leave him for a moment.

Marion returned to the city, and informed Madame Vigne of the real state of the case. She was alarmed, but kept the matter secret. Tom's apartments were fumigated, and no other case occurred. Mr. Monck visited the Island and made daily inquiries after Tom, but did not see him. A week told the story. Thomas Granville was dead.

While he was ill, Clotilde never slept but for an instant or two at a time. He was raving and did not know her; but just before he died, he became perfectly sensible. He knew her.

"God bless you, my own dear Clotilde. It is hard to part with you, hard to part with life, just as I have learned how to live and to enjoy it; and you, of all the world that I have known, are the only one by my side in this awful crisis. Don't weep —don't quiver. Bear up as well as you can. When I am dead, go and draw the money in the bank for your own purposes. It is yours. If there is any objection, the will I made and gave Madame Vigne is good. That is not all. When a week has elapsed, go to my brother, and tell him all. Tell him how you have been devoted to me to the bitter end of my useless life, and he will be softened—he will—O, my God!— it's dark—get a light—Jesu "—

Clotilde had lifted his head up, but with the partly uttered word of our Saviour's name, he fell back upon the pillow a corpse, and his nurse—the beautiful Clotilde, faithful to the last, fell senseless upon his body.

She witnessed the burial of Thomas Granville, which was solemn and immediate. Then she left the hospital where he had died, and came up to the city, a stern, beautiful woman. She was no longer the passionate, loving, laughing girl. She went directly to the Hotel de Paris, and the Madame gave her the old apartments, which had not been rented. She waited a week, and then called on Pitt Granville. He was bowed down, and took poor Tom's death much to heart. She narrated all that had passed, and showed Tom's bank book and his will, and the other papers. Mr. Granville rang the bell, and then ordered the carriage.

"I will go with you to the Savings Bank," he added; and when the carriage was ready, they entered it together, and proceeded to the bank. Mr. Granville was well known there. He asked if there would be any difficulty in Clotilde receiving the money—the twenty-four hundred dollars?

"None whatever. Whenever she wishes she can draw it out," replied the official.

"Then add this to her credit in the book," said Mr. Granville; and when Clotilde saw the entry in the book, she discovered that Tom's brother had given her twenty-five hundred dollars. He begged her to use his name, and to call upon him whenever he could be of service to her; and he conveyed her to the Hotel de Paris in his own carriage, and there left her. He never saw her again. Neither did Clotilde remain but a few days longer at the Hotel de Paris. She then left, and what her fate was did not transpire for many years.

Our readers may be anxious to know what that fate was. Twelve years after the event of Tom Granville's death, a beautiful woman called upon Marion Monck. She had just returned from California, where she had amassed a large property. She called herself Mrs. Granville, and she went with Marion to a French banking-house and bought bills of exchange on Paris to the extent of eight hundred thousand francs. She was older, and more majestic than formerly. She went to France, but what became of her is a mystery; and what had been the manner of her earning so large a property in California was a still greater mystery.

Tom Granville was soon forgotten, and our narrative will now return to its regular course.

CHAPTER LXI.

The Globe Hotel and Blancard—John O'Docmall—The Colonel Clairfoot and Lady Clairfoot—A Horrible Seduction and Robbery of £3000—The Bloomingdale Asylum and an Inmate.

For many years a large hotel called the "Globe Hotel" was maintained in the lower part of Broadway. It was located a few doors below Wall street, extended from Broadway to New street, and the name of the proprietor was "Blancard."

At this hotel Mr. O'Doemall was sometimes a boarder, but at all times a visitor. The "Globe" was the home of many distinguished Englishmen, who came to this country to travel, or of English officers on their way to Canada, or on their return from Canada to England.

To this hotel came an English lieutenant-colonel, with his wife. He was on his way to Canada, and had arrived in the city in the month of January. It was bitter cold weather. His name was Clairfoot. Among the first acquaintances he made was Mr. O'Docmall. The latter gentleman in the most disinterested manner informed Colonel Clairfoot that the weather was so cold in Canada that he stood in danger of freezing to death. This had no effect, so far as the colonel was concerned, but it alarmed him on account of his wife, and he became anxious that she should not accompany him; and the more so as his stay in Canada was not positively determined. He might be able to get through the military business with which he was intrusted in a few weeks, and he might be detained months. In the latter case, he knew that he could speedily send to his wife to join him in Canada, whenever he might be located for any length of time. When Colonel Clairfoot had decided upon this course, he consulted with his friend O'Docmall in reference to procuring handsome apartments in a private house. He did not like the idea of leaving his wife at a public hotel. Mr. O'Docmall soon procured the desired quarters for the lady, and to them the colonel removed. The house was a boarding-house in Chambers street, and the colonel had taken the whole of the second floor for his lady. She was a peer's daughter, and, of course, a lady in her own right. She was a very fine showy Englishwoman—not over twenty-five years of age, while the colonel was a man who had nearly reached fifty. In the course of the proceedings, O'Doemall had been introduced to Lady Clairfoot, and when the colonel left for Canada he partly entrusted her to the care of his friend O'Doemall, who on his part promised to do all and every thing that could possibly conduce to the comfort of the lady. The colonel started for Canada quite satisfied with his arrangements. His wife had money in her own right when he married her, besides ample funds left with her by the colonel for her own use. She had brought a letter of credit upon the agents of the Rothschilds for three thousand pounds sterling. A knowledge of these facts had been picked up by O'Doemall, and no sooner had his friend the colonel started for the North than O'Doemall went adroitly to work to carry out his plans and purposes, whatever they may have been. He found out the weak points of Lady Clairfoot in a very short space of time. He soon managed to get up a quarrel between her ladyship and the family in whose house she had rooms, while he apparently was the pacificator and friend of the landlady. The lady was induced to have her meals in her own apartments, and Mr. O'Doemall continued to be a regular visitor both at the dinner hour and at tea, for hardly an evening passed that he did not escort her to a place of public amusement. After the play was over, Lady Clairfoot—who was extravagantly fond of a good hearty supper, which she could not get in her boarding-house—would accompany O'Doemall to "Taylor's," "Thompson's," or some other well-known restaurant. She was gay and lively, perfectly innocent, and somewhat independent, and just the person with whom a gentlemanly unprincipled rascal like O'Doemall could make rapid headway.

Fortunately, for the success of Mr. O'Doemall's efforts to victimize the worthy lady, her husband was detained in Canada from day to day, and as he was not a great letter writer, and expected to return speedily, he did not write his lady at all.

It is useless to conjecture the arts used by such a man as O'Doemall to destroy a woman. He could resort to the very basest in the seducer's calendar, and there is no doubt but that some vile drug was used to accomplish his designs upon Lady Clairfoot. She had accompanied him to the theatre, then to a supper, and from thence to her home. At her home he persuaded her to join him in a glass of bottled ale, of which he had sent to her room a dozen bottles, with a story that he had imported it himself from London. She drank one or more glasses, and then remembered nothing more until she awoke the next morning in her sleeping apartment, and Mr. O'Doemall was by her side. The lady was indignant, and the man was impudent. She threatened, and he coaxed until she became aware that further efforts against him were futile. She was in his power, and she submitted. He had obtained, under various pretences, all the ready money she had with her, and when she asked from O'Doemall sufficient to pay her board at the house, he made frivolous, lying excuses about his having used her money until his own remittances came. She believed him, and then he suggested that she should draw on her letter of credit.

He accompanied her to the agent of the Rothschilds, and she took up a hundred pounds. Mr. O'Doemall had now the lady under his control. He persuaded her to leave the house where she had been placed by her husband, and he engaged rooms for her in a distant part of the city. There they lived as man and wife.

Mr. O'Doemall had had an understanding with the bankers that they would cash her drafts, if brought by him, without requiring her presence. Again she signed a draft for a hundred pounds. She did not read the draft, and with perfect recklessness she plunged into every species of dissipation. He introduced to her a man named John James (since in the Illinois State Prison for forgery), also an Englishman by some distinguished name, and then O'Doemall introduced cards, and the lady lost. In giving a draft to O'Doemall for the usual amount of a hundred pounds, as she supposed, she actually signed a draft for one thousand pounds. This money O'Doemall placed with a respectable commercial firm as his own.

Not a night passed that all hands were not engaged in some revelry. Lady Clairfoot was hardly ever sober, and she drank apparently to drown remorse. Again was she induced to draw for money. Again did she sign a draft for a very large amount, supposing it a small one, and this game was played successfully until all the money, excepting two hundred pounds, had been drawn out by O'Doemall, and secured over two thousand pounds, or about ten thousand dollars to his own credit in the hands of this responsible commercial firm, with whom he had never been known to have had any dealings.

O'Doemall was hardly sober a moment, except when it was necessary to accomplish his plans. His partner, John James, had no knowledge of the extent of the villainy which was being perpetrated upon Lady Clairfoot. Mr. James supposed that O'Doemall was victimizing her to the extent of a few hundred pounds, and he was satisfied with a small share of it. Had he known the game was thousands, he would have claimed more. Mr. O'Doemall was not asleep in reference to Colonel Clairfoot. He felt guilty, and knew there would be a terrible reckoning when the Colonel made his appearance in New York, and was informed of the facts. He kept Mr. James constantly employed in seeking news of the Colonel's movements. He himself changed his haunts, and when he had obtained and secured two thousand pounds, and had, besides, seven hundred dollars in cash, he made up his mind to abandon the lady to her fate, and quit the city until the storm blew over.

One of his haunts was the Shakespeare Restaurant, then kept by Windust. Here he was found by Mr. James one morning quite intoxicated, and utterly incapable of taking care of himself. Mr. James informed him that Colonel Clairfoot had reached New York, and was at the "Globe Hotel." This alarming news produced no effect upon the hearer, except to make him extremely pugnacious. He was at once desirous to go and fight Colonel Clairfoot, and avenge his wrongs and protect Lady Clairfoot. Luckily, he was too drunk to get off his chair or to walk across the bar-room without assistance.

Mr. James was in a quandary. He dreaded an explosion or an explanation, for he was fearful that he should be called upon to disgorge, or perhaps explain before a magistrate his share in the infamous seduction and plunder of the English lady.

Under these circumstances he passed into the street, hoping to find assistance. He had not proceeded more than a block before he encountered Marion Monck. O'Doemall had once introduced Mr. James to Marion, and now he renewed the acquaintance. Marion received his advance somewhat coldly. He knew nothing of Mr. James, except as a friend of Mr. O'Doemall, and since the robbery of Colonel William Mac Neil he had been unable to free his mind from an impression that O'Doemall was the robber, and indirectly the assassin of the Colonel. Mr. James asked Marion if he was disposed to do an act of kindness for one who had been friendly to him when sick.

"Most certainly. Who is he? and where is he?" inquired Marion.

"It is Mr. O'Doemall. He is down in Windust's cellar, extremely drunk. And that is not all; he has been drinking for several weeks, and unless he is placed under immediate restraint, I fear he will injure himself or some one else. He is now so drunk he cannot stand. He has plenty of money about him," observed Mr. James.

Marion was about to say "Send him to the hospital," when poor Mac Neil's hasty fate crossed his mind, and he hesitated. "Has he nobody to look after him?" he asked.

"Not a soul but me," replied James.

Marion thought that Mr. James was not a very trustworthy friend, and he at once offered his services. "Take me to O'Doemall," he said. The two descended to the cellar where O'Doemall was seated, his head lying upon the table.

"Hullo, old fellow, what is wrong with you? Wake up, and speak to your friends. Mr. O'Doemall, I say," said Marion.

The drunken man roused up. "I tell you I have not got the lady's money," said O'Doemall, and then recognizing Marion, who had spoken to him, and who was shaking him, he added, "Why, Marion, is that you? I have not seen you for ages. What is out?"

"Nothing out, O'Doemall, except yourself. You are all out. You are drunk. You must go with me," added Marion.

"Mr. James, will you clear out, and leave me with my friend Monck," said O'Doemall.

Mr. James went to the extreme end of the room

"That is a most infernal rascal, Marion Monck. Have a care of him. I am sober—quite sober. You don't believe it. Very well. I have got a great deal of money with me. Count that,"—and as Mr. O'Doemall said this he pulled out bill after bill, and when one pocket was emptied he tried another, and when Marion finished counting the money so placed upon the table, he observed, "Why, O'Doemall, you have over six hundred dollars with you. It is not safe to carry such a large amount with you."

"I know it. I wish you to take it, and keep it for me. Will you oblige me? You are as safe as the Bank of England. That's a good fellow. I am not sober, and I am not drunk. I have not slept for many nights. I have been worried very much," said O'Doemall.

Marion took all the money except the surplus over the six hundred, which he handed to O'Doemall. "I will keep it, O'Doemall, but some thing must be done for you. You are very ill. The fact is, you require good nursing, or you will die," said Marion.

"I am perfectly aware of it," replied O'Doemall. "Can't you take me to some nice place—in the country, for instance, where I can be out of the way until I get well? You can pay the shot out of my money."

Marion agreed to the proposal. He went at once to Mr. James, and told him his plans. Mr. James was delighted. "Nothing could be better," he exclaimed with delight.

Marion did not see what there was to be delighted about, but he told Mr. James to go and engage a carriage to go out a few miles into the country. The carriage came, and O'Doemall and his two friends entered it. Marion handed the driver a ten dollar bill, and told him where to drive and what to do, and shortly after the carriage and its contents were on their way to Bloomingdale. When they reached the gates of the asylum, Mr. O'Doemall was asleep. Marion got out, and went up to the building. There he paid sixty dollars, or three months' board for their patient, whose name was duly entered. Marion Monck fully explained the case, and satisfied the chief physician that it was all right. He then returned to the carriage, and almost immediately it was driven inside and up the main entrance. Servants came out of this country hotel to assist the guest to his quarters. Mr. O'Doemall was woke up. He gazed at Marion, then at the hotel. Memory recalled a part of his previous conversation, and he exclaimed with glee, "Ah, you have done as I requested. Got me a country hotel. Where is it? What's the name of the place? Let's go in and get a drink, and then I will go to bed."

They entered the hall. O'Doemall began to notice some things. It was too late. "Good-bye," said Marion; "I will come and see you in a few days."

"I say. Stop. What does this mean? Keep your hands off me,"—and with a hundred oaths and protestations and requests to be let loose, Mr. O'Doemall was sent, or rather dragged to his apartments. He was a patient in the "Bloomingdale Asylum," vulgarly called a mad-house.

Marion Monck and Mr. James returned to the city. Had the former dreamed that his humane intentions were to be the means of letting a villain escape from the punishment he so richly merited from a wronged husband, he would have cut off his own hands for the act.

It was so. Colonel Clairfoot made every effort to discover O'Doemall. Mr. James went over to Jersey and staid three months, to keep out of the way. There was no clue to O'Doemall's retreat. The husband found his wife almost a maniac. He learned how deeply he had been wronged, and how largely she had been robbed of honor and of money. But time was precious. He waited a month to catch the rascal O'Doemall. He was not to be found anywhere. Satisfied that he had escaped his vengeance, the Colonel and his lady returned to England. What became of her was never known by any one on this side of the water. He was heard of some years after, for he committed suicide in the city of Dublin without any apparent cause (so the papers stated that gave an account of the melancholy transaction).

Marion Monck was, of course, ignorant of any transaction of a guilty nature in which O'Doemall had been engaged. He supposed he had drank to excess, and placed him where he was safe.

A week elapsed before he visited him, and then he hired a carriage, and taking with him the balance of the money left in his hands by O'Doemall, he went out to the Bloomingdale Asylum. That visit and the finale of our history of Mr. O'Doemall must be left for another chapter.

CHAPTER LXII.

Mr. and Mrs. Wilson—Mr. Bennett sends Marion Monck to South Carolina as Correspondent of the Herald—Two Months with Mr. Calhoun—Departure from Charleston for New York, and Safe Arrival with Mrs. Ferguson.

RARE and unfrequent were the visits that Marion Monck paid to the comfortable residence of Mr. and Mrs. Wilson. He was ever welcomed there by both husband and wife, and it would be difficult to decide why so old a friend did not visit them oftener. There was one reason, however, which Marion hardly understood himself. He was not at home in the presence of Mrs. Wilson. He remembered the young wife of Mr. Nordheim, and there was something he could not forget—and yet he could hardly understand what that something was. The Count Falsechinski, who was a perfect man of the world, had on one occasion enlightened him as to the past feelings of Mrs. Nordheim, but yet he could not reconcile the opinion with the fact, that the widow Nordheim had married Mr. Wilson.

It was a happy marriage. They had become parents to two children, both boys, and the second one was named "Marion."

Marion Monck had called up one evening, and Mrs. Wilson announced the fact to him in the presence of her husband.

"We have named our second darling after you, Marion, and

the young gentleman's name is Marion Monck Wilson. We are not unmindful that we owe our happiness to you. Had it not been through your instrumentality I had never known my present lord, and I am grateful, Marion. We only wish that you could point out to us some way in which we could really be useful to you. We desire anxiously to see you settle down in life. You have sown all your wild oats. You have a marked capacity for business; and let me beg of you, dear Marion, to think seriously of what I say. You have not two truer friends in this wide and wicked world, than Mr. Wilson and myself." There was feeling expressed in these few words from the lips of the graceful woman, which reminded Marion of old times, and he was affected deeply. He replied,

"If it would give you any pleasure to see me settled, I can only wish that I was in a regular business. I hope soon to be. The Count Falsechinski has hinted to me an arrangement, by which I shall soon have a partner, with plenty of cash capital. I am under a promise not to mention any names, or I would tell you more."

"That is good news. The Count is in a situation to make good any promise that he gives," said Wilson.

"Are you aware, Marion, that we are going to move into the country?" asked Mrs. Wilson.

"Indeed I was not. To what part of the country are you going?"

"To the Connecticut village where I staid during the cholera year. We are not going to break up in town. You remember my aunt, Mrs. Ferguson, in Charleston—of course you do; we have written her to come on and make a permanent home with us. She will keep the house in the city, and we shall only be absent during the hot summer months. It is better for the children. Poor boys, I cannot bear to have them cooped up in town, when there is fresh and pure air to be had by a short journey."

When Marion made these visits he was asked all sorts of questions about those persons they had mutually known, and in this manner an evening passed very quickly and happily to all parties.

"Come oftener, Marion," would be added by the lady in the kindest manner when he was leaving, and he would make up his mind that his visits to this delightful family should henceforth be more frequent. But something always turned up to prevent it. He was literally very busy—doing nothing. He wrote occasionally, and he idled still more, but his mind was constantly employed. He would sometimes go to an old haunt and remain there for hours, drinking a solitary glass, and then he would dream out a thousand beautiful thoughts and fancies. He thought much, and though he had no definite plan but to pass away the time, and the stimulus he drank helped out his ideas and thoughts, yet he never wrote them down. He *thought* them, and they pleased him, and were stowed away for use in after years. In these places he saw life. He listened to the conversation of others without mixing in it, and whether these conversations related to a dog fight or a rise in cotton, he gleaned information.

Sometimes he visited drinking places where the worst of the male sex congregated, and often had he volunteered to keep the slate when a lot of thieves were raffling for the first chances in the fruits of joint robberies. He was thanked, never molested, and often invited to drink. The slang language of these people, and their motives of conduct, amused him. When he had a few spare dollars he would go to a new spot, where poor broken-down drunkards congregated, men who had not a copper towards paying for a three cent drink. Here he would pick up and stow away in his iron memory any quantity of useful information. He would treat, and treat, the strange crew until his funds were exhausted, and the men themselves wondered at such folly and extravagance. But he gained his point. He was deeper into the mysteries of life after all such night expeditions.

One lovely April morning, Marion Monek was passing up Nassau street, when he was met by the editor of the Herald. The latter asked in his hasty manner,

"Well, are you doing any thing?"

"Nothing in particular."

"Will you go South for me?" asked the editor.

"What to do?" asked Marion.

"I wish you to travel through the Southern States, or at least to spend the summer months in your native State, South Carolina, and write me a series of letters giving me all sorts of information—its agriculture, manufactures, society, scenery, great men and little men; in fact, about every thing; will you go?"

"I will: when do you wish me to start?" asked Marion.

"At once. Come up to the office and I will give you funds. Leave to-day if you can, and go by the land route to Charleston. From that point I wish you to commence writing me letters," said the editor.

"I will be ready in an hour, and will then come to your office," replied Marion.

"Good morning—that will do," and they parted.

Marion went at once to his boarding house, packed his trunk, paid his bill, and made arrangements that his trunk should be sent to the Philadelphia depot at five o'clock.

An hour after he was at the Herald office, received the necessary funds from Mr. Bennett for his journey, and general instructions as to what he was to do, and then bade him farewell.

Marion Monck was delighted with the prospect of leaving New York; he was sick of the city, and beside the prospect of several months to be passed away in pleasant travel, he was to see his parents once more, after an absence of many years. He did not bid any one good bye, but wrote a note to Count Falscchinski, and another to Mr. and Mrs. Wilson, informing them of his purpose.

The journey was a pleasant one, passing through Philadelphia, Baltimore, Washington, Richmond, and Wilmington, North Carolina, by land, and thence to Charleston by steamboat. He reached Charleston the fourth day after leaving New York. The next day he went up to the residence of his parents at Monck's Corners. To give any idea of the reception he met with there would vastly exceed our limits. He found his parents and aunty older, but still hale and hearty, and in the most independent circumstances. He did not leave his home for two weeks, and then he returned to Charleston, and commenced writing letters to the Herald. These letters made a sensation at the time. They were all signed "Commissioner," and dated Charleston, Augusta, Columbia, Camden, Greenville, Sparta, Glen Springs, Unionville, Winsboro', Cæsar's Head, Flat Rock, and other points of interest in the State, not excepting Fort Hill, near Pendleton, the residence and home of the great Calhoun. There Marion spent two months, for he was an especial favorite of the great statesman. These letters can all be found in old files of the Herald. There were six published in the London Herald, written by " Commissioner," who was Marion Monck, and who wrote these letters as *flyers*. The series, if collected and bound in a volume, would have a great run, for it is now no secret, that in writing these letters Marion had assistance from the highest source in the State. Mr. Calhoun himself furnished most of the ideas, (and some were brilliant,) for these Southern letters.

While a resident at Mr. Calhoun's mansion, Marion Monck

became acquainted with a lady and her daughter who were up on a visit to the great statesman's family,—in fact were distantly related. The young girl was not twelve years of age, and a regular wild one. She would ride with ease the most skittish horse on Mr. Calhoun's plantation, and would drive into Pendleton and back again in a buggy, with perfect safety. When she rode about the place, or visited any of the neighbors, she rarely troubled the negroes to open gates for her, but made her horse leap the various fences.

"That tom-boy will break her neck," exclaimed Mrs. Calhoun, on one occasion, as "Cara" came full tilt with her horse over the fence of the door yard. Mr. Calhoun was also on the piazza of his residence, standing by the side of his wife, and was a witness to the feat.

"Don't call her tom-boy. It is not a proper title. I like to see it. Cara by such exercises is developing her physical powers, and one day will be able to become such a wife and mother as God intended women to be. There is no weak, sickly effeminacy about her, engendered by being shut up in a parlor, without pure air or healthy exercise. I like to see a girl educated in that manner. It is an education worth more to her and to society than it is even to be able to read and write, if she could not have both physical and mental education."

Marion listened with interest to these remarks about a little girl that he escorted to various places, leading her by the hand. These remarks probably led him in after years, when Mr. Calhoun had descended to the tomb, to make this ci-devant little girl "Cara" Mrs. Monck. But we are getting on too fast with our story.

It was late in October before Marion Monck had finished the tour of South Carolina. Then he returned to Monck's Corners, and spent another happy month with his parents. His father was extremely anxious that he should give up New York and remain at home.

"You have seen the world, my son. Why not now settle down and live at home? We are not rich, but we have every comfort that a reasonable young man can desire. Where else can you find more substantial happiness?"

It was all in vain. Marion's mind was made up, and no inducement held out by his father could persuade him to give up for a moment his long dream of ambition, which was to succeed as a merchant in New York.

"I will make a spoon or spoil a horn in that city," was Marion's quiet rejoinder, quoting a favorite axiom of his father.

"You say, Marion, that you desire to go into business in New York. Let mother and I make up what capital you need. By selling cattle and stock of various kinds, and adding to it some bank stock that we have put by, we could give you some seven or eight thousand dollars, and not miss it much if you were to lose it all," said his father.

"God bless you, dear father. I would not touch your hard earnings if it was to be the means of making me as rich as all the Ravenels and old Wade Hamptons to boot. No—don't say a word about it. I shall not starve in New York, and I may succeed," said Marion.

"And if you do succeed, my son, what does it all amount to? You can't eat any more—you can't drink any more—you can't sleep any more, if you succeed, as you call it, and get to be worth millions, than you can up here at Monck's Corners in our own comfortable homestead, which will be all yours when we die. Besides, there is no such hunting in New York city as here. There are no such deer—there are no such wild turkeys; and you can catch more fish in the Santee Canal and Biggin Creek in half an hour than you can catch in the New York waters in a week," exclaimed the honest old father.

Marion laughed and replied, "True as gospel, my dear father; and you might have added, there are no such live oaks in any New York door-yard as there are about this house—no such magnificent forests, and all that. Still I must try my luck in the city for a while longer. I should stagnate here—die from actual want of something to do."

"A wilful man will have his way," replied the elder Monck, and left Marion, while he went to look after his horses.

The mother, who loved her son devotedly, was equally unsuccessful in her endeavors to persuade him to give up New York, and settle at Monck's Corners. When the time came for his departure, both parents accompanied him to Charleston, and did not return to Monck's Corners until Marion had sailed for New York.

While in Charleston, Marion called on his early friend Mrs. Ferguson. She was delighted to see him once more, and he expressed his gratitude for the success which her letter of introduction many years previous had brought to him. The good lady said,

"I have sold out everything, and am ready to go to New York to live with Bessy. She has written for me."

"So she told me before I left New York. In fact, I had no idea that I should find you here. Why not go on to New York with me?" said Marion.

"I certainly will do so if you will take charge of me," was the reply of the worthy landlady.

It was so arranged, and Marion secured a passage for Mrs. Ferguson on board the ship Saluda. They had a pleasant passage to New York, and when the ship reached the dock Marion hired a carriage, and conveyed the lady to the residence of Mrs. Wilson, her niece. He remained only long enough to shake hands, and then went to the Herald office, where he found Mr. Bennett. He was cordially received.

"Capital letters you sent me. I published every one of them. They were very interesting," observed the editor.

"I am very glad that they pleased you. I should have sent you more, but I was detained several weeks at Mr. Calhoun's residence," added Marion.

"I am not disappointed. What money have you received while you were absent?"

"Just enough to pay my current expenses. I have not been very extravagant," replied Marion.

Mr. Bennett took a slip of paper, wrote a few words upon it, and handed it to Marion, observing, at the same time, "How would you like to go to Washington?"

"I don't know at present. I have to see a person, and then I will tell you," replied Marion.

"Very well. Call upon me when your mind is made up," said Mr. Bennett, and Marion left him to go with the slip of paper to the cashier. It was for three hundred and fifty dollars. When Marion had pocketed the money, he said to himself, "Well, that is not bad, considering that I have had some fun. In fact, I did not expect to receive a cent, and am rather surprised at the liberal amount. The fifty must answer my needs, and so I will invest the three hundred in a check on Charleston."

He went at once to the office of Spofford & Tileston, large merchants engaged in the cotton trade. There he bought a draft on Charleston for three hundred dollars, made payable to "Henry Monck," or order. When Mr. Tileston saw the name, he asked Marion if he was not the author of the letters from the South signed "Commissioner?" Marion hesitated before he gave a reply.

"Mr. Bennett told me so," added Mr. Tileston.

"Then I shall not deny it, if that is the case. I did write the letters," said Marion.

"And extremely interesting they were. I am glad to meet with you," said the merchant.

When Marion took his leave he went up to his old Spanish boarding-house, and re-took his room. His pretty senorita friends Inez and Isabella were delighted to see him, and he was glad to see them. He at once wrote a letter to his father, after the following fashion:

"NEW YORK, *Dec.* 1, 18—.

"*My Dear Father*—

"I am safe back in the great city that you so honestly detest. I was agreeably surprised on my arrival to find that my Southern letters have proved to be worth three hundred and fifty dollars. The fifty dollars I shall spend—the three hundred dollars I do not need. When I was last with you, I noticed that you were very anxious to own the magnificent stallion "Santee," belonging to your friend Schopman. The price asked was three hundred dollars. The enclosed order will just pay for that horse, and I beg you will consider it a gift from your affectionate son. Give my love to mother and to aunt Mary, and give a pound of tobacco to Mann, Phillis, and Daddy Jemmy respectively. They will appreciate tobacco more than a love message. Your affectionate son,
"MARION MONCK."

When Marion had finished this document, he inclosed the draft in it, and then mailed it himself at the post-office. Then he went up town, where he met a friend who told him that he had been earnestly sought after by the Count Falsechinski. So Marion left a card at the residence of Mr. Grasper, for the Count was not at home when he called. Then he went around town to places where he was known, and at a late hour returned to his boarding-house.

CHAPTER LXIII.

The Count Falsechinski's Position—Scene at Breakfast—Meets Walter Granville—Scene with Clara Norris—Pitt Granville becomes insane, and is taken to the Bloomingdale Asylum.

FEW persons could be found who appeared to enjoy life and his position with more satisfaction than the Count Adolph Falsechinski. Every thing that he had meddled with had turned out successfully from the moment he met Marion Monck. If he gambled, he became a heavy winner. He sought a clerkship, and it gave him habits of business, and a position; he taught languages, and he made money and valuable acquaintances; he speculated in stocks and doubled his money—in real estate, and it brought him a fortune. He married, and obtained beauty, dignity, rich relations, and a large amount of cash; and even while these successes were being achieved by his own diligence and exertions, his patriotic brother died, leaving him the head of an old noble family in Poland; and a slight fine restored to him his title of Count, and the estates unincumbered.

After his marriage with Miss Grasper, the Count travelled with his bride for several weeks. On their return to the city they made their residence at the granite palace of Mr. Grasper. The Count had won the heart of the old gentleman, who became more pleased with the match as he became better acquainted with the sterling qualities of his son-in-law. The Countess became devotedly attached to her husband; he was kind and attentive, and his devotion did not end with the honeymoon—he commanded respect wherever he went, and every hour's intimacy taught the bride to respect more and more her lord and master.

Over the mind of Francis Grasper, his brother-in-law, the Count was not long in obtaining a complete mastery. The former admired the latter as much as one man could possibly admire another, and was pleased to have him for his relative. He made his sister happy, and what more could be desired?

"Frank, I wish you to go and dine with me to-day where we can be alone by ourselves," said the Count one morning, when all were assembled at breakfast.

"Nothing would give me more pleasure; when and where shall it be?"

"At Delmonico's, time three o'clock," and turning to the old gentleman, he added, "The fact is, Mr. Grasper, I have a place for Frank which I think he will like, and after I have made sure of it by a private conversation with him, I will explain the matter to you. I detest seeing a fine young fellow like Frank, although he may come into a fortune some day, without any visible means of exertion. I should like to see him employed—useful, doing something."

"Count, you have hit my ideas precisely. To tell you the truth, I would like to have Frank do something for himself—he is quite old enough to settle down. If you can arrange it, you will oblige me very much."

"Then do not forget your own appointment, Frank;—and now I must leave you."

With this sudden closing, the Count passed into the street

and wended his way down town, stopping at Centre street, in the hope of meeting Marion or of learning his whereabouts. Although he did not find Marion, he discovered a person whom he remembered very well, notwithstanding his features were altered. It was Walter Granville, smoking a cigar and drinking a glass of hot toddy. Somewhat fiercely he addressed the Count.

"Well, Count, you have got up a little higher in the world than when I first knew you. Then I believe you taught languages?"

"I have no reason to be ashamed of my profession, when I had the honor to teach a lady who is now I believe Mrs. Walter Granville," and the Count bowed.

"Yes, you did teach my wife, and I am much obliged to you. A good many of our old friends have stepped out since I first met you."

"Colonel Mac Neil is dead—Mr. Nordheim is dead—your uncle Thomas is dead. Yes, we all have to die. Have you seen your father?"

"No, I have not; he does not trouble his head about me, and I see no reason why I should fret about him. They say you are rich, Count. Is it so?" asked the young man.

"I am not poor, and I am not ashamed under my altered circumstances, to say I was once very poor. Can I be of any service to you, Mr. Walter?"

"Not a bit, not a particle.—I can steer my own canoe: will you take a drink?"

"Excuse me, I rarely drink in the morning, and I must hurry down town; good morning, sir," and with these few words the Count took his departure.

"That is a proud, haughty cuss; he was once humble enough, but he has pluck and I like him. I wish my old governor would kick the bucket, and then I would hold up my head as high as any of them," muttered the son to himself after the Count's departure. "Jemmy, give me another drink. I wonder what the devil keeps Harry away so long. Sure he has not been here, eh?"

"I am certain he has not been here, and he will probably be along soon. Who was your friend that just went out?" asked the bar tender.

"That is a real live Count—the Count Falsechinski—and he has got the brads, too," was the reply.

"I saw him give Colonel Mac Neil a hundred dollars one day—it was just before the Colonel died," said Jemmy.

"The deuce you did—why, what claim had the Colonel on the Count?"

"I do not know, but the fact is as I tell you. There is your friend Robinson."

At this moment Henry Robinson entered the store from the rear, and without a word took a chair and seated himself by Walter Granville.

"What the old Nick makes you look so moody—any thing gone wrong?" inquired Walter.

"Yes, every thing seems to me wrong. I have just called on your wife. I am getting too much in her debt. It is a shame, but I can't help it. Rose, poor thing, is an awful expense, but she can't help it. I was obliged to get funds from Mrs. Granville this morning."

"Well, that is all right. Did she shell out freely, or hesitate?" asked Walter.

"Not in the least, and I do not like riding a free horse to death, when I have rich relatives of my own. I told Mrs. Granville so this morning, and asked her advice. She gave me a plan to work upon, and curse me if I don't try it on. I am going to have an interview with my parents—what do you think of that?"

"If Clara—my wife, I mean—has suggested a plan, it is a good one. She is clever. What an infernal shame that such a woman should ever have been a ——. Blame it, I cannot pronounce the word when I am speaking of my own wife. But she is honest now, and the old devil we live with!—a'nt she a sanctified old sinner? don't mention it," said Walter.

"I shall try the plan, and if it succeeds you shall know all about it. If it does not, there is no harm done. Answer me one question. Do you think Rose would pass for a Spanish girl?"

"Blame me if I don't think she would. If she only spoke Spanish you could not tell her from a genuine pretty senorita—black hair and eyes, and all that sort of thing."

These two young men continued together for some hours, drinking and smoking, until Walter was "pretty tight."

"Harry, I shall not see you very often after this. I think you will get all right with your parents—if so, the less you see of me the better, and the less Rose has to do with Clara the better. In fact, old fellow, don't think hard of me if I should soon be among the missing. This getting money from a woman as I do, is not the thing for me. I shall cut it before a great while, and then I am off to sea again. I like independence."

"But your wife—what will she do?"

"She be blamed. She has always taken care of herself without me, and can do it again. Not a word about what I have said to you, to her," observed Walter Granville.

He parted with Robinson at the door of the grog-shop, and went at once to his wife's apartment in Bond street. When he entered the room, he flung himself upon the sofa, saying, "How are you, Clara? All alone, eh? That is right."

"Beast," was hissed through the lady's teeth, and then she continued, "Walter Granville, you are drunk again. In fact, it is nothing but drunk from morning until night. I will put up with it no longer. Either stop it or quit," said Clara, firmly.

"Quit—that's the word, is it?" Walter raised himself upon the sofa. Then he sat up. "Quit—is it to be? You infernal wicked prostitute. Your acts have inveigled me into a marriage, and now because I don't please you—because I try to drown my degradation in drink, you want to cry 'quit,'"—and as he said this he sprung at her, and closing his hands about her neck, he choked her until he himself got scared, for when he removed his hands she sank down upon the sofa without sense or motion. He stepped to the washstand, seized a jug of water, and threw the entire contents over her person, drenching her completely. "Now live or die, curse you. I don't care which. I ought to kill you, and rid the world of a female devil. Would to God I had never seen you, and I hope that to-night is the last that I shall spend within a thousand miles of you. You are getting around again, eh?" exclaimed Walter.

Clara opened her eyes and gazed at him. "Walter, I did not expect this from you. You hurt me cruelly," she exclaimed.

"Did I? It will do you good—teach you to keep a civil tongue in your head, for it is a bit of a foretaste of what I will do with you if ever I put my hands about you again in real anger. I would choke you as I would a bad hen. You spoke of parting. I am ready. What have you got to say to it?" asked Walter.

"I was only vexed for a moment, dear Walter. I did not mean to hurt your feelings. You know I love you, and have tried to be a good faithful wife to you," said Clara, weeping.

"Oh, fol-de-rol, I say. I am going in earnest, old gal, and

it's no use talking. If you have got any spare change, give it to me, for I shall never ask you again. I am going to be independent, if I ain't any thing else," continued Walter.

It was in vain that Mrs. Granville remonstrated, begged, and even prayed Walter to remain. Threaten him, she dare not do, after the experience she had had of his choking propensities. She handed him her purse. He took from it a few dollars, and handed the rest back to her.

"I want a rig and enough to carry me to Alexandria. There I am going to ship before the mast in a vessel bound round the Horn. That is between you and me. The fact is, you will hear of my death in about a fortnight. Then you can play the gay widow, and no fear of my ever turning up again. I will do you that justice, for ever I do come this way, it will be years hence, and under some assumed name. Keep up a stout heart. It's no use talking, Clara. It has got to be as I have said. You are tired of me. I am tired of you. That is honest. If I stay here, all your money won't keep me from a drunkard's death. It will force it on me. Now let us part friends," said Walter.

Clara Norris was, for once in her life, affected. She knew the determined will of Walter Granville. She knew that she should see him no more—that he was going to sea on a long voyage. She burst into tears.

"Oh, Walter, I cannot bear this. Do not go, or take me with you."

"Nonsense. Now mark my words. You will see my death in the papers before long. I want to be dead to all here. But I tell you there will not be a word of truth in it. I shall continue to live under some assumed name. Now good-bye. No nonsense." Saying this he kissed her, and was about to leave when he seemed to remember something. He then said, " Clara, if you have one tender spot for poor Walter, and want to do me a kindness, lend a helping hand to Harry Robinson and Rose,"—and before she could reply he was out of the room, down the stairs, and in the street. What direction he took after leaving her, she never heard.

More than a fortnight elapsed before she heard any more of him. Then a notice appeared in the morning paper, copied from a Philadelphia paper. It was as follows:

"Walter Granville, a sailor on board the ship Liberty, was lost overboard on the 17th inst. The ship was dropping down the river, and had anchored near Wilmington. The body was not recovered. The young sailor was a son of Mr. Pitt Granville, an eminent New York merchant."

Clara read and re-read the article. "He has complied with a part of his promise. I suppose he went ashore at Wilmington, and then proceeded on to Alexandria by railroad," she thought aloud. But there was one house in which that article was read where its effects were fearful. It reached No. 9 State street, and was read by W. Pitt Granville. He at once screamed with laughter. Then he called the rest of the family. Read the announcement of his son's death, making, at the same time, the most ludicrous grimaces. He said it was "funny," "rare sport," "Walter was always fond of swimming," "better to be drowned than married." He was not violent, but his mind had failed—or, at least, had temporarily given way.

Colonel Benson came, and his son also. Mr. Granville was insane. There was no question about it. Physicians were called in. A person was appointed to take temporary charge of him, until some permanent provision could be made to cure him if possible, or, at least, for his safety, should his madness assume a violent form.

It was found that Mr. Granville was, at times, quite insane, and on one of his sane days he himself proposed that his friends should take him to the Bloomingdale Asylum. This was eventually done.

CHAPTER LXIV.

Marion Monck pays a second visit to Mr O Doemall, in the Bloomingdale Asylum—Curious Fun among Mad People—Surprising number of Respectable rich People in that Asylum—Arrival of Pitt Granville at the Institution—Mr. O'Doemall comes out—Invests his ten thousand dollars, and leaves New York—His Villainies.

WHEN Marion Monck paid a second visit to the Bloomingdale Asylum, he found the patient, Mr. O'Doemall, quite convalescent. As soon as he saw Marion approach, he shook his head pleasantly, and exclaimed, "Ah, you precious fellow, are you not ashamed of yourself to have trapped me into a mad house so nicely. Country hotel, eh ?"

"I do not think I could have acted better for your own good than I did. You were in a shocking state, perfectly incompetent to take care of yourself, and I did precisely as I would have wished a real friend to act for me. Are you under any restraint now ?" asked Marion.

"None whatever. I needed sleep, and I obtained it the second night. What a horrible thing this drink is! The medical genius has had to keep me under lock and key for two days. Now tell me the circumstances under which you brought me here. I have a faint recollection of them, but am not clear," replied O'Doemall.

Marion related the manner in which he met O'Doemall at Windust's cellar, his interview with Mr. James, and the receipt of money; and added, "You seemed perfectly cool. You counted your money. Bye-the-by, I wish you to relieve me of further charge in the matter. I received six hundred dollars. I paid out hack hire ten, and three months' board here for you is sixty dollars more, and here is five hundred and thirty."

Here he handed O'Doemall that sum, who counted it deliberately, and observed,

"All as right as a twist. It is not every man that would have acted in this manner, but I flatter myself, Mr. Monck, that I understand human character pretty well. That Mr. James would have robbed me of every cent and cleared out. By-the-by, where is that precious chap? I wish you to answer me another question. Does anybody beside you and James know that I am here?"

"Not a soul. James has left New York from some cause or another, and has gone over to Jersey. He left his address in case you wished to write him, and told me to tell you that there was an English mad dog in New York, and that you had better keep from being bit by keeping out of the way," said Marion.

"Ah yes, I understand—the mad dog I suppose is liquor. It has bit me, and I will keep out of the way. I rather like this place, and as my board is paid, I shall stay some weeks, or until my nerves get so strong that I can resist the temptation to drink. What do you think of it? It is rather discreditable to be in a mad house, but as no one of my city friends is aware that I am here, my character is safe, eh?" said Mr. O'Doemall, who had very powerful reasons for keeping shady. He deceived Marion completely, and the latter replied to him,

"The very best thing that you can do. Your business will not suffer, and your health will be really benefitted. I will do anything that I can for you in the city."

"Thank you. There is but one thing you can do. I wish you to call at Blancard's Globe Hotel, and ascertain if Colonel Clairfoot is stopping there. If you find that he is, or that he is in New York, I want you to ascertain when he leaves the city for England or Canada. I will do as much for you if I ever have the chance. In making inquiries about the Colonel, do not let any one know why you ask about him, and promise me that you will not cover me with eternal disgrace by letting a soul know that I am in this mad-pen, or in existence. Will you promise me that much?" asked O'Doemall.

"With all my heart. Not a living soul shall be aware that you are alive, from my lips," replied the good-natured and unsuspicious Marion, who had no idea that placing O'Doemall in the Asylum had saved his life perhaps in more ways than one. It certainly was a secure and unsuspected refuge for the guilty man; for Colonel Clairfoot had applied to the police for aid to discover O'Doemall, and the city had been searched from one end to the other.

"What sort of a time have you had here? Do the keepers treat you well?" asked Marion.

"Like a prince; and it is the funniest institution on Manhattan Island. Of course I am not mad, but all these people are as mad as March hares, and yet are unconscious of it. Now we have all sorts of amusements—a billiard table, a ninepin alley, and these mad chaps go and have a game. Fancy my going to play ninepins with one of them! I made a match to play a 'pony game.' It all went on very well for some time until I noticed that my opponent hesitated. He held in his hand a good sized pony ball, and his eyes began to flash fire. 'I am Jupiter, the Thunderer. Look out for my thunder, mortal! and he fixed his frenzied eyes upon me, and lifted up the pony menacingly. You can bet high that the mortal sloped, and I ran out the back way as fast as my legs would carry me; but I was chased for some distance by Jupiter the Thunderer, who let fly a pony ball that whizzed with an inch of my head. If it had hit me, my brains would have been scattered. One of the alarm-keepers heard the noise, and Jupiter was seized, made fast, and carried to a private apartment, where he might thunder as much as he pleased, but where his thunder could not take the shape of an iron-wood pony ball.

"I frequently walk about these beautiful grounds, and enjoy the pure air. I meet on such occasions both ladies and gentlemen. Of course they are mad, or they would not be here. You are apt, however, to forget the fact. Yesterday a gentleman met me in one of my walks, and as he came opposite to me, he raised his hat in the most respectful manner, observed that it was a fine day, and wished to know if he could serve me. Upon my soul I took him to be one of the physicians or Board of Directors, as the latter frequently come here, and I turned to join him in his walk. I asked him many questions, and he answered them all with marked politeness. He was an amiable fellow. Finally he asked me to come and take a seat in an arbor. I complied; and had no sooner done so, than he placed himself in the open doorway, and asked, 'Do you know me?' 'I suppose I do. You are doubtless one of the Managers or Board of Directors.' He began to regard me rather more savagely than I liked, and replied, 'Wrong, sir. I am one of the Board of Directors of Heaven. I am the archangel Gabriel, and I will scorch you up like a feather with one of my wings, if you move;' and with this he began to use one of his flippers like a wing. I started to get out, but he sprang upon me like a wild-cat, uttering, with a most fearful yell, 'Wretch —you murdered my brother angel!' I did get out—how, I don't exactly know; but I left the archangel Gabriel with the claret flowing down his face pretty freely. I am somewhat given to pugilism, and the poor maniac got a sample of it. But the cases I have mentioned, Mr. Monck, are the quiet, gentle mad people. O, if you want to see the bad ones, go up where they chain them, and lock them up in cells. You can see frightful cases enough there, if you wish," continued Mr. O'Doemall.

"I have seen quite enough—I have no wish to make a more intimate acquaintance with any of the species of madness; but can you go out when you please?" asked Marion.

"Certainly, if you are once pronounced sane. I could go out with you in five minutes, if you wished. How do you do, Mr. Foster?"

This was addressed to a very gentlemanly looking man, nearly sixty years old, who approached them. O'Doemall introduced Marion. The three conversed for some time, and then Mr. Foster left them.

"Good God!" said Marion, "I know him well. Why, he is a large merchant in South street. Is it possible that he is mad? Why, he has a family—keeps a carriage, and has a pew in Dr. Spring's church!"

"The very same man, Mr. Monck; and if he were to give you a check at this moment for twenty thousand dollars, it would be paid like winking. He is perfectly sane now," said O'Doemall.

"Then how in the arch fiend's name does he happen to be here?" asked Marion.

"Because he has drank his wine at dinner for years. He has drank his brandy and water of an evening, and he is liable to the same tumble as meaner men. Feather beds won't give him sleep when his blood is half alcohol. As soon as his family perceive what is coming on, they send him up here for a week or a fortnight, and give out in the city that he is sick. When he gets well, he remains up here several days longer than is necessary. He is a little ashamed of it, but will soon get over that. If he was to kick the bucket up here, nothing would be said about it, and his corpse would be sent down to his own house. At this moment there are thirty cases of delirium tremens in the Bloomingdale Asylum of men of wealth and standing in society—professors, merchants, lawyers, judges, and even drinking physicians, are cured temporarily here. It costs but sixty dollars, and a ride in a hack. Men frequently come here in their own carriages, brought by their wives, sons or brothers," said O'Doemall.

"I am somewhat surprised, I assure you. Can it be true?" asked Marion.

"Don't trust to me. Get in with the officials of the establishment, or watch with your own eyes, and you will meet men here that it would be an honor to know elsewhere. Poor devils that drink and get delirious go to the Tombs, Almshouse and Hospital. The rich and respected in society, who can pay sixty dollars and not feel it, come here to get cured, and silence is the watchword for all such cases."

The two persons had now approached near the main entrance, and Marion asked Mr. O'Doemall if he had any commands in town. The reply was in the negative.

"I do not want anybody living to know that I am here. I am not quite well, and I shall remain here until my general health is completely restored. Come and see me as often as you can, but do not be surprised if I am not out of this for some weeks."

While they were conversing, a carriage, or rather two carriages, drove up to the main gate.

"Some new customer for the mad-house," observed O'Doemall.

Neither spoke for some time, until Colonel Benson and his son Middleton came out of the first carriage.

"As I live, there is Colonel Benson," said Marion, and added, "I will wait, and see who those people are."

A moment after a well known physician came from the carriage, leading another man. In a moment he was visible.

"The mad chap is Mr. Granville, as I am a sinner. There is no mistake about it," said O'Doemall.

From the second carriage came Mrs. Benson and Isabella Benson and Mrs. Wilson. The group entered the gate, and proceeded to the asylum.

"A regular family party," said O'Doemall.

"Walter Granville's death has done the work for his poor old father," added Marion.

"Is Walter Granville dead? That is news to me. When did he die?" asked O'Doemall.

"He was drowned from a ship in the Delaware river," replied Marion.

The two followed the procession up to the asylum, and after Mr. Granville had been disposed of, and his friends had returned to New York, Marion made inquiries of the superintendent. He ascertained that the physicians had pronounced the case of Mr. Granville to be a melancholy species of insanity, and that being uncertain what form it might take, it had been deemed advisable to place him under a mild restraint, and where he could have the best of mad medical advice.

It may be as well here to state that Mr. Granville continued to reside at the asylum for months, and then for years. He confided the closing up of his affairs to his son-in-law and Col. Benson. He signed his own papers in liquidation, and even the checks with which he paid his quarterly dues of sixty dollars were signed by himself. When he wishes to leave the asylum, he does so, and not unfrequently, after a visit of two or three days to the city, his own carriage conveys him back to the asylum. He is never violent, but for days is quietly insane. He is still wealthy, for his business was closed up, and his capital invested in real estate and stocks in his own name. His daughter treats him the same as in his palmiest days. His grandchildren are objects of his deepest love, and he never speaks of his son but in a sentence of two words—" Poor Walter."

To return to Mr. O'Doemall and Marion. They commented freely as they walked about the grounds after Mr. Granville had been received upon his insanity. Marion was unable to realize the fact. He was so many years with that merchant, and respected him so highly, it seemed impossible he could fall from his lofty position. He was abruptly startled from his reflection by the voice of O'Doemall.

"That sweetheart of yours, Miss Isabel, is quite a little ugly old woman. I suppose seeing her has touched a soft spot, eh?"

"Not at all. I am pained to see the head of the family inside of these walls, and I am sorry that his daughter should be a witness of her father's incarceration. But she has shown that she has filial feeling in her heart by coming here with him, and I respect her the more for so doing," observed Marion, quietly.

"I have no wish to hurry you, but it is time for you to go. The hour of visitors is passed," said O'Doemall.

Marion bade him good-bye, left the asylum, and returned to town.

It was some days before he could execute the commission of Mr. O'Doemall in reference to Colonel Clairfoot. When he returned to the asylum, he carried with him a newspaper in which, among the list of passengers by a packet ship that had sailed for Liverpool, were found the names of the Colonel and Lady Clairfoot. When O'Doemall read this, he asked Marion if he came out in a carriage. The reply was in the affirmative.

"Then I will return to the city with you. I am quite well."

Marion had no objection to offer, and the two came to the city in the same carriage. O'Doemall ordered the coachman to drop him at the "Waverly," a hotel on the corner of Broadway and Exchange street.

With Mr. O'Doemall our story will soon finish. New York got too hot for him. He had committed acts that, fairly investigated, would have sent him to the State Prison. He had escaped the immediate danger from his wrongs to Lady Clairfoot, but how soon an avenger might return and hold him to a stern account, was not to be calculated upon. With such dangers staring him in the face, he made up his mind to leave New York for a time, if not forever. He called upon the respectable firm with whom he had deposited ten thousand dollars, being a portion of the money he had robbed from Lady Clairfoot. He requested the firm to obtain for him ten certificates of deposit in the Bank of New York, payable to his order, for one thousand dollars each, and he called and left his signature at the bank and received the ten certificates. Armed with this sum and the ready cash he had about him, he left New York without a word to a living man or woman as to his destination.

He was seen not many months afterwards in the streets of New Orleans by one who had known him in New York, and still later, when the California excitement broke out, a vessel said to be owned by him left New Orleans for San Francisco in California. He arrived there in safety, and sold the ship.

His adventures in that gold region were of a spirited character, and if ever they are published, if his character did not change from what it was in New York, they will be a chapter of rogueries, rascalities and villainies unequalled in any annals save the volumes of the English Newgate Calendar.

CHAPTER LXV.

Henry Robinson introduces Rose to his Parents as a Spanish Girl Clara Norris Granville Returns to her Farm in Sussex—Her Parents, Brother, and Sister—Reflections upon the Career of Clara.

HENRY ROBINSON did not rest long after her conversation with Walter Granville before he put the plan he had proposed into operation. He called upon his parents. They were delighted to once more behold their truant son. The mother gave way at once, and clasped him in her arms. All was forgotten and forgiven. The father hesitated, but as he looked at his son, more manly than ever, and bronzed by exposure and hardships, he too forgave, and all was well.

"Now, Harry, will you give up all your follies, stay at home, and be a good boy?"

"Father, I will; but I am no hypocrite. Mother, join with me in asking forgiveness for one act more. I have concealed it, but I will do so no longer. In my travels in South America at one of the ports of Peru I met with a lovely girl. She loved me. She was an orphan. She abandoned home, and came with me to America. I have married her. I could not do less. Will you forgive me? Say but this. Receive my Rosa, and I will do all that you wish me to do. She is at a hotel waiting for your decision. Forgive me this act, for it brings you a lovely daughter, as well as a repentant son."

Long and painful was the suspense. Then Mr. Robinson inquired if she was of good family?

"The best; but all her relations are dead. She has now no one but her husband to love, and—if you forgive me, then she will have two good parents to love and respect, as I do," said Harry, and he knelt to his parents and bowed his head almost to the carpet.

"Does she speak English?" asked the father.

"She does. I have taught it to her, and made her pledge her solemn word that she will not speak a word of Spanish for two years. This will make your son forget that she is a Spanish girl."

"Harry, we forgive you. Go at once and bring your wife here. We will receive her with open arms.—Mother, you agree to this, eh?"

Of course the mother agreed to it, and Harry hurried off for his wife. When he reached her and informed her of all that had occurred. She shrank from the task. "Oh, if they should find me out. I cannot speak Spanish," pleaded Rose.

"I have told them that you have promised not to do so for two years, so that you will have to keep from Spanish for that length of time," laughingly observed Harry.

At last poor Rose was equipped properly for the expedition. Her baggage was packed, and she entered the carriage that was to convey her to the house of her husband's parents with a shrinking, palpitating heart. She was beautiful, and Harry, as he clasped her to his heart, whispered words of encouragement and endearment at the same moment.

Again he entered his father's doors; and leaning on his arm was the pretty but confused trembler. They entered the parlor, and the fair girl was kissed and embraced by both parents. It was a happy day. That night, before the family retired, Henry was called into a room by his father: "You have sown your wild oats, I hope, Harry. You have married a charming wife, and, you dog, if you don't make her happy, I will never forgive you. You must go into business. I know a large broker who needs a partner and capital. I will furnish you as his partner, and the necessary capital. Do you agree to it, my son?"

"I agree, dear father, to any thing you propose. I can only regret that I ever disobeyed you in any thing," said Henry, with real feeling.

"Let all that pass. Your wife is a lady if she is Spanish. I can see that she has got the old Hidalgo blood in her veins; make her happy, you dog," said the father.

The happy husband was once more upon his feet. His father placed him in business, and rented and furnished a house for him. The son devoted himself to business, became in due time a parent, and in a sweet domestic home found happiness and respect. He made money in business; his wife becoming an ornament to society; and few who witnessed the Spanish beauty, dressed in white, with her long dark hair, and covered with diamonds as she appeared in the parlors at a large party, that she had ever been an 'outcast' in New York. No one knew it but Clara Norris and Mrs. Woodruff. The latter knew very little about Rose or her husband—and though she once met the beautiful and fashionable Mrs. Robinson, she never dreamed that she had known her as Clara's friend Rose.

The change in her position in life never leaked out, and if it had, it could never have been proved. As years rolled on Robinson felt more at ease, and when his father died, leaving him a splendid fortune, he feared no longer.

This ends his connection or that of Rose with our story. We must now return to Clara Granville. Her advice had led to this happy result.

The melancholy intelligence that Walter Granville had been drowned was no sooner communicated to his wife Clara Norris than she prepared to make the most of it.

Properly handled, it would add to her respectability in one quarter, and that was at her home in Sussex County, New Jersey. She caused his death to be noticed in all the Jersey newspapers, as she had on the occasion of her marriage had a notice to that effect widely circulated. The widow Clara Granville had a large quantity of the most suitable mourning dresses made, and in that regard her conduct was unexceptionable. When the dresses were finished, she took her departure from New York for Sussex County.

She did not for one instant believe that Walter was dead. She knew better, but it suited her plans and purposes to act as if he were.

This woman was still gloriously beautiful. She had not lost one charm. Age seemed in her case to improve all that she originally possessed. She had taken the greatest care of her person and her health; she dressed with elegance, and aimed at the simplicity and innocence of a girl of sixteen.

It has been mentioned to her credit, that one of her first acts, so soon as she had the means, was to elevate and place in an independent position, her parents. This she had accomplished. She had purchased a large and valuable farm, and stocked it well with cattle and agricultural implements. Her father had proved an excellent farmer, and in nine years he had almost doubled its value.

Clara had a brother and sister named James and Augusta. These children when she left home were respectively six and eight years old. The boy James was the eldest. Clara herself was but fifteen when Mr. Nordheim removed her from her home; she was twenty-five when she returned thither a widow—but oh, to what a different home! And the new home was of her own creating. She had sent both brother and sister away from home—the one to a Female Academy at Newark, and the other was now a student in Princeton College. James was a handsome, intelligent young fellow, and Augusta was a full grown girl of sixteen, and as handsome as Clara was at that age, and they strongly resembled each other.

The home to which Clara resorted when she became a widow we will attempt to describe. It was a large mansion, with plenty of out-buildings, many of them erected by Clara's orders. In front of the residence was a level lawn, consisting of about twelve acres, and at the edge of this lawn was a fresh water lake of fifty acres, filled with fish of every kind. There was a bridge at the outlet of this lake, and crossing this bridge you drove for some distance on the main road, passing through fields of corn, grain, clover, and pasture grounds, the latter filled with cows of the best stock. You descended a hill, and then came to another valley. At the side of the main road at the foot of the hill was a gate which opened into a side private road. This led to the mansion, which was located about a quarter of a mile from the main road. As you drove to the house by this private road, you passed barns, and carriage, tool, chicken, and cow houses, and then came to two artificial fish ponds. A little farther on was a large spring, ten feet deep, surrounded by willows whose roots helped to strengthen the dam of the spring, over which poured the pure cold water, making a fall of several feet. This water glistening in the sun's rays, was a sight worth seeing. It formed a little brook which meandered through the meadow we have described, and emptied into the lake.

To the north of the dwelling were large orchards, and in all directions were fruit trees of every description. A hundred white ducks were swimming on the lake, and as many geese sporting in the brook. The garden was well laid out and filled with rare flowers. The poultry was of choice breeds, and had been selected by Clara in New York. She had also made her purchases of wagons, bridles, harnesses and saddles, and sent them up. In the stables or in the fields were several valuable horses. Nothing was wanting—and when the widow reached her home and looked abroad over the beautiful scene from the piazza, and felt that she had created all this, she said to herself, "Well, well, if I have been what the world calls bad, I have not lived in vain—I have made others happy." Then she tripped down to the large dairy house, which was built of stone, and stood upon one corner of the spring, and drank buttermilk, while she looked at the revolving water wheel which was turned by the water from the spring, and churned all the butter made in that dairy.

She was listening to the music of the falling water when her lovely sister came down the road with a pail of milk. As she left the dairy, Augusta came and stood by her sister upon the large flat stone by the brook.

"Dear, darling Clara. how beautiful you look. But what makes you cry—do you miss brother? Oh, he will be here in a few days, and then we will all be so happy. How I should have liked to have seen my brother-in-law Mr. Granville. But he is dead—and I, a foolish girl, ask you why you weep. Come, dearest, the spray from the water will wet you through; come and take a stroll down to the lake, and I will unfasten the boat and row you out. I can row the boat as well as brother."

Clara threw her arms around the waist of the fair speaker, and accompanied her to the lake. There was on it a beautiful boat, which Clara had sent up the year previous; she entered it, and her sister rowed her into the middle of the lake. Not a wavelet disturbed that mirror of glassy water, so calm and still. Not a sound was heard except the chirping of some bird, or the lowing of some cow.

The sun had just set. Clara sat motionless in the boat, and at last she spoke.

"Dear sister, here ought to be happiness, as there is peace. Oh, I will never leave this place again. I have been in the world—seen its hypocrisy, frivolity and heartlessness. Here is home, and true, fond, loving hearts No, I will never leave you more. Now, darling, row the boat ashore, and we will go up to the house. The dew is falling fast, and I am not yet used to it."

The fair young sister complied, and they landed, and walked linked in each other's embrace up to the house. There the evening meal was ready, and Clara partook of it with a silent happiness she had never known before.

Few fair girls who have been forced into the life that Clara Granville had led for ten years, ever retired from it so successful. She was purchased—willingly sold herself to better the condition of her parents. She succeeded. There was no phase of the life she adopted that she did not experience. She was the kept mistress. She had her costly appointments in the highest class of assignations, and she lived respectively in brothels No. 1, No. 2, and No. 3, where she was accessible at the regular prices of those establishments. From one of these she emerged to entrap a young man of good family into marriage. From that hour she became virtuous, and when he left her to roam upon the ocean, and had his death announced in the public prints, she retired to her home in the country—to the bosom of her family, to the respect of her parents, and the love of sister and brother. She owned a beautiful house. She owned property in New York that was rapidly rising in value. She had money in stocks, and she had cash in bank. Her beauty was unimpaired. She had acquired accomplishments by hard labor. She could play upon the guitar and the piano, spoke several modern languages, and an ordinary education in other respects. She had read every thing. When she left home she was ignorant of all education. She had educated herself, her brother and her sister. She had redeemed a father and a mother who both drank.

There is a moral in such a tale as this. We may condemn the means she used to accomplish such great results in her limited circle, but we cannot withhold praise from them.

Contrast her position with the thousands who sink every year into the gutter and the grave in the great city of New York. Many enter upon the life of a harlot under as favorable auspices as Clara Norris did. They are kept by men of wealth, but the foolish, unthinking girl spends what she could save with a lavish hand, and when the lover or keeper becomes cold she has no resource but to take a step down. Again she is the idolized, petted, caressed, and money-making girl in the most aristocratic house of ill-fame. But prudence deserts her here. Money is flung into her lap by handfuls, and she tosses it out again for dresses and jewelry, and becomes indebted to the principal of the house or landlady until disease or accident sends her down another grade. Here she is equally improvident, and drinks like a fish. There is a lower and a lower deep until she reaches Water street, the Hook, or the Points, and there she has but one step more to take, that is to the alms-house, and from there she is eventually carried in a white pine box to an unknown grave.

There is hope for the prostitute, but it rests with herself. She is the arbitress of her own destiny. She wields a power she little dreams of. She commences her career with money, She earns it in quantities. Did she but know enough to save it, she could fight the world with its own powerful weapon, *money*. The unfortunate girl who is forced into such a life for any cause is too apt to be cut off by her own connexions, unless her parents or relatives are very poor, so poor that money, earned in any manner, is a balm for disgrace.

Clara Norris owed her salvation and success to one fact. She went into a life of infamy armed with a holy love for her parents and her brother and sister. She earned and she saved. It was for them, and as money accumulated she became more and more anxious. She bought and paid part—she had a motive to pay the rest until she owned property that paid an income of itself. Her sin was great, but it was redeeming. She did good to others, and first to her own household.

When she returned to reside in her parents' home did the finger of scorn point at her from any quarter? No. She would have shot that man with looks alone that had dared to approach her in her own home with infamous thoughts or proposals. Neither was she a hypocrite. To her young and beautiful sister she unfolded the secrets of her past life, her motives, and by her conversation, impressed her with the awful sanctity of virtue, and the happiness of a fair girl, whose position was such, that she need not deviate from its paths, and after the conversation, that younger sister, in her robe of purity and beauty, walked forth into the green fields and into the wild forests with a character as stern and proud as if contamination had never approached the sister she loved, who had sacrificed all she had done for the good of the drunken parents and the poverty struck, unrespected children. Augusta, as she listened to her sister's exposure, loved her dearer than ever. So when James came home, a glorious educated boy, she was his companion, talked freely with him, instructed him against the wiles of the sex, told him of the power of money, what it had done for all of them, and how it was powerful enough to beat down the darts of scorn from the most respected and respectable in society. Mrs. Granville, at her home, was the perfect lady. She devoted herself to making her sister as accomplished as herself. She sought no society; and she treated with kindness all those who approached her home with feelings of respect.

Her brother was armed against the false opinion of the world. The sister installed into his mind the highest ambition. She led him to think that success in the world was nothing, and that with books and a home and healthful work he could be far happier than in any other sphere of life.

"When your father dies the place shall be yours, and you can make it a paradise. The world may blame me for my own life. Conduct yourself properly, and blame will never attach itself to you."

Such was sister Clara, and she commanded the respect of all in her vicinity. We shall leave her in her country home with every material for future happiness, and nothing to mar it, save it be some unpleasant memories of the past.

CHAPTER LXVI.

The Count Falsechinski dines at Delmonico's with his Brother-in-law—Proposes that he should be a Merchant and go into business with Marion Monck—The Count seeks out Marion—Tea at Mr. Grasper's—The affair arranged—Marion Monck calls upon Mr. Bennett at the Astor House—Mr. Bennett's opinion of the London Times and Journalism generally.

DELMONICO'S establishment was at the corner of Beaver and William street, and the Count Falsechinski met his brother-in-law Francis Grasper at the appointed hour, as agreed upon at breakfast. The Count was there in advance of young Grasper, and he occupied his time until the latter arrived in the coffee-room of that famed and still famous establishment. A dinner had been ordered in a private room. When Francis arrived, they both repaired to the room, and soup was soon placed before them.

"Brother of mine, I don't feel much like dining, and I did not fix upon a dinner as a means of very great enjoyment, but rather as a means of securing your time and attention, while I open to you a plan that I think you will be pleased with," observed the Count.

"I am quite sure, Count, that I shall be pleased with any project you should suggest for my advantage. I know you have my good at heart, and I know you would propose nothing that would not be pleasant to me," said young Grasper.

"Do not be too sure of that, my amiable brother, but listen to me. The American people must have something to do, if they would be respected. You may be as rich as Crœsus, or your father—it won't answer for respectable purposes, unless you do something in this country, where people *all* work. People ask 'Who is that young man?' They also ask, 'What does he do?' To the first question, the reply, 'He is the son of the President of the United States, or of John Smith,' is alike unsatisfactory, unless the second is properly answered If the reply to the second should happen to be, 'O, he does nothing,' it is tantamount to saying, 'O, he is a natural born fool, and has got nothing to do, for he is incompetent to do anything.' A man, particularly a young man, has no position if he is idle, no matter what his means may be. He had better open an oyster saloon, a cigar shop, or a penny milk depot. He must do something. What do you say to that, Francis? Am I not correct?" asked the Count.

"You are not only correct, but I have already experienced its truth. Many a time have I been asked, 'What business are you in?' and when I have replied, 'I am in no business,' the question has been repeated in a different form: 'Clerking it yet?' and when I have said, 'No, I am not a clerk;' there has been a pause, as though I had insinuated that I lived by petty larceny, or something that was criminal. You are right, Count, I need something to do. What is it you have to propose?" asked young Grasper.

"My dear Francis, are you willing to become a lawyer?" asked the Count.

"No," replied Francis.

"A doctor?" asked the Count.

"No, no," replied Francis.

"A parson?" asked the Count.

"No, no, no. Worse and worse," replied Francis.

"Then, my dear fellow, there is only one decent employment left. Will you consent to be a merchant?"

"What sort of a merchant—a dry goods, shoe store, silks, groceries?" asked the youth.

"No—none of these. They are mere shopkeepers, not merchants. I mean a merchant in the largest and most extensive meaning of the word. To do a business with foreign ports—to export and import cargoes. To sell cargoes, and foreign or domestic produce on commission. To own ships, and send them laden to the ports of the world, and bring back return cargoes. That is the kind of merchant I mean," said the Count.

"And that sort of business, Count, would suit me to a nicety. But how am I to get into any such large concern?" asked young Grasper.

"You need a partner. Now I have in view a young man like yourself, only several years older. He has no capital, but he has business capacity of the highest order. He is capable of conducting just such a business as I have described," said the Count.

"What is his name? Do I know him?" asked Gasper, Jr.

"His name is Marion Monek. He was for many years in the

counting-rooms of Granville & Nordheim. There are very few young men more capable of successfully carrying on a large business than my young friend. He has no capital, but if you think you and he could get along as partners, I will give him a capital, and there will be no trouble in getting your father to give you a still larger capital," observed the Count.

Young Grasper reflected a few moments, and then replied,

"I am perfectly willing to go into such a partnership for the purpose of doing the commercial business you have described, but I am not at all acquainted with it. Would Mr. Monck be content with such a commercial ignoramus as I should prove to be for a partner," asked Francis Grasper.

"I have no doubt of it. He would of course understand that you could not regulate business, or conduct it as he could now do. But you would learn in time to do that. I know you possess perseverance, and have nothing to interfere with a devotion to your new business. I thought I would have a free and frank conversation with you before I said anything definite to my young friend Monck, or to your father. Now if you will say that you would like to try the experiment, I will go to work and complete all the necessary arrangements," said the Count.

"Then I say at once, go ahead. I am willing to place myself in your hands, and am really quite anxious to see my partner that is to be," said Francis Grasper.

"Let us finish our dinner, then and go and find Mr. Monck. He has been absent in the South for some time, or I should have proposed this matter to you long ago. He has been back a few weeks. I have seen him but two or three times since," observed the Count.

The brothers-in-law finished their dinner at Delmonico's, and then went to look after Marion Monck. They went to his boarding-house and to several of his haunts, but did not succeed in finding him while they were in company. At last the Count proposed that young Grasper should leave him, and that he would seek Marion Monck alone. As soon as Francis had gone home, the Count turned down town, and went to 46 Centre street, and not finding Marion there, he took a seat, and waited. He had not to wait long. The young man he was seeking soon entered, and frankly extending his hand to the Count, observed,

"Well, Count, I am glad to see you; for it affords me an opportunity for thanking you for past kindness, and to say, at the same time, that I am obliged to ask you to be more definite in the proposal that you have hinted to me. I know you have my interest at heart. I have received a proposal to leave the city and to write letters to a leading newspaper this winter; so if you have not some thing for me to do, I shall accept it."

Marion hesitated as he made this communication, but the Count relieved his mind at once.

"Well, Marion, hear what I have to say, and then decide. I owe you a debt of gratitude that money cannot repay. I know that you are ambitious to get into mercantile business. I have had a plan for this a long time, but I was unable to carry it out until last spring, and then you were gone South before I knew it. I would furnish you with money freely, but I know also that you accept it reluctantly, and I doubt whether you would have done that had you not supposed I was paying to keep you along for purposes of my own. So I was. Now let me explain my design. I have a brother-in-law, a fine young fellow—his name is Francis Grasper. Did you ever see him," said the Count.

"Very frequently. I know him by sight, although I have no particular acquaintance with him," replied Marion.

"I wish to put this young man in business with you. He is intelligent, but inexperienced. What do you say to it?" asked the Count.

"How can I go into business? I have no capital—and he would not go into partnership with a young man penniless, like me," said Marion.

"I am not so sure of that, my young friend, but be that as it may be, I am not going to let you go into business without capital. How much capital would it require to do a safe and successful commission business—have you any idea?" asked the Count.

"I have sir, because it is a subject I have thought deeply about. If I was to go into business, and had thirty thousand dollars, we could do a smashing business," replied Marion.

"I hope you will not do a *smashing* business—that would be bad. But seriously. You shall have thirty thousand dollars. I will give you ten thousand dollars, and this sum, with your superior business abilities, shall be deemed equal to twenty thousand dollars, which Frank shall put in the concern, or rather his father shall put in for him. Now, sir, consider this matter as arranged. Does it meet your views?" asked the Count.

"I can hardly speak, Count—I do not know what to say. Yet if you think I shall not disappoint your expectations, I will cheerfully enter into a partnership so much to my benefit, and I will do the best I can. My whole soul shall be in the work," observed Marion Monk, very earnestly.

"My dear boy, I do not doubt it for a moment. You will succeed, I am sure; but if you do not, it will not be a great loss to any one but yourself. I can afford to lose ten times ten thousand dollars, and not feel it; and even if you do not succeed, old Mr. Grasper would pay willingly that sum to see his son in business with a good partner. Is it a bargain?" asked the Count.

"Decidedly, so far as I am concerned," said Marion.

"Then you must go up with me to Mr. Grasper's. Francis has been hunting with me for you for several hours, and went home expecting you would come up as soon as I found you."

"But, my dear Count, I am not exactly fit for a visit," said Marion.

"Bah! Come with me and make no apologies. You will be welcome. We go to talk business, and not to a dress ball. Come along."

Thus urged by the Count, Marion made no further refusal, but walked up to the grand palace of the Count's father-in-law.

"Is Mr. Francis Grasper in?" was his first inquiry, after they reached the house.

"He is, sir," replied the servant; and followed by Marion, the Count passed into the parlor, where the object of their search was seated by one of the windows. He received Marion in the most cordial manner.

"I will leave you two young gentlemen to get acquainted. Francis, I have agreed to give Marion Monck ten thousand dollars. You don't know quite as much about business as he does, and so your worthy father must make it up by giving you twice that amount. I will go and see him. Make Marion remain to tea. I wish to introduce him to the senior Mr. Grasper."

With these words the Count passed out of the apartment to an office, where he found his father-in-law. To him the Count explained his plans. They were at once cordially embraced by the old financier. At the tea-table, Marion Monck was introduced to the old gentleman, and to the rest of the family. All were pleased, and ere he left, he had made an appointment to meet young Grasper early in the morning, to arrange further matters in reference to the new commercial establishment.

When he left the house of Mr. Grasper it seemed to Marion that all must be a dream. He could hardly realize the fact that from being almost without a dollar in a few days he would be a partner of a "firm" worth thirty thousand dollars. "But I must not forget old friends while I am making new ones, and I will call upon Mr. Bennett on my way down and decline his kind offer." With this intention he stopped at the "Astor." The editor of the Herald had recently married, and with his young bride was stopping at the Astor House. Marion Monck called to pay his respects and express his good wishes for the happiness of the new-married pair, and to decline the offer of going to Washington. He was introduced to Mrs. Bennett, and enjoyed a pleasant chat with the fair dame. Other visitors entered and occupied the attention of the lady, and Marion had Mr. Bennett to himself. He thanked the editor for his kindness, and for his fair offers for the future, but added: "I have been so long an apprentice to commerce that I have no ambition to succeed as a writer. I have had an offer to go into partnership under very favorable auspices. My partner has capital and connexions, and is a very amiable young man."

"I certainly wish you success; but I have my fears. I think that there is a great uncertainty about a merchant's success, and the day may come when you will regret not having made up your mind to connect yourself permanently with the business of journalism," said Mr. Bennett.

"It may be so; but the position of a merchant is much more creditable than even that of a newspaper writer," was Marion's reply.

"Simply because the position and power of the pen is not yet properly appreciated. What is his power in the world who can merely count that two and two are four, and that twice four are eight, and goes on to make or lose money on that basis—who knows how to eat, drink and sleep, and carry on a routine business—when placed in comparison with the man who writes articles that are read and will tell upon the minds of thousands?—of a man who can make public opinion, or who can direct it, where it does exist, into healthful channels? Such a man in reality should hold a far higher position than the so-called merchant or successful shop-keeper. Look at the circulation of the Herald. It issues over ten thousand copies, and is read by at least one hundred thousand persons. Yet it has only commenced its existence. I will increase its circulation to ten times what it now is, before many years are passed; and it will command an influence upon this continent equal, if not superior to what the London Times now does in Europe. Few people understand the true theory of journalism. I am but a pupil in it. When I started the Herald I thought I had no more to learn. Every day convinces me that I do not even now know anything. Not a day passes but I acquire some new knowledge of my profession, and I suppose I shall continue to learn as long as I live."

Marion made no reply for some time to a prophecy uttered by the editor, for he did not then appreciate its force. He asked a question: "How can you make the Herald as successful as the London Times? That paper is a stock concern, and is very rich."

"It was started and placed on its present footing by the mind of one man—John Walters. He stocked it—that is true—but he divided the stock among his own family, and the income is enormous. The family, or the stock-holders, rarely interfere with the course of the Times. It is edited by a man who never writes a line for its columns, while he superintends the matter for the paper, and rejects or admits the editorials written by the most powerful writers in England," said Mr. Bennett.

"Why does not the powerful editor write himself?" asked Marion, with some curiosity.

"Simply that it is human nature for a writer to harp upon one subject too long. He runs it into the ground. An editor who is a clever, judicious man, and who does not write himself, becomes impatient with the writings of others. He has no hobby of his own, and his rejections of articles from the pens of the principal writers give no offence and excite no disaffection, because there is evidently no jealousy on the part of the chief editor. His decisions are wise and prudent ones. Before I leave the Herald, it shall be equally well and firmly established, so that when I die it can walk along alone to fulfil its destiny. Now you try merchandising, Marion, but mark my words, you will not succeed, and when you get sick of your mercantile ambition come back to me. You have talent, and will succeed as a newspaper writer. It has been my opinion for years. I have tried to develope the genius you possess, and I have at least made you aware of the fact that you *do* possess it. Some day it will come out, and I hold it to be a great pity that you do not commence at once, instead of wasting your time in the shipping or any other commercial business. See who is right in the long run." Thus spoke Mr. Bennett, and his words sown there produced fruit in after years, but not until a long series of mercantile losses and disasters had made Marion Monck sensible that the editor was right.

Marion left 'm that evening with feelings of the truest respect and esteem, and was almost convinced that the best course he could pursue would be to refuse the kind offer of the Count Falsechinski. But—

> "There is a destiny that shapes our ends,
> Rough hew them as we may."

Marion's destiny seemed to be a merchant's life.

CHAPTER LXVII.

The Conclusion.

THE lady who has figured in these pages as Mrs. Woodruff, continued in her business, respected by those who did *not* know her well, and retained her standing in society, and in the religious community into which her unparalleled impudence had forced her.

Her establishment was the most choice and the most distinguished of any in the city of New York. It had no equal. Her management was such that she never came in contact with the authorities, and she had among her acquaintances and friends, many persons high in official power and influence, who would have protected her from harm had complaints ever been made against her. Such was never the case, however—and now that years have passed, she is still as flourishing as ever.

We must now return to Marion and the Count. The meeting between Marion and Francis Grasper was satisfactory to both—and after several days, the basis of their partnership had been arranged to their mutual satisfaction. Of course it was equally satisfactory to their respective friends. Mr. Wilson had been consulted by Marion, and his advice was of great service to the new beginners as merchants on their own hook.

The Count Falsechinski paid in a cash capital of ten thousand dollars for Marion Monck, and Mr. Grasper paid in the sum of twenty thousand dollars for his son. This was the cash capital of 'Monck & Grasper,' and on the first day of January, 18—, they commenced a general commission and commercial business. Their office and counting-room was in Broad, near Beaver street.

No young House ever started under more favorable auspices—they had a sufficient cash capital, and thanks to the elder Grasper, who wrote to all his business correspondents in different parts of the States and in Europe, they formed commercial connections of the strongest kind.

The Count had determined to leave New York with his wife immediately after Francis and Marion had commenced business. It was further decided that young Grasper should accompany them, and after his arrival that he should visit the principal ports in Europe, and endeavor to secure business to the New York firm of Monck & Grasper. This plan fully met the views of his partner, and also was approved by the senior Grasper. Old Mr. Prime was consulted, and consented to become one of the references of the firm.

Our history will now leave Marion Monck settled firmly in his seat as a merchant in New York. He had been through a great variety of good and evil fortune, and had withstood the temptation of both. He was twenty-five years old—ambitious, energetic, and determined. He had a good share of commercial experience—enough to justify his taking the charge of a commercial house. One of his most valuable counsellors was Mr. Wilson, who came daily to the counting-room of his young friend Marion.

After the departure of the Count Falsechinski, his wife, and Francis Grasper, the old Mr. Grasper never failed to call and see how the young Marion Monck, his son's partner, was succeeding.

We shall not continue the history of our hero beyond this point; he had succeeded in establishing himself as a merchant, and that is the second of the four great epochs of every man's life.

The other characters in this work have all been fairly disposed of—and in tracing out their various careers, a deeply impressive moral may be drawn in each case.

Colonel Benson and his lady were in the enjoyment of all those blessings which wealth confers, induced by a fair and easy conscience.

Middleton Benson was a steady, prosperous, and prudent merchant. His wife, Isabella Granville that was, became devoted to him, an excellent mother to the children, and quite a domestic woman in her way. No tidings had ever reached her of her brother, since his death had been announced in the newspapers.

The old gentleman Pitt Granville continued to be busy about his affairs, and an inmate of the Asylum at Bloomingdale, where he could receive medical treatment when his quiet fits of insanity made their appearance.

From his parents Marion Monck heard frequently. They lived on in their quiet Southern home, glad to hear of his success in getting into business, but profoundly ignorant of its advantages. His aunt Mary had become a very scientific woman, and frequently wrote to her nephew on such subjects — although he would have valued her letters more had they quoted the price of Sea Island or upland cotton.

Mrs. Tom Granville resided in Baltimore, and rarely troubled her head about the Granville relations. She was divorced from Tom by a double divorce—the Maryland Legislature was the author of one, and grim Death of the second. She called herself a widow, and spent a great portion of her time in the city of Washington, where she was one of the most influential politicians. A bill could be got through both houses of Congress with more ease with her aid than without it—consequently she became a very popular and a very useful woman in legislative affairs.

Old Josiah Cubson, the laughing Englishman, settled on Staten Island, and became the father of a baker's dozen of daughters.

The widow Gaillard, after her husband's death remained in South Carolina with her mother-in-law, devoting herself to the education of her son. Her father, Colonel Benson, visited her occasionally.

The two Peruvian girls, with whom Marion Monck was a great favorite, returned to Peru, where they married revolutionary generals—and as their husbands were shot within a year after their respective marriages, they became widows.

Forty-six Centre street was broken up by the death of its proprietor, and is now a second-hand furniture store. Jemmy the bar-keeper got a situation on the Police.

Of the descendant of the old Dutchman Van Hagen we have given a full narrative up to the hour when we leave him a merchant in New York, where he must "do or die."

Their subsequent career must be the subject of a future volume, should it ever be written.

THE END

www.ingramcontent.com/pod-product-compliance
Lightning Source LLC
Chambersburg PA
CBHW030543300426
44111CB00009B/835